Dear Eyal,

All the best to your thirtieth birthday! Enclosed you'll find some of the good things that shall remain in your life! Happy birthday and thank you for an amazing party with you!

Tom

Dear Eyal,

Heureux anniversaire, I wish you all the best. It was a great, great pleasure to celebrate with you.

Audrey

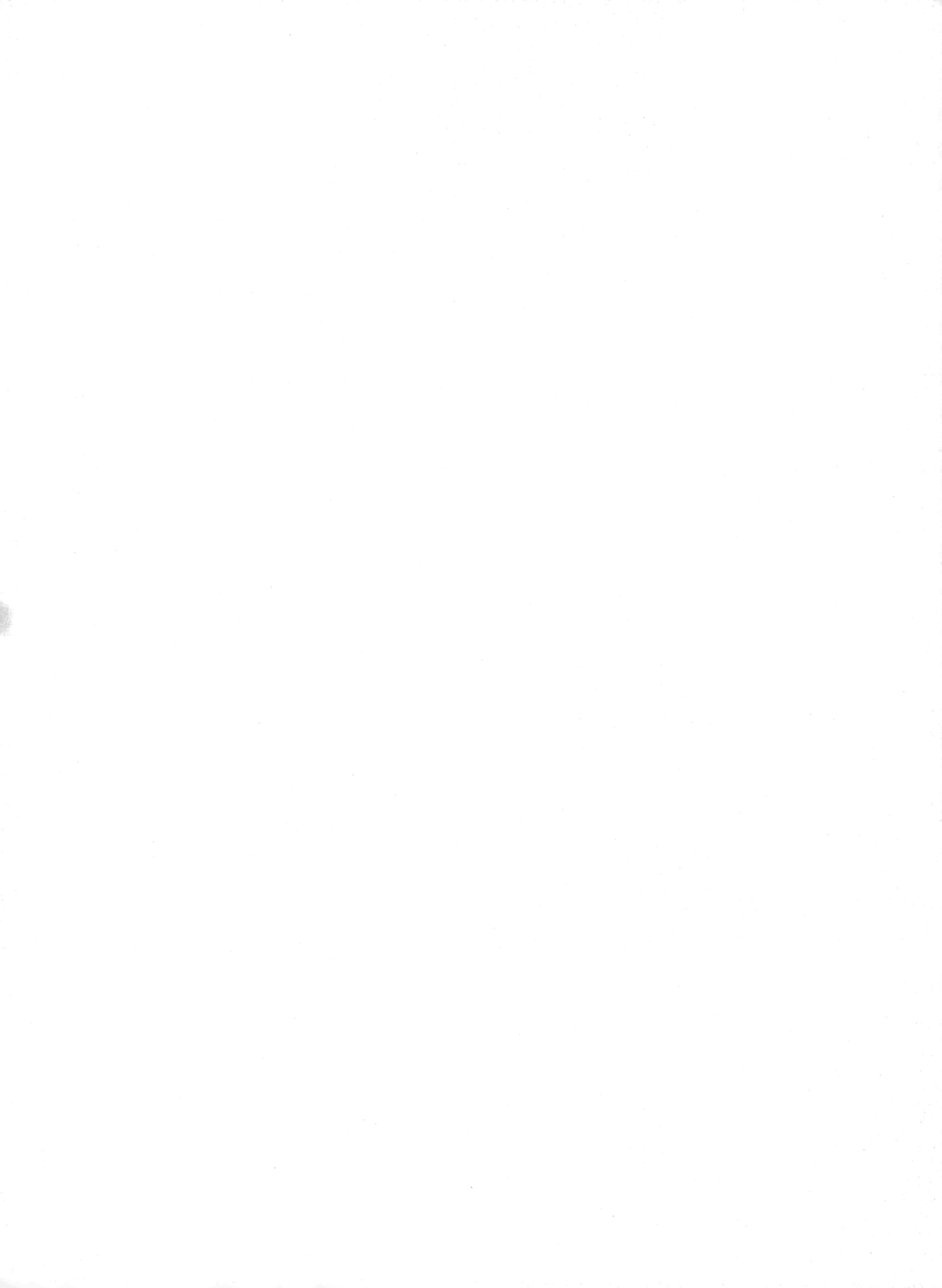

DAVID DREBIN
BEAUTIFUL DISASTERS

DAVID DREBIN
BEAUTIFUL DISASTERS

teNeues

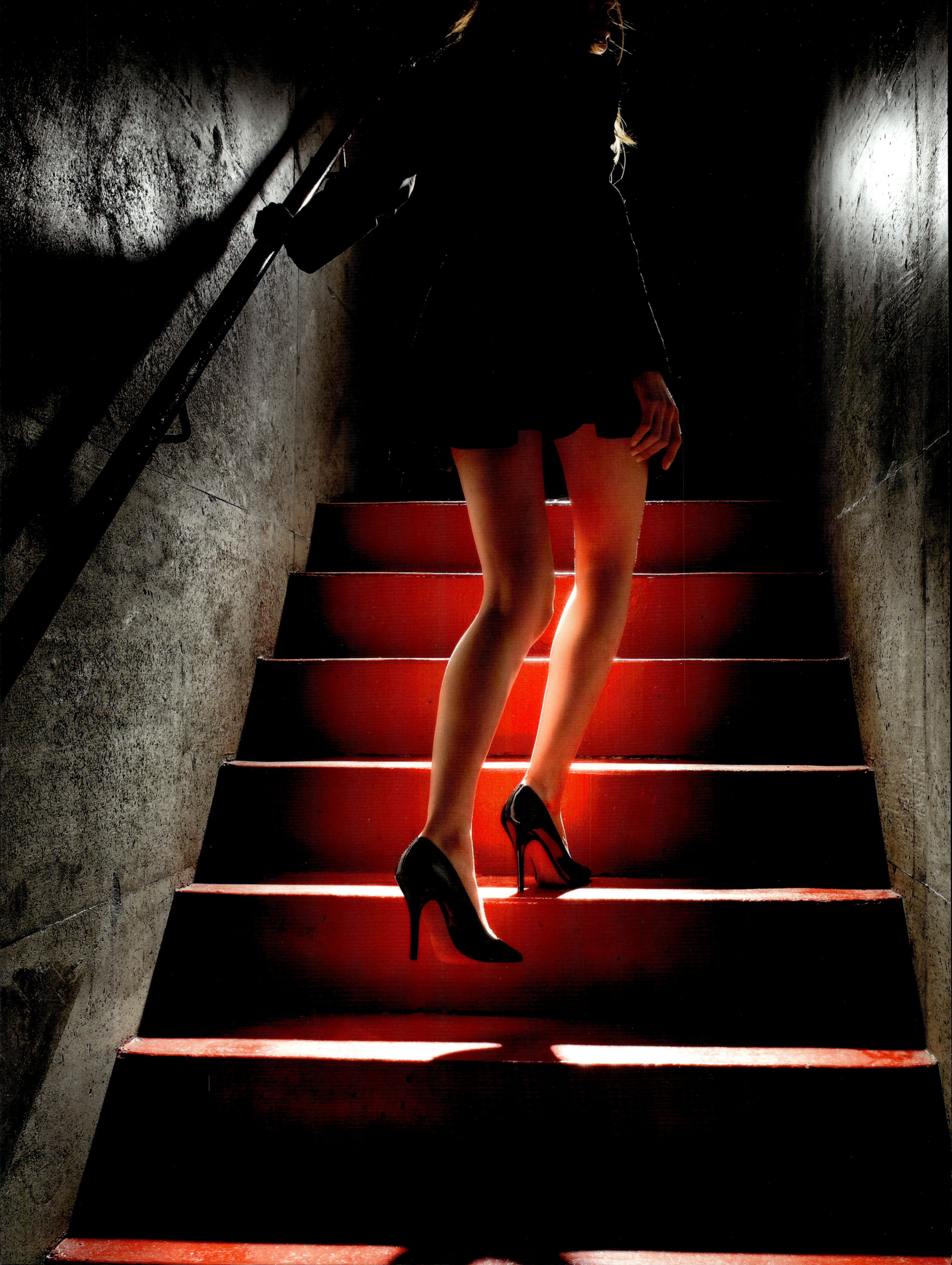

PREFACE

I discovered David Drebin in 2005, when I was won over by his fresh approach to photography somewhere between painting, photographic art, and cinema.

He uses highly sophisticated staging to breathe new life into beauty, fashion and landscape photography. He places the woman, sublime and solitary, in urban landscapes and in front of magnificent panoramic backdrops, creating mystic. Such an atmosphere feeds the imagination of the spectator who is able to lend it his own interpretation, sometimes stepping right into voyeurism.

Some of these fashion shoots in natural settings are reminiscent of Guy Bourdin, while the more erotic pictures recall the work of Helmut Newton. All the while, Drebin manages to retain that personal touch with a style that is very much his own.

I am sure that David Drebin will be the great photographer on the market in the years to come.

I published his work in 2007 and again in 2011, in *Photo*.

Beautiful Disasters is, for me, the culmination of his talent.
I value his simplicity, his friendship, and his loyalty.

Eric Colmet Daâge

Director of *Photo* Magazine, France

VORWORT

Ich entdeckte David Drebin im Jahr 2005 – die ungewohnte Art seiner Fotografie zwischen Gemälde, Kunstfoto und Filmszene überzeugte mich sofort.

Er versteht es, der Glamour-, Mode- und Landschaftsfotografie durch raffinierteste Inszenierungen neue Impulse zu geben. Erhaben schön und einsam, präsentiert sich die Frau bei Drebin inmitten großartiger Panoramakulissen geheimnisvoller Stadtlandschaften. Diese Stimmung regt die Fantasie des Betrachters an, lässt ihn eine eigene Deutung suchen, was zuweilen an Voyeurismus grenzt.

Einige der in der Natur aufgenommen Modefotografien erinnern an Guy Bourdin, andere – erotischere – an Helmut Newton, wahren aber trotz allem in hohem Maße die Originalität seines Stils.

David Drebin wird in meinen Augen der große Fotograf auf dem Kunstmarkt der nächsten Jahre sein.

In den Jahren 2007 und 2011 brachte ich seine Arbeiten in *Photo* heraus.

Beautiful Disasters ist für mich das Resultat seines Talents.
Ich schätze seine Natürlichkeit, Freundschaft und Treue.

Eric Colmet Daâge

Herausgeber des französischen Magazins *Photo*

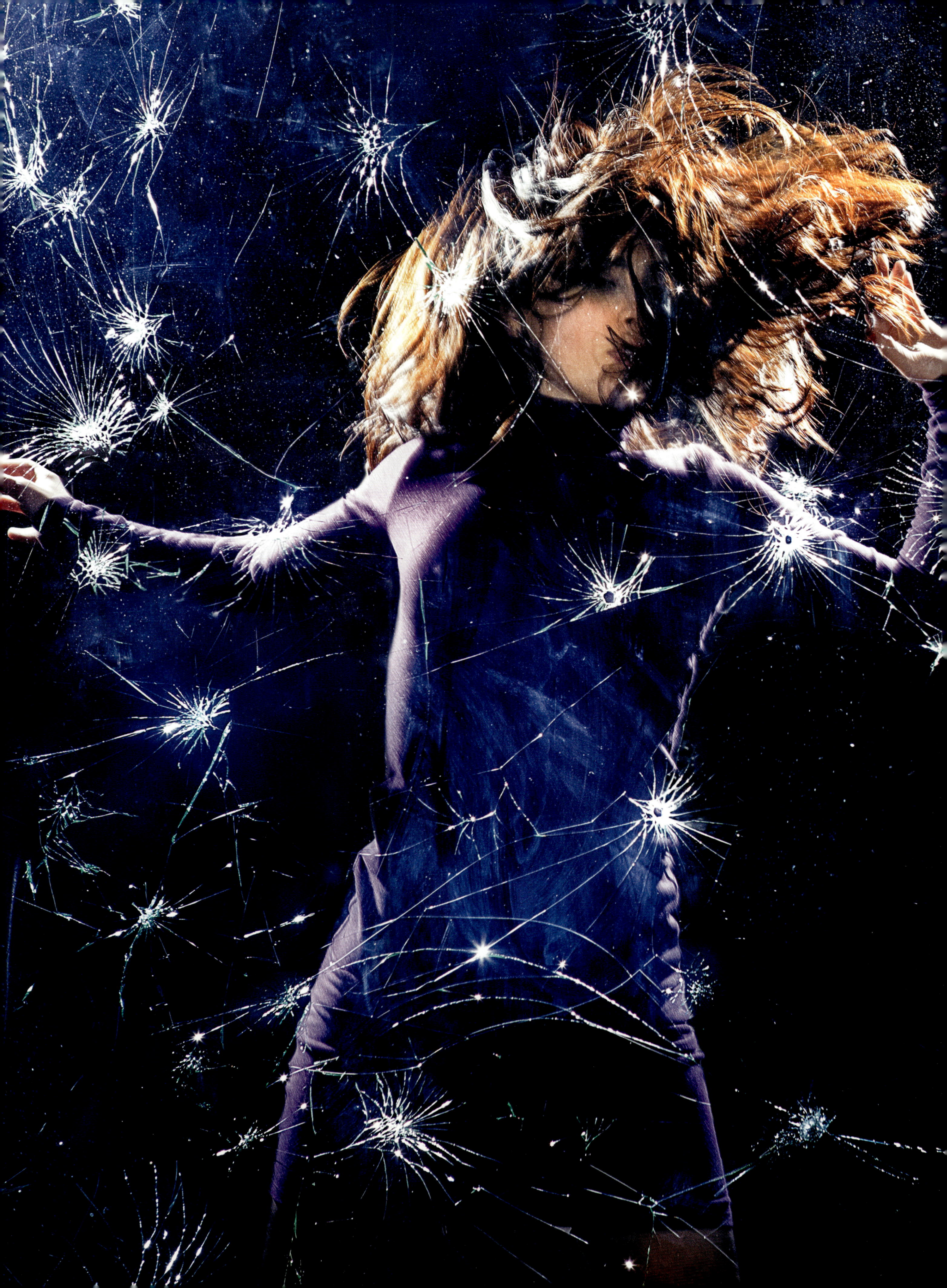

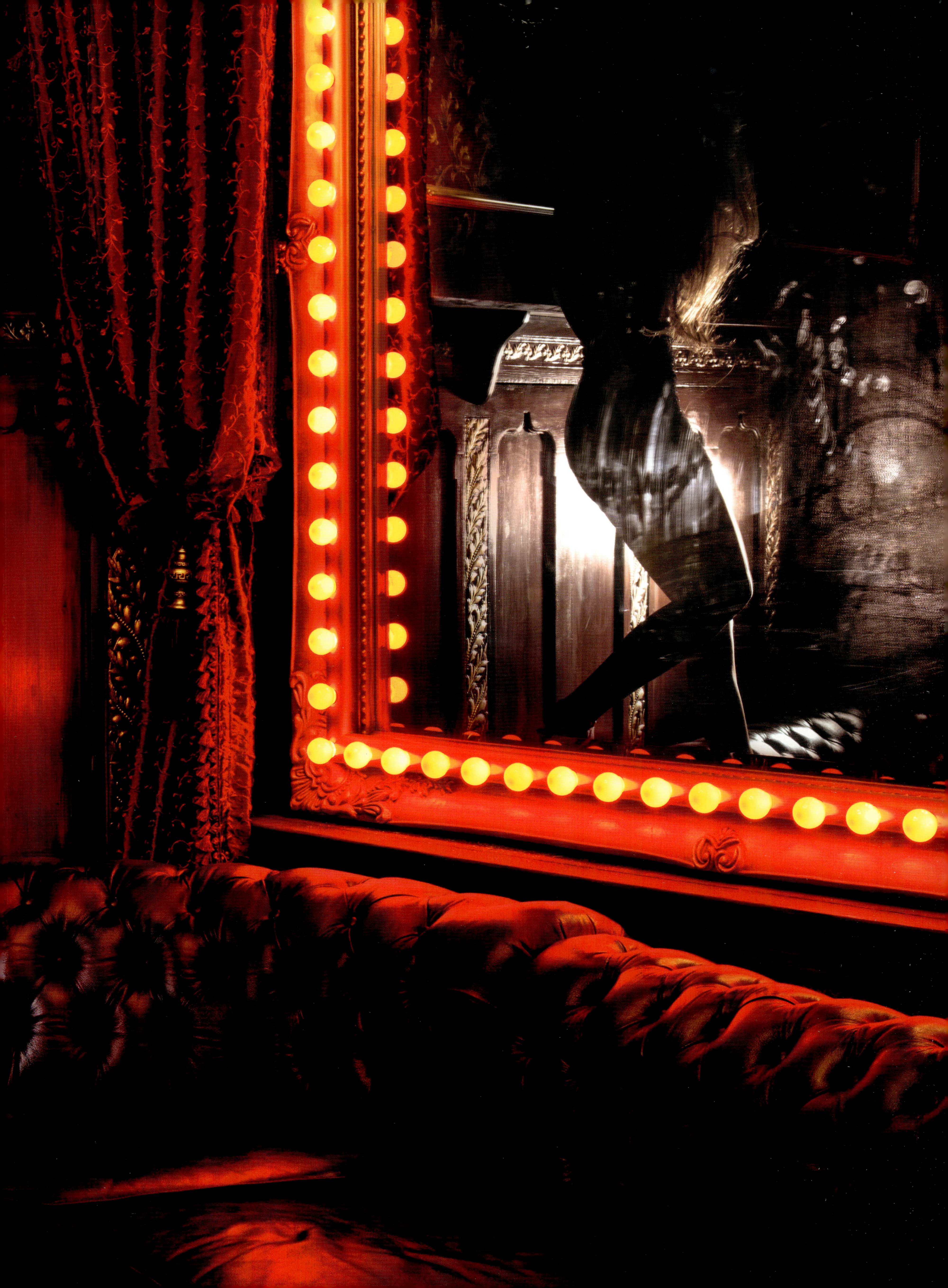

PRÉFACE

J'ai découvert David Drebin en 2005, conquis par sa nouvelle façon de photographier entre peinture, photo d'art et cinéma.

Il a su renouveler la photo de charme, de mode, de paysage, grâce à des mises en scène très sophistiquées. La femme, sublime et solitaire, est située dans des paysages urbains et de magnifiques décors panoramiques qui créent le mystère. Cette atmosphère excite l'imagination du spectateur qui a sa propre interprétation, allant parfois jusqu'au voyeurisme.

Certaines photos de mode dans la nature font penser à Guy Bourdin, d'autres plus érotiques à Helmut Newton, tout en restant malgré tout très personnelles dans un style bien à lui.

Je pense que David Drebin sera le grand photographe de ces prochaines années sur le marché de l'art.

Je l'ai publié en 2007 et en 2011 dans *Photo*.

Beautiful Disasters est pour moi l'aboutissement de son talent.
J'apprécie sa simplicité, son amitié et sa fidélité.

Eric Colmet Daâge

Directeur du Magazine *Photo*, France

PREFACIO

Descubrí a David Drebin en 2005 y ya entonces caí conquistado por su novedosa manera de plasmar imágenes, a un tiempo pintura, fotografía artística y cine.

Drebin ha sabido renovar la fotografía del desnudo, de la moda y del paisaje gracias a una puesta en escena extremadamente sofisticada. Coloca a sus mujeres, sublimes y solitarias, ante paisajes urbanos y extraordinarios fondos panorámicos que las envuelven en el misterio. Esta atmósfera enardece la imaginación de quien las contempla y le lleva a buscar interpretaciones propias, al tiempo que lo lleva a terrenos próximos al voyeurismo.

Algunas de las fotografías de moda en plena naturaleza traen a la memoria el trabajo de Guy Bourdin; otras, más eróticas, a Helmut Newton. Pese a ello, todas conservan siempre una personalidad muy propia y un estilo inconfundible.

Creo que David Drebin será el gran fotógrafo a seguir durante los próximos años en el mercado del arte.

Publiqué ya su obra en 2007 y 2011 en las páginas de *Photo*.

Beautiful Disasters supone, en mi opinión, la culminación de su talento.
Aprecio mucho su simplicidad, su amistad y su lealtad.

Eric Colmet Daâge

Director de la revista *Photo*, Francia

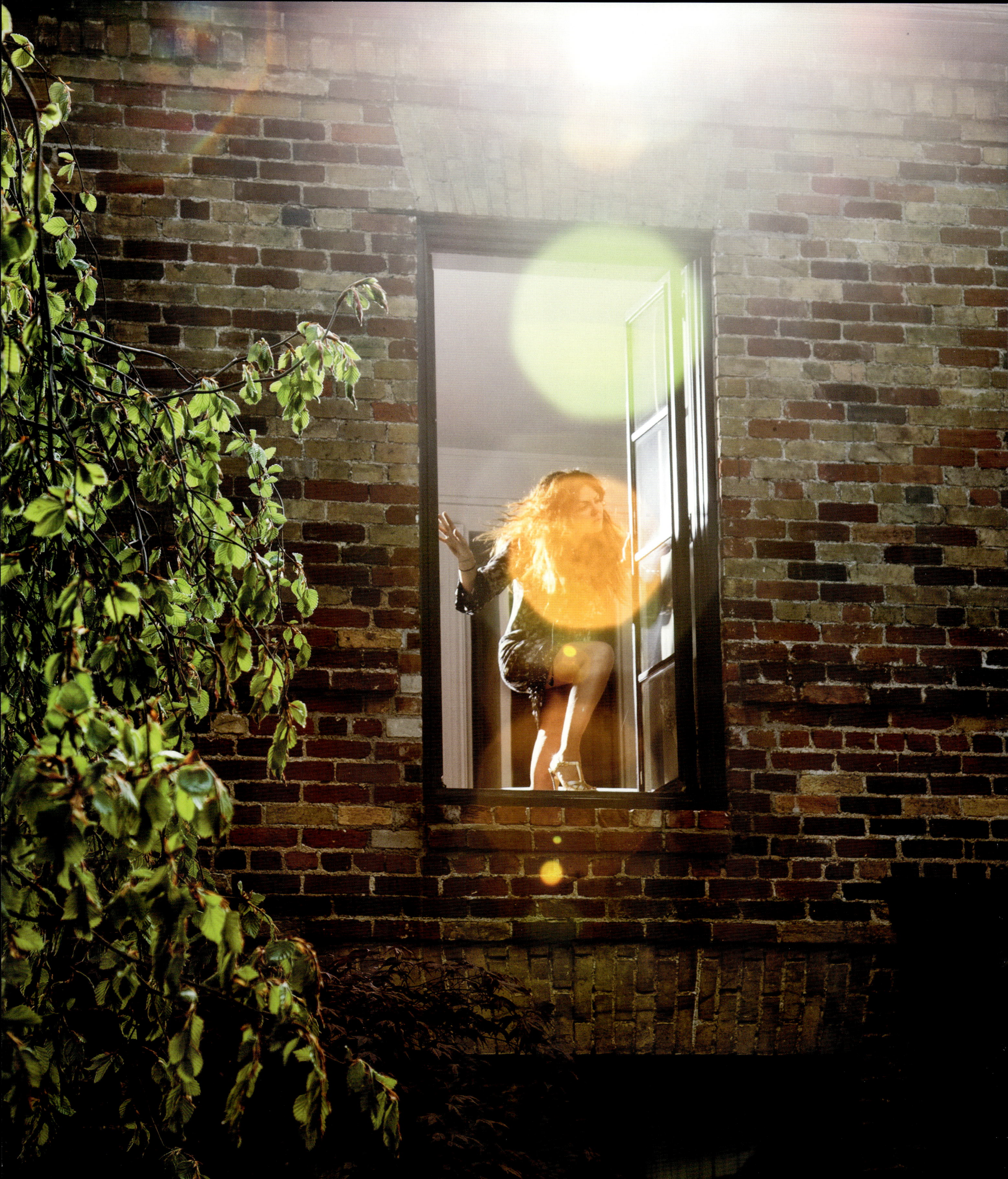

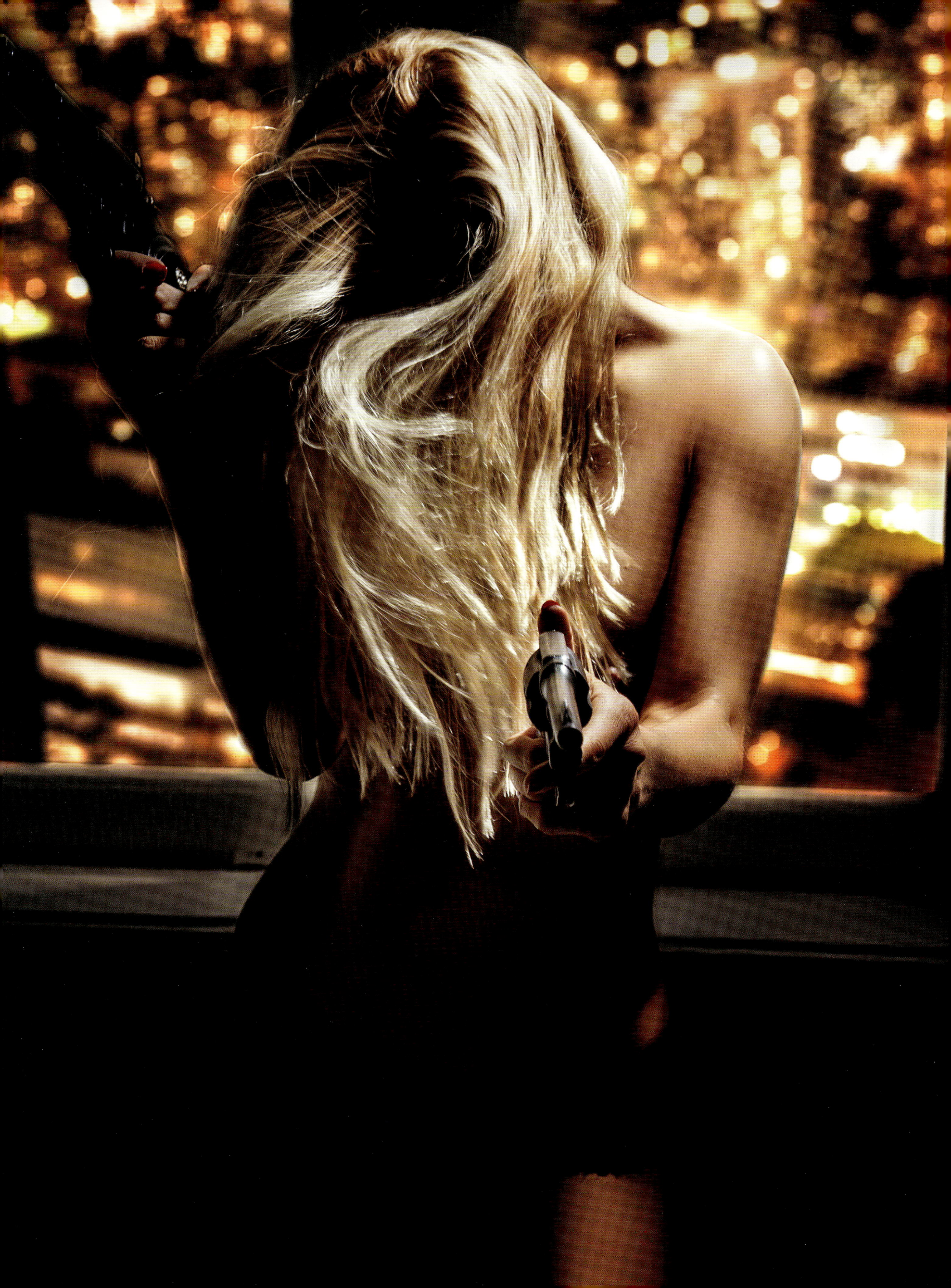

PREFAZIONE

Ho scoperto David Drebin nel 2005 e sono stato conquistato dal suo modo originale di fotografare, uno stile fra pittura, fotografie d'arte e cinema.

Ha saputo rinnovare le foto glamour, di moda e di paesaggio grazie a messinscena molto sofisticate. La donna, sublime e solitaria, è fotografata in paesaggi urbani e magnifici scorci panoramici che creano mistero. Quest'atmosfera stimola l'immaginazione di colui che guarda e dà la propria interpretazione, che a volte sfocia nel voyeurismo.

Certe foto di moda nella natura fanno pensare a Guy Bourdin, altre più erotiche a Helmut Newton; nonostante queste associazioni, lo stile di Drebin è del tutto personale e originale.

Credo che David Drebin sarà il grande fotografo dei prossimi anni nel mercato dell'arte.

Io ho pubblicato le sue foto nel 2007 e nel 2011 nella rivista *Photo*.

A mio avviso *Beautiful Disasters* è il coronamento del suo talento.
Apprezzo la sua semplicità, la sua amicizia e la sua lealtà.

Eric Colmet Daâge

Direttore di Magazine *Photo*, Francia

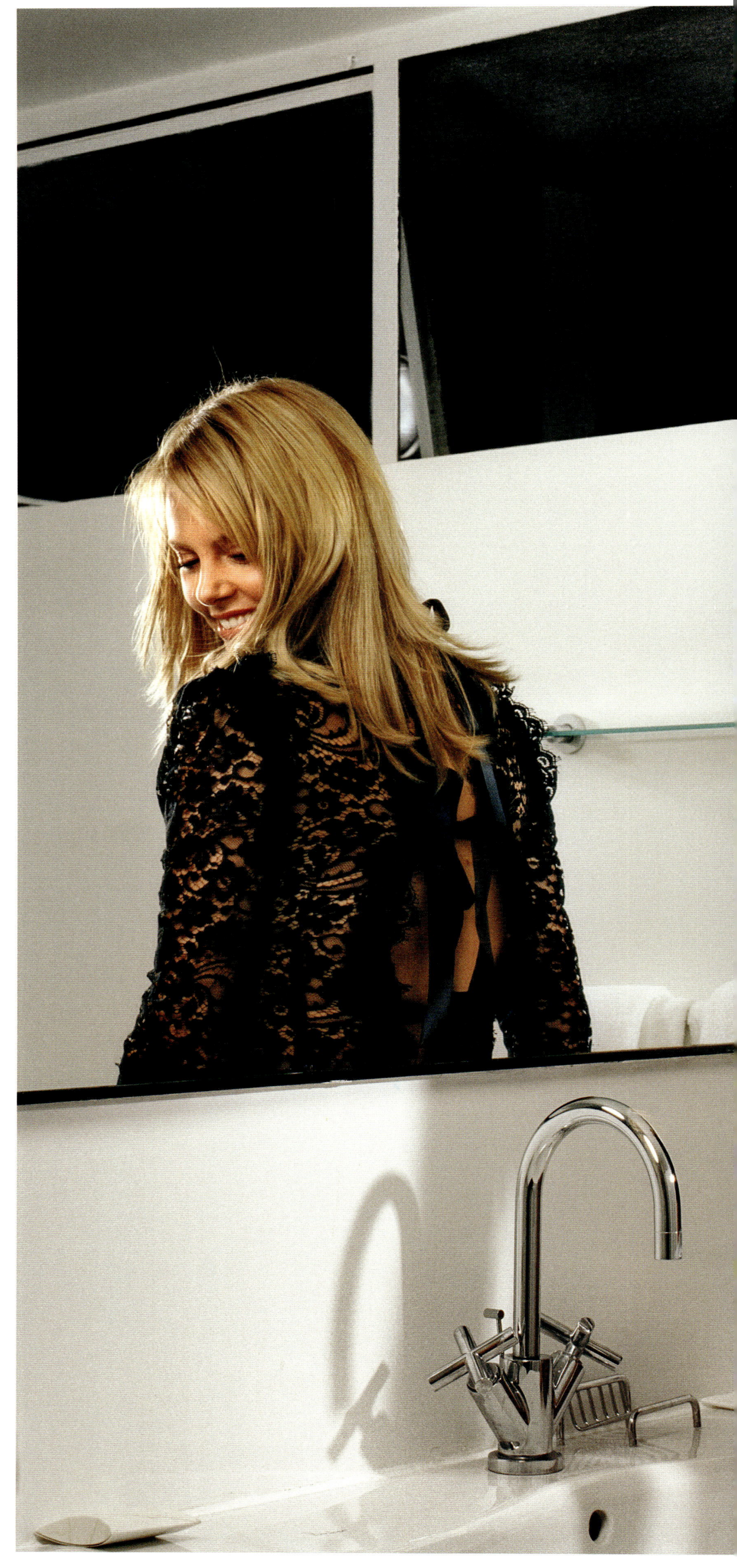

CHARLIZE IN MIRROR | 2003

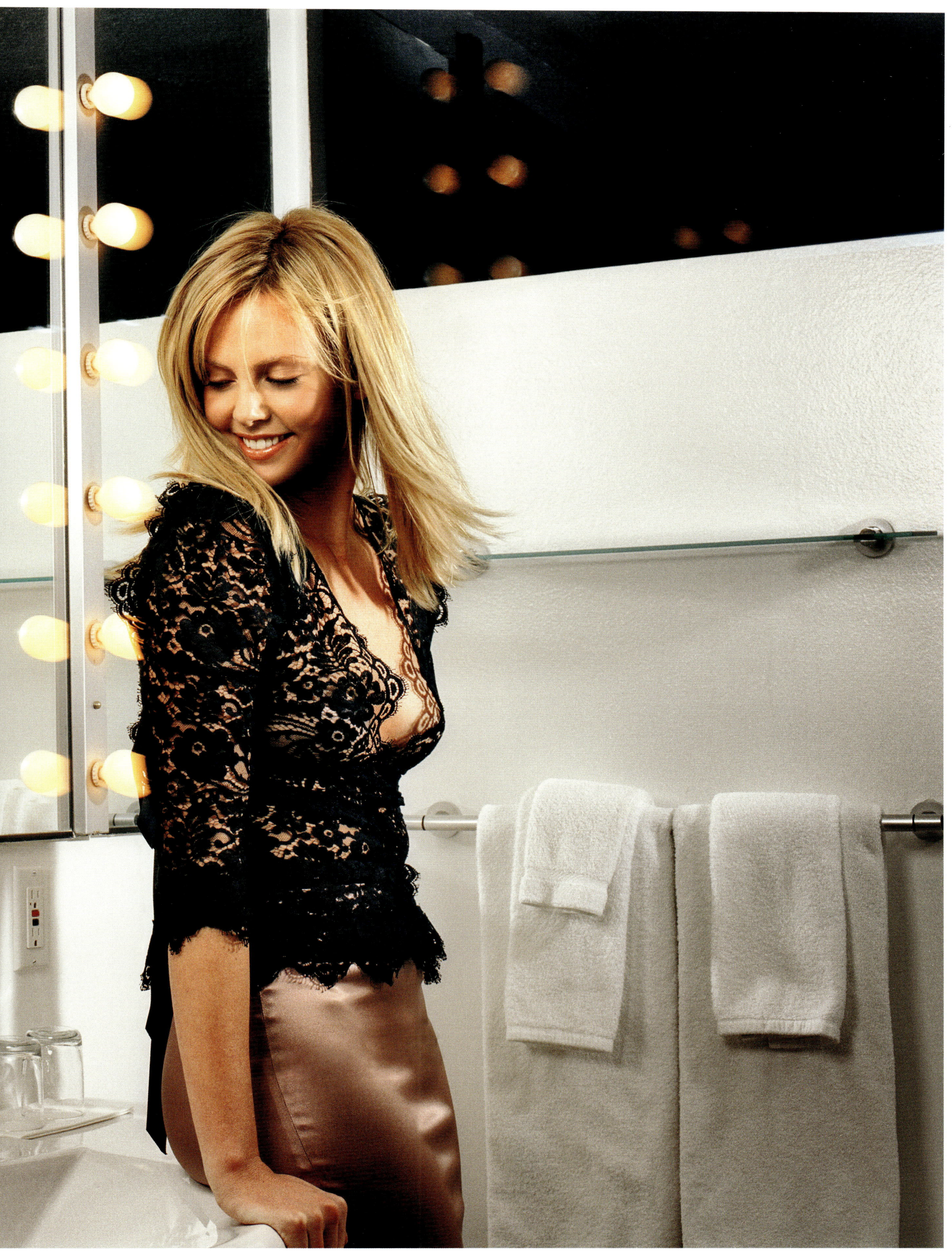

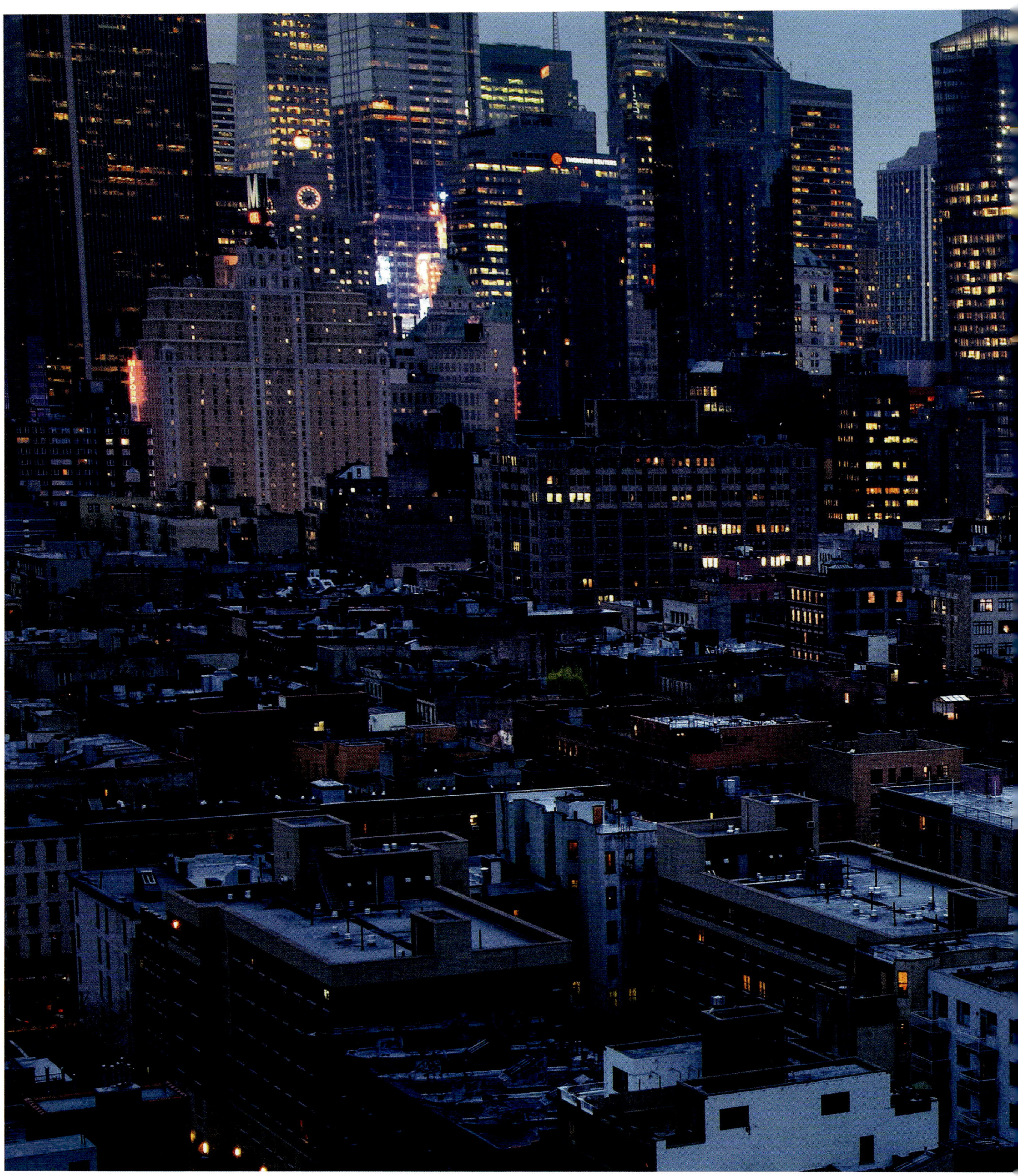
THOMSON REUTERS
MILFORD

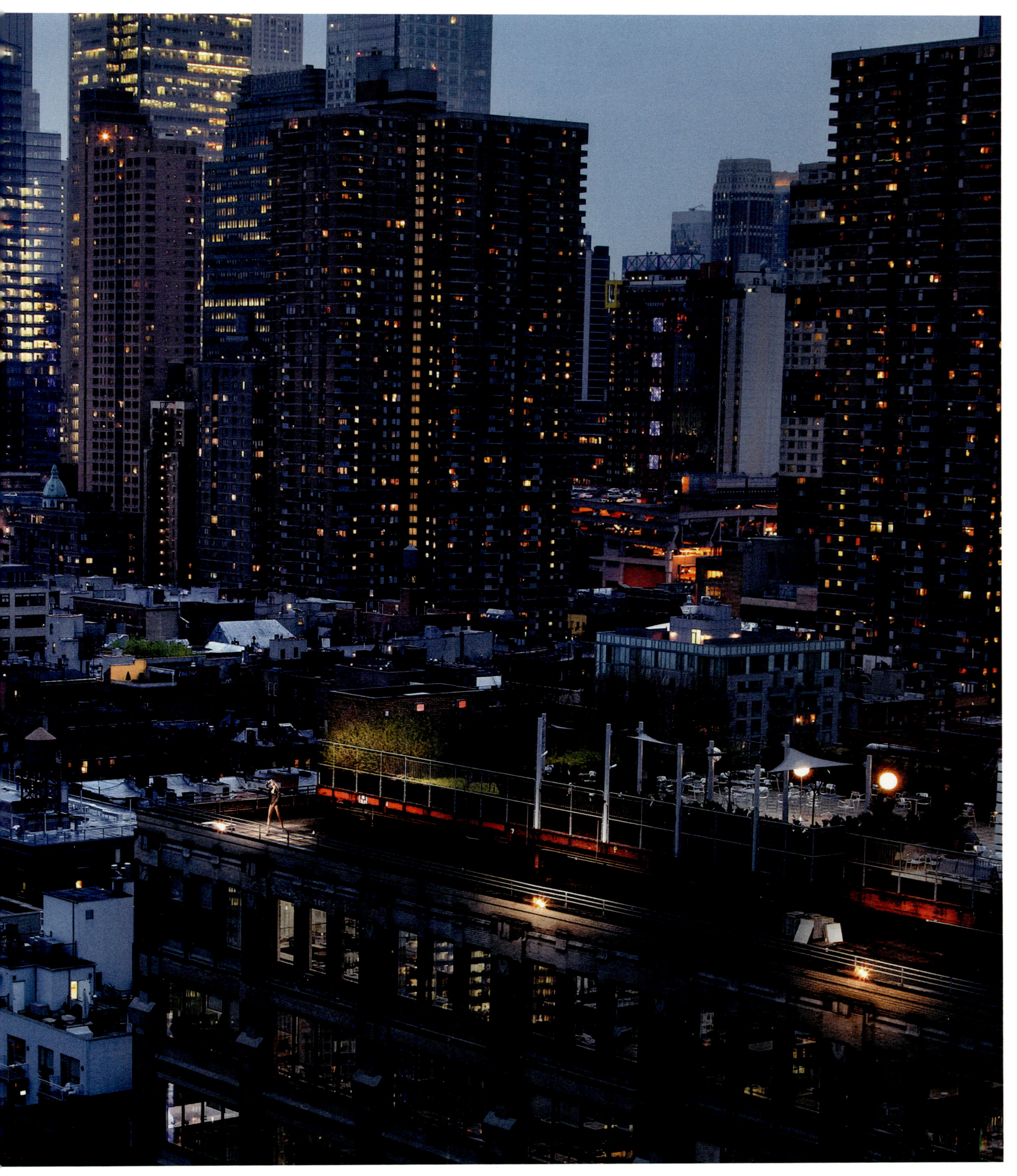

GIRL IN NEW YORK I 2011

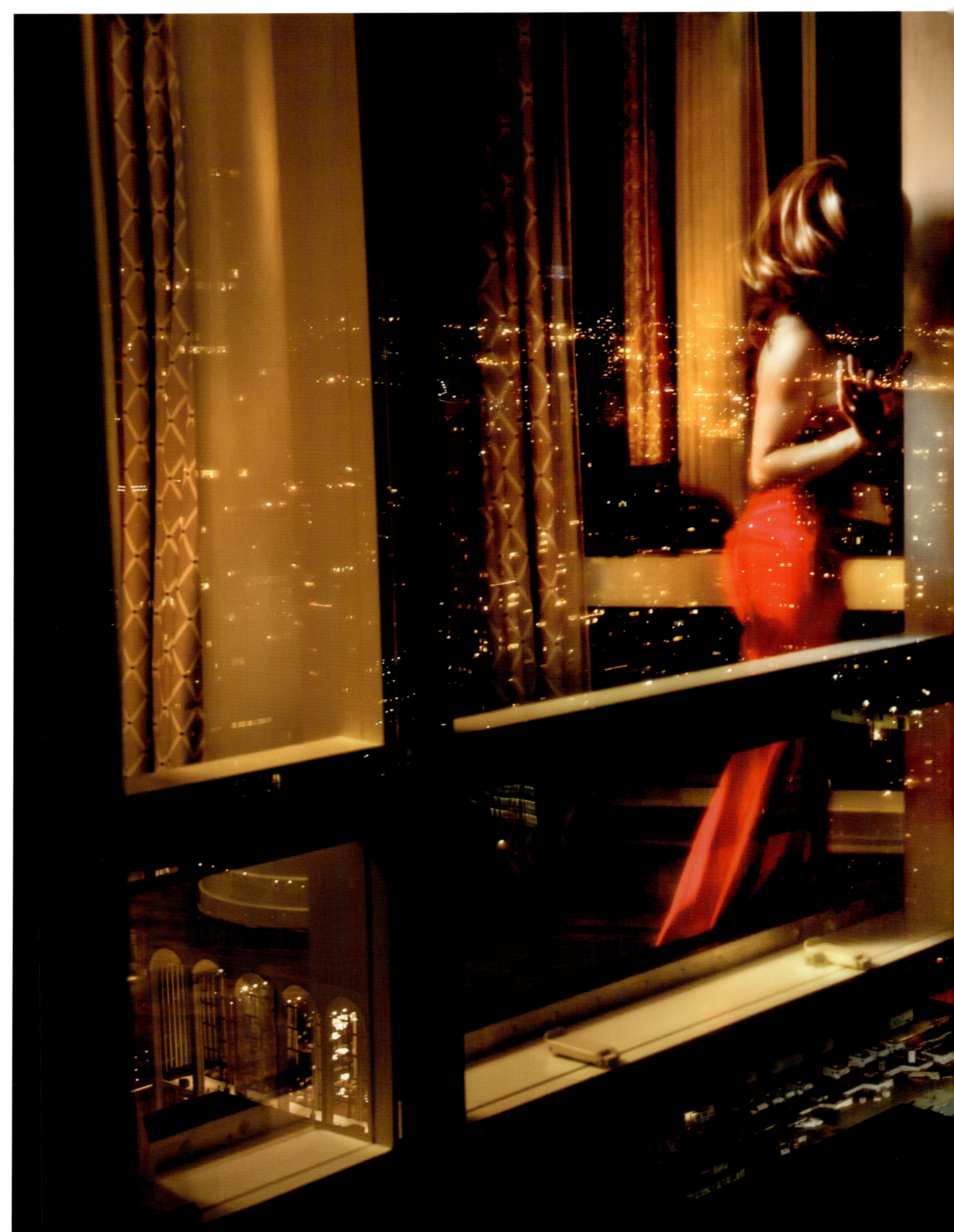

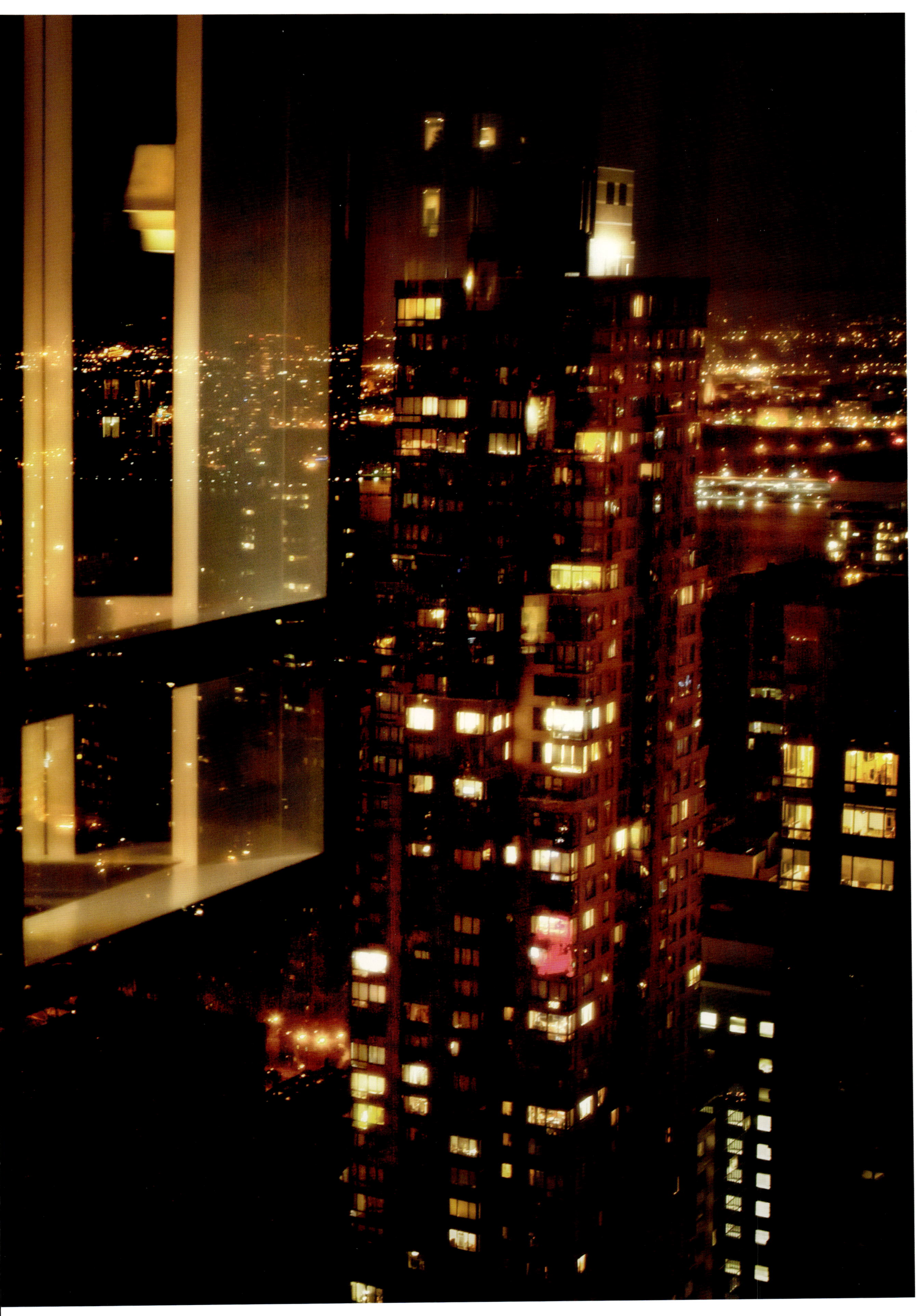

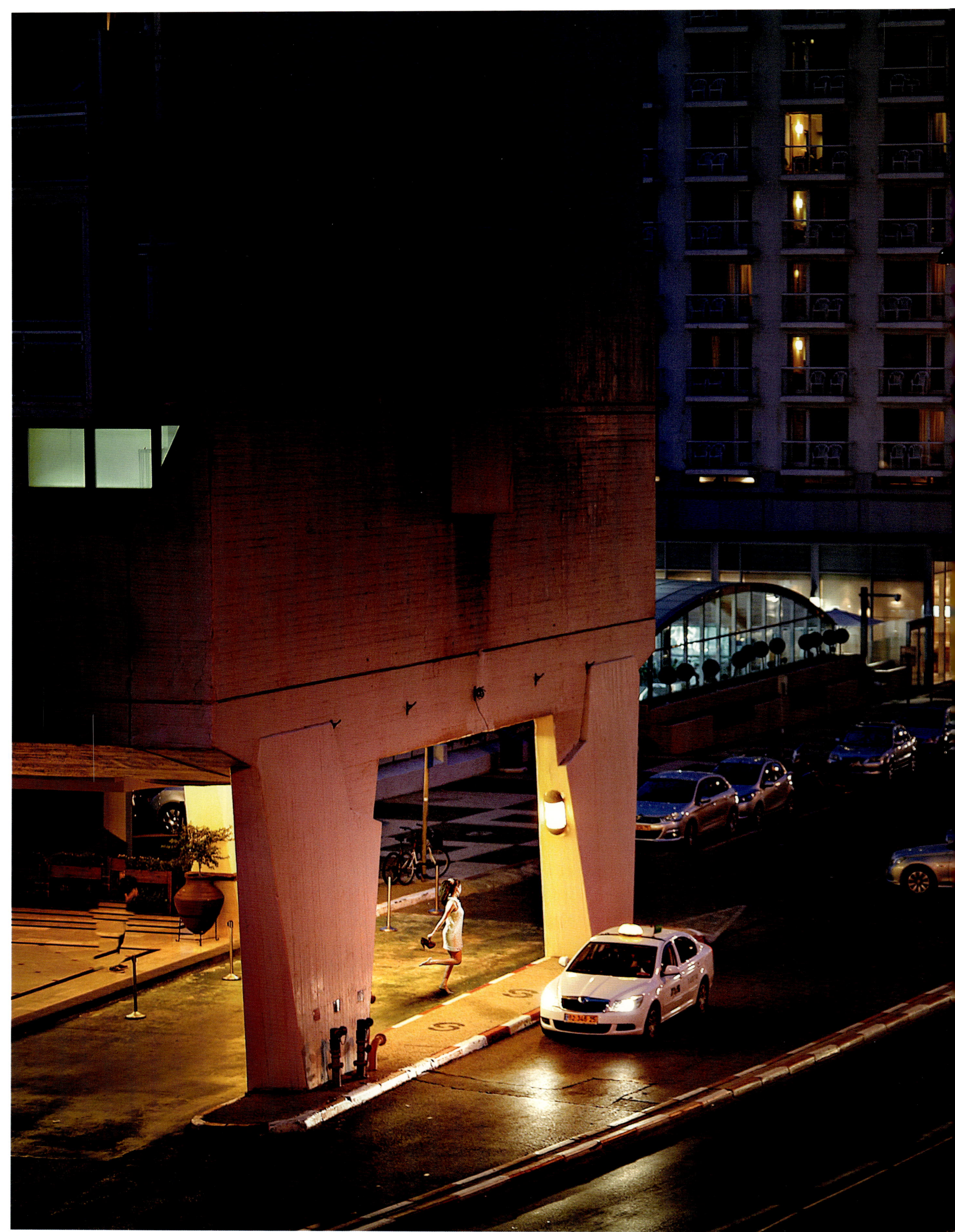

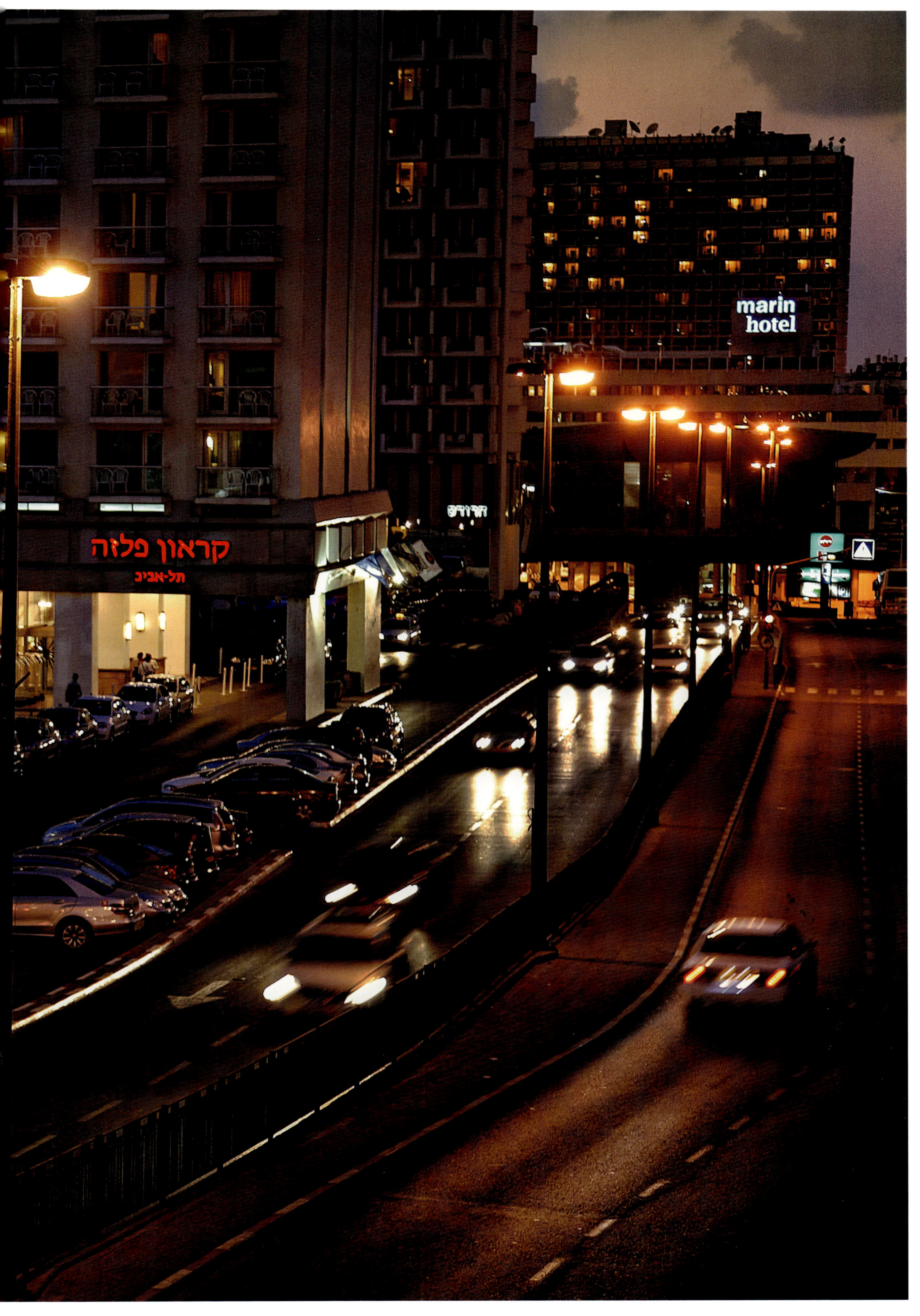
marin
hotel
קראון פלזה
תל-אביב

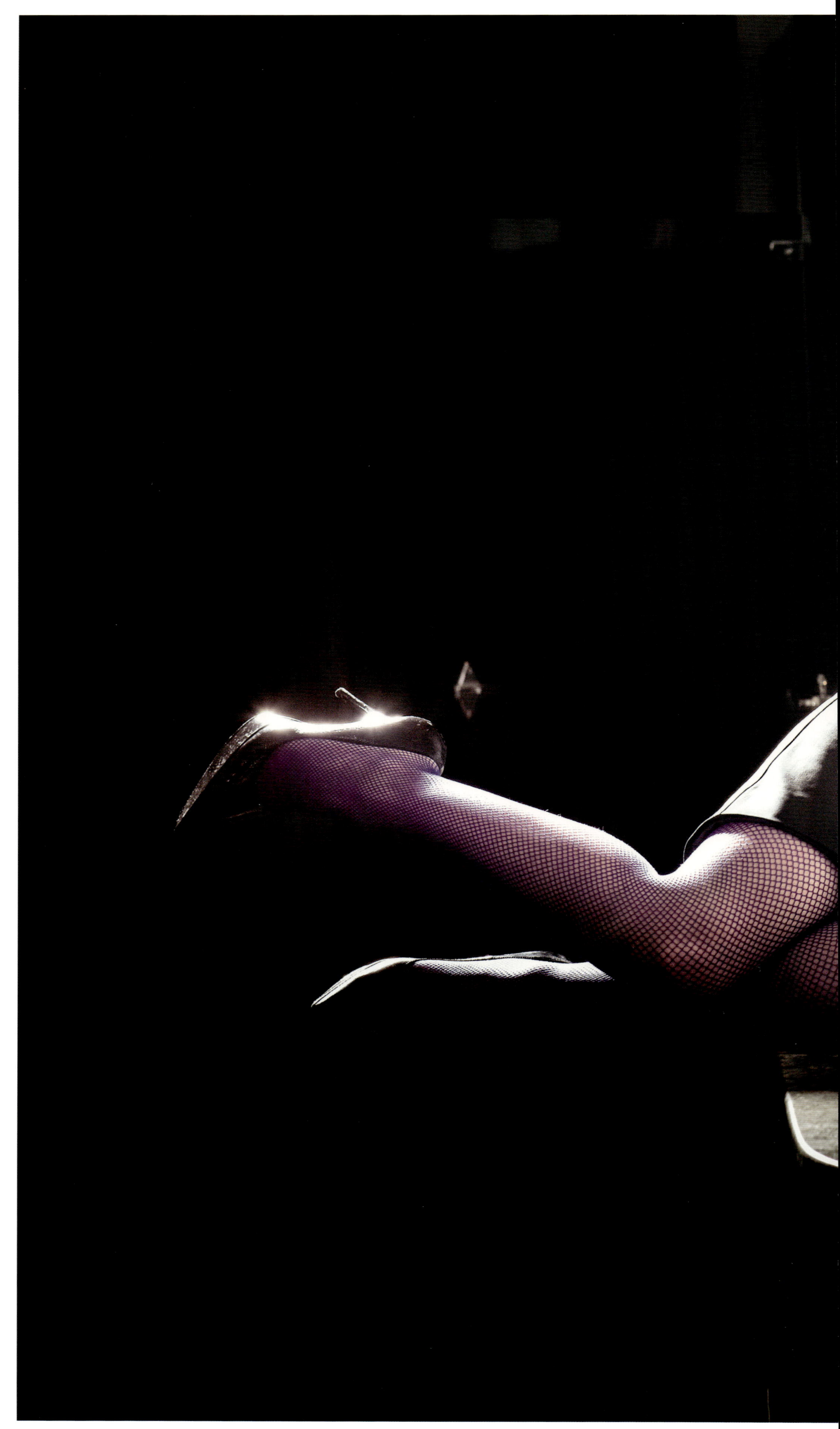

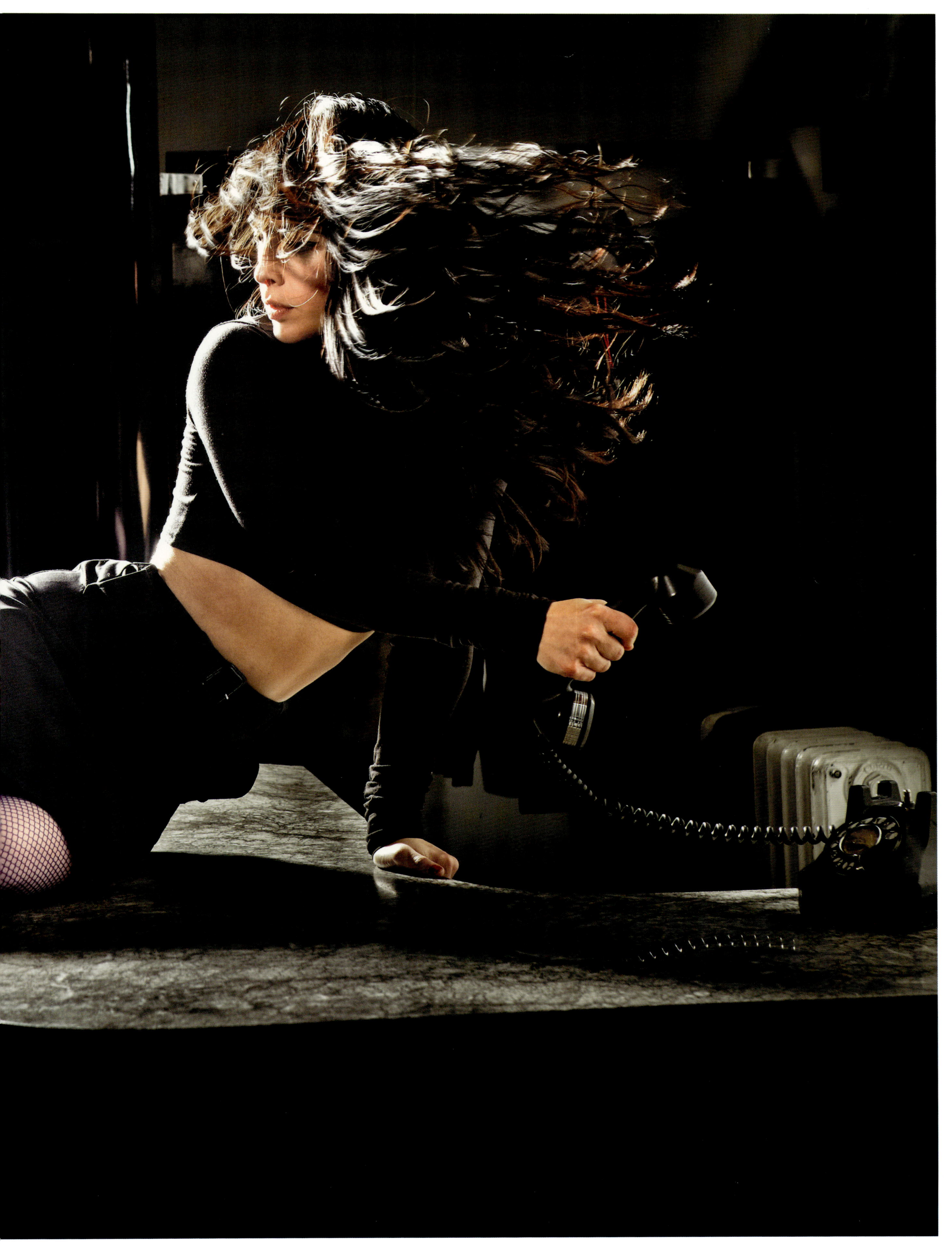

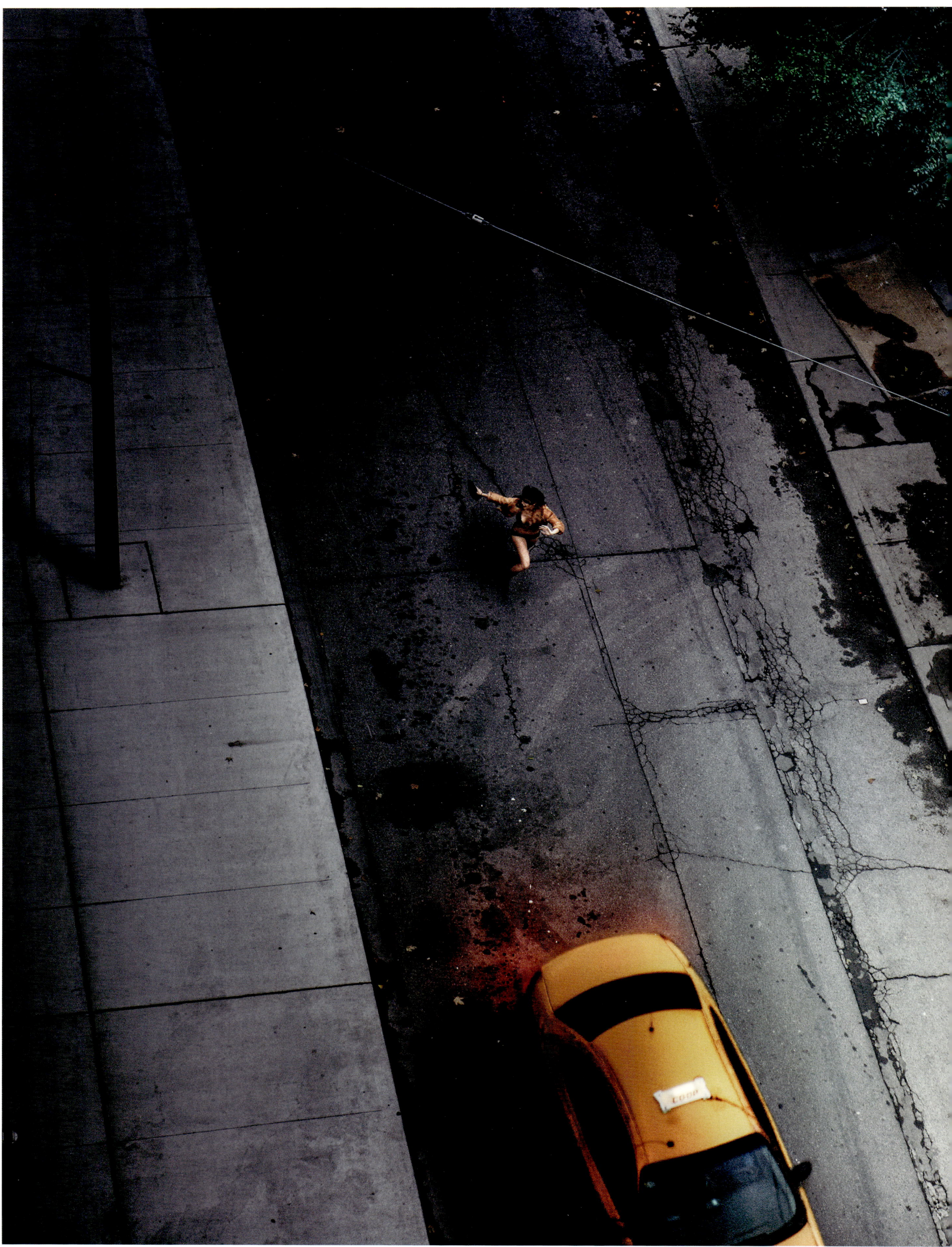
LOOP

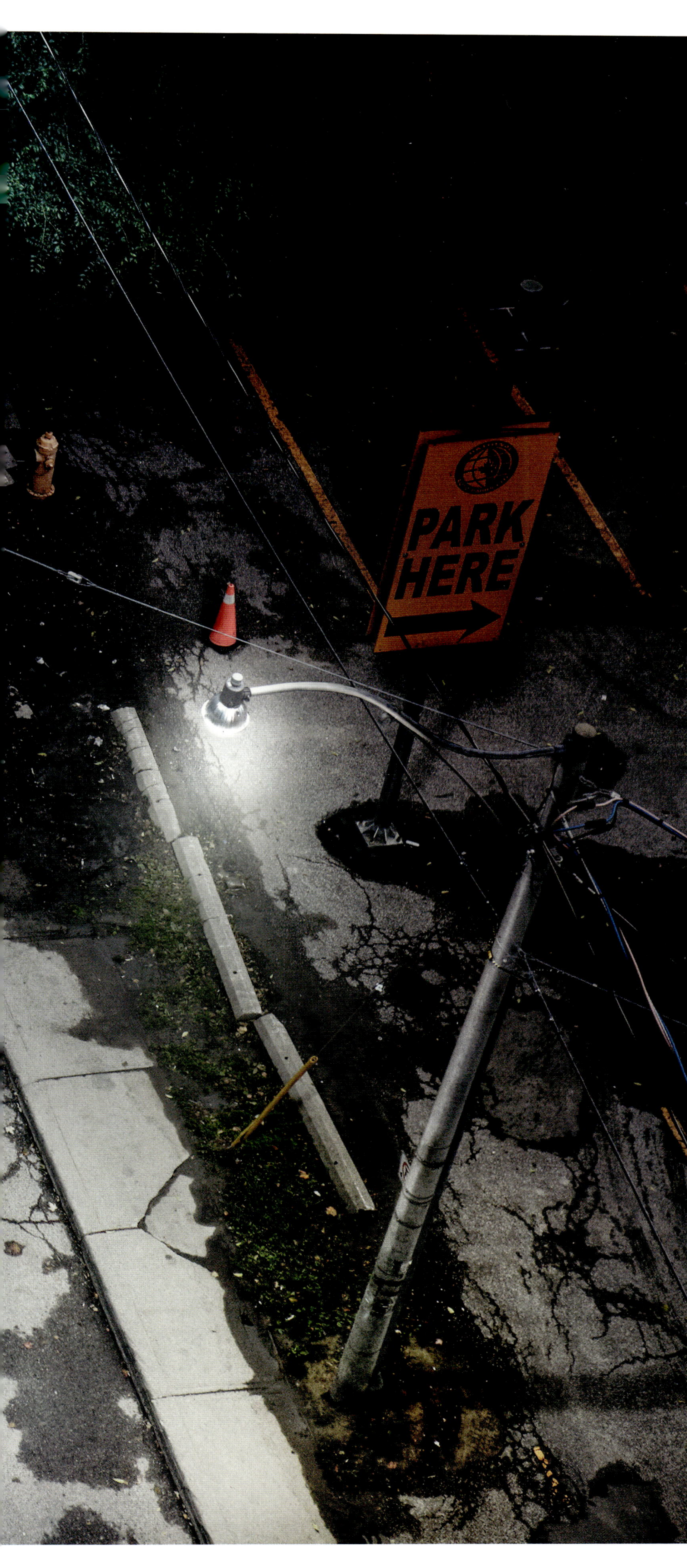

LOST CHANCE I 2011

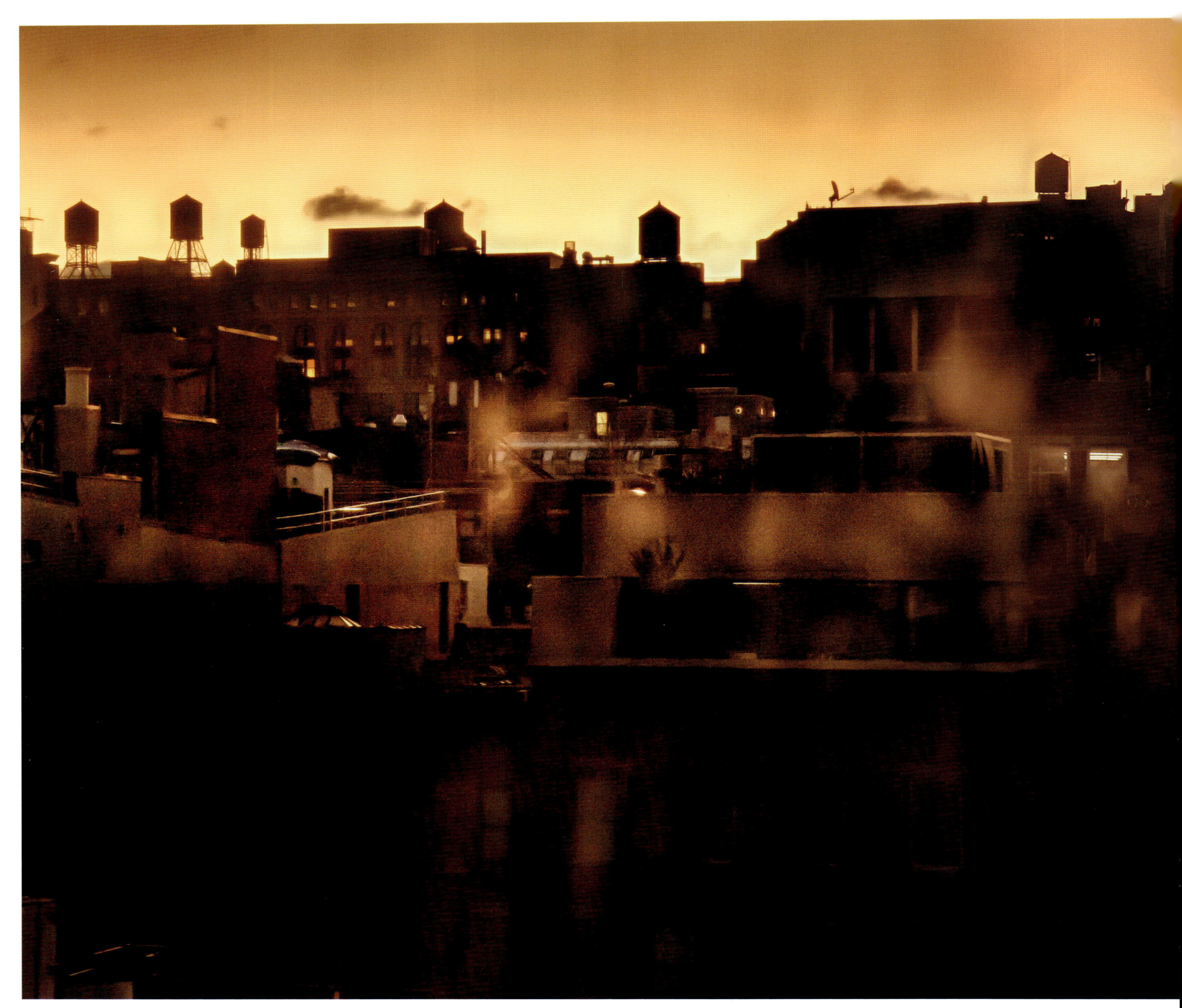

DAWN IN NEW YORK | 2012

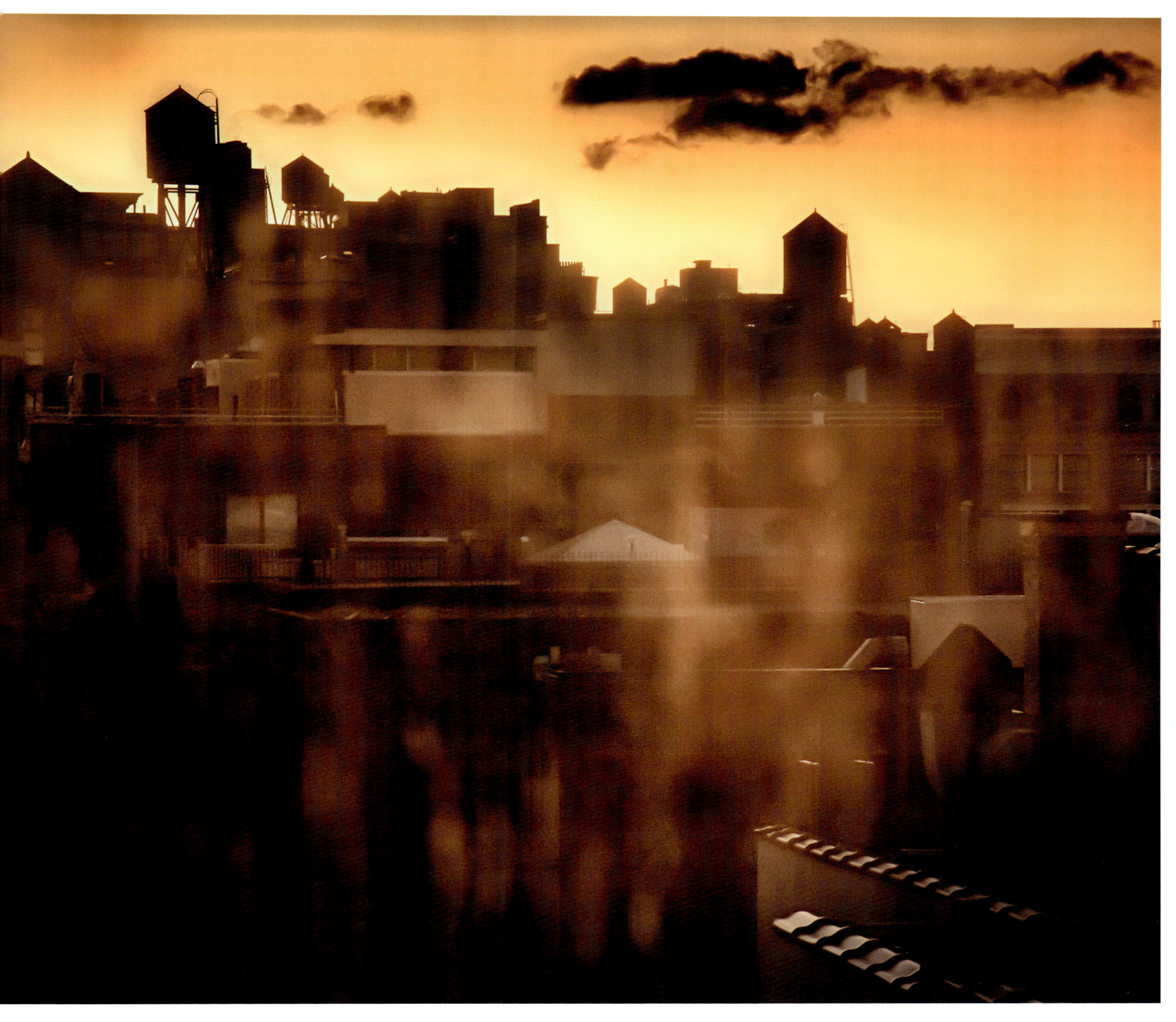

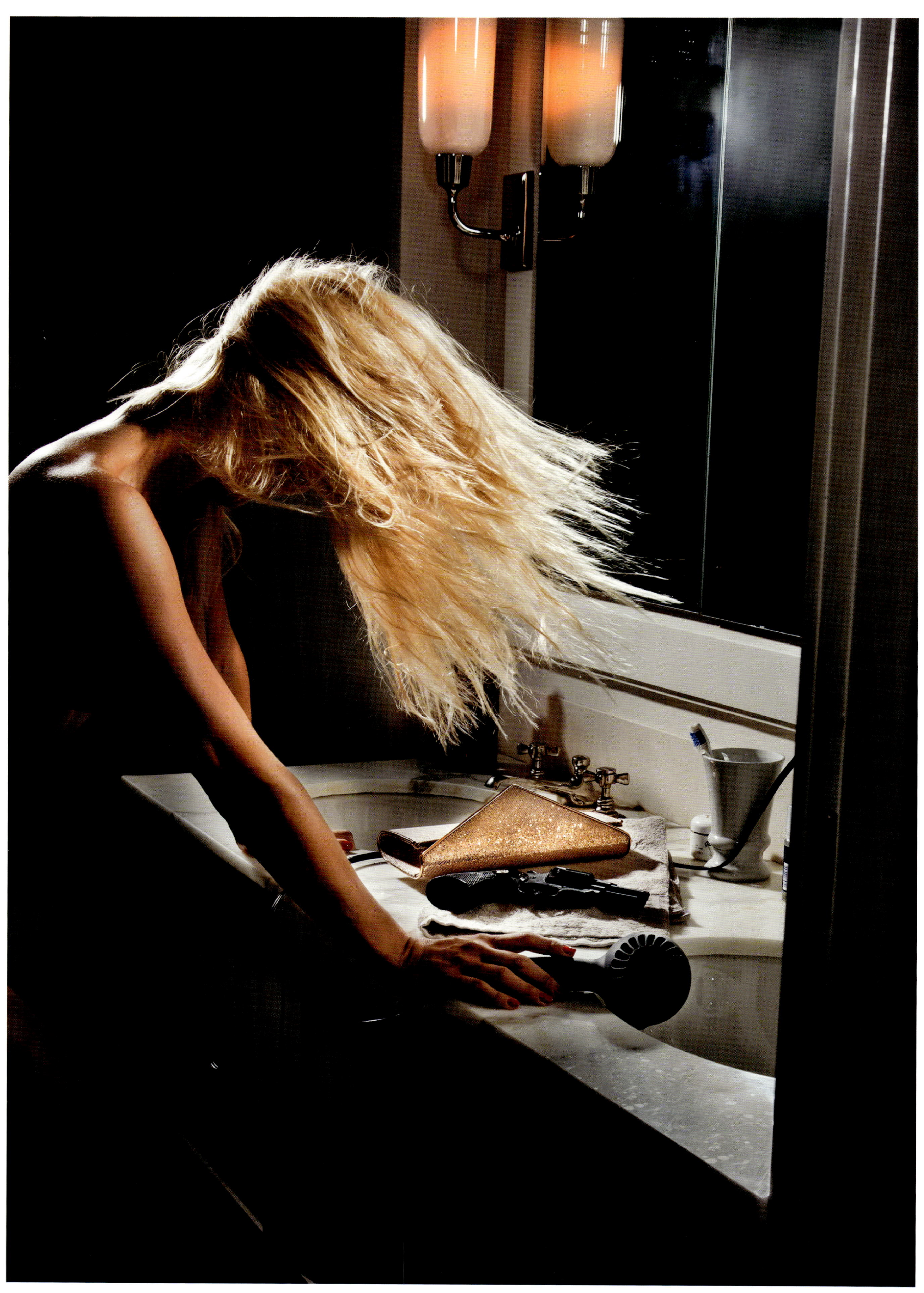

GETTING READY | 2012

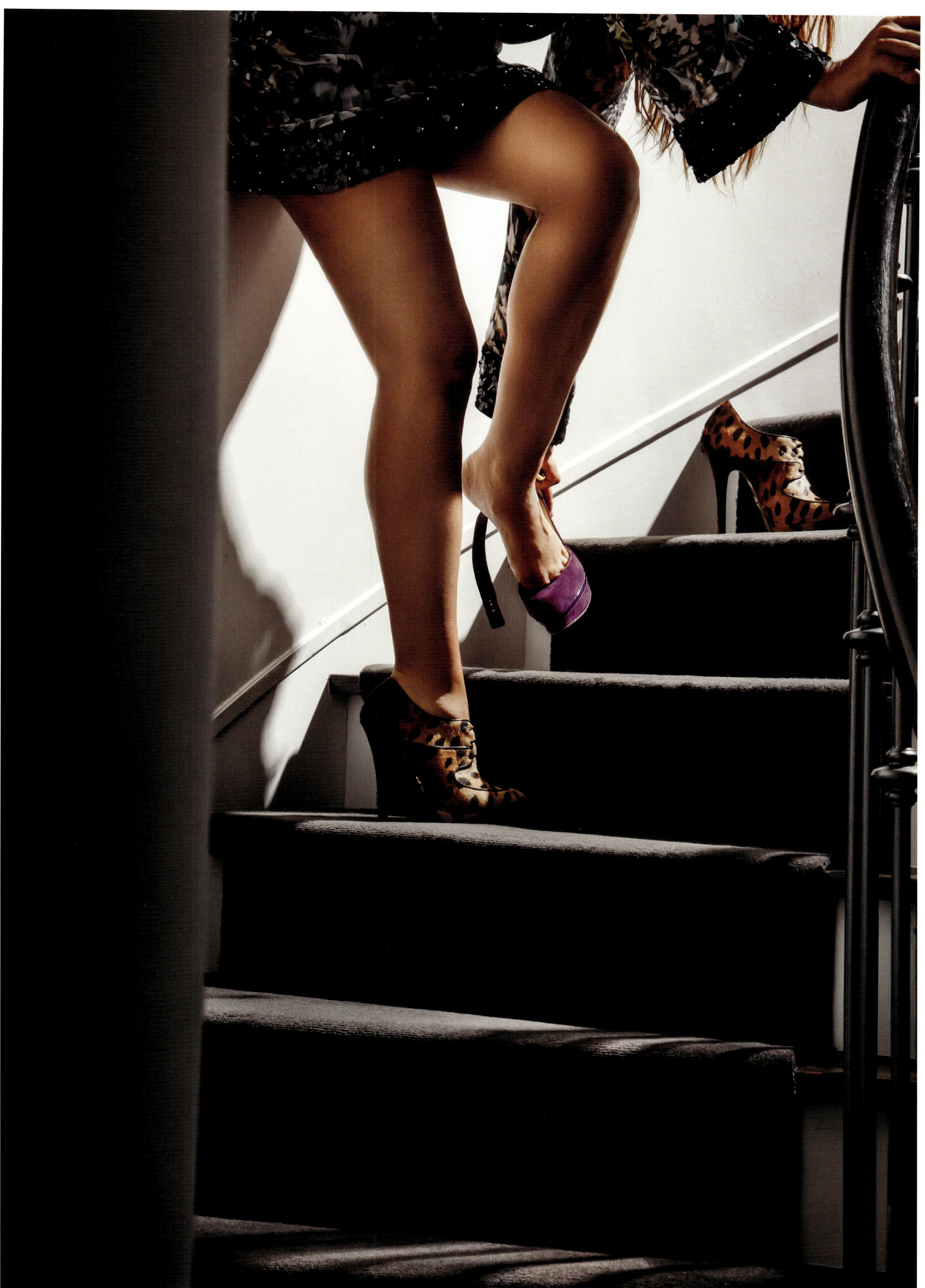

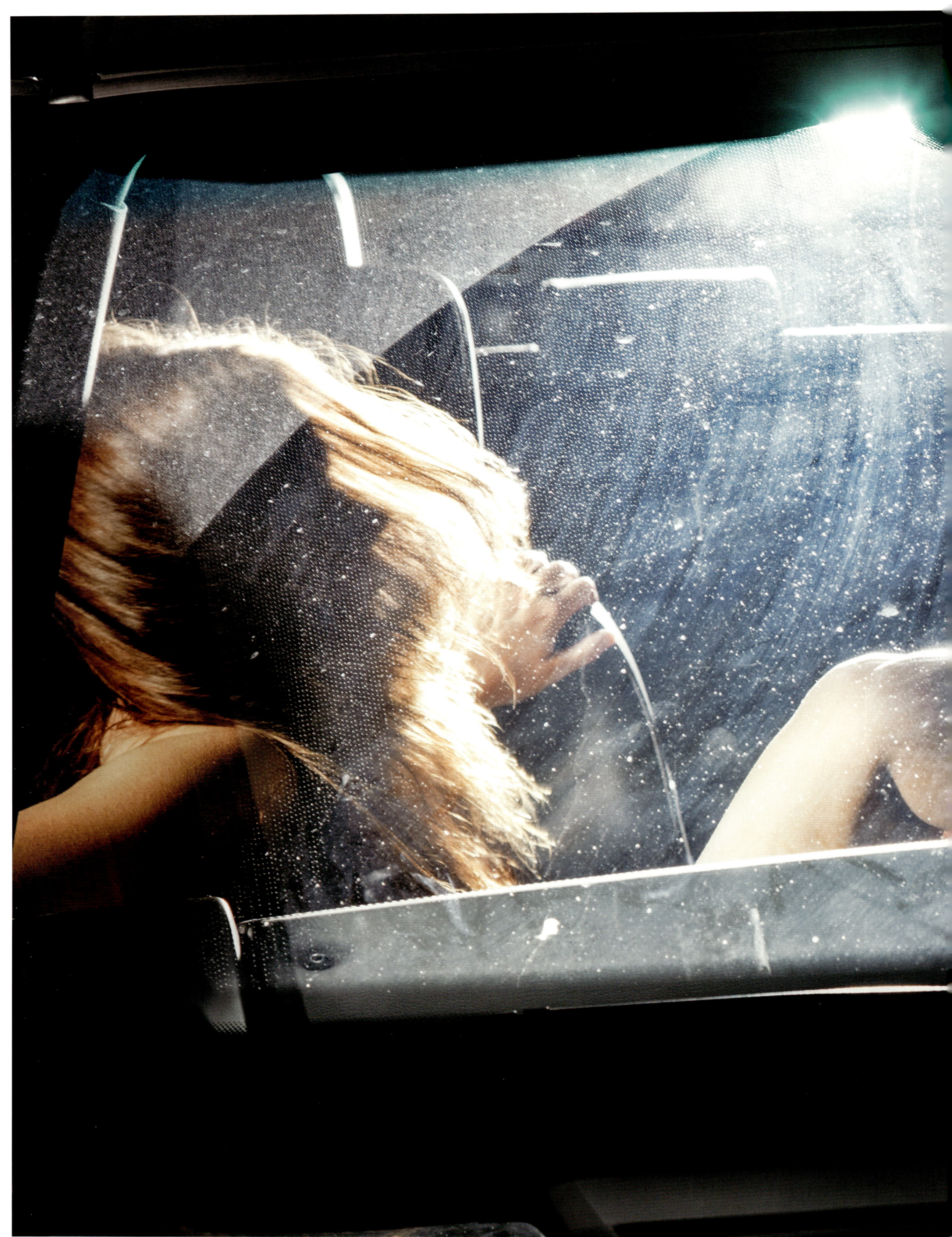

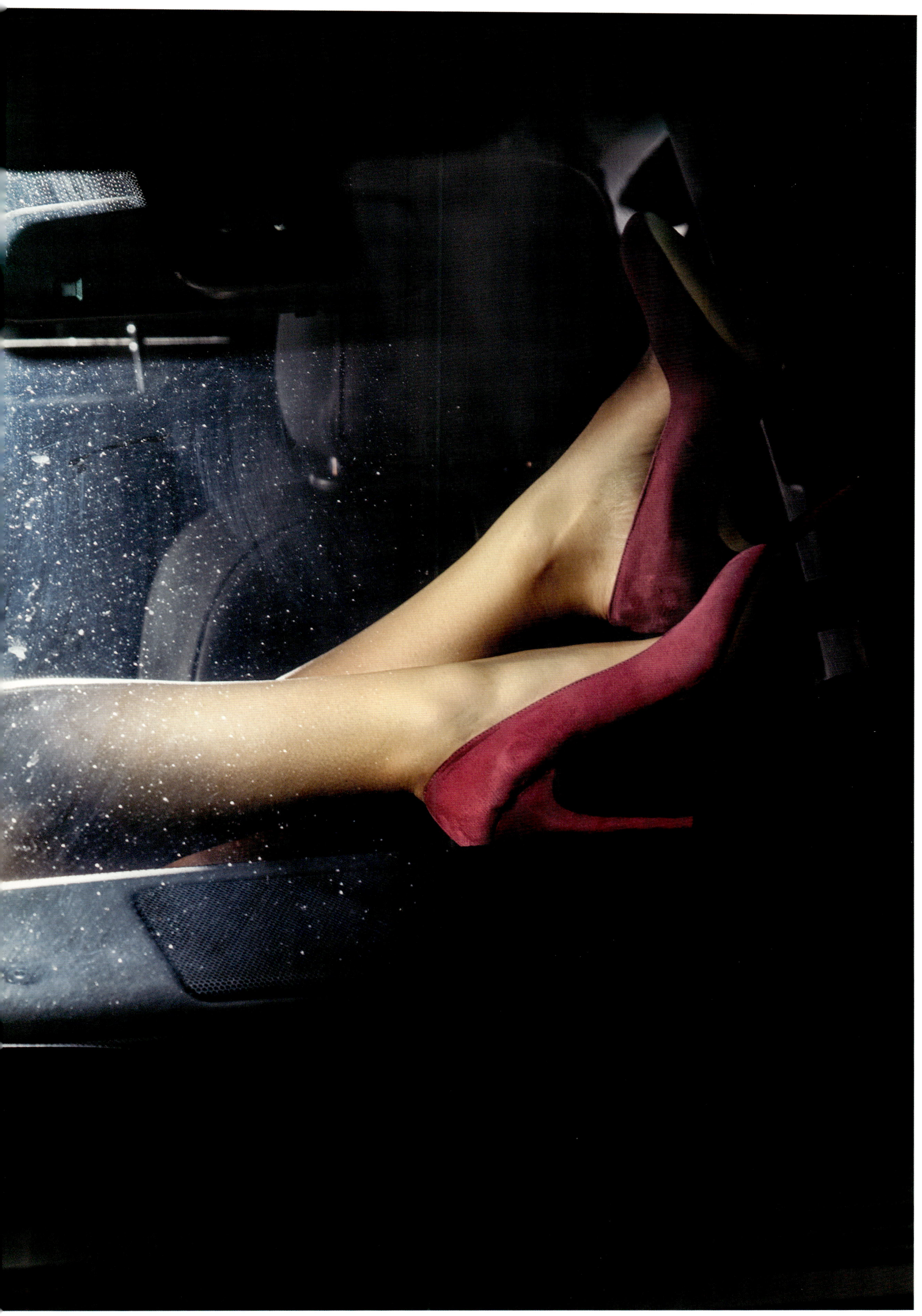

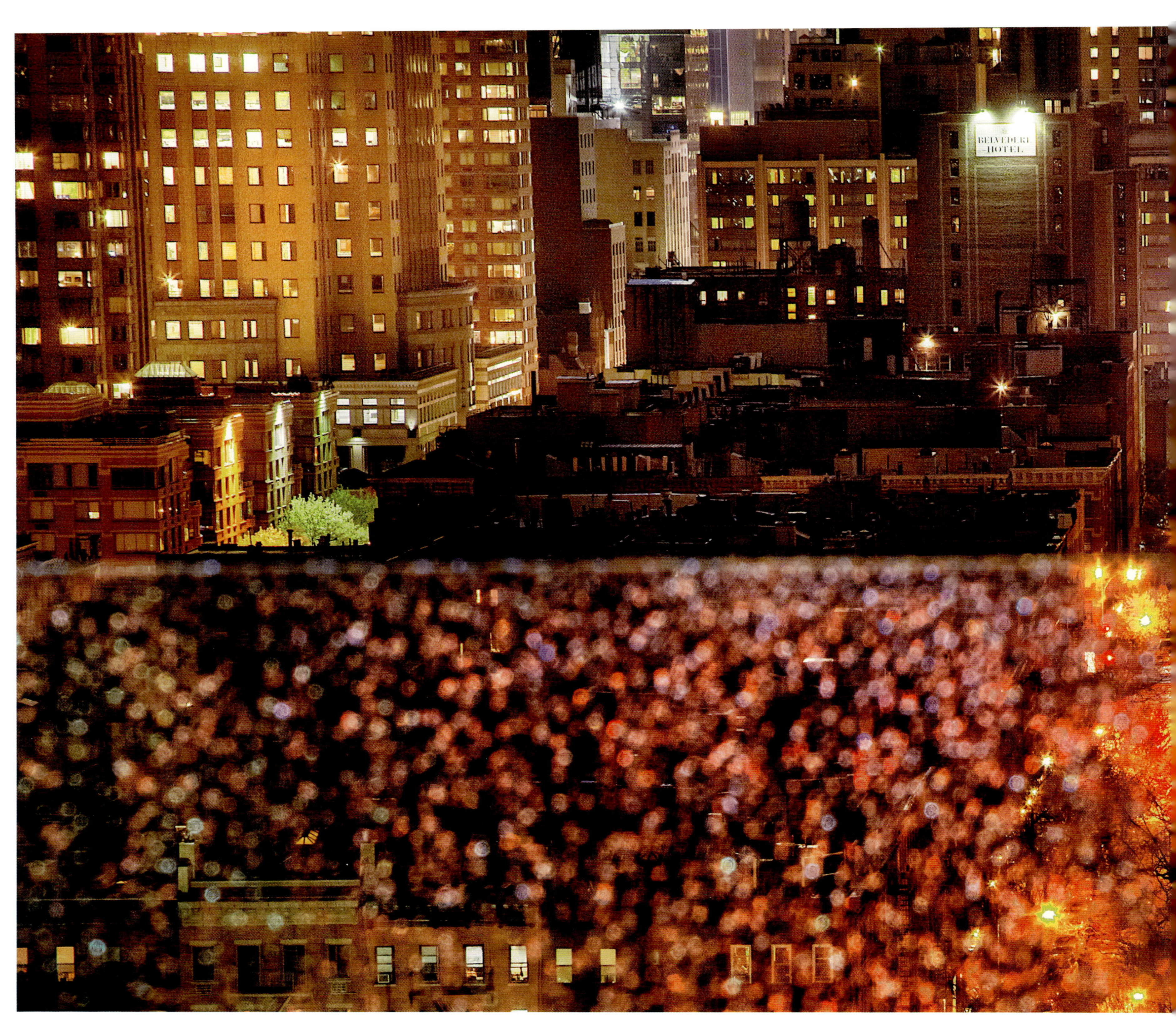
BELVEDERE
HOTEL

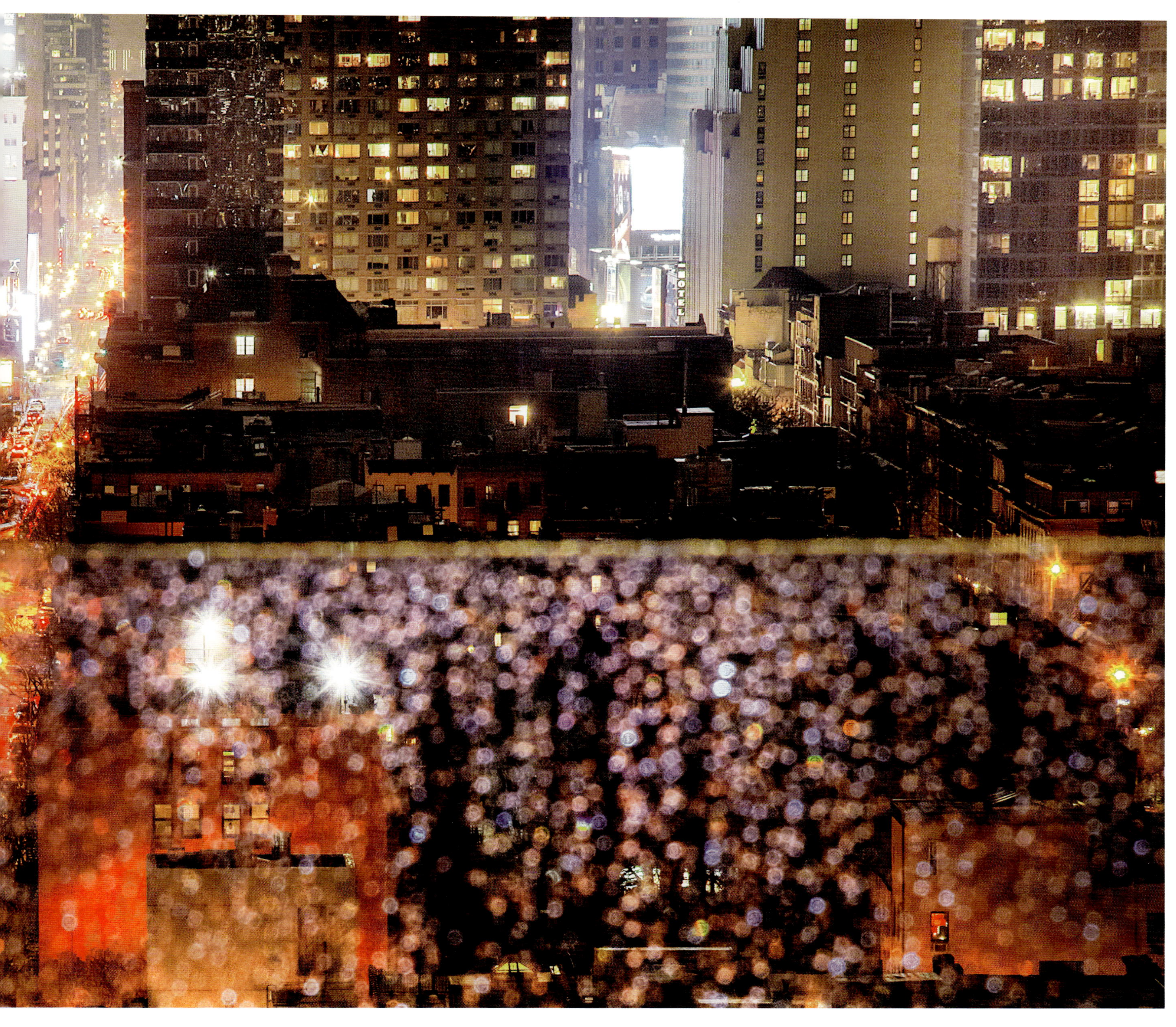

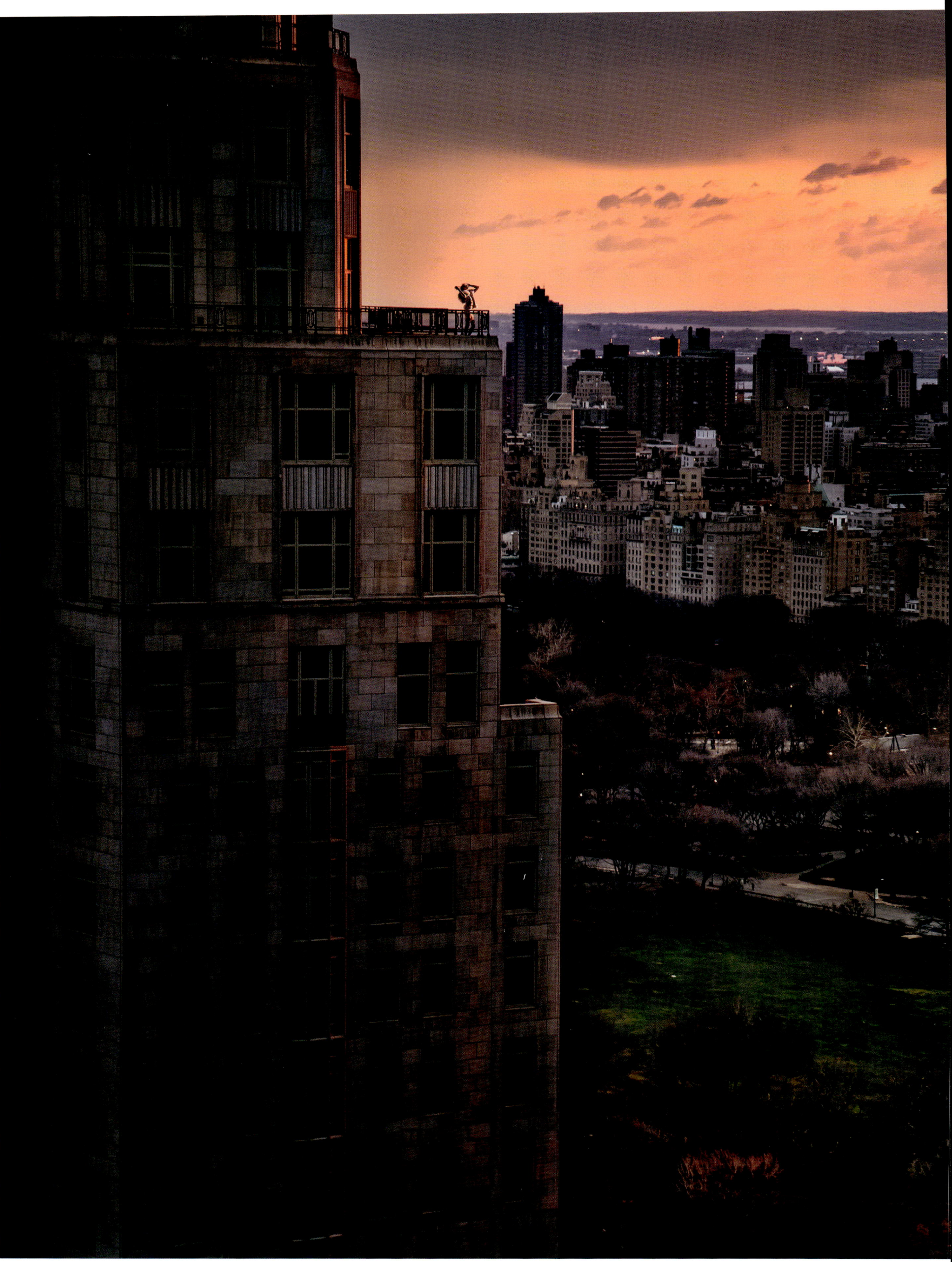

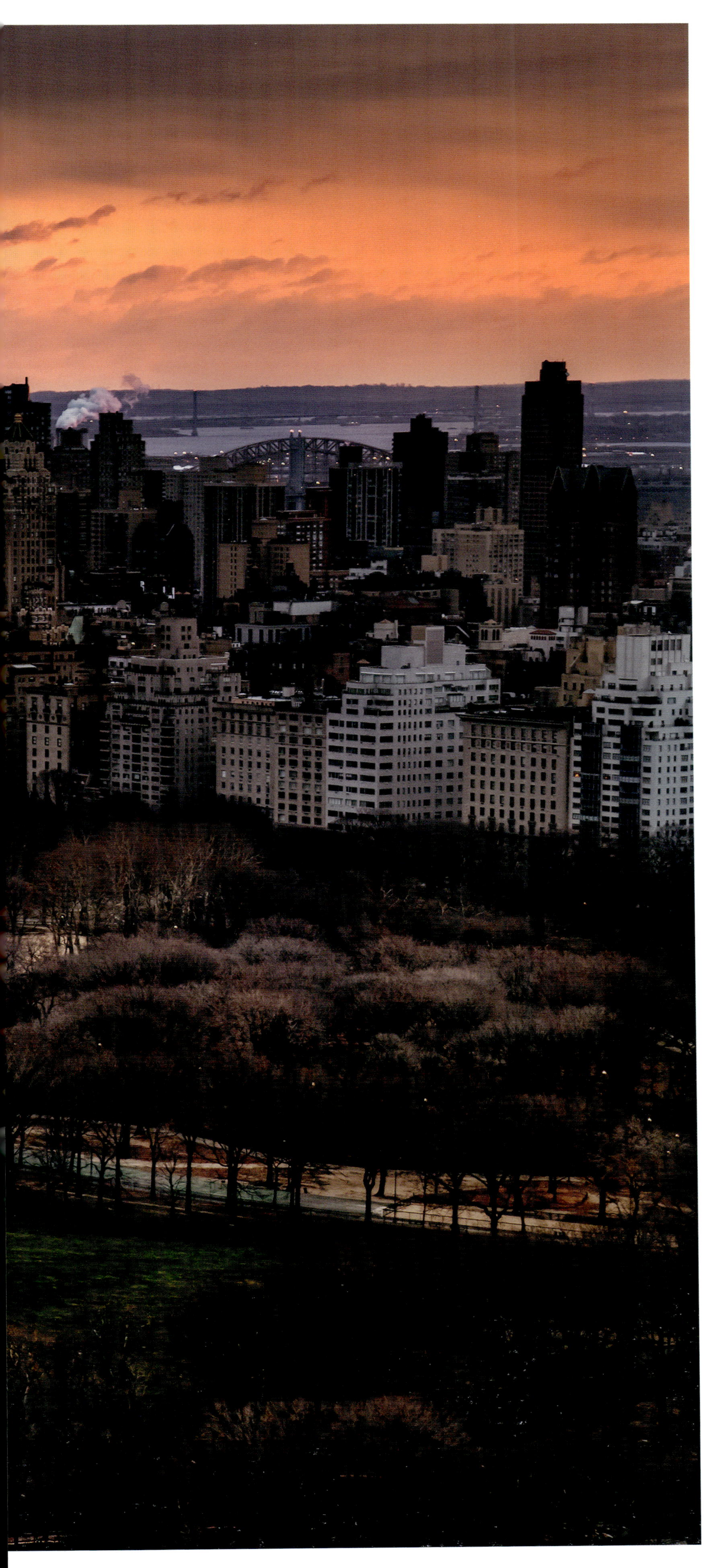

GIRL OVER CENTRAL PARK | 2012

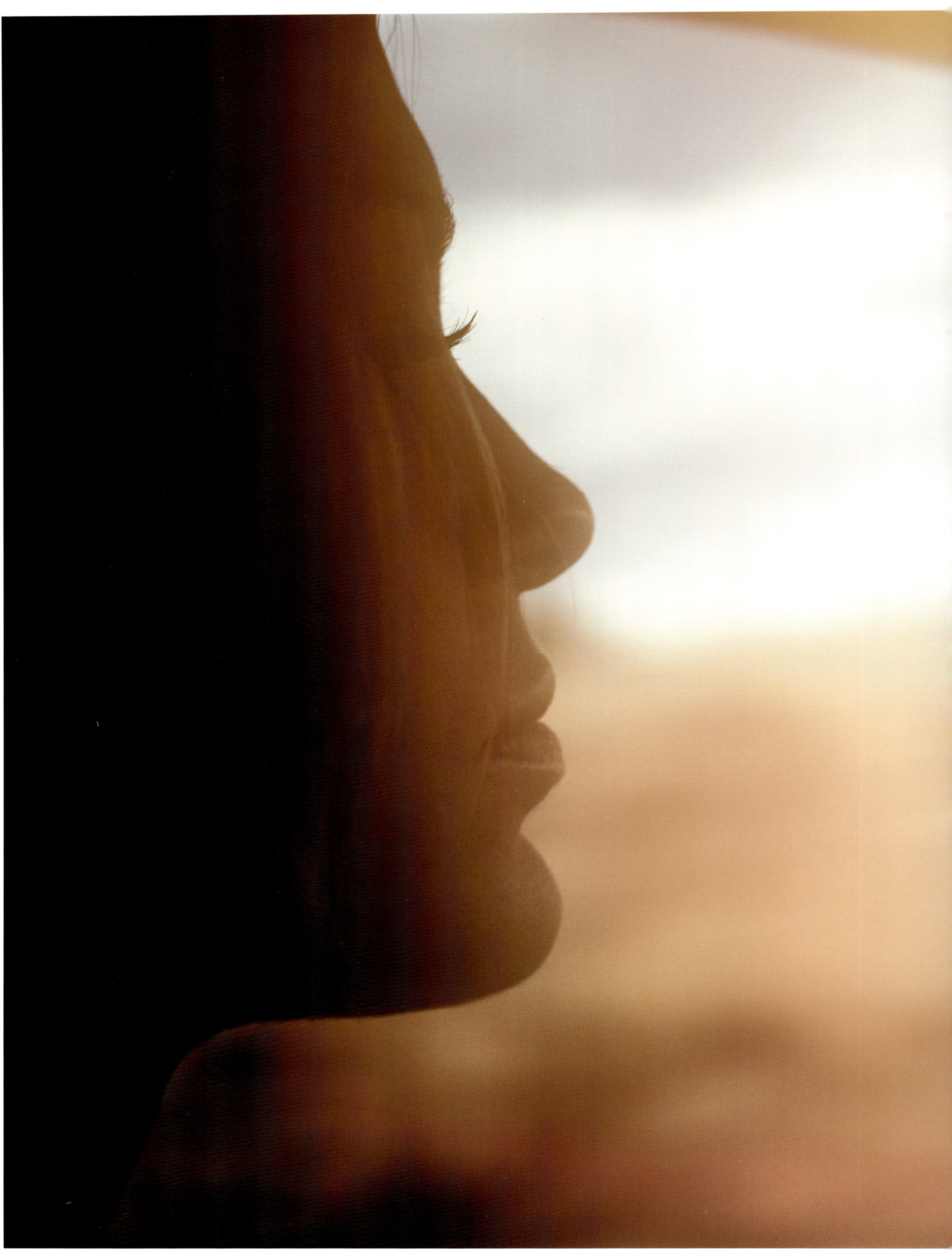

HAZY DREAMS I 2012

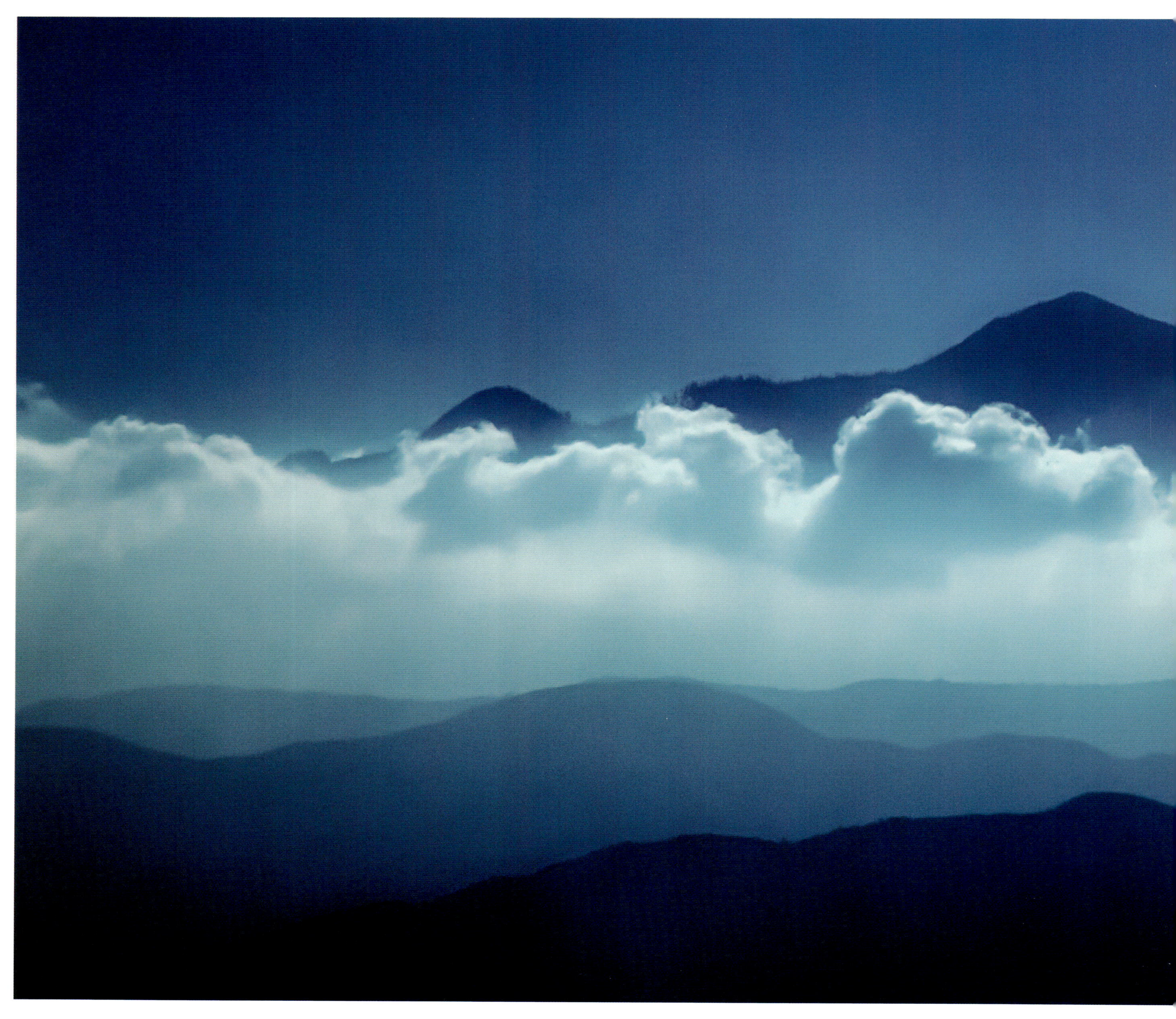

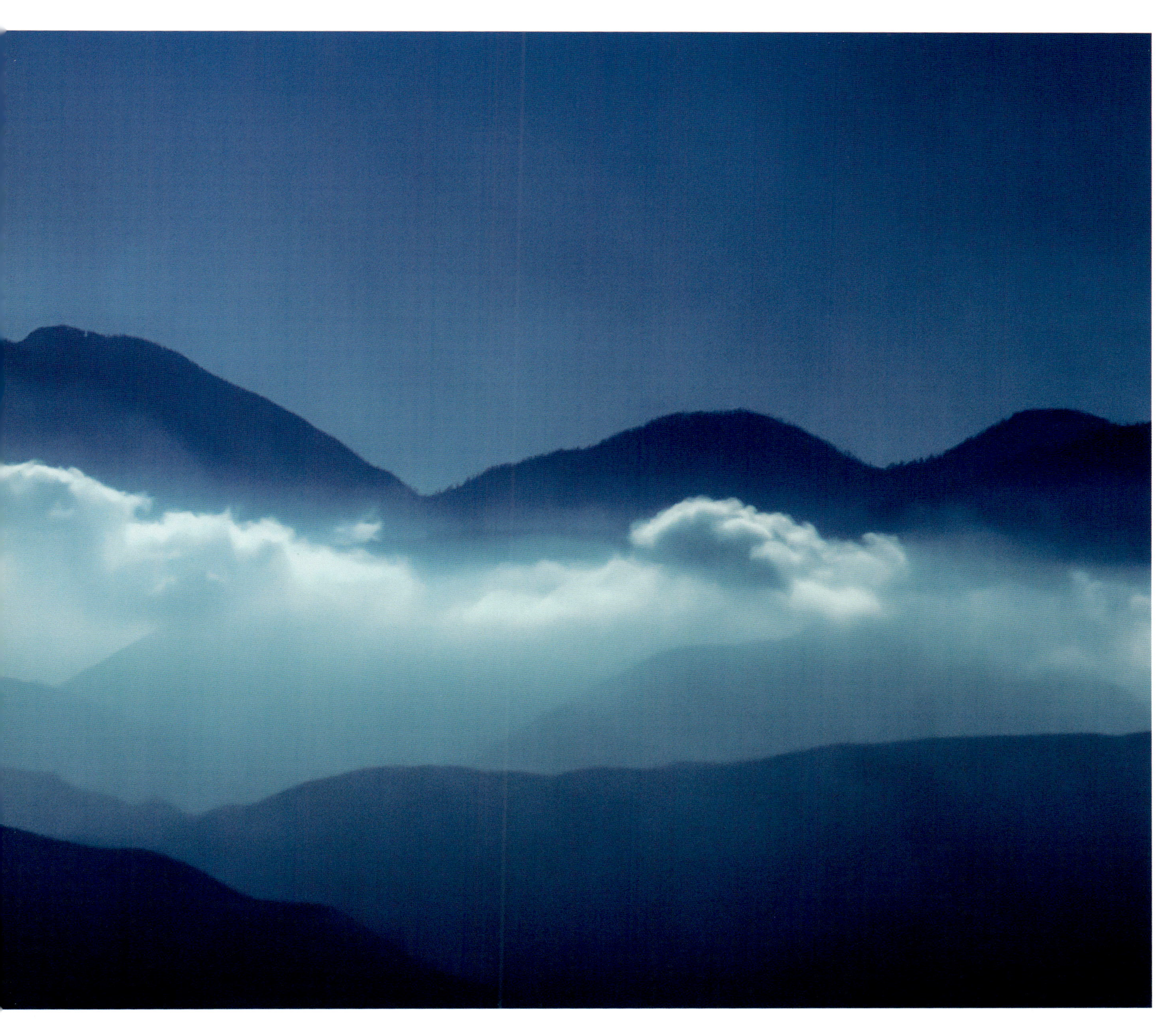

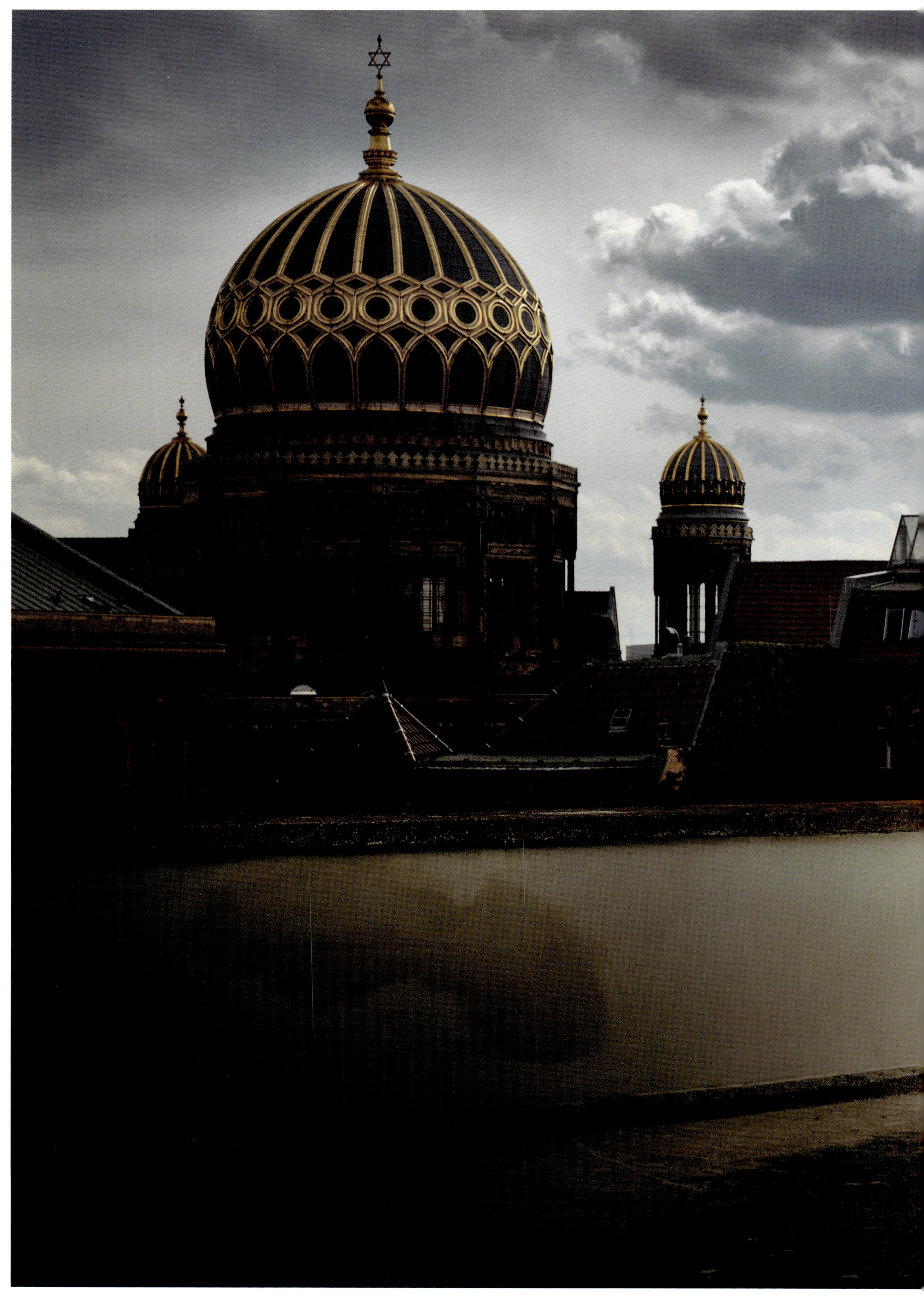

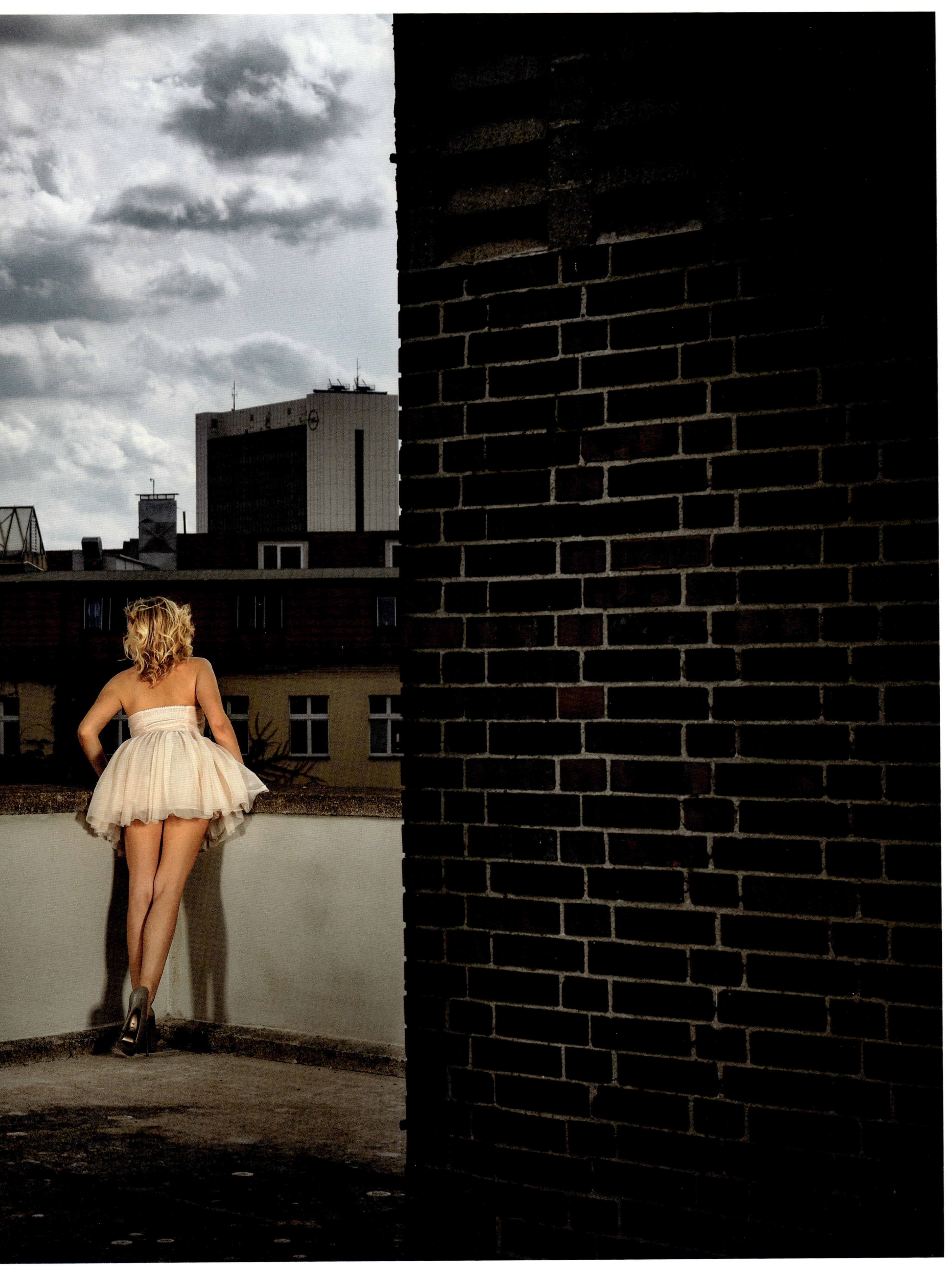

AFTERNOON FROM BERLIN | 2011

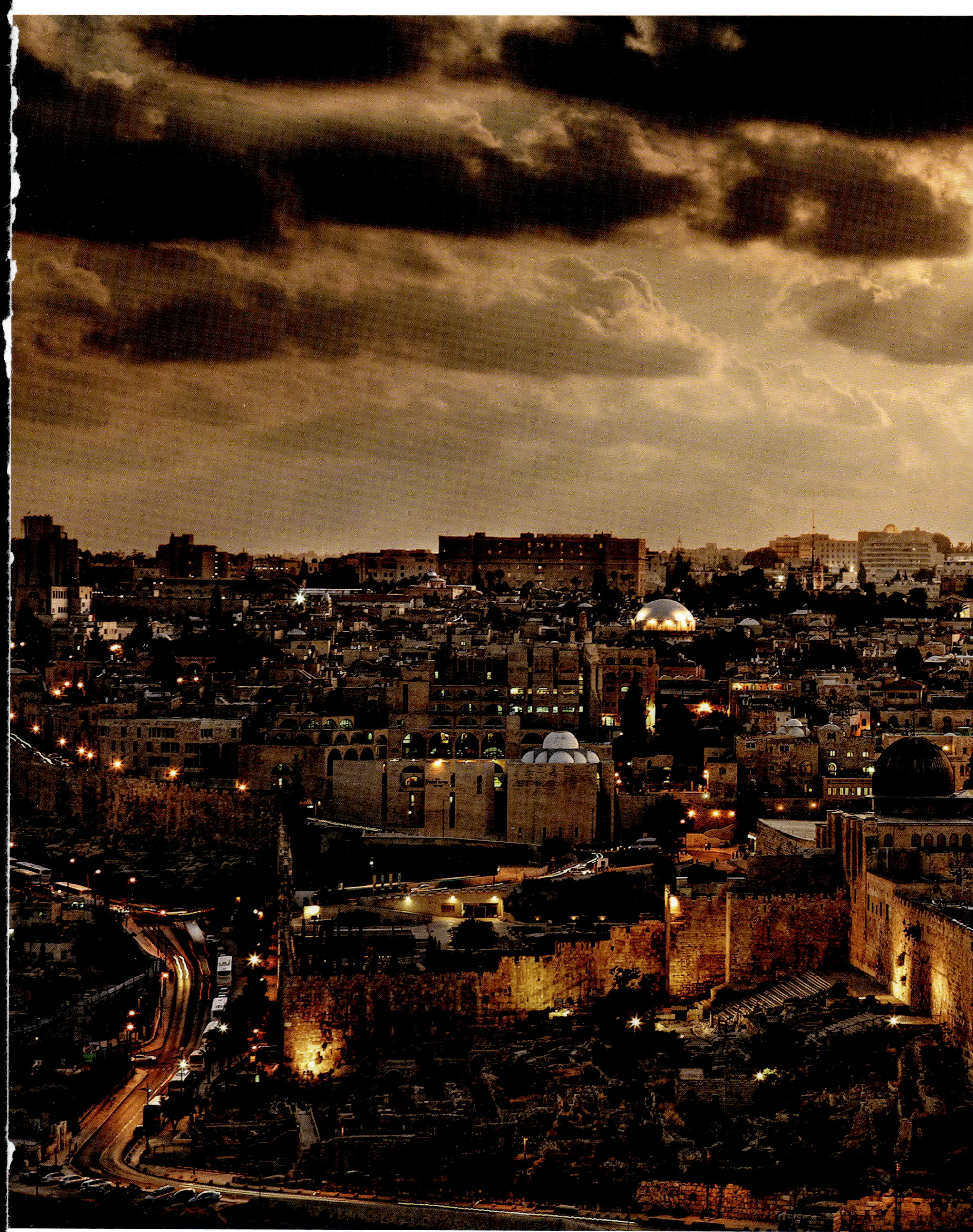

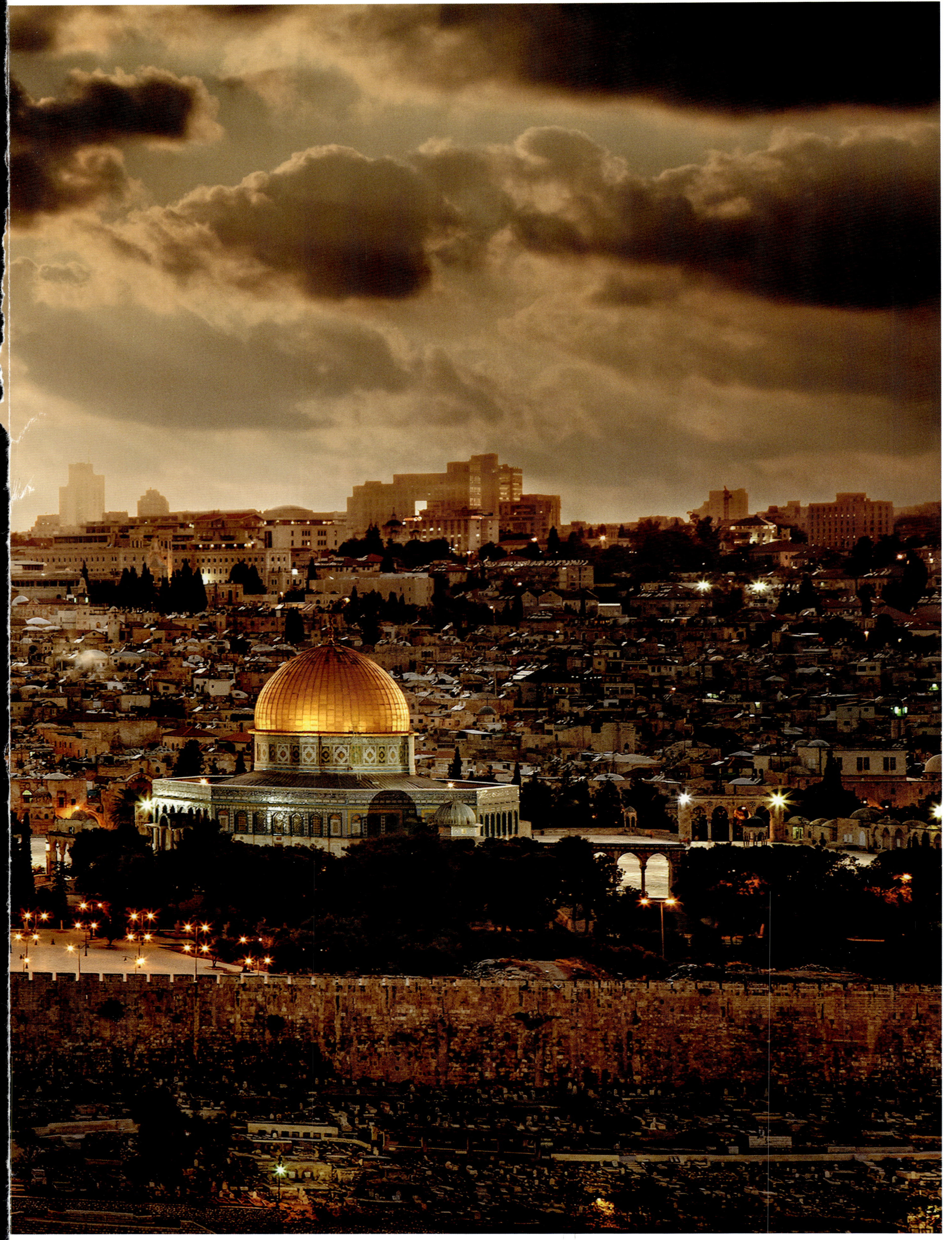

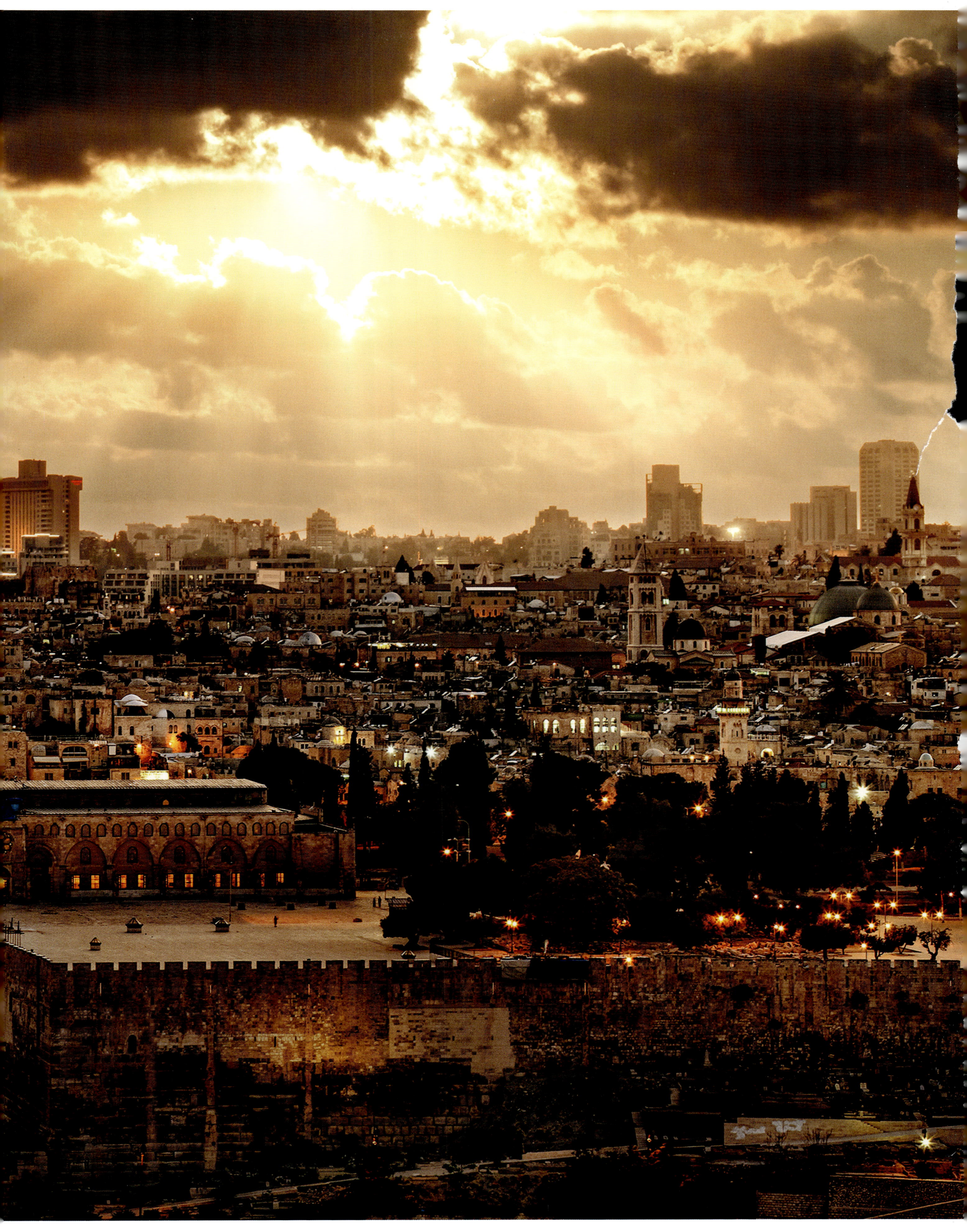

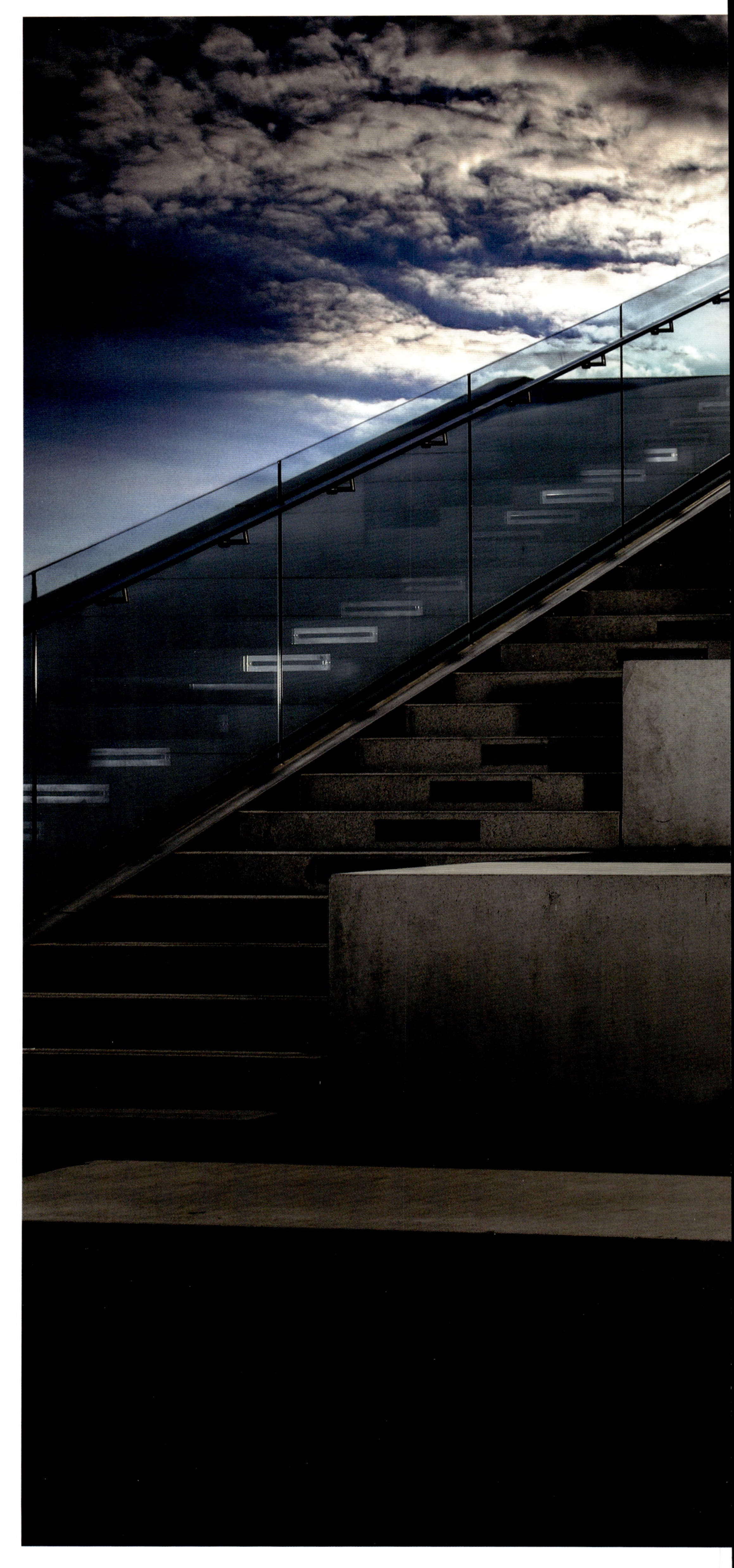

THE GIRL IN THE BLACK DRESS I 2011

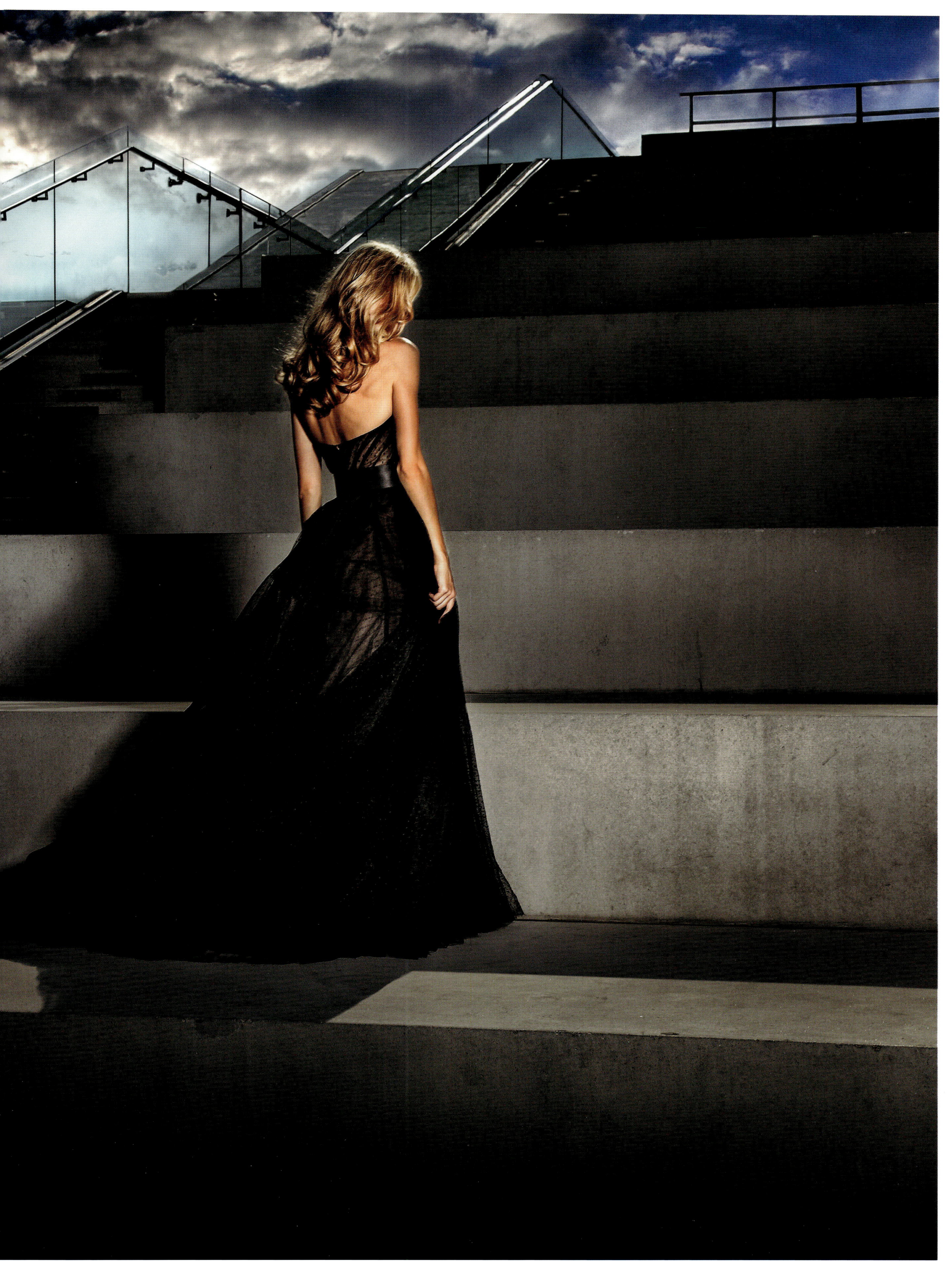

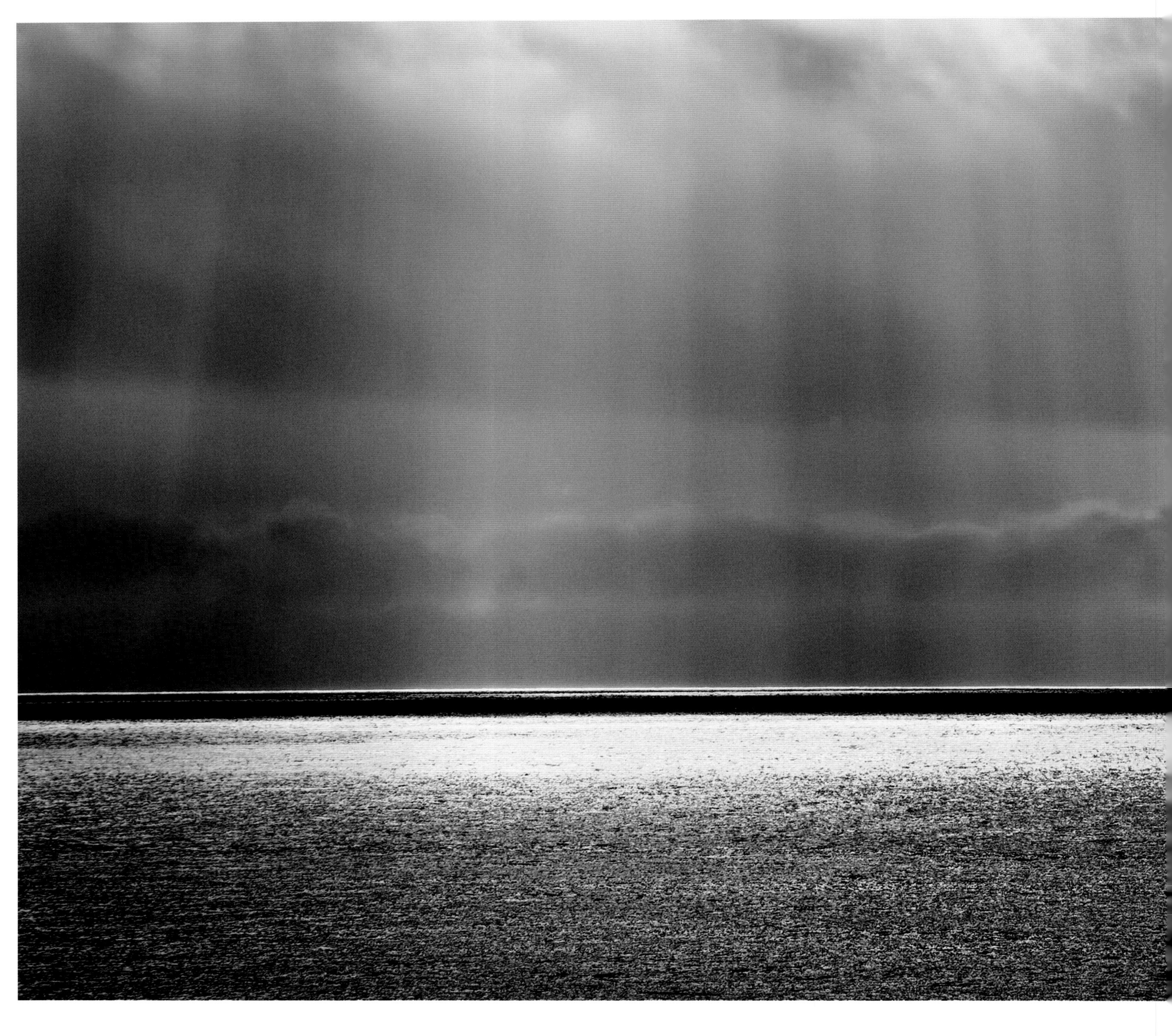

HEAVEN CAN WAIT | 2011

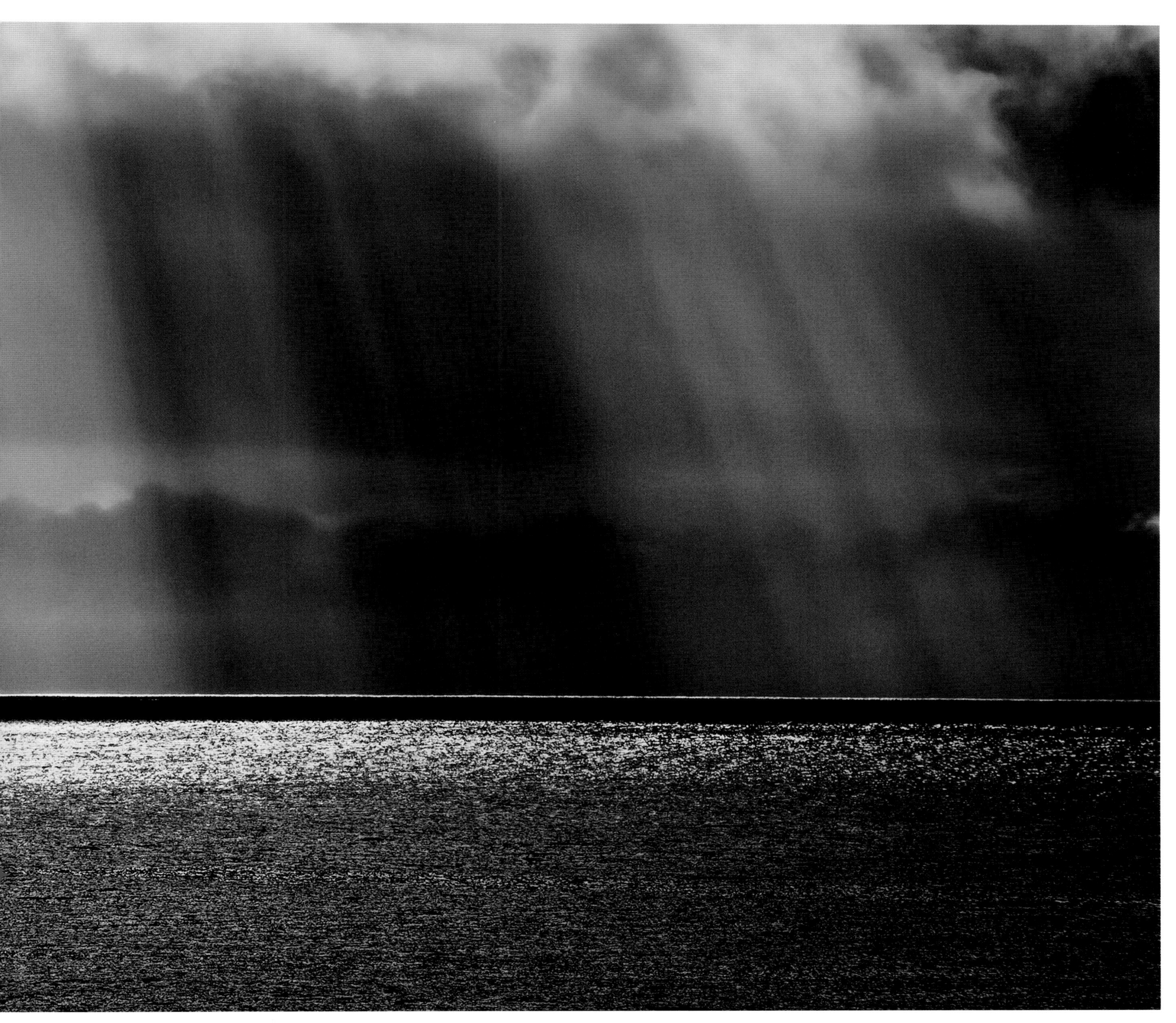

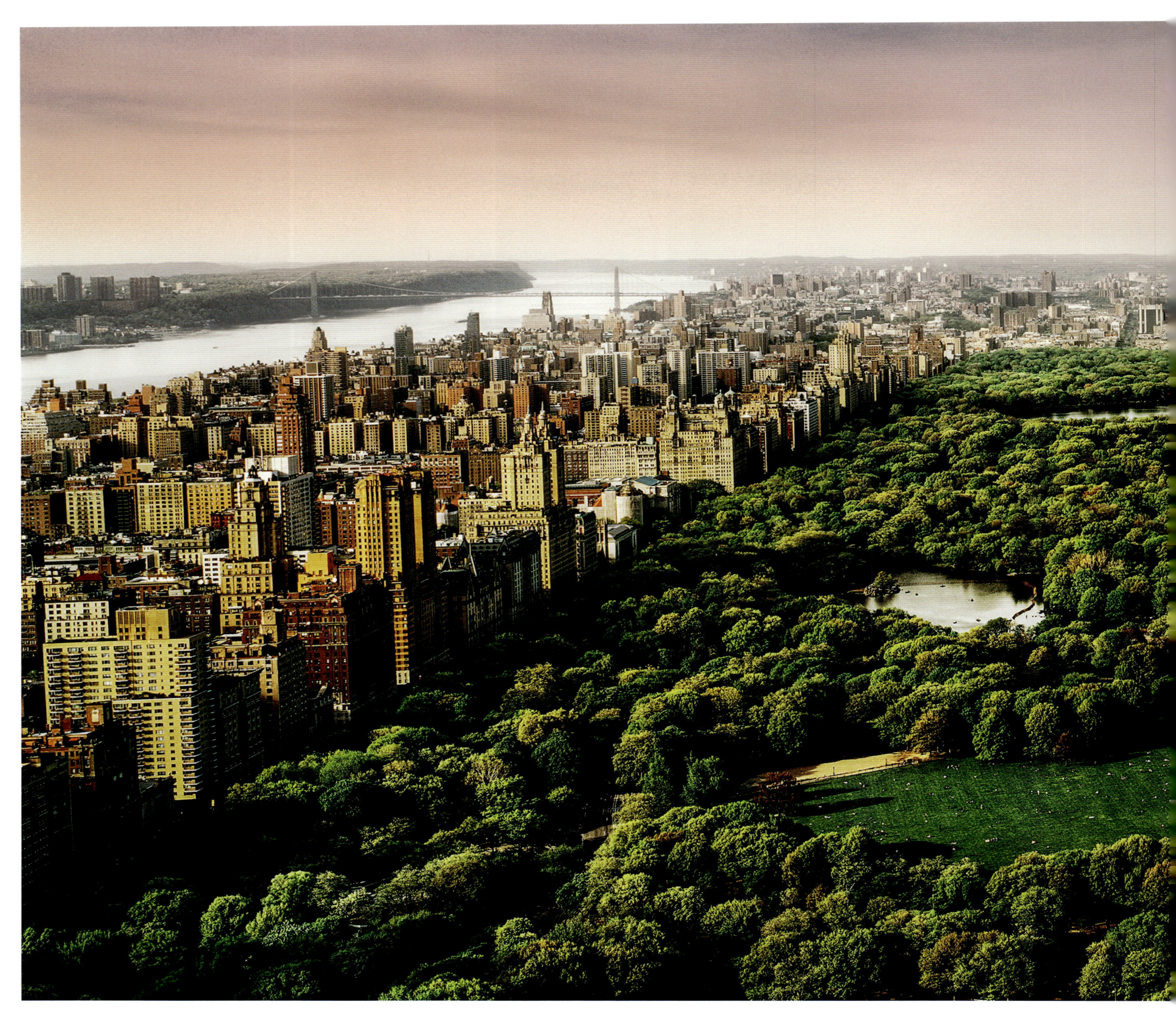

DREAMS OF CENTRAL PARK | 2006

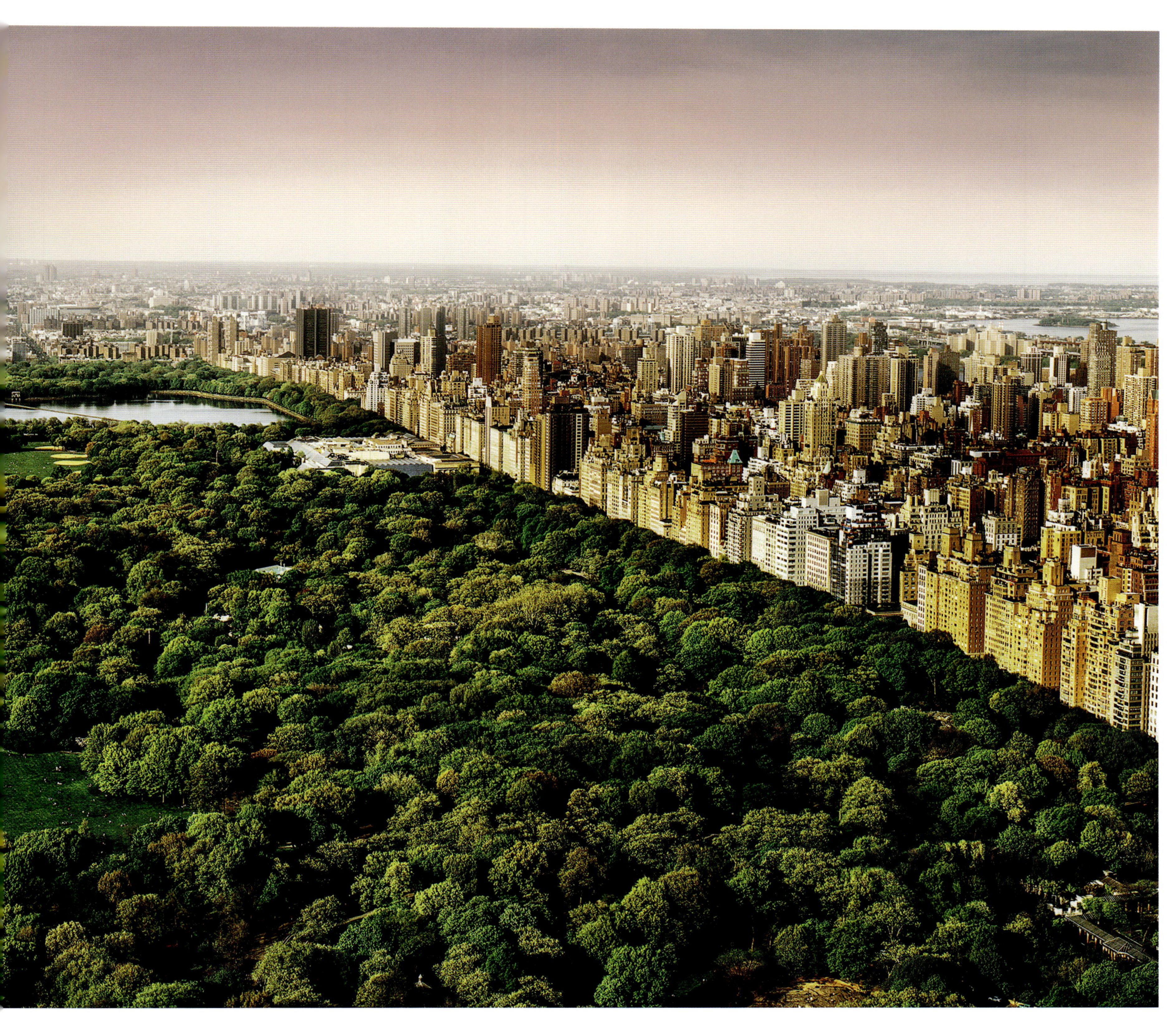

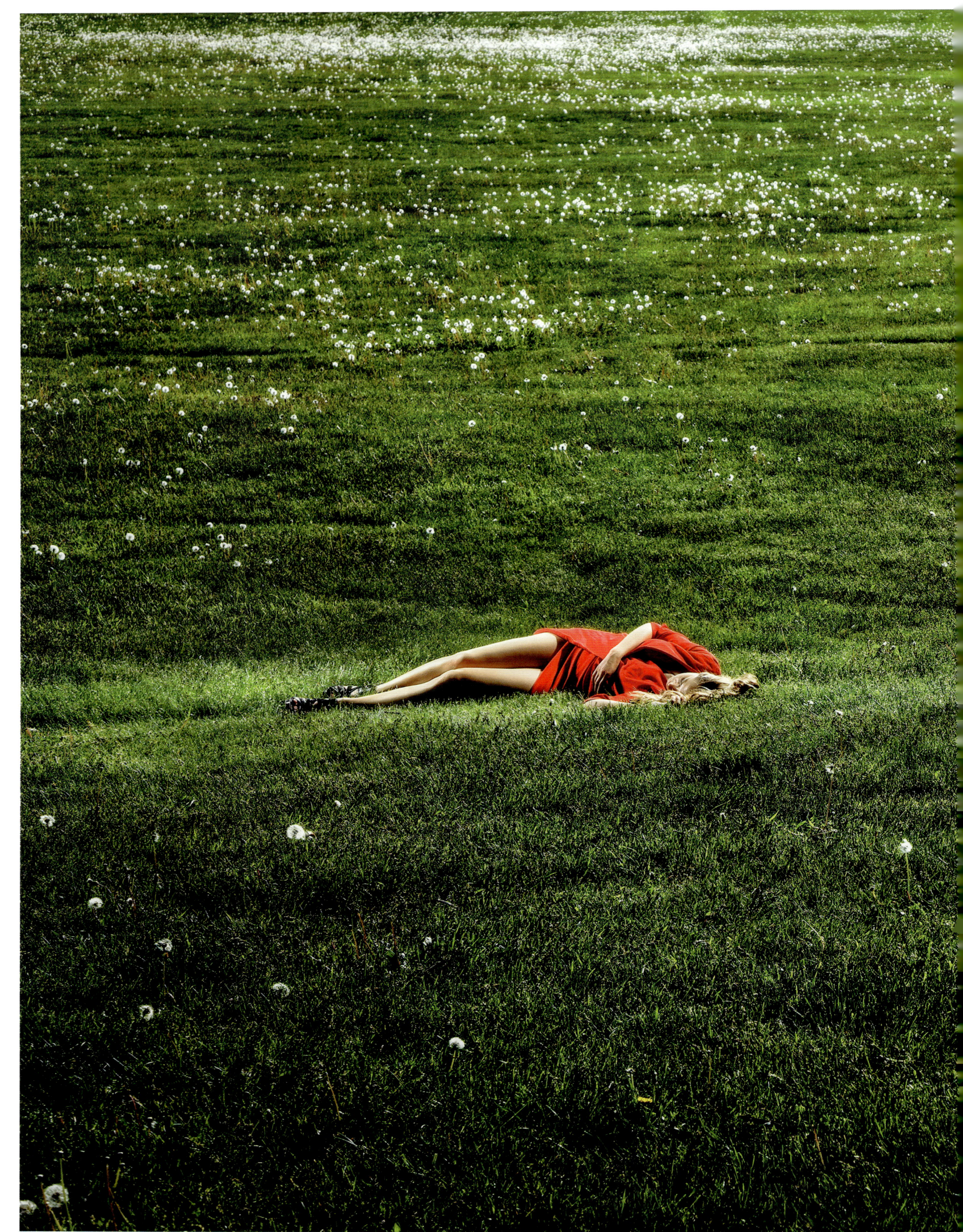

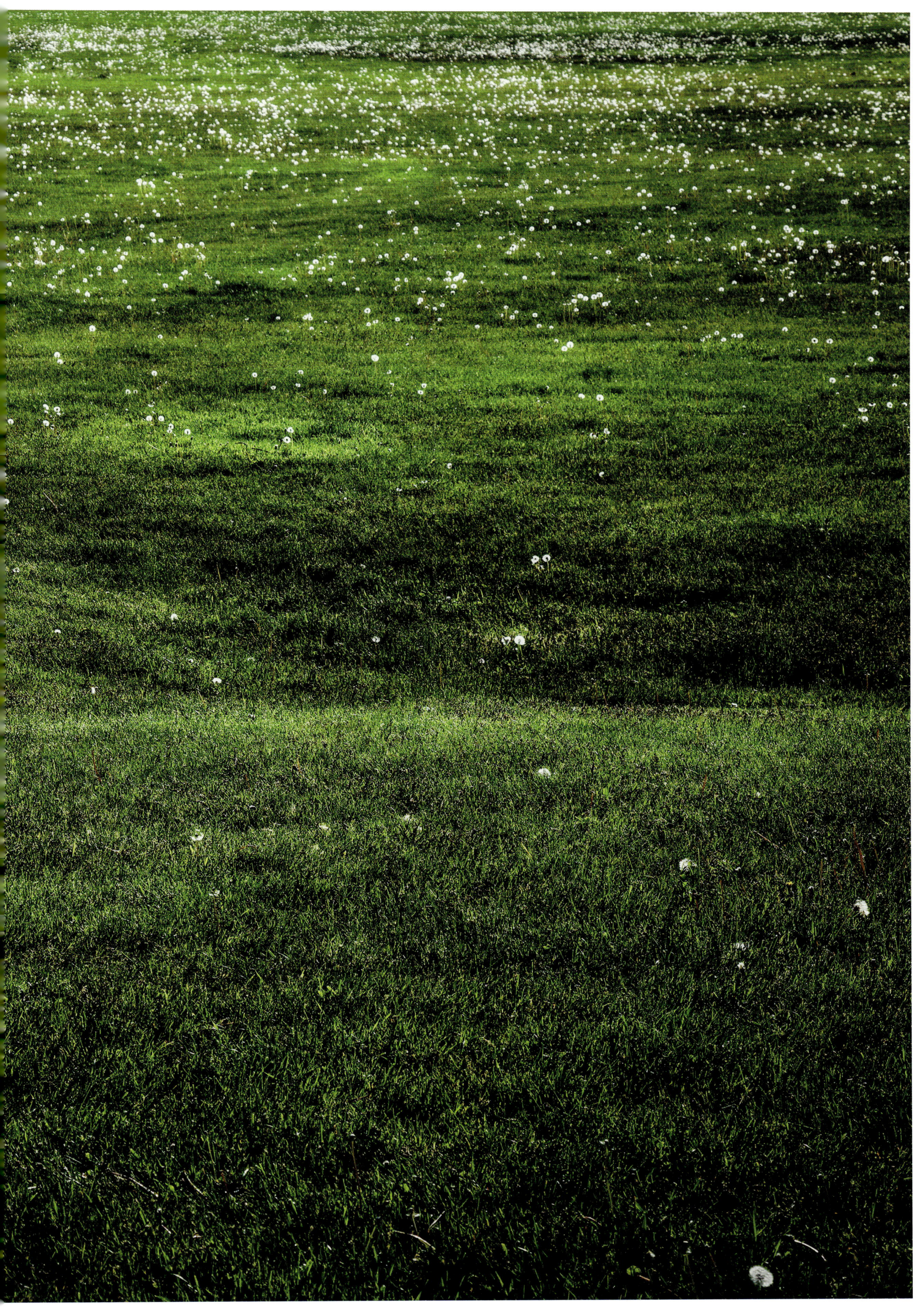

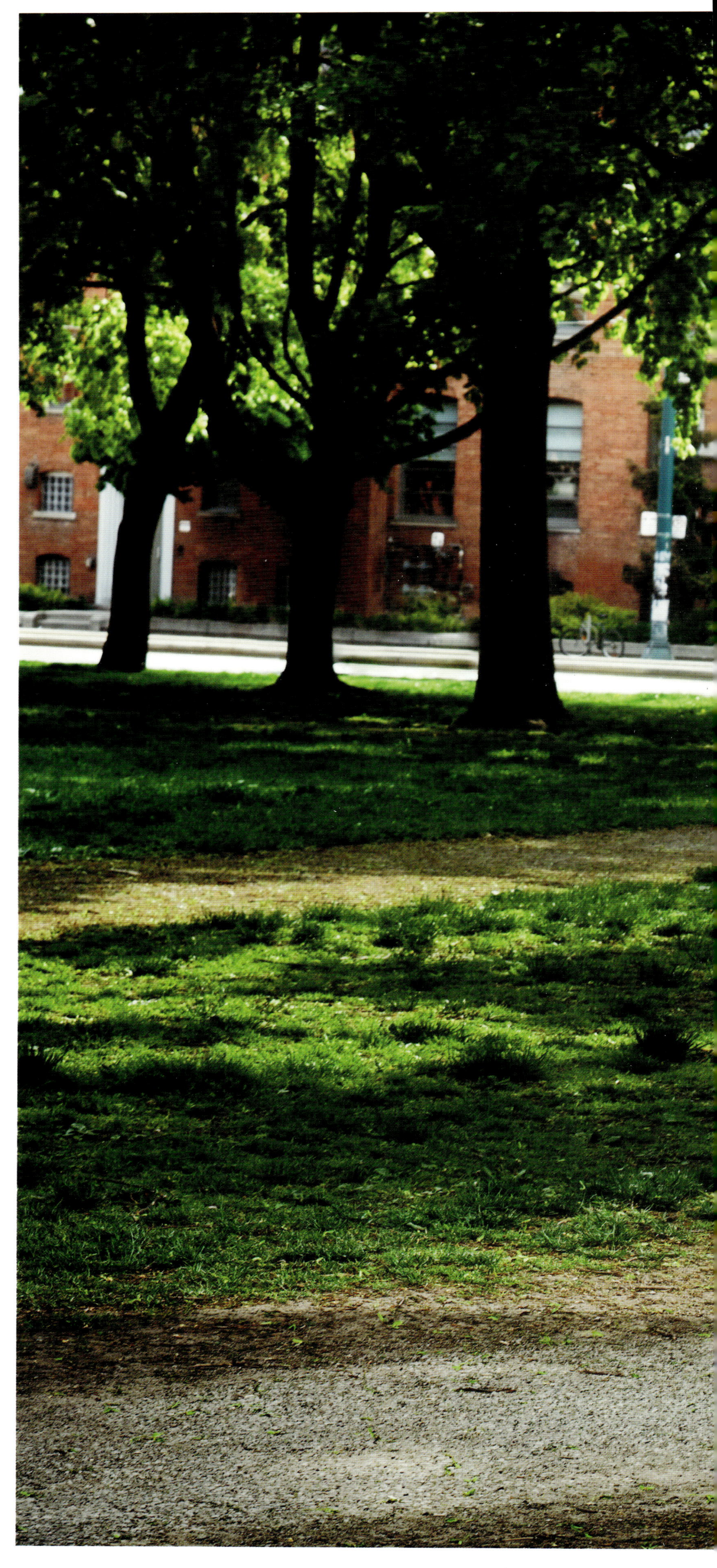

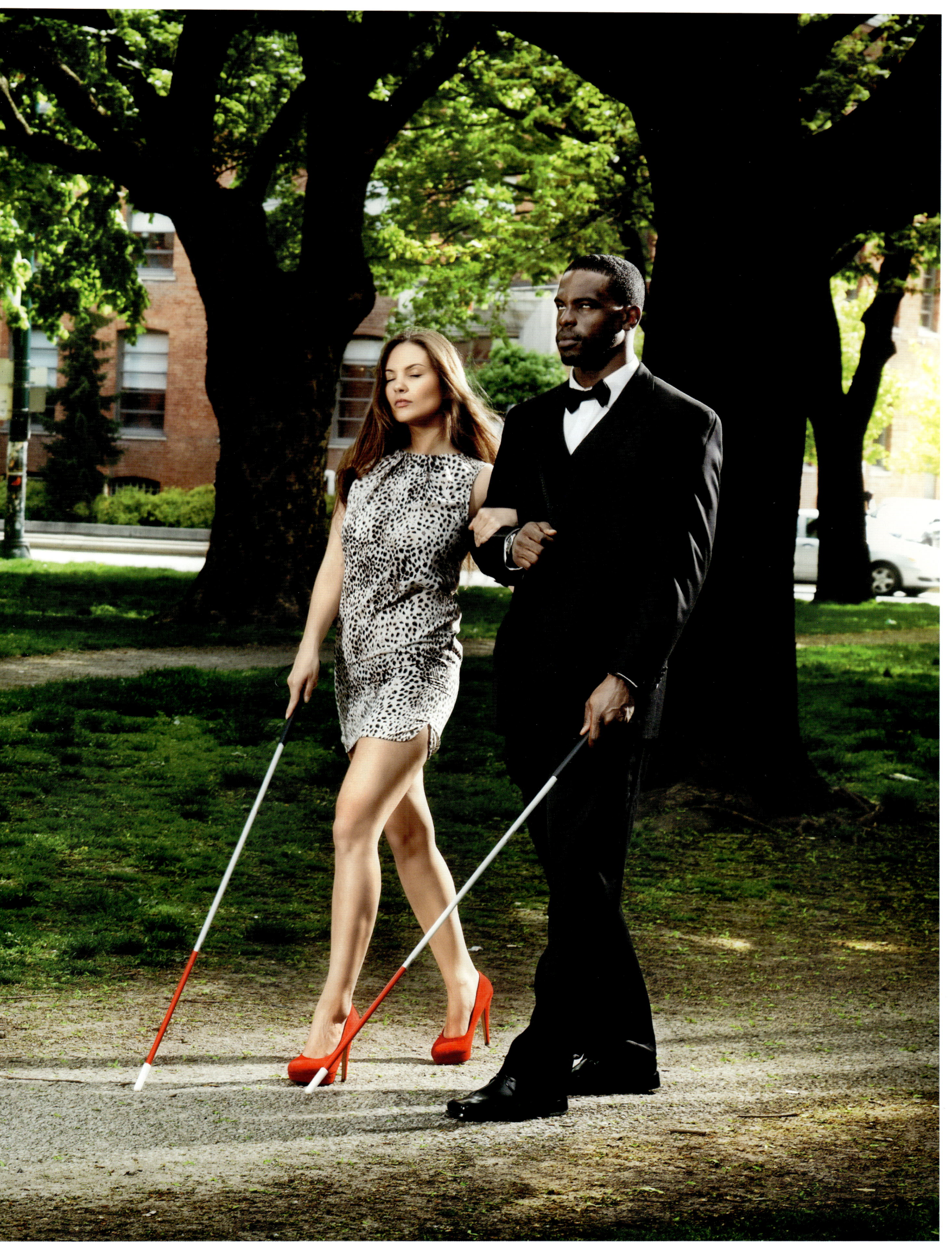

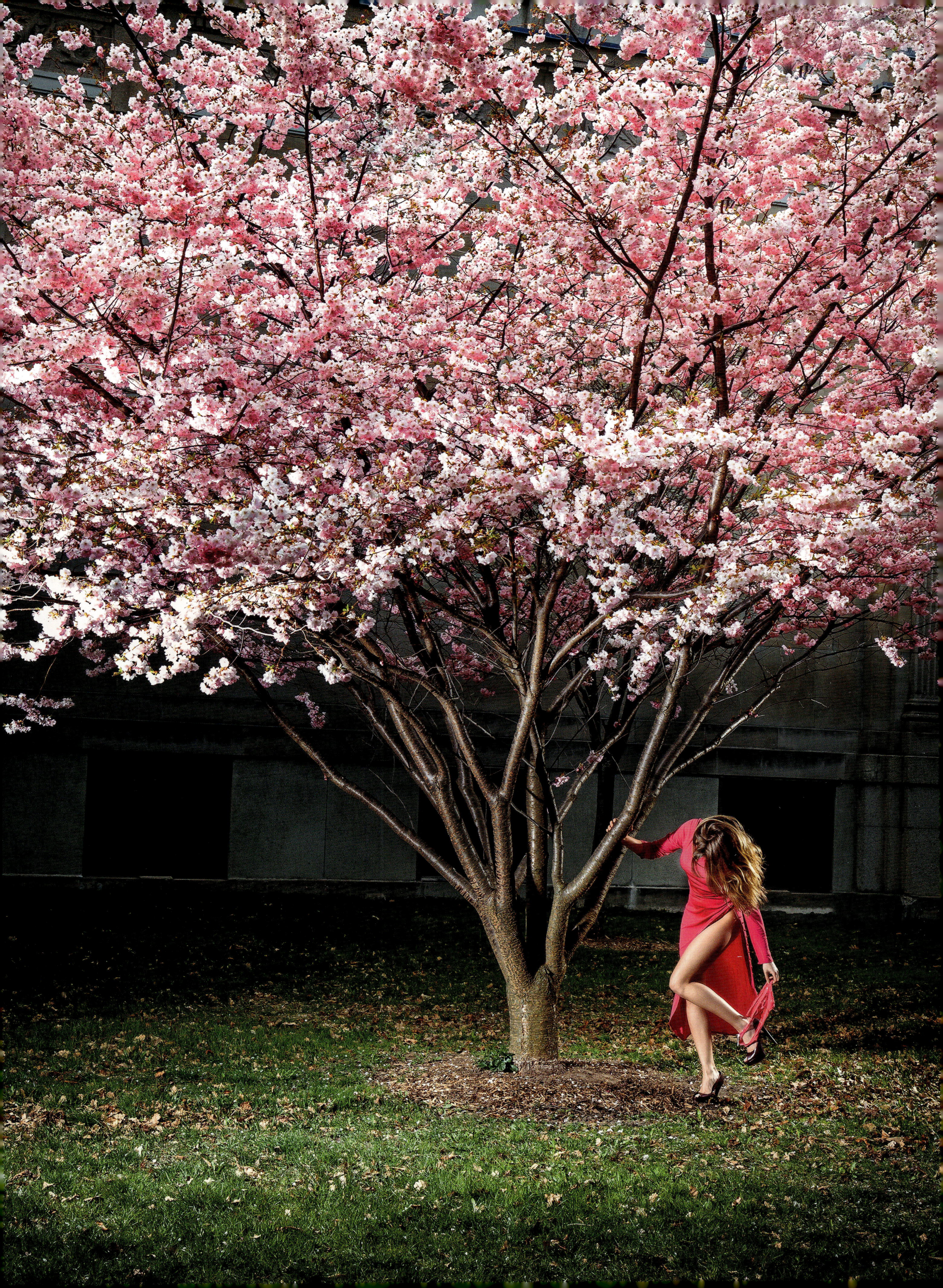

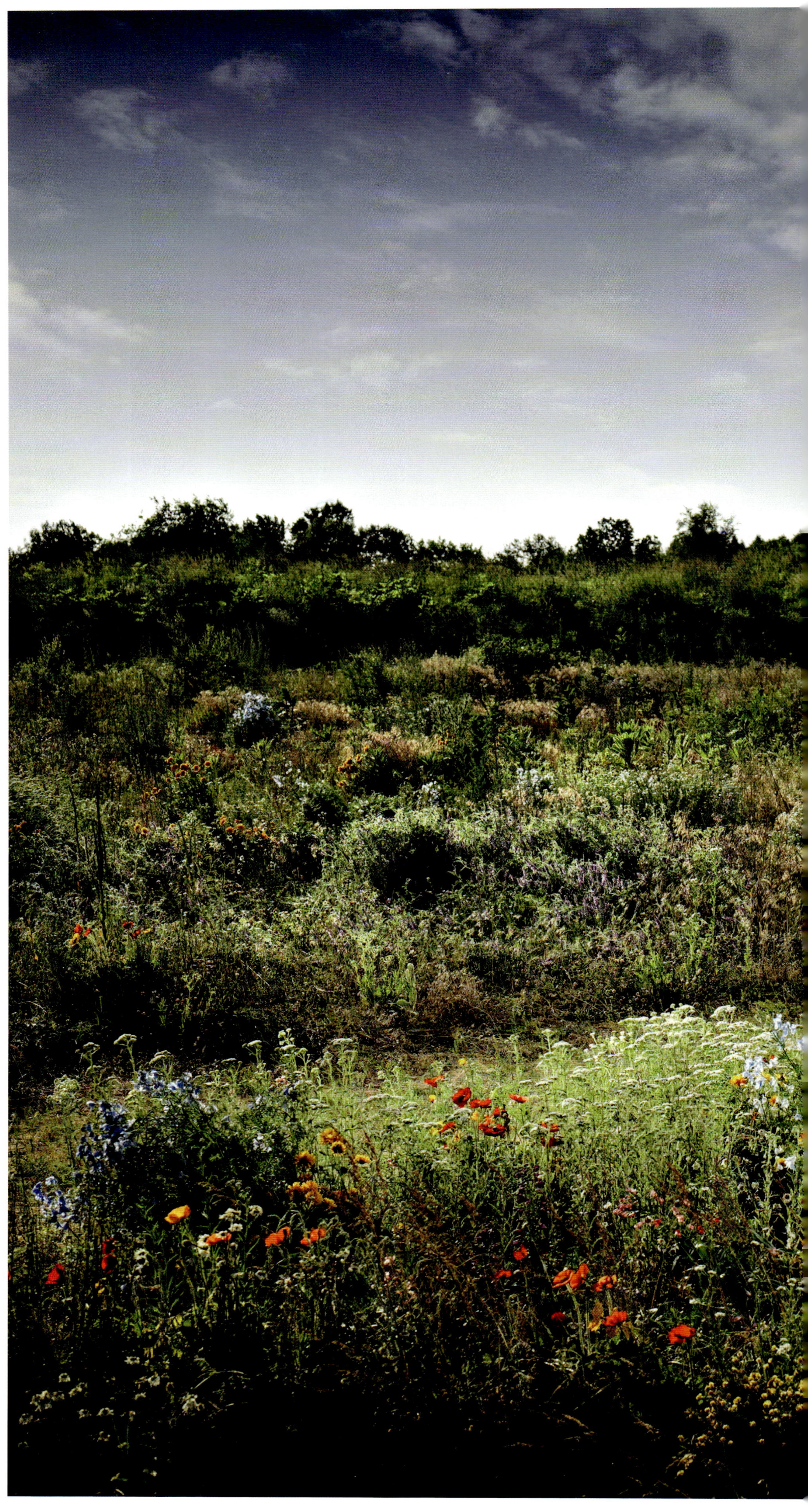

FERGIE | 2007

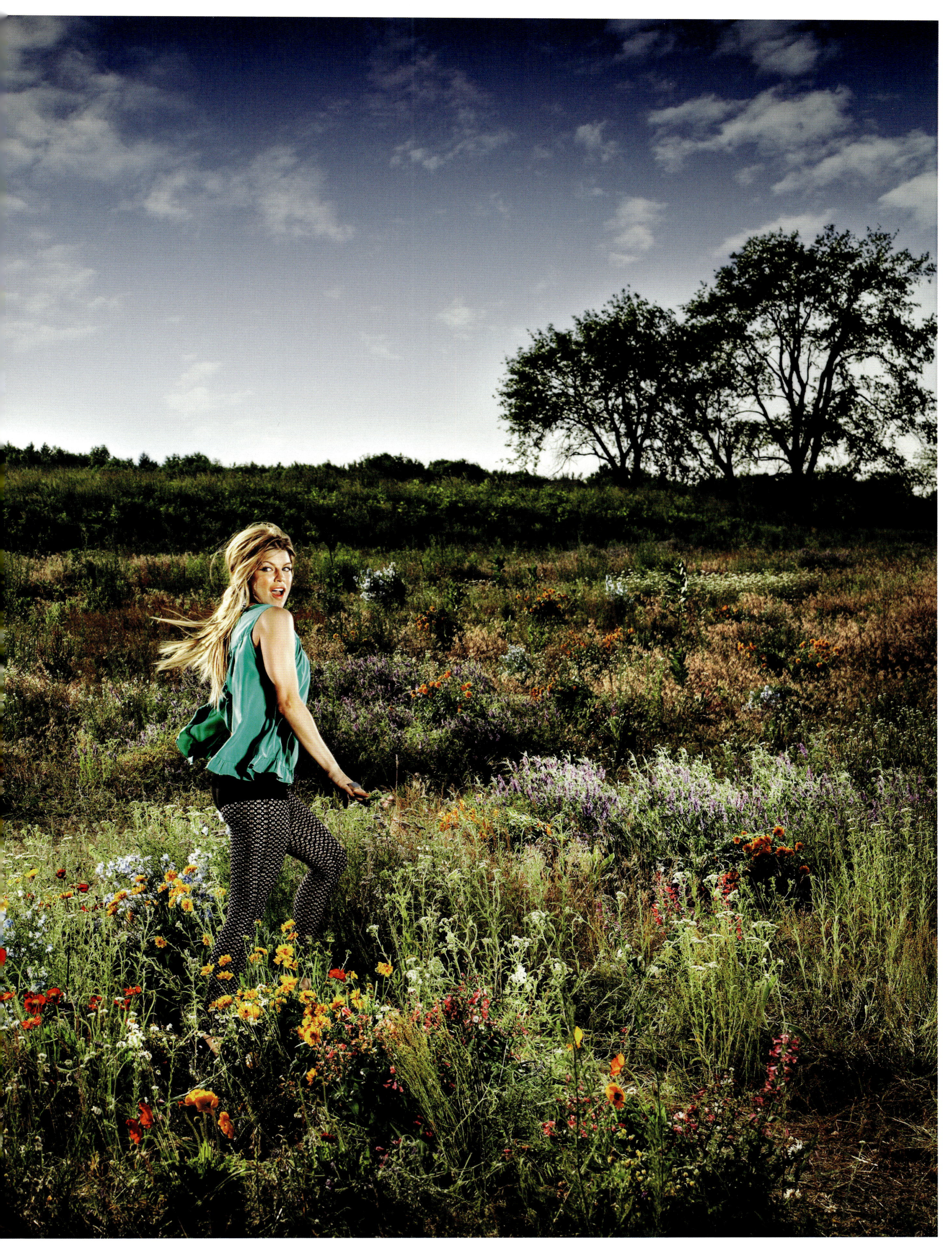

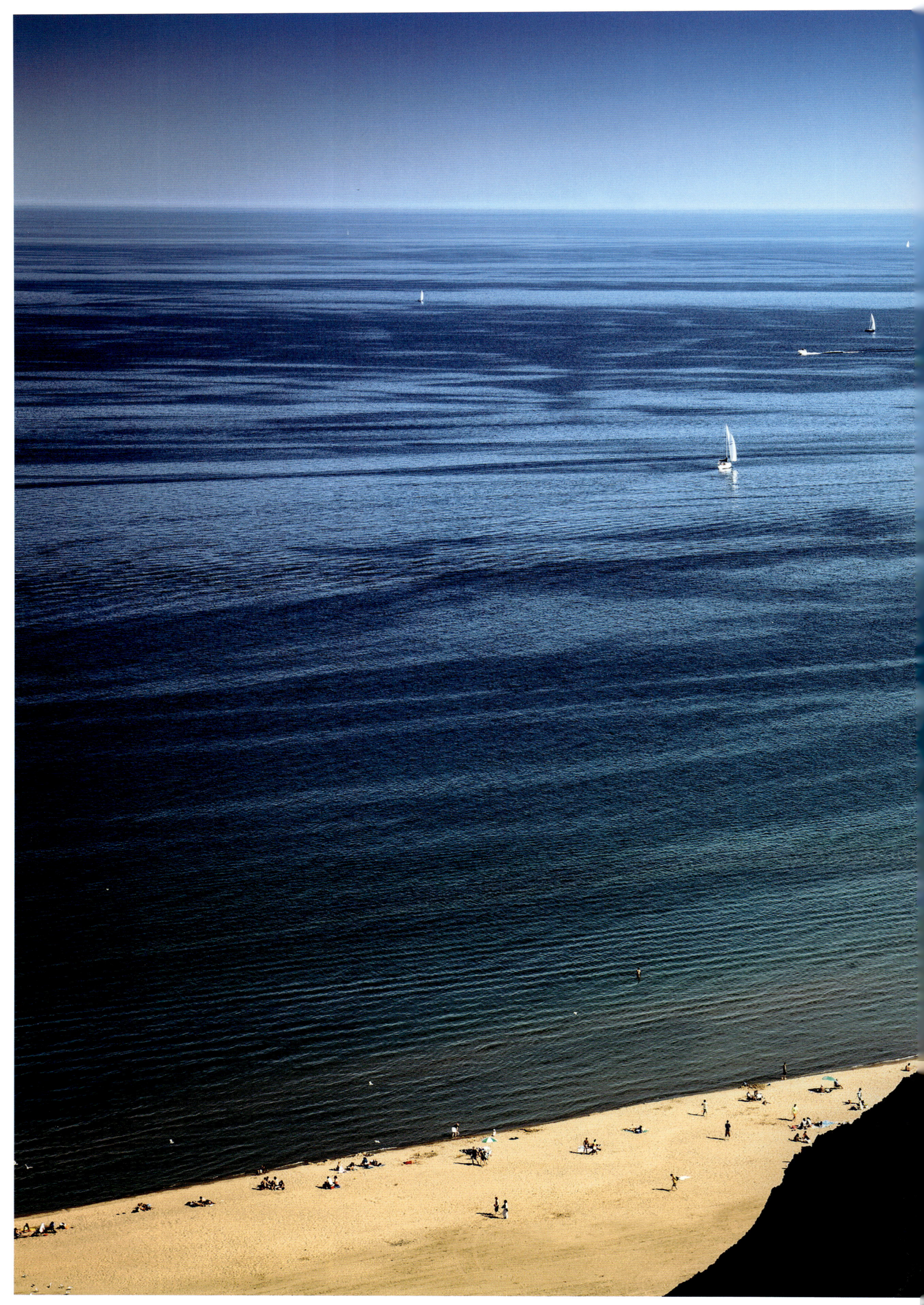

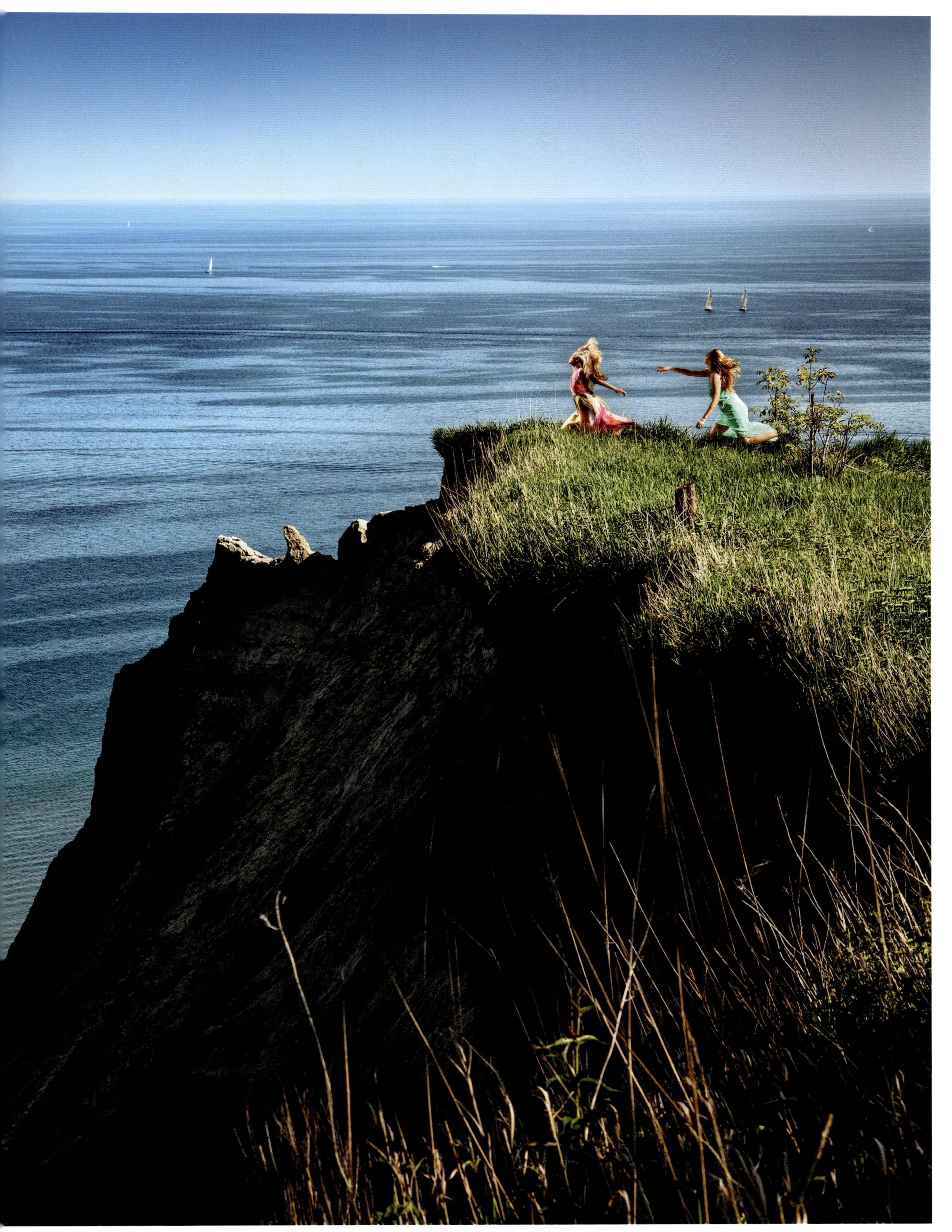

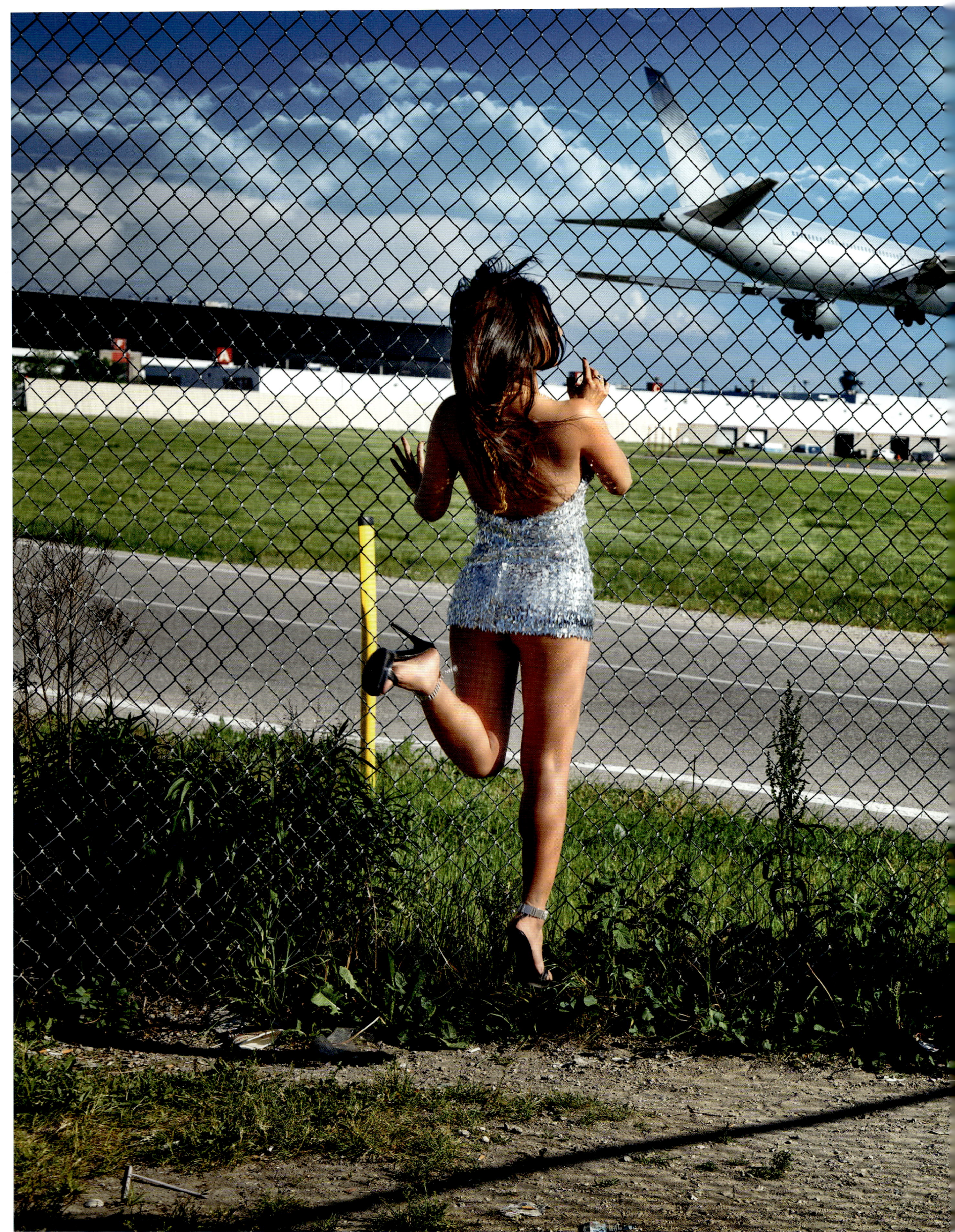

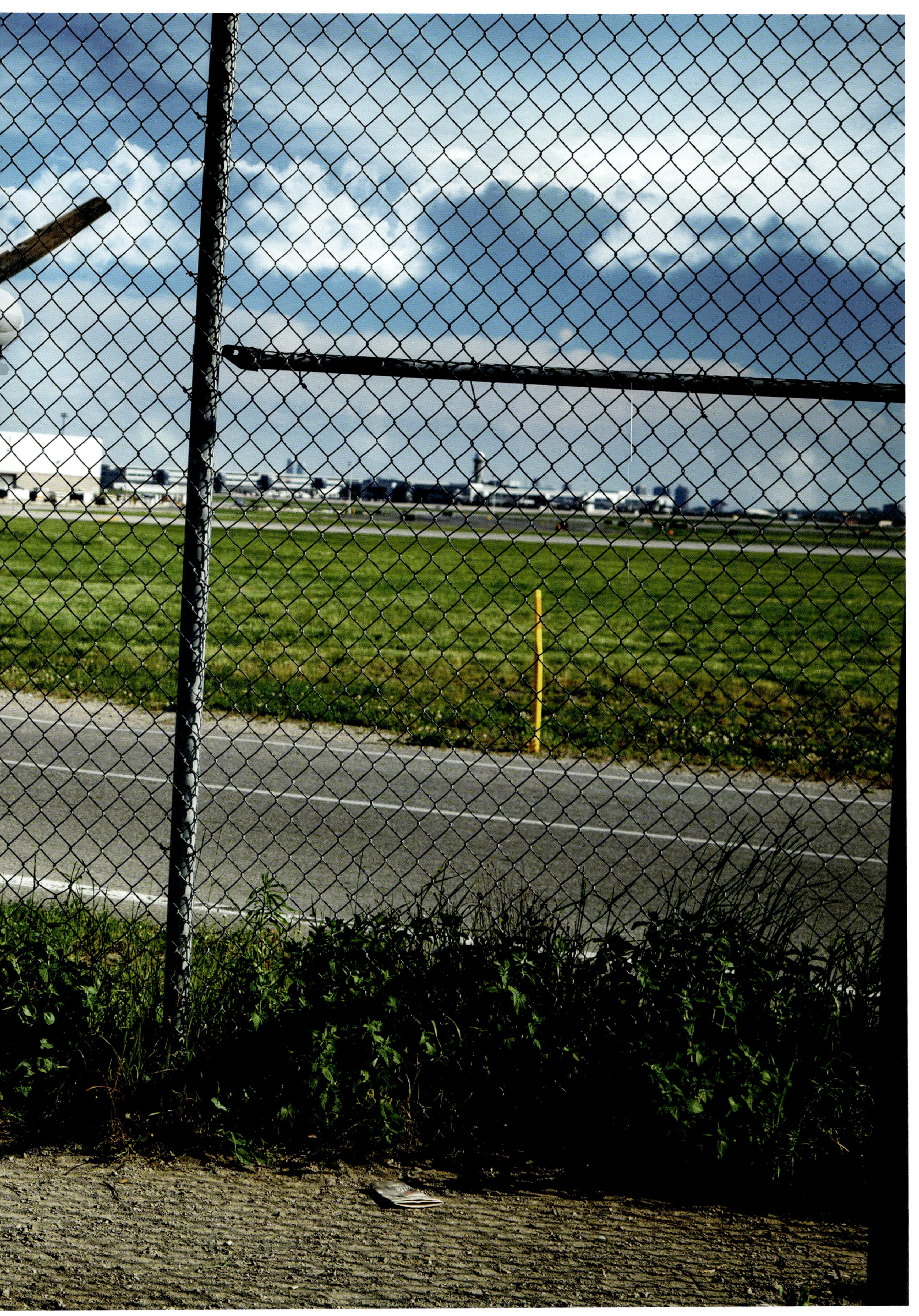

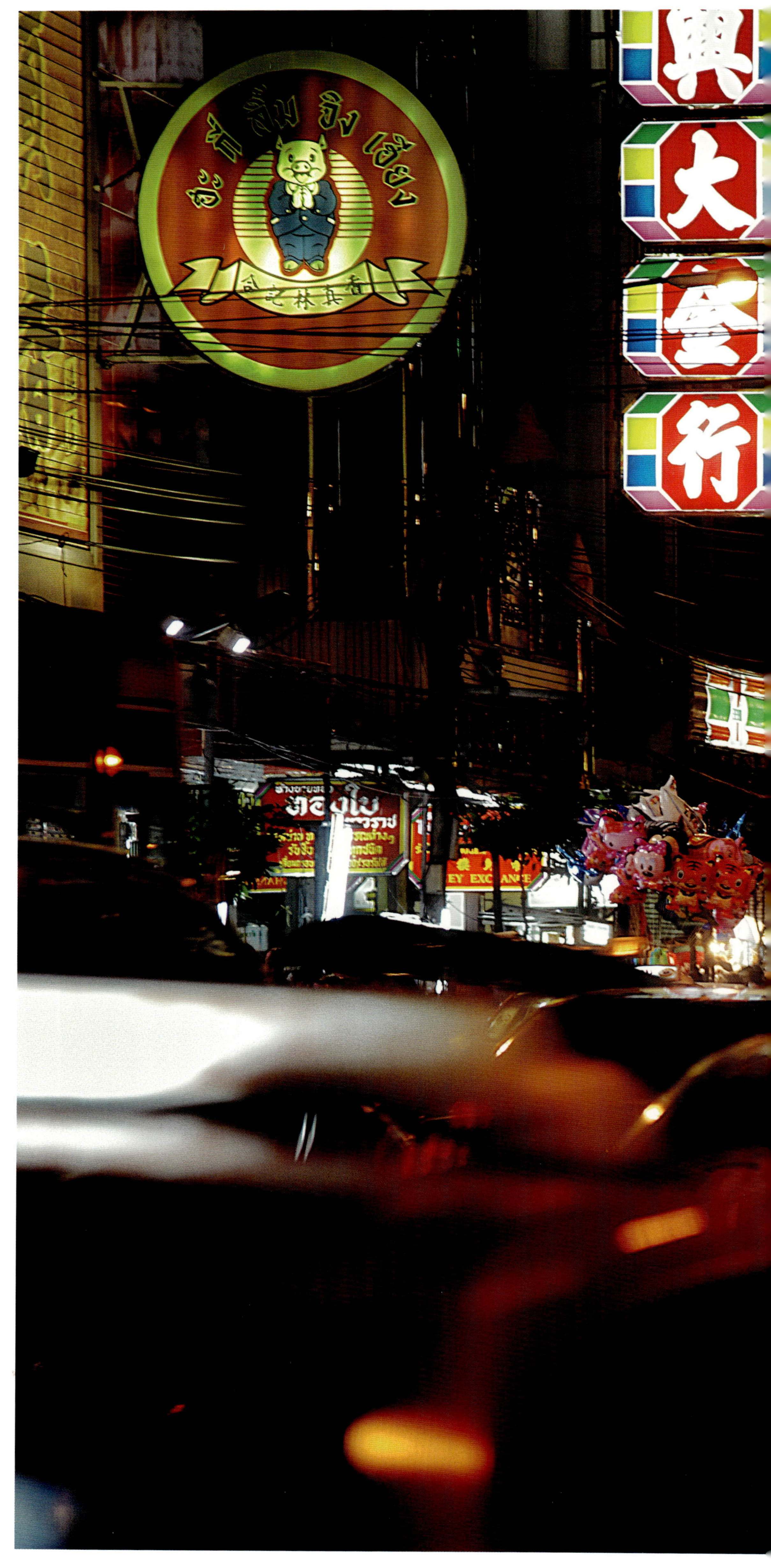

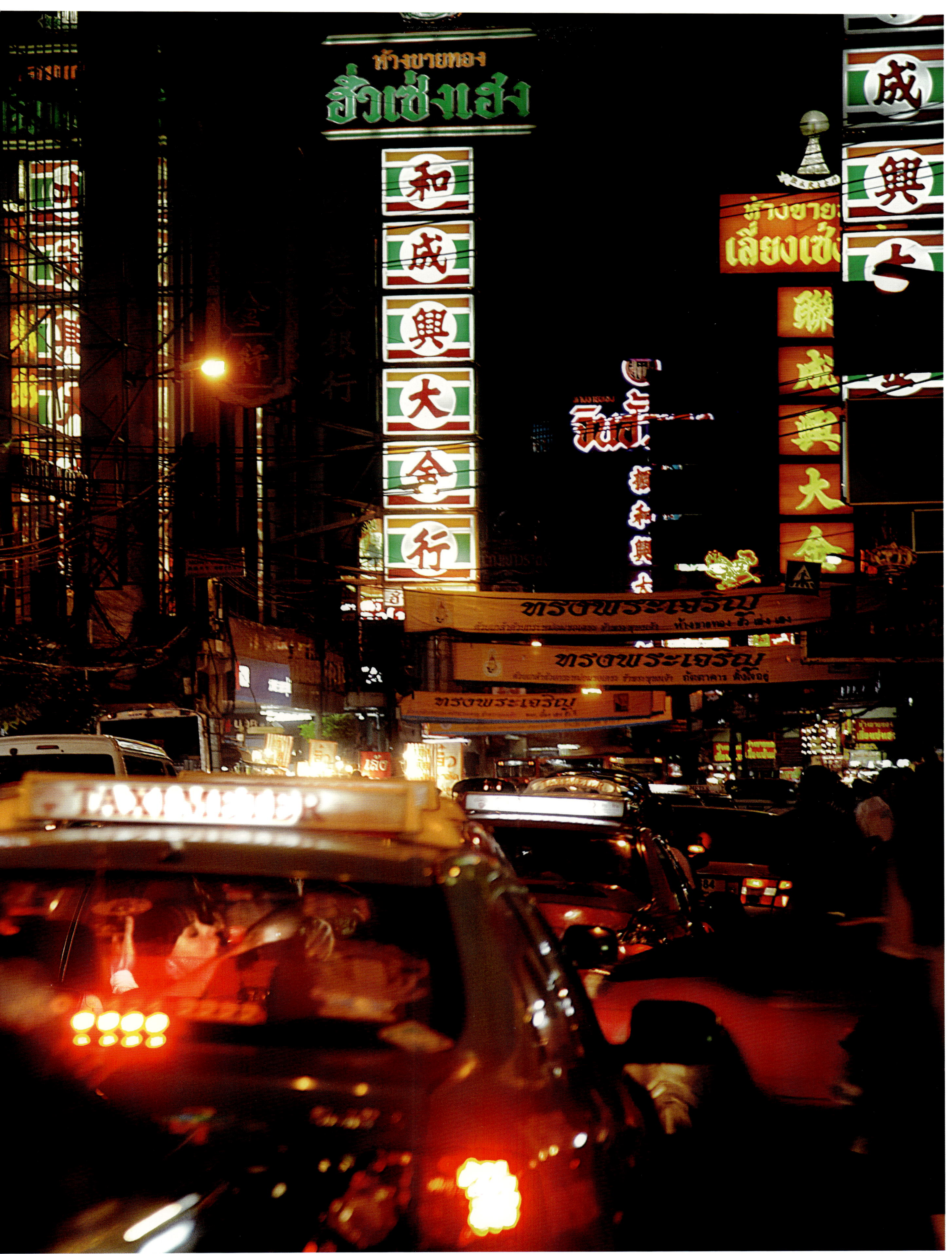
ห้างขายทอง
ฮั่วเซ่งเฮง
和
成
興
大
金
行
ทรงพระเจริญ
ทรงพระเจริญ
ทรงพระเจริญ

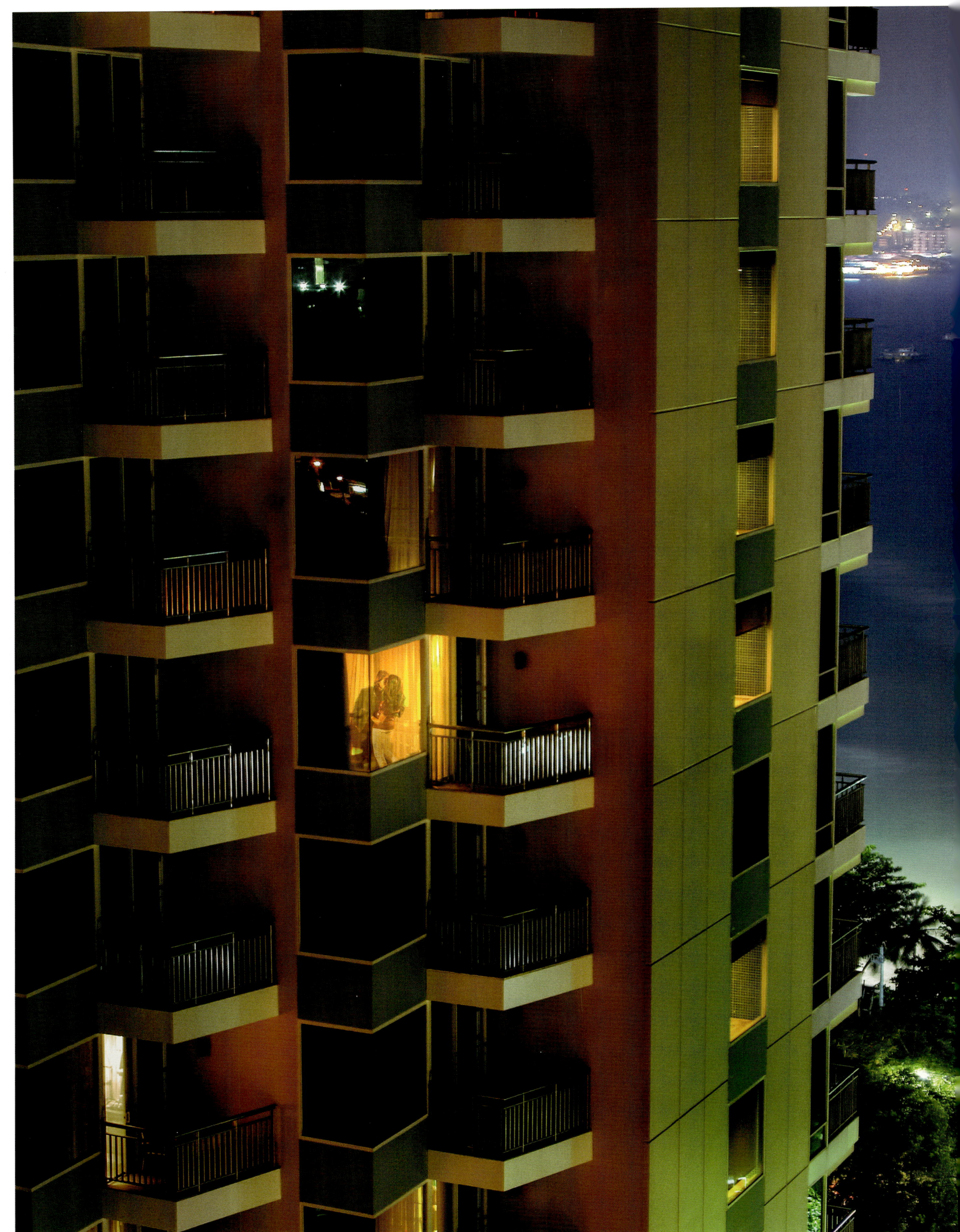

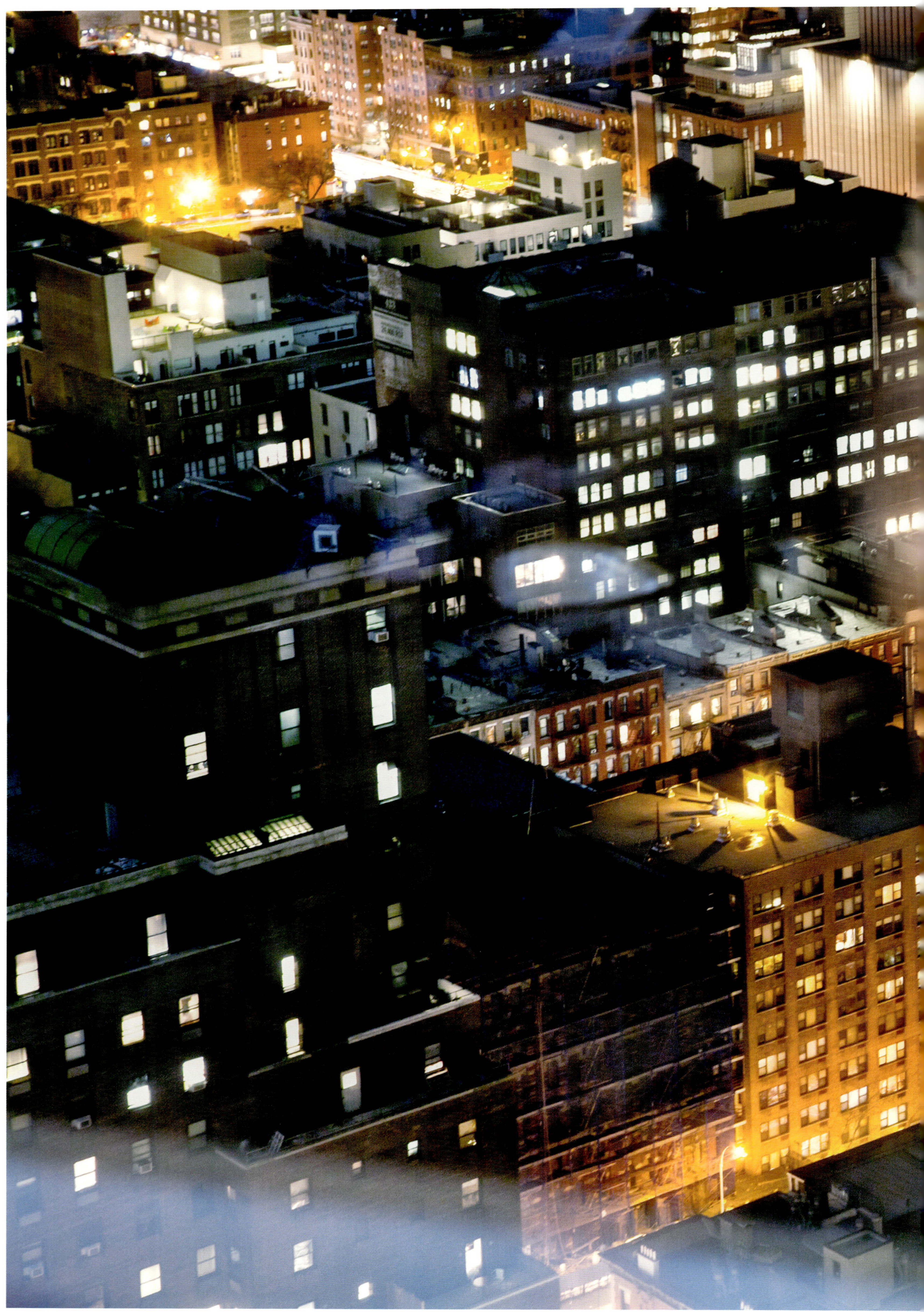

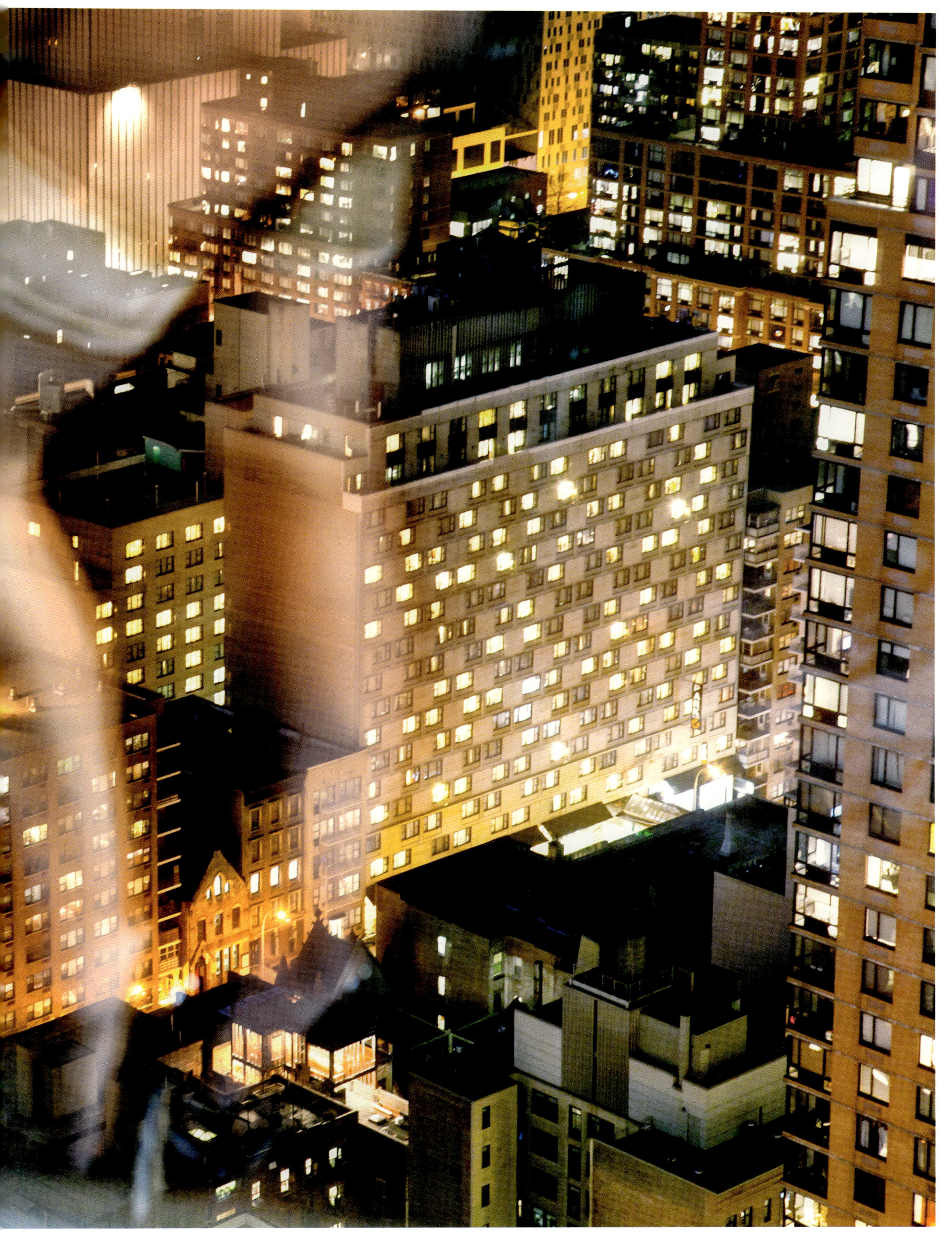

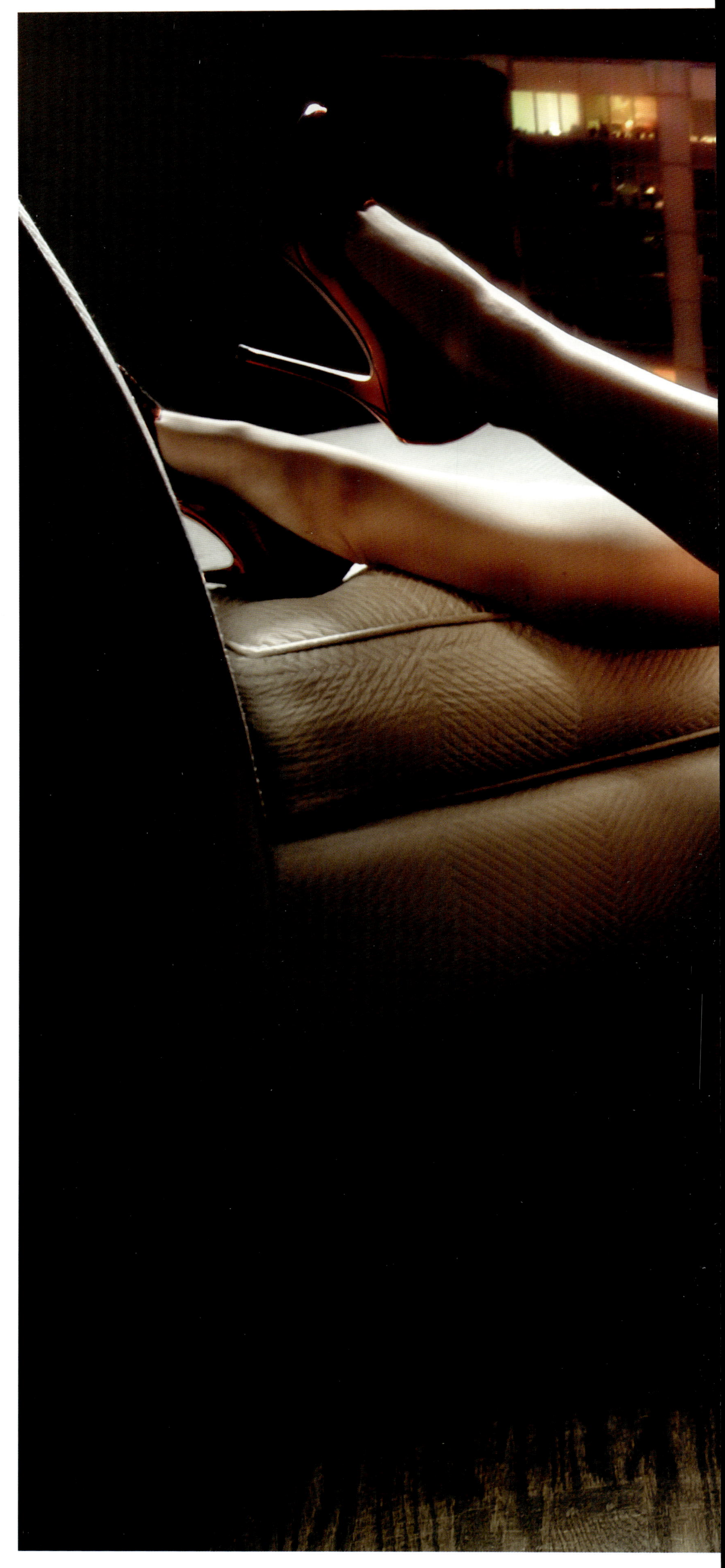

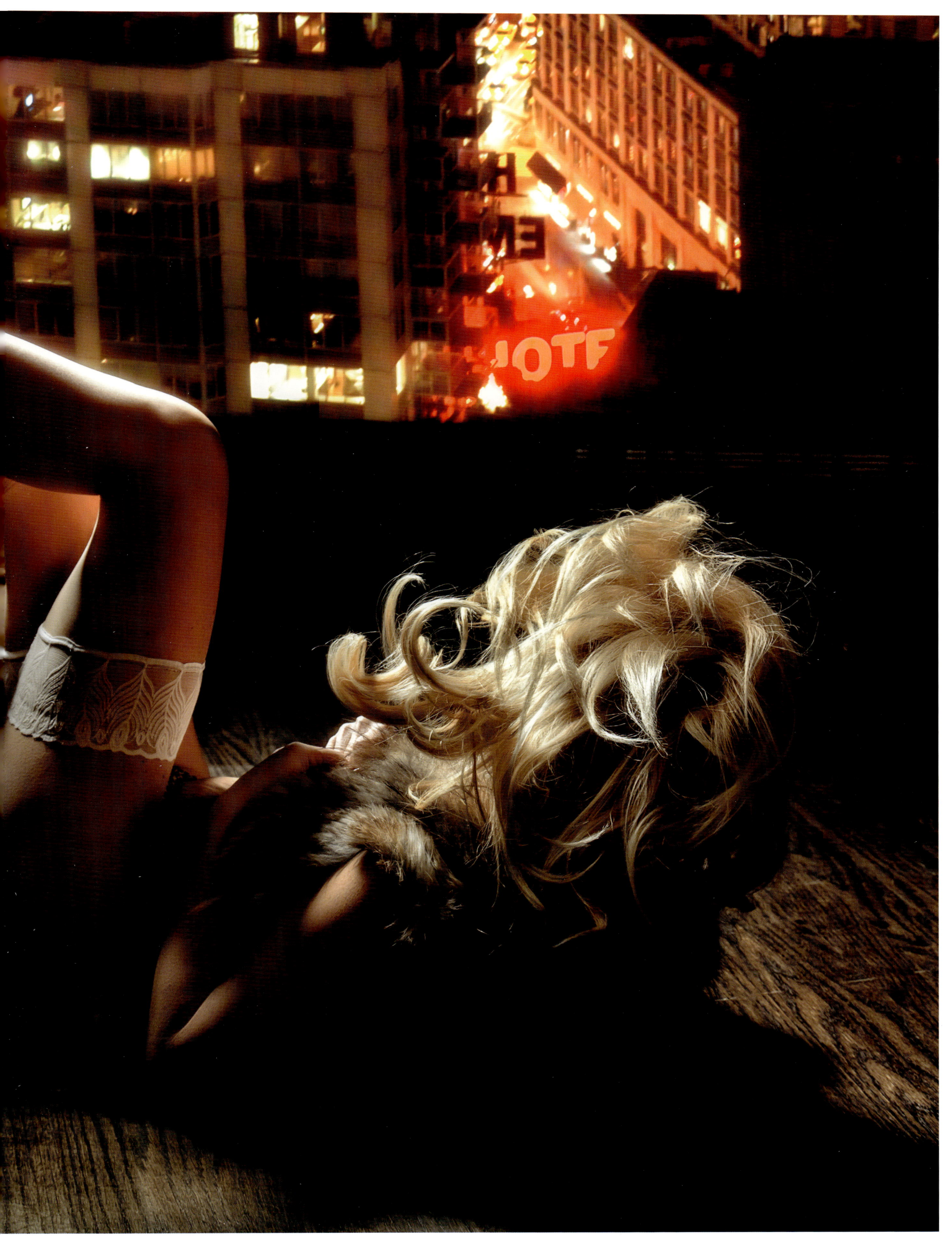

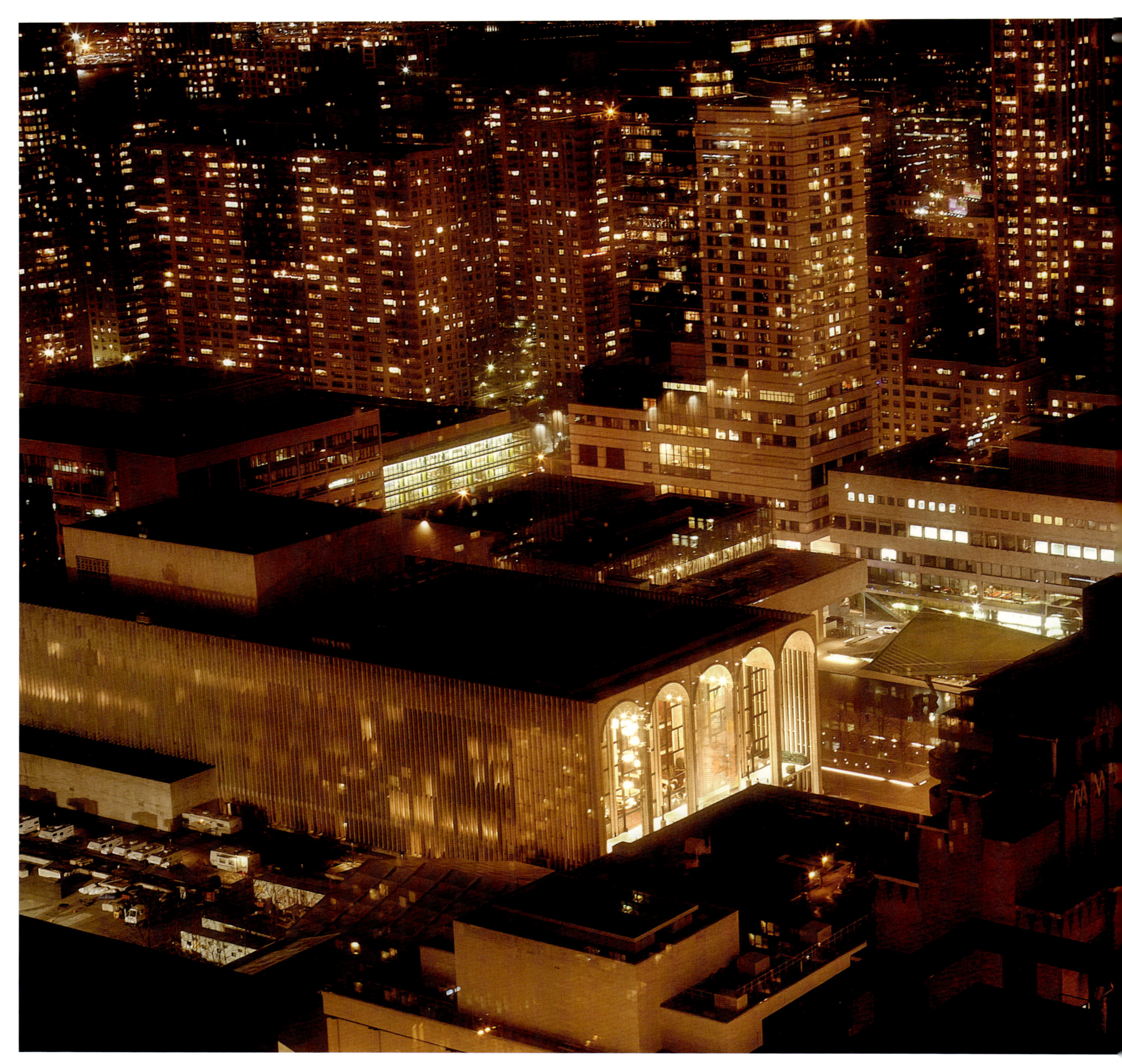

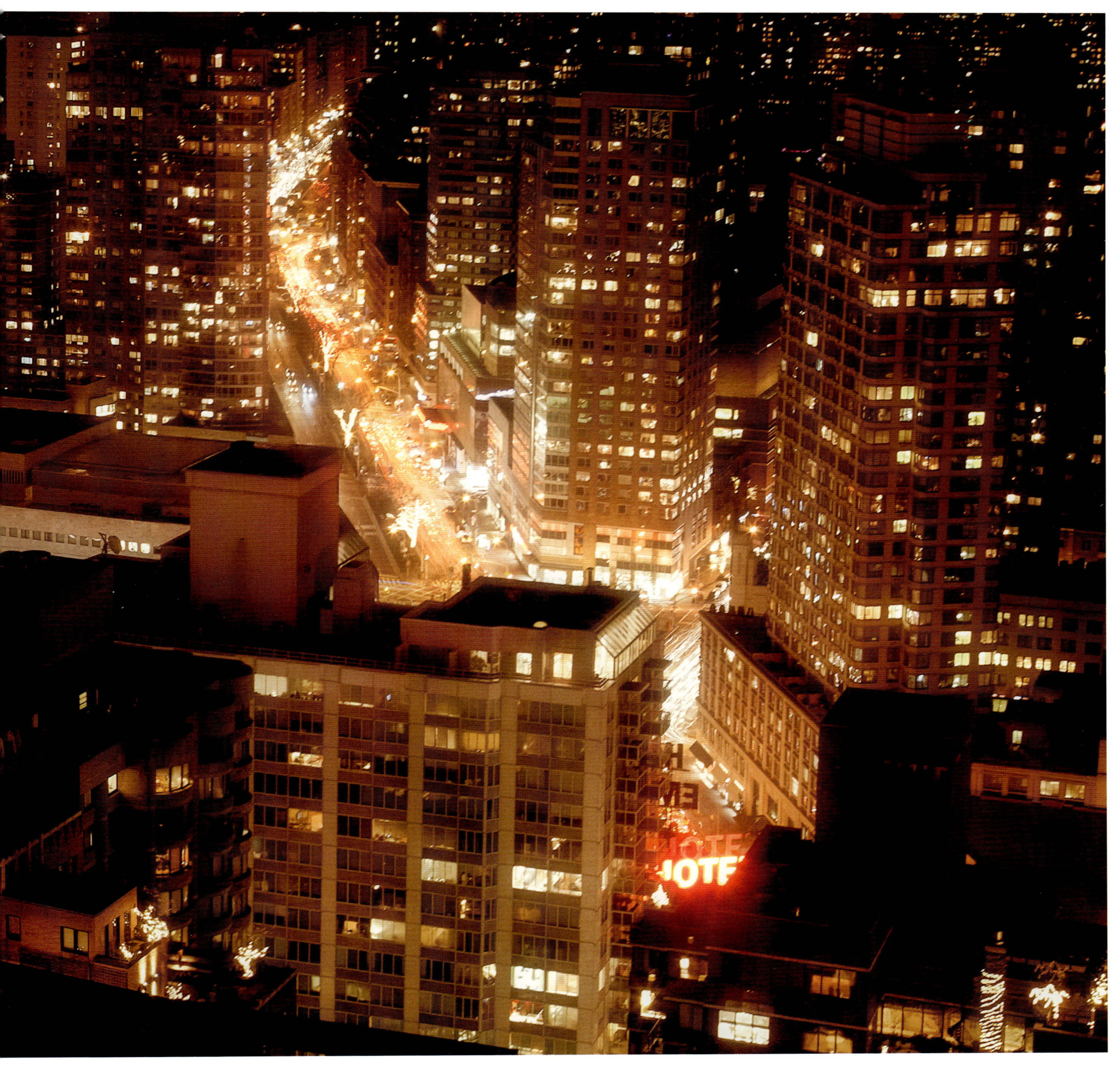

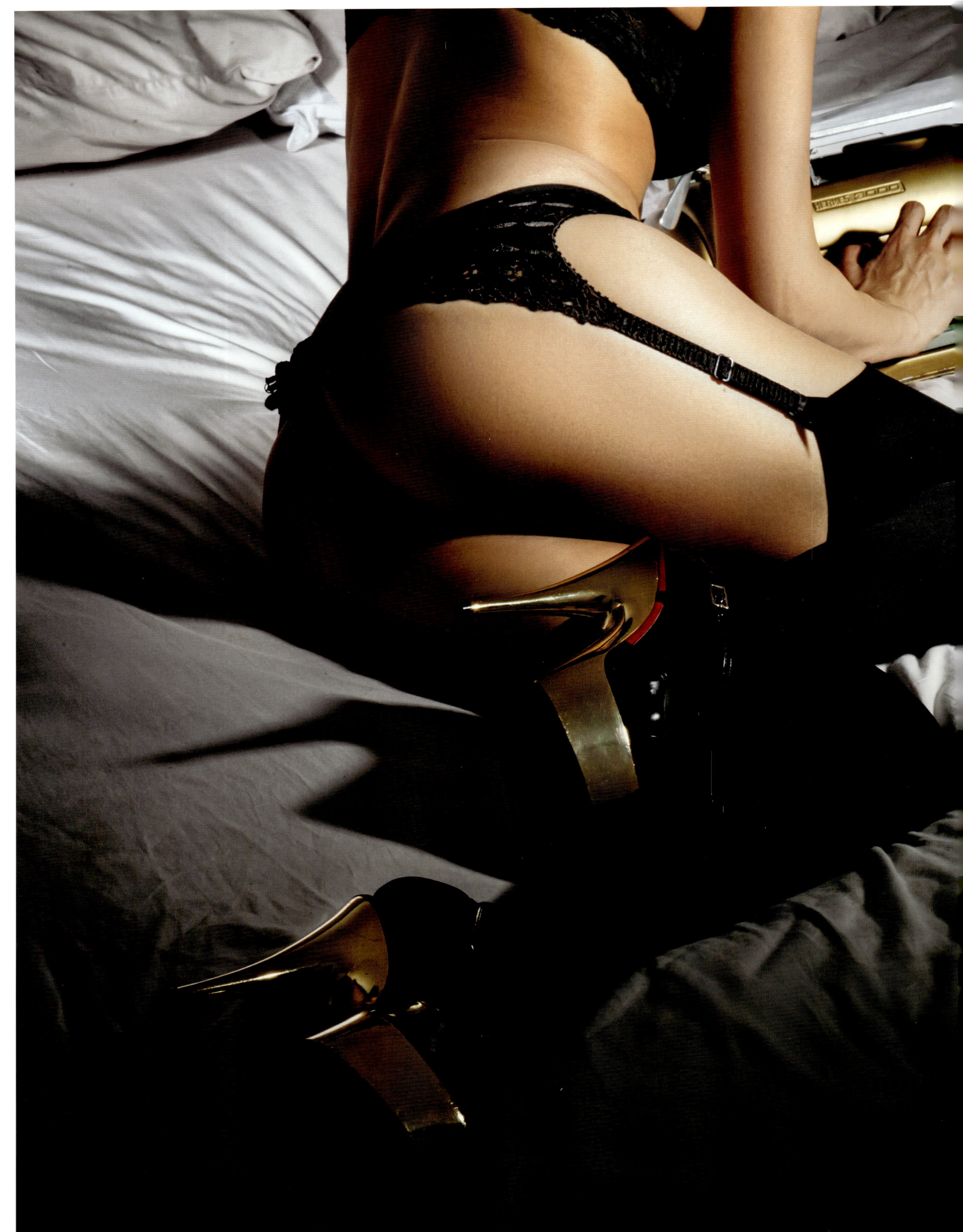

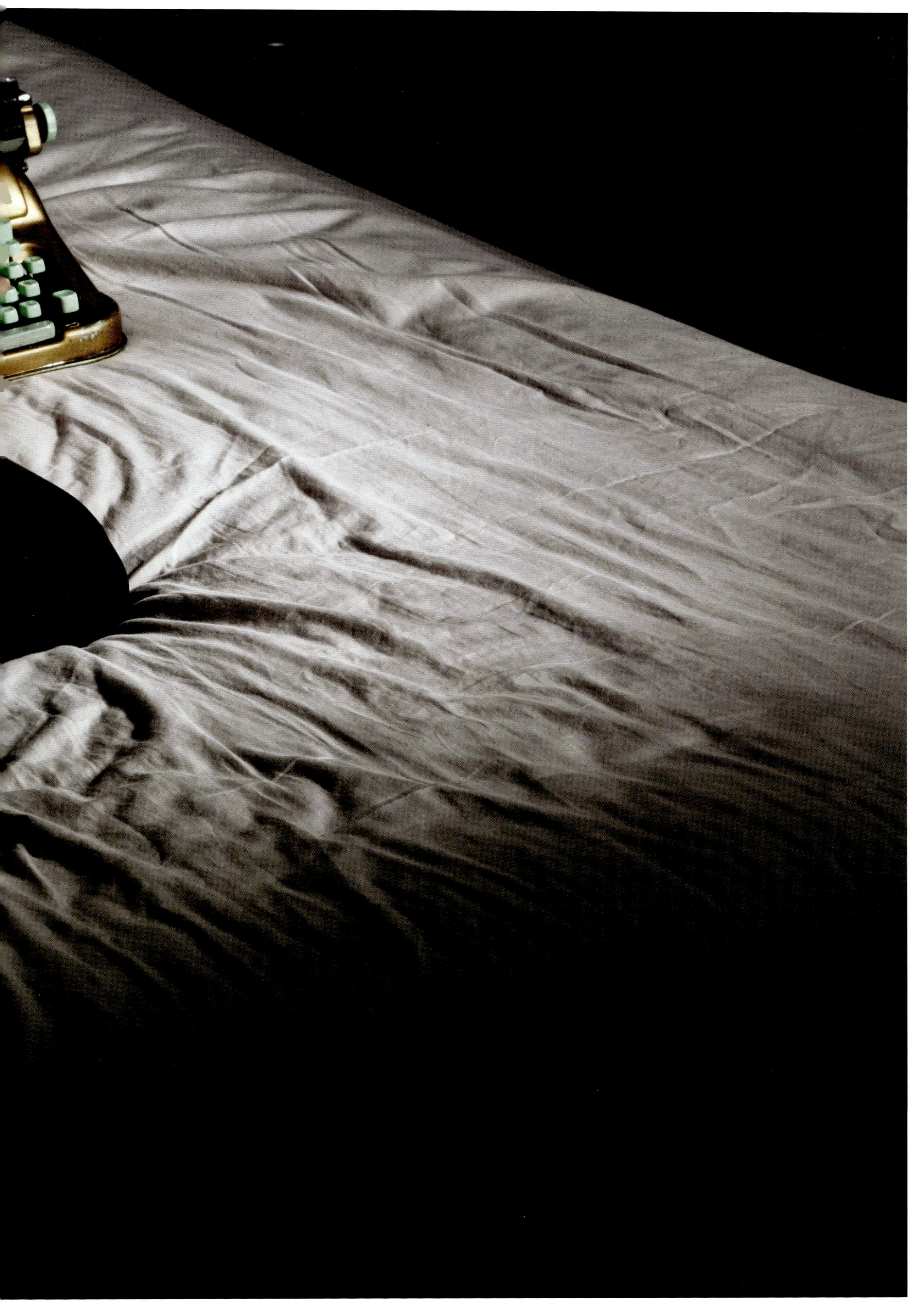

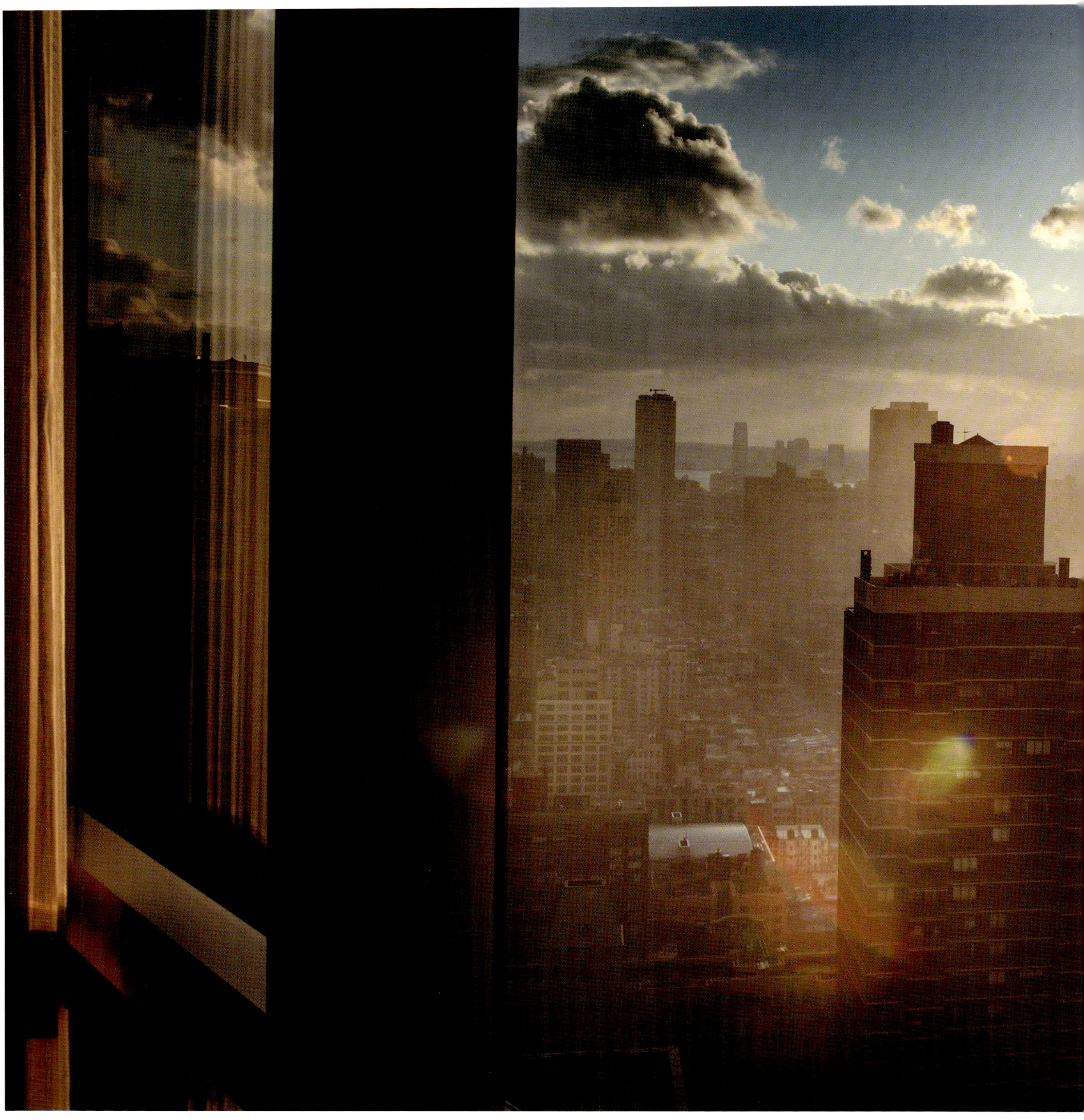

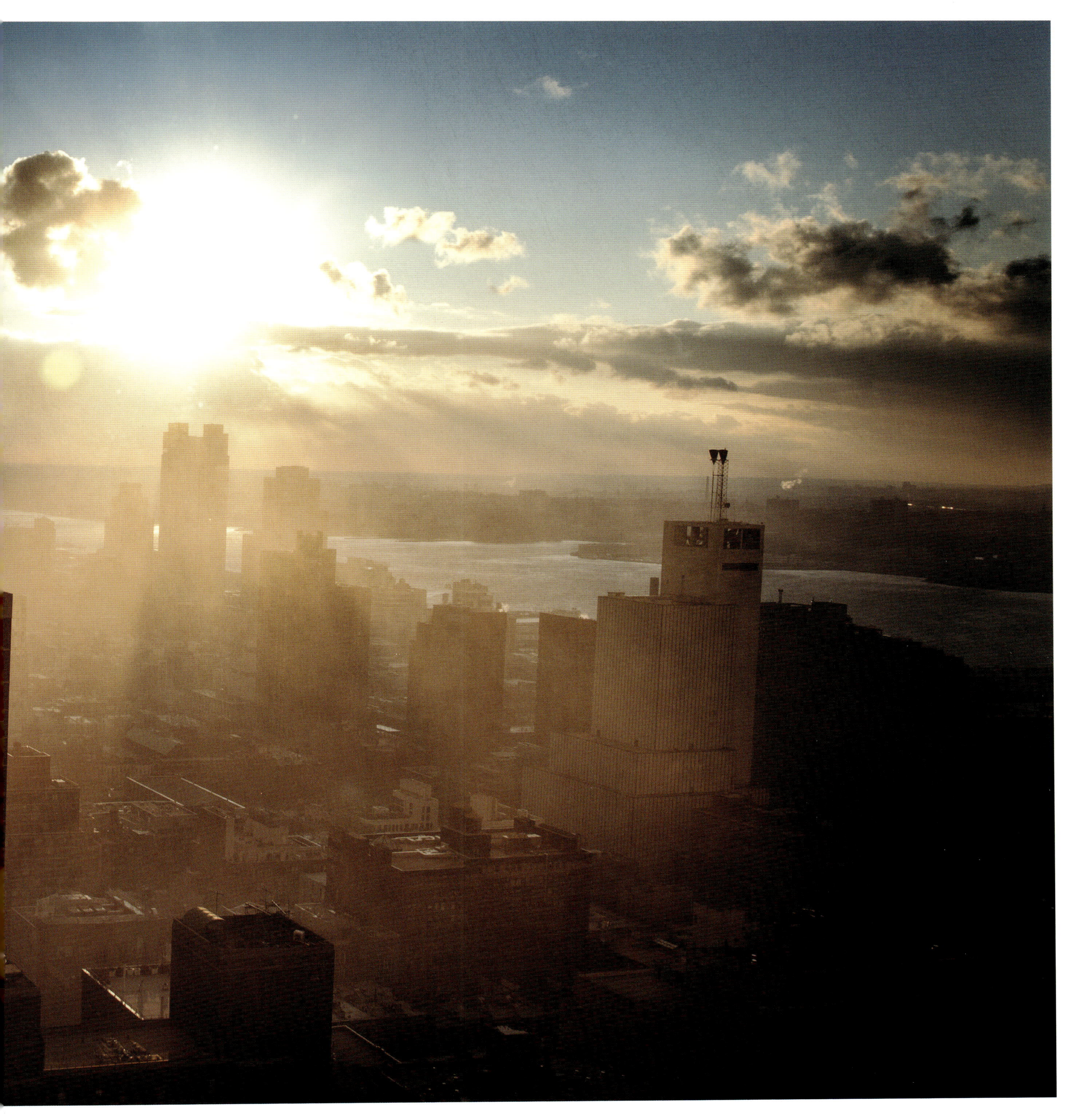

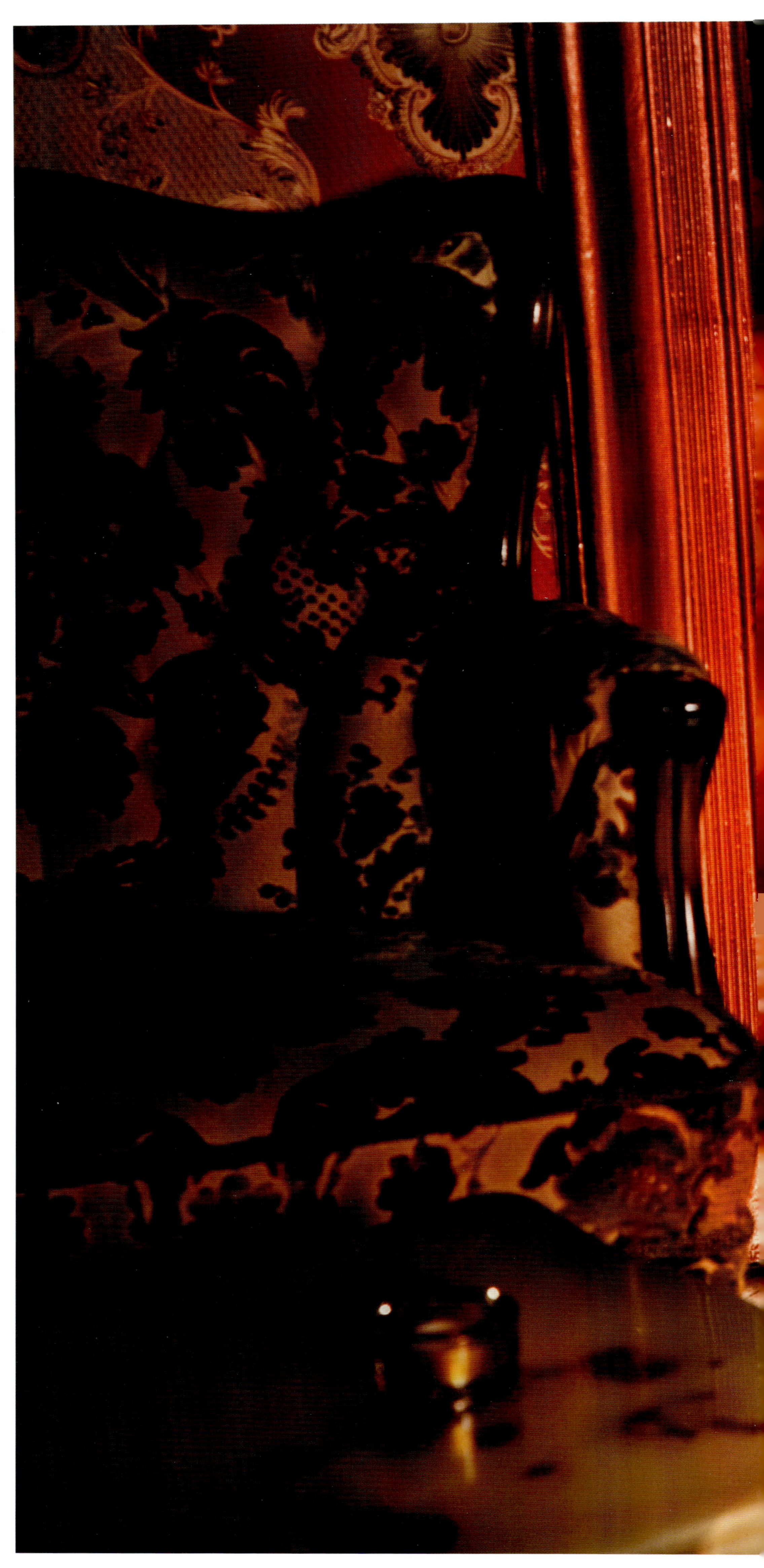

GIRL IN THE RED MIRROR | 2011

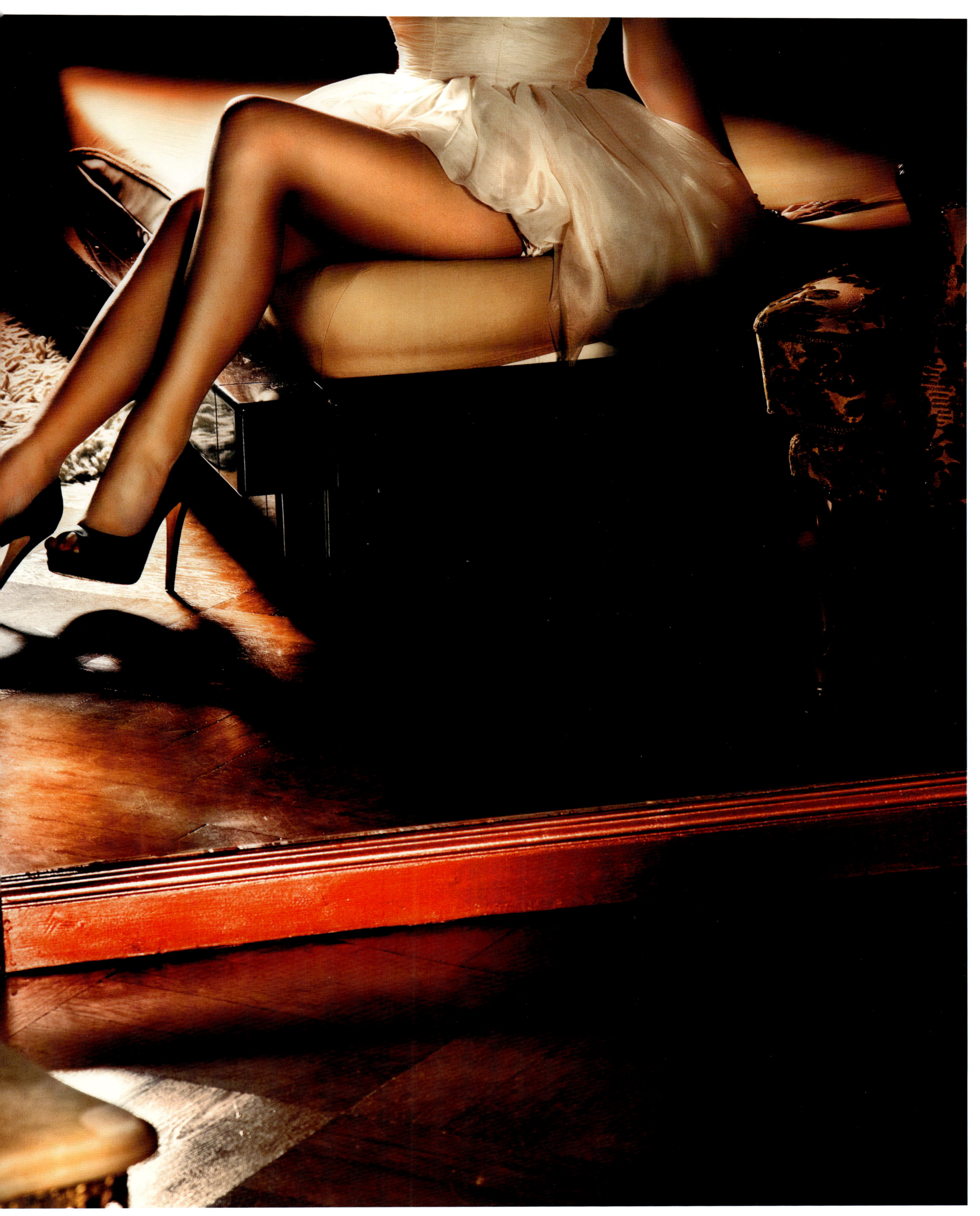

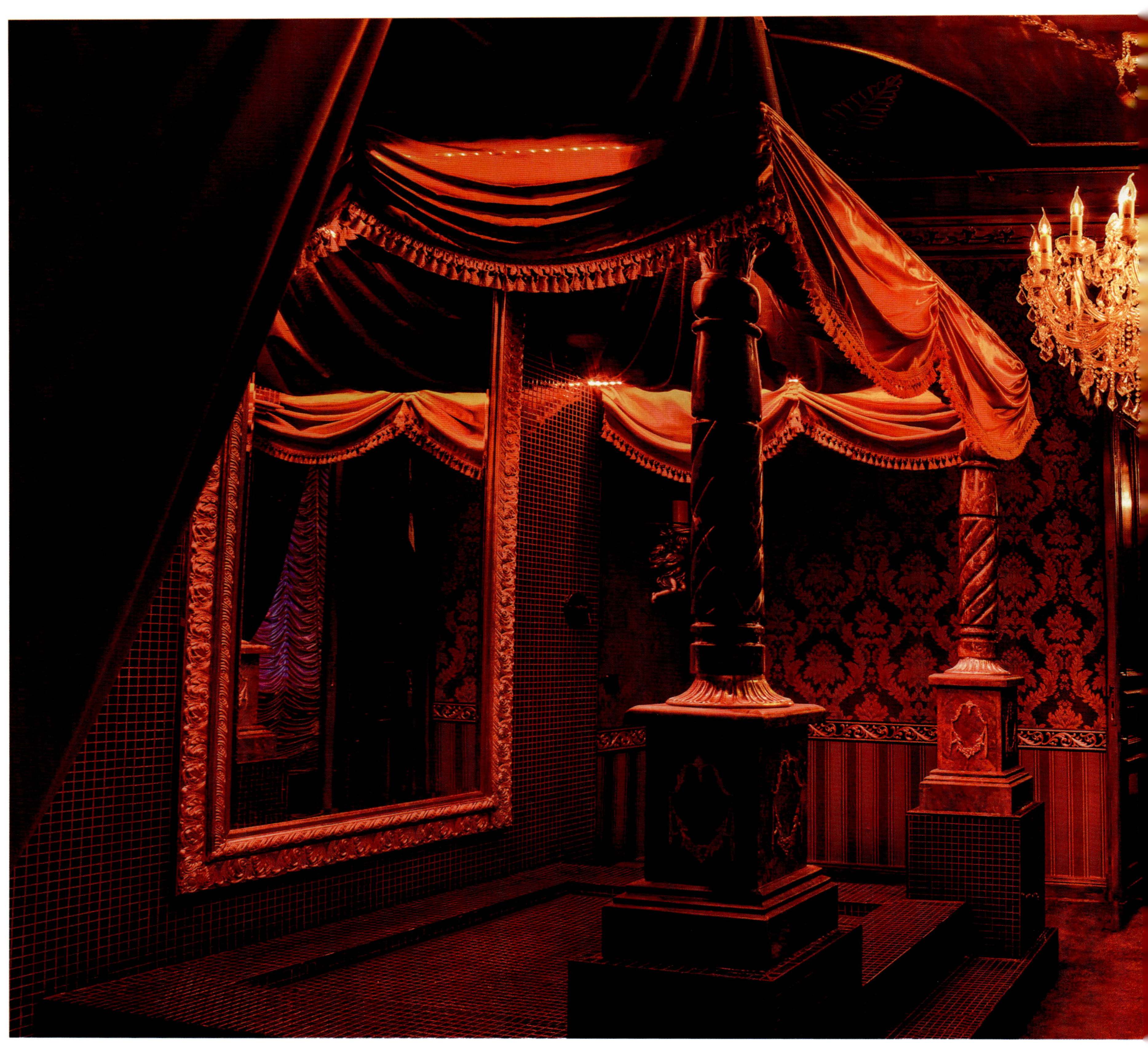

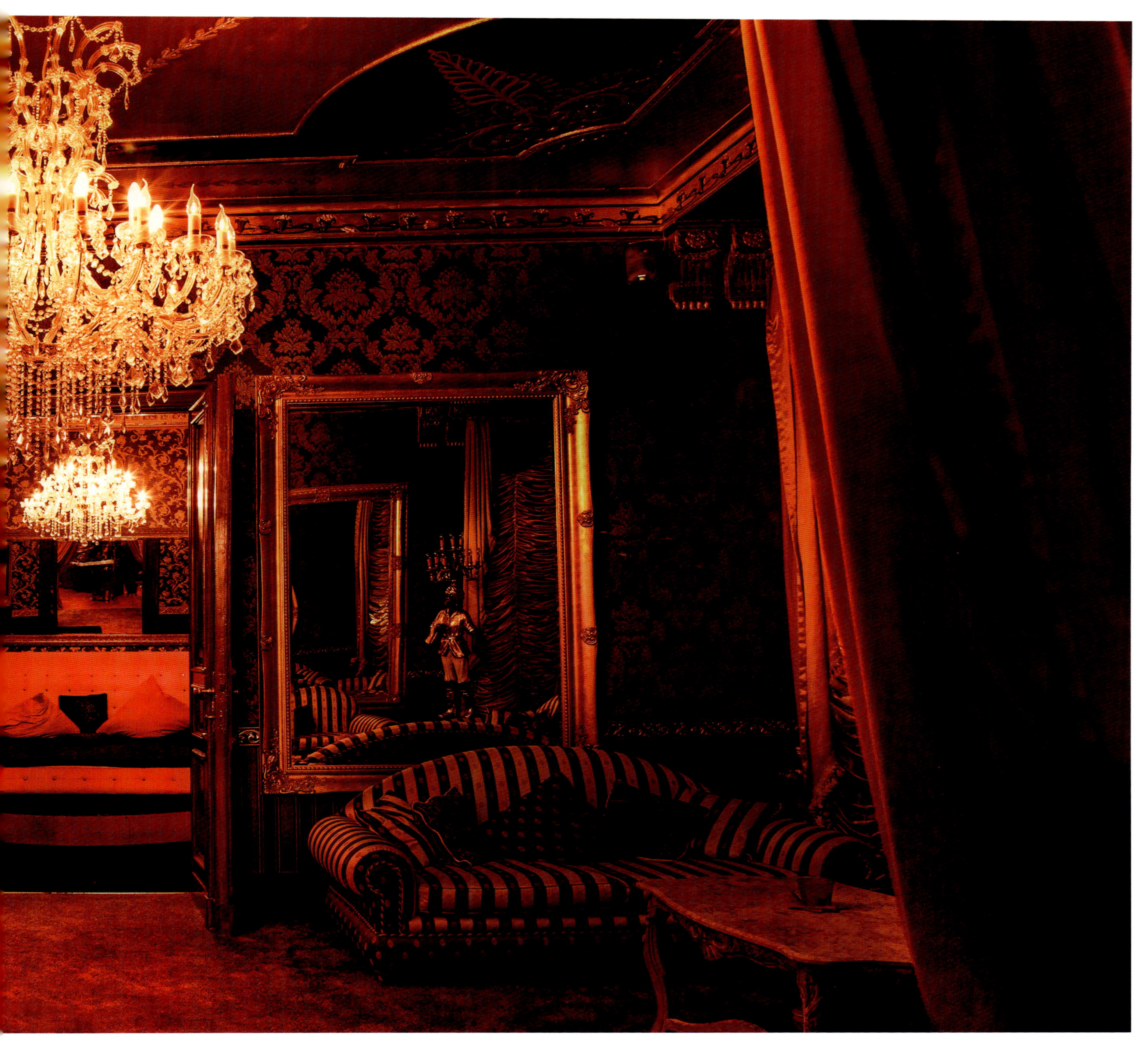

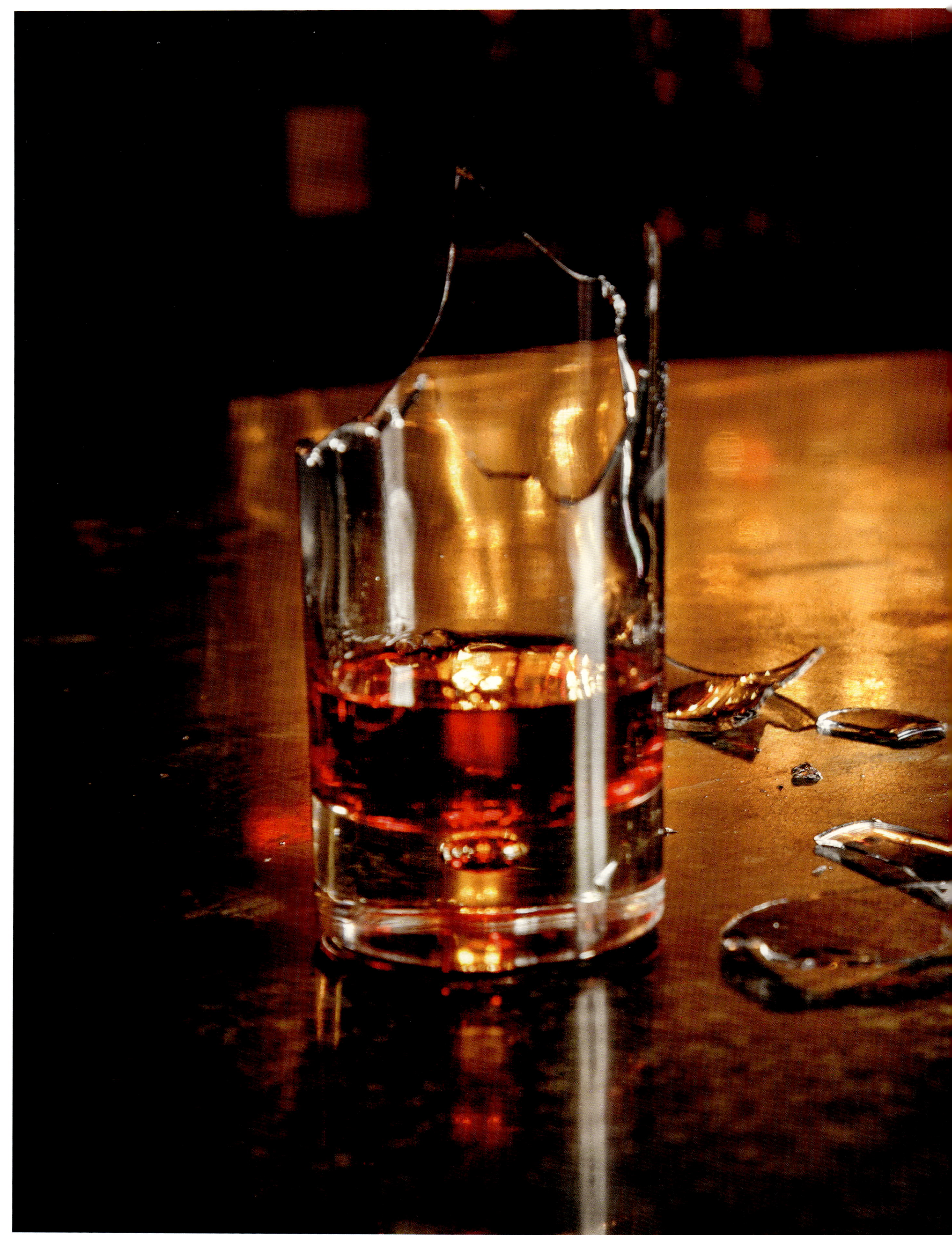

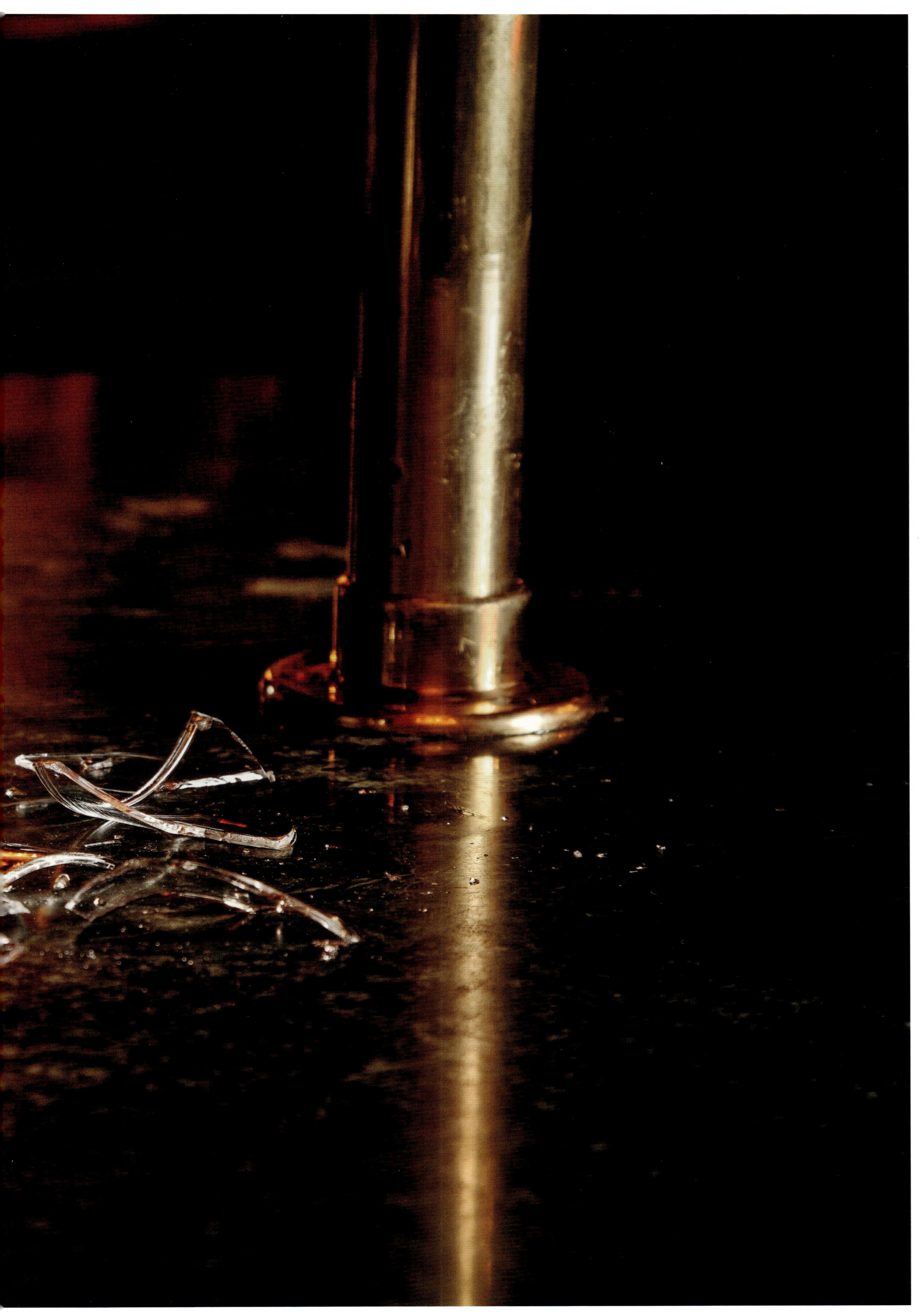

DANCING IN MIRROR I 2012

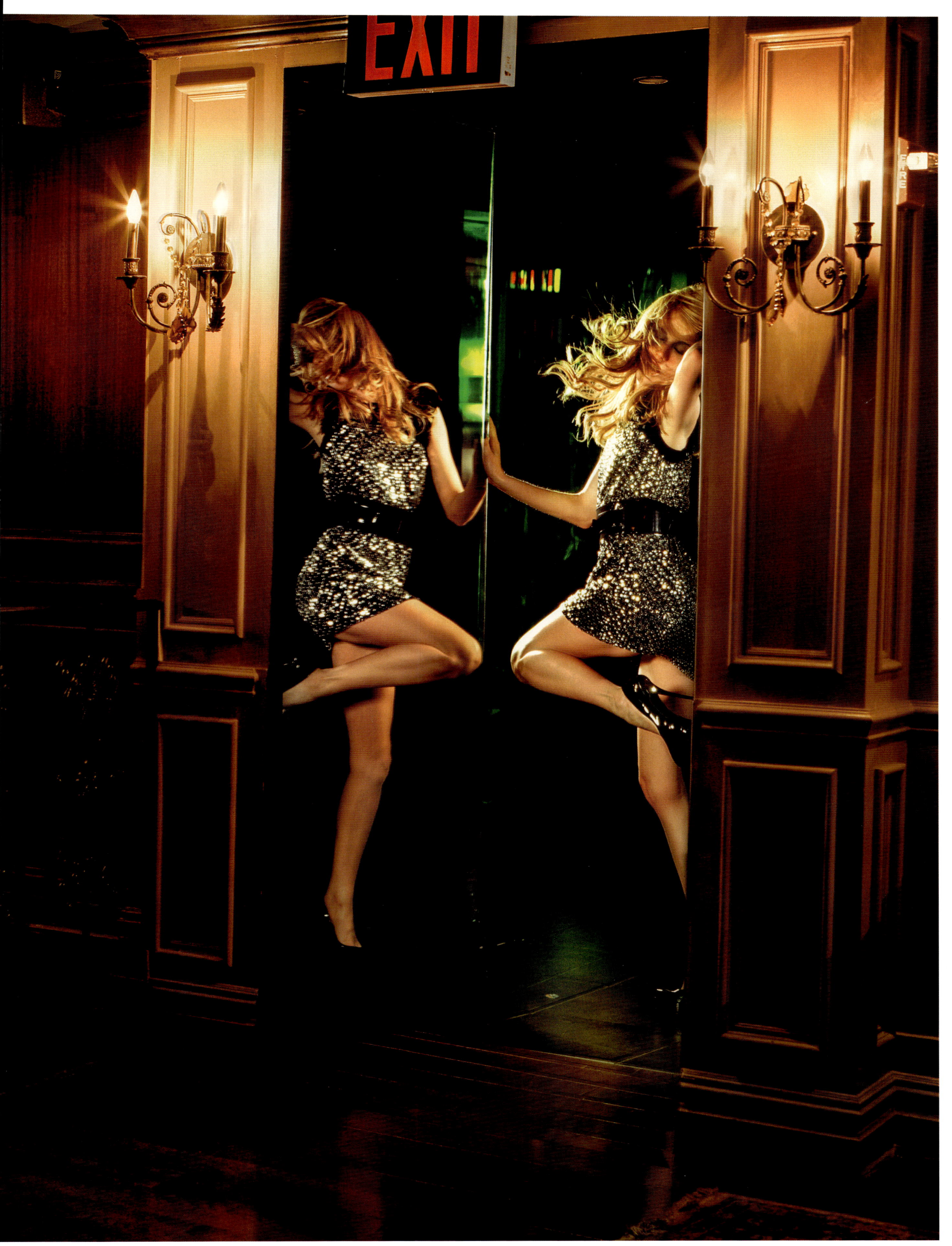
EXIT

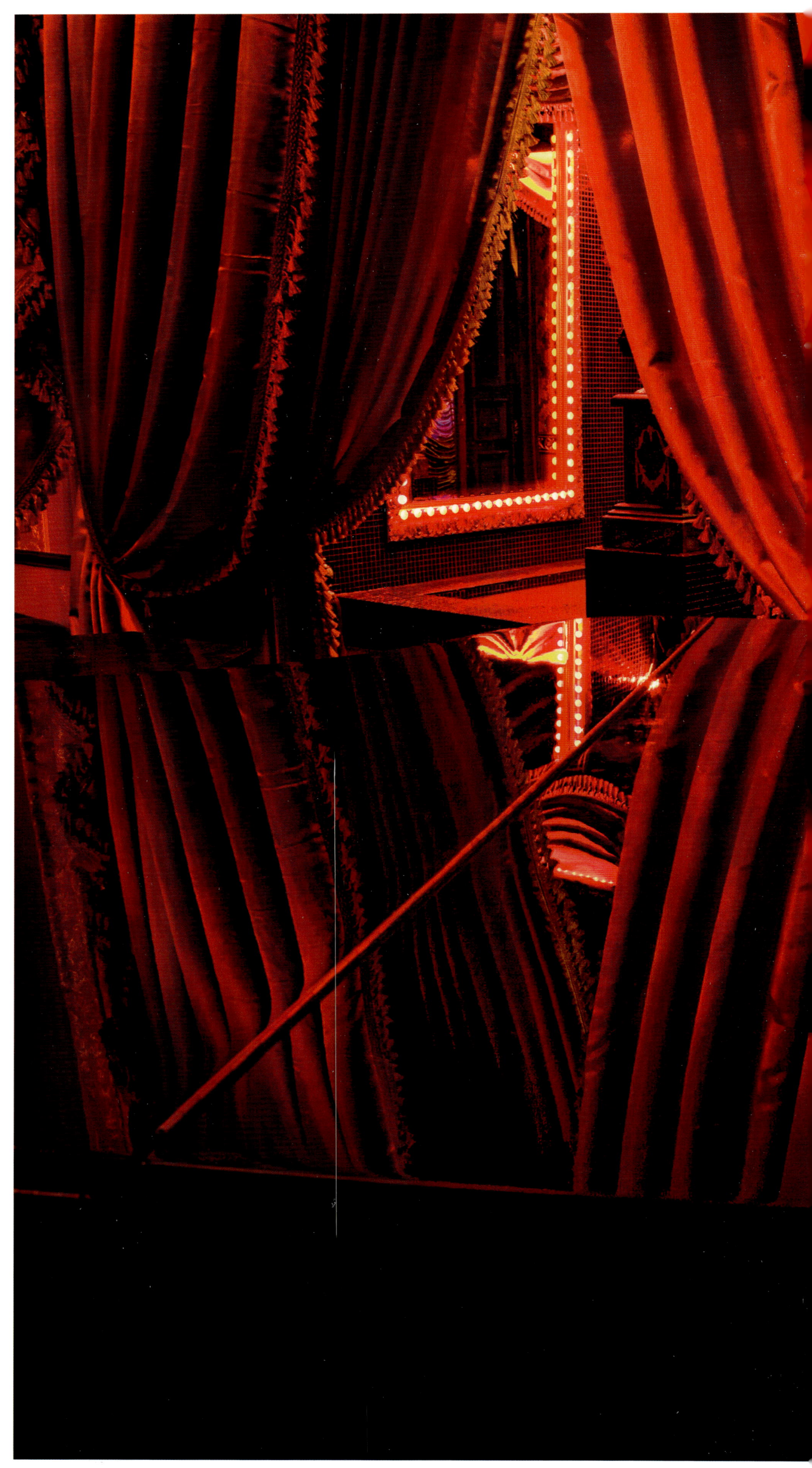

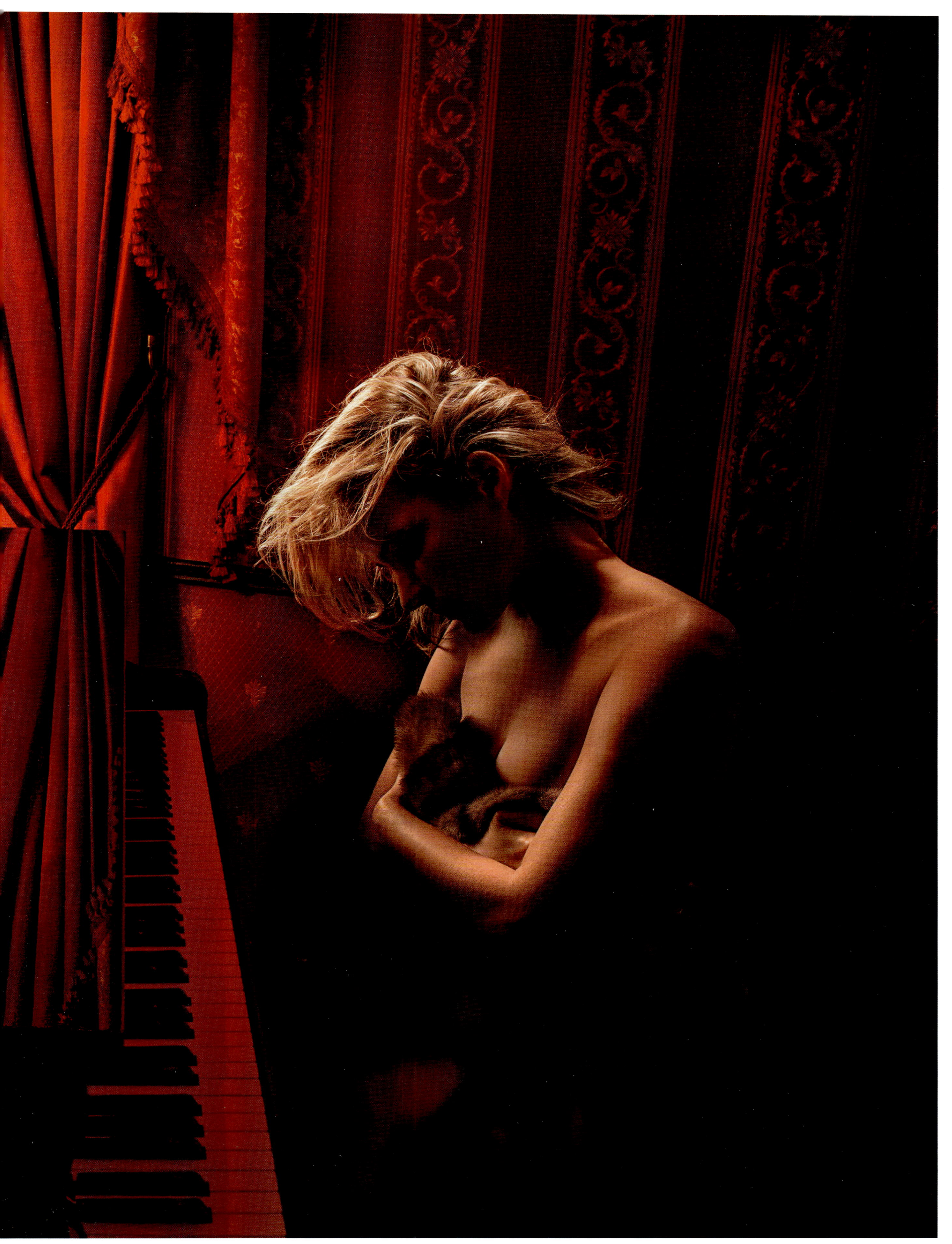

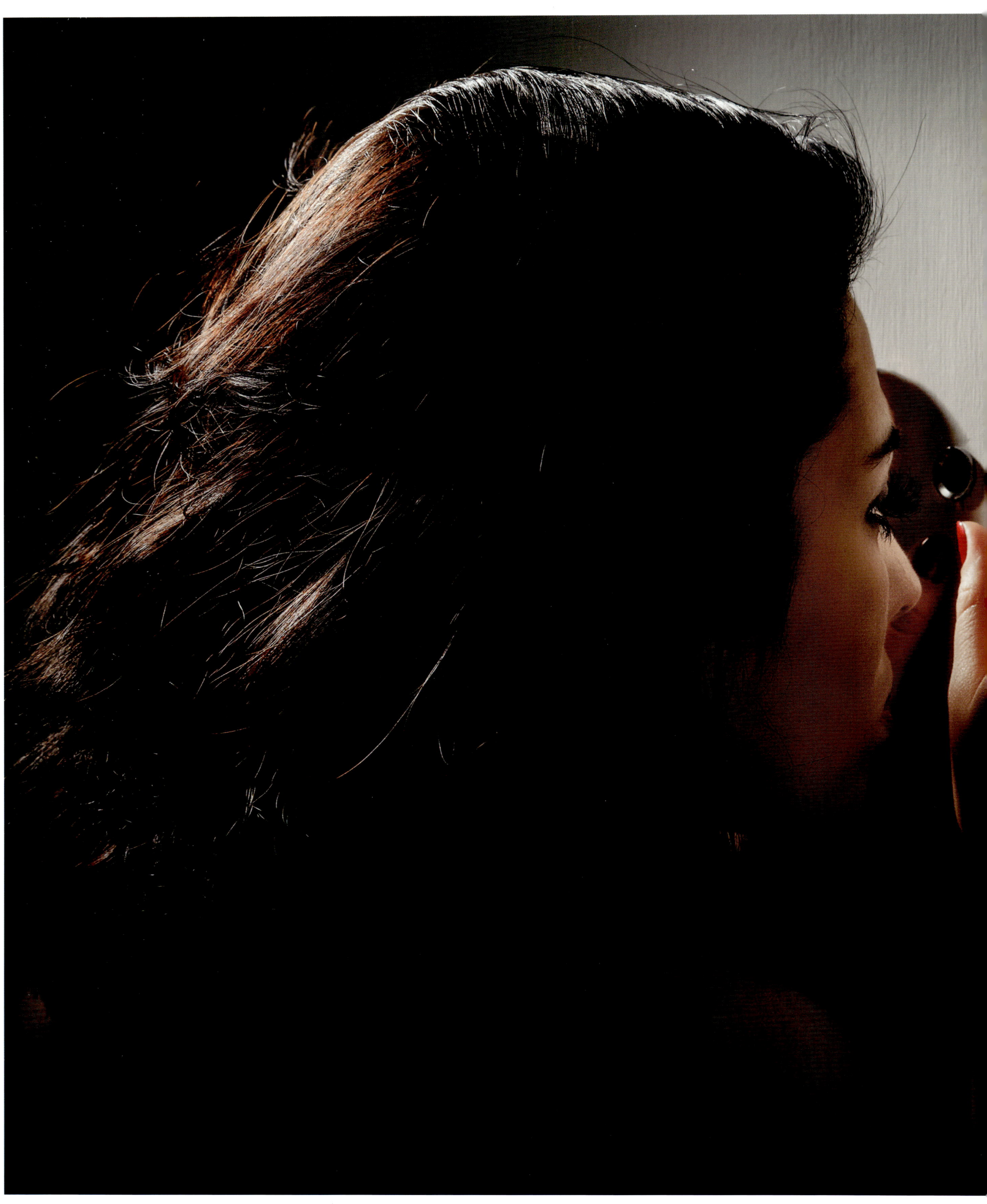

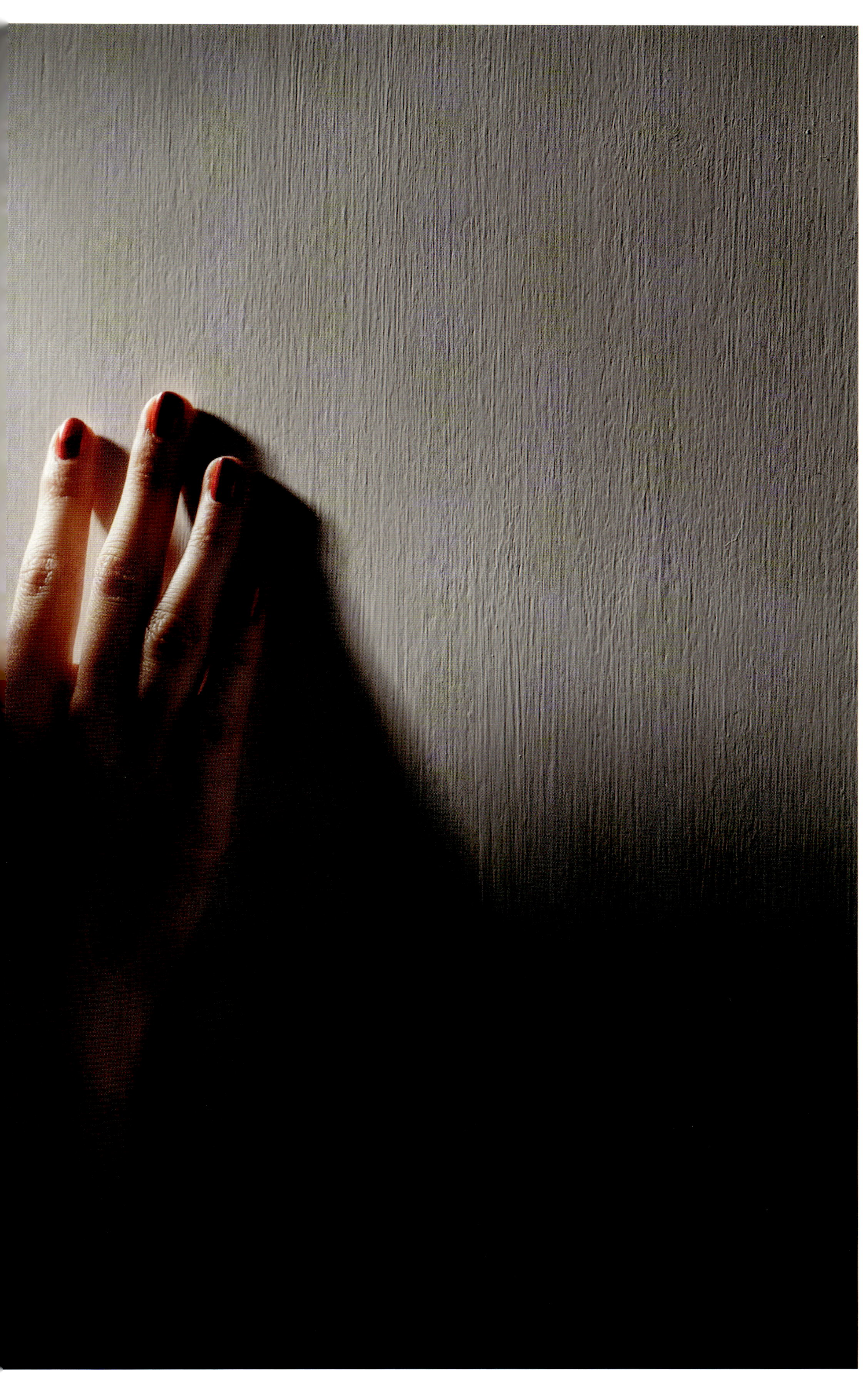

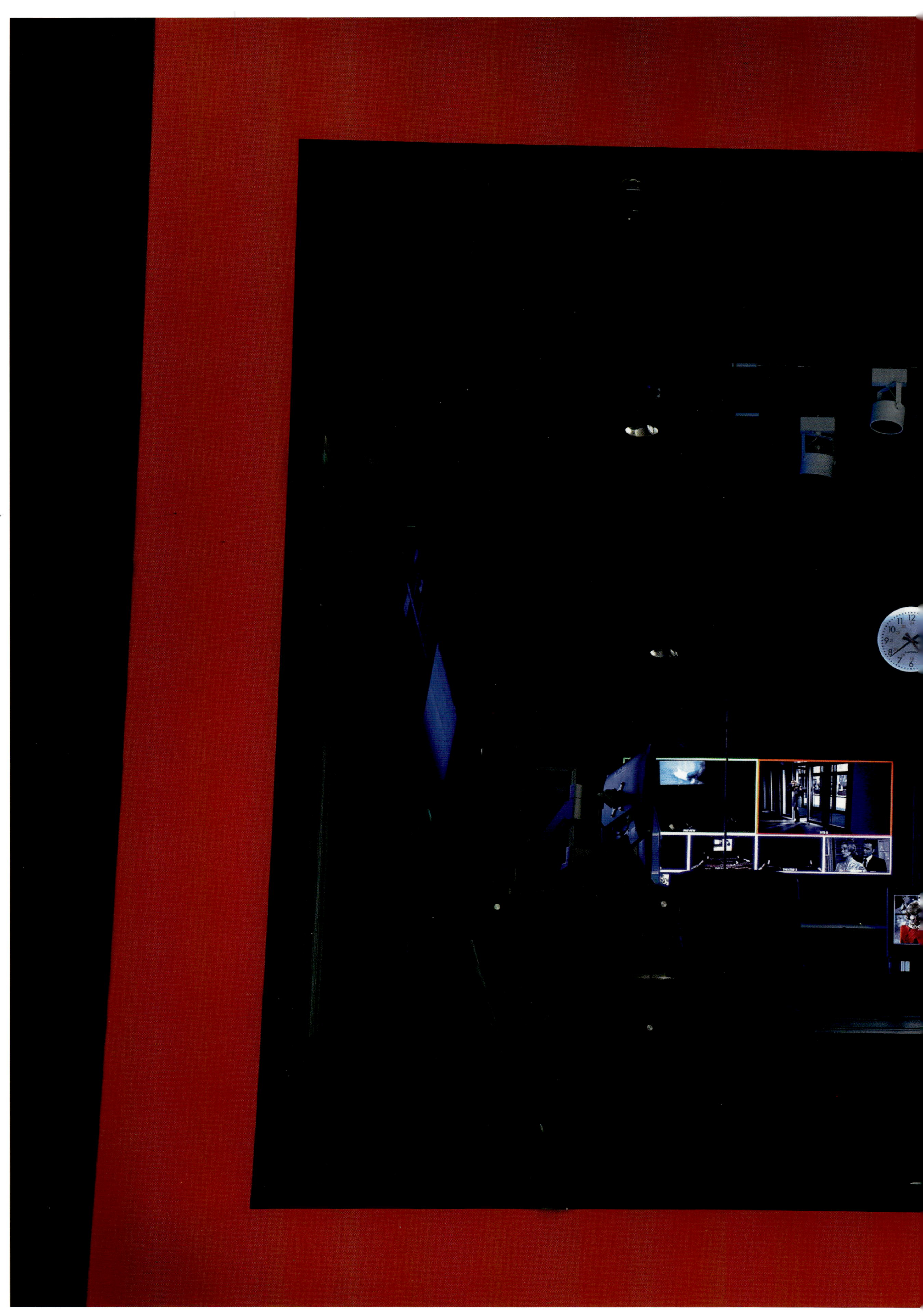

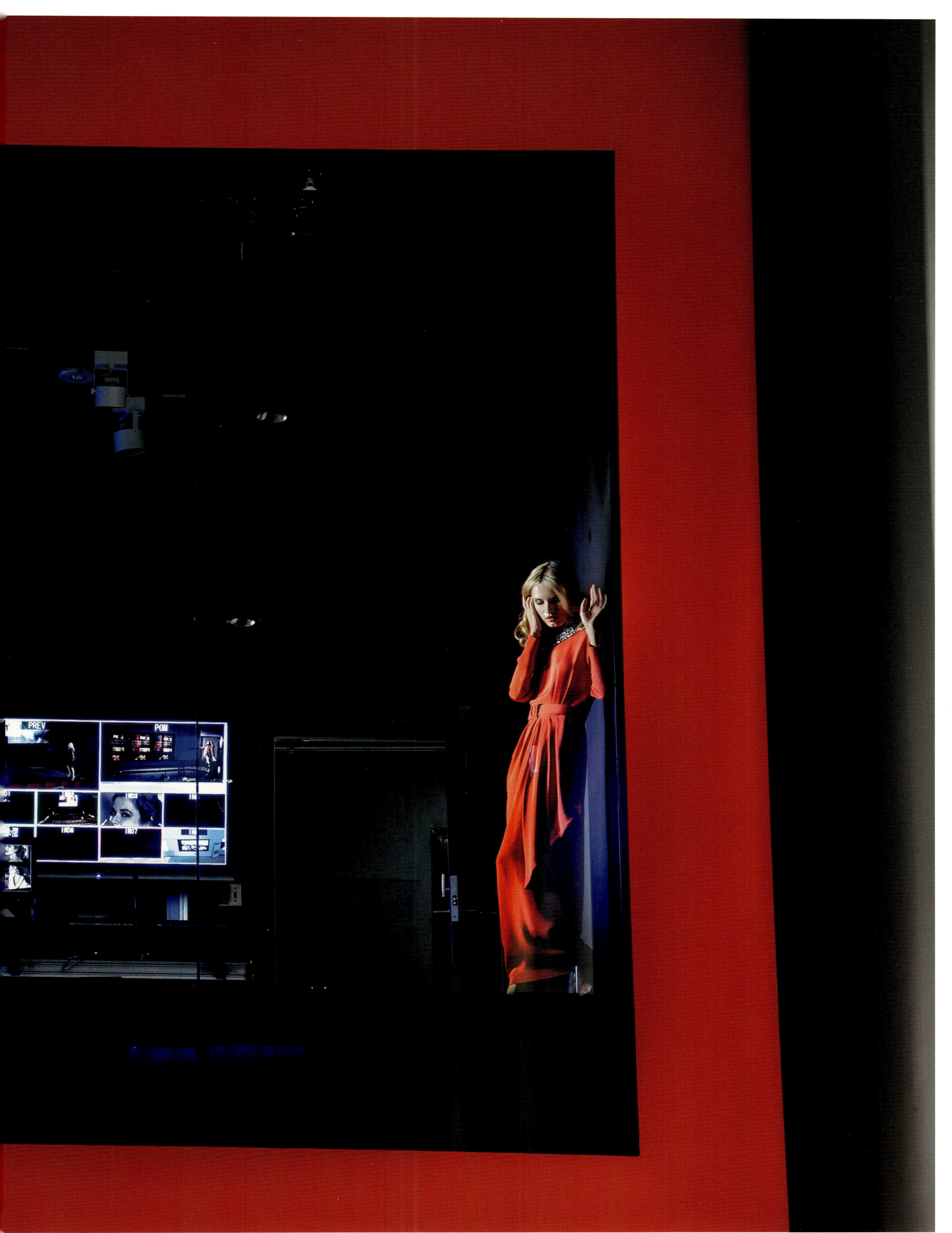
PREV
PGM

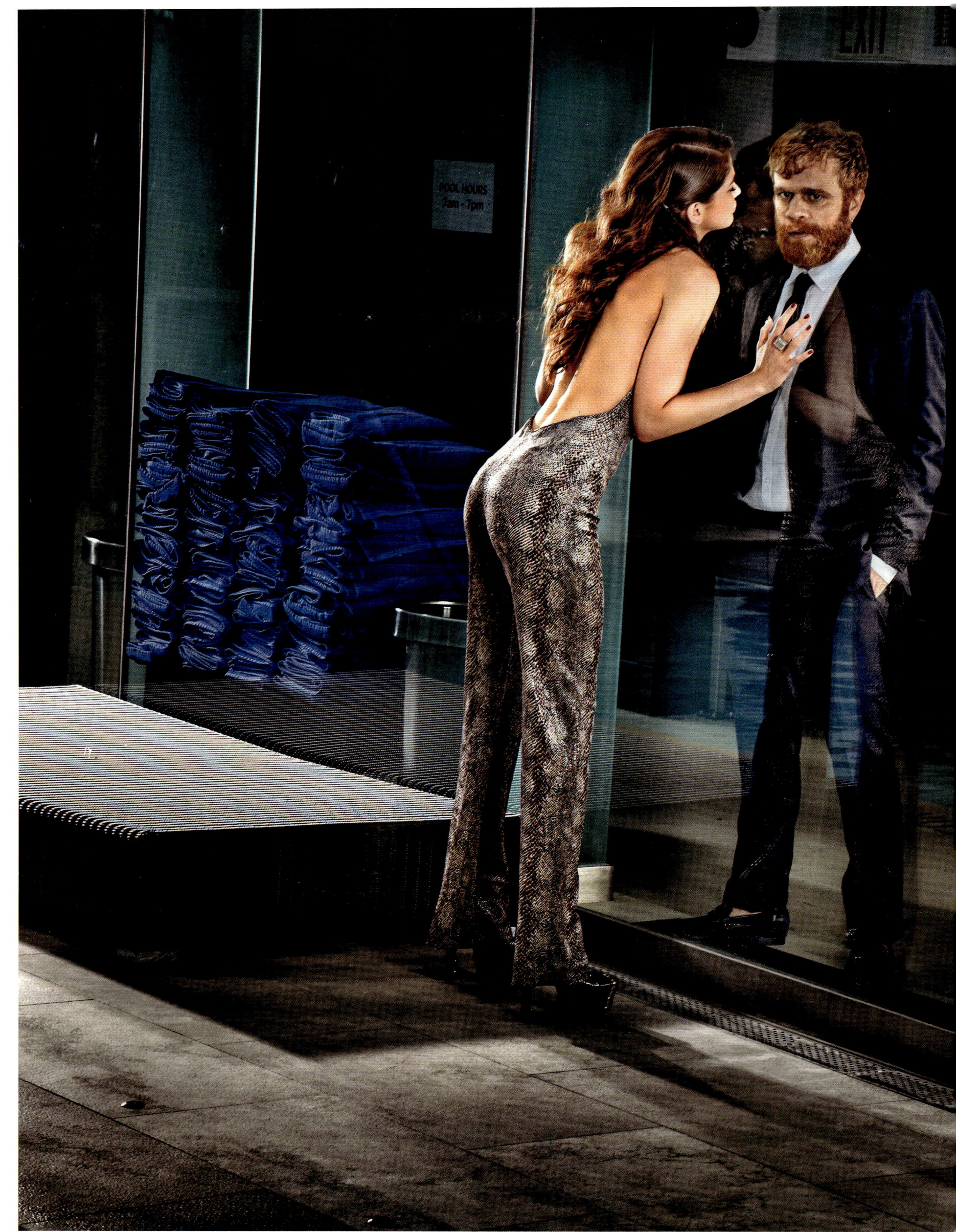
POOL HOURS
7am - 7pm
EXIT

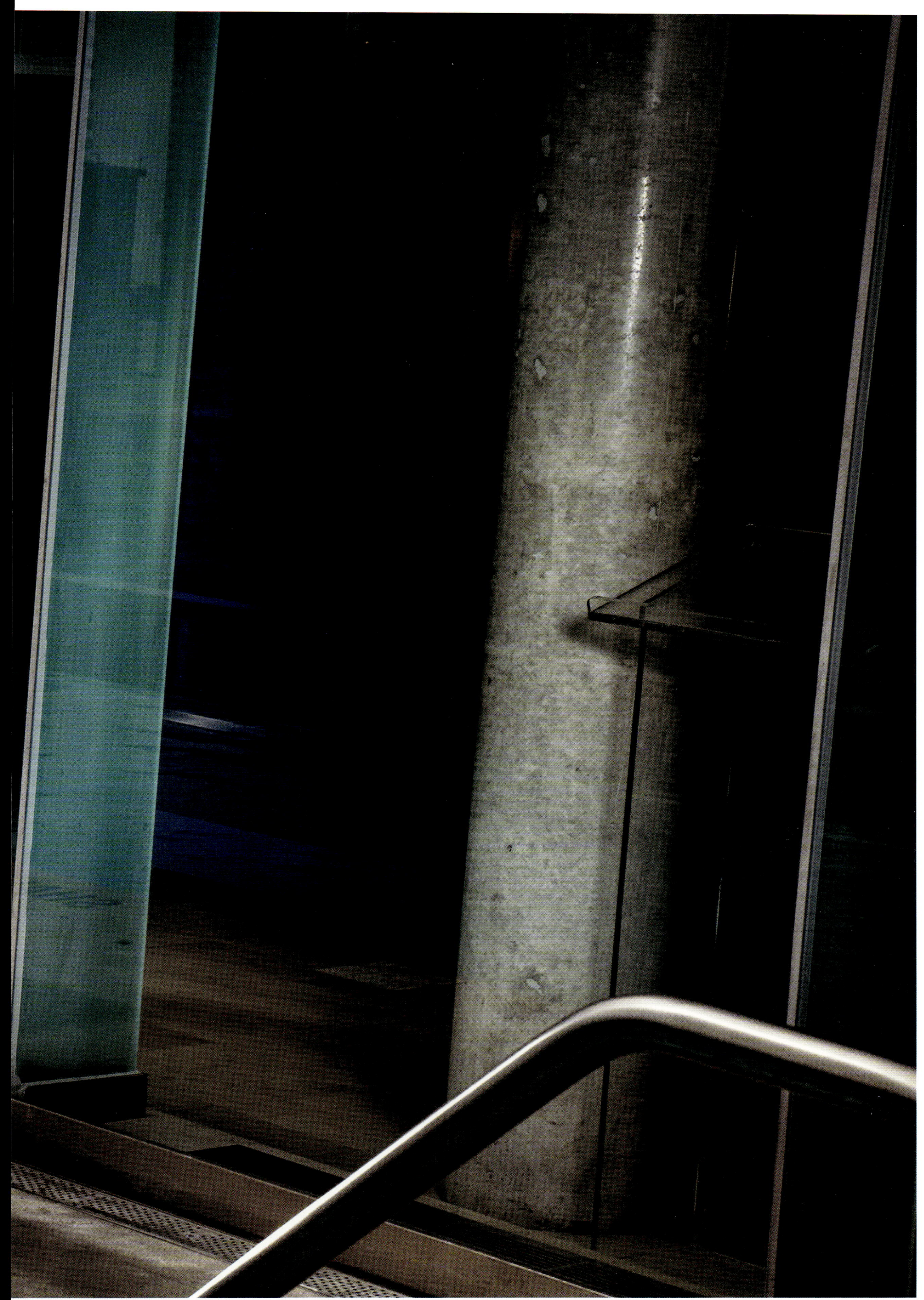

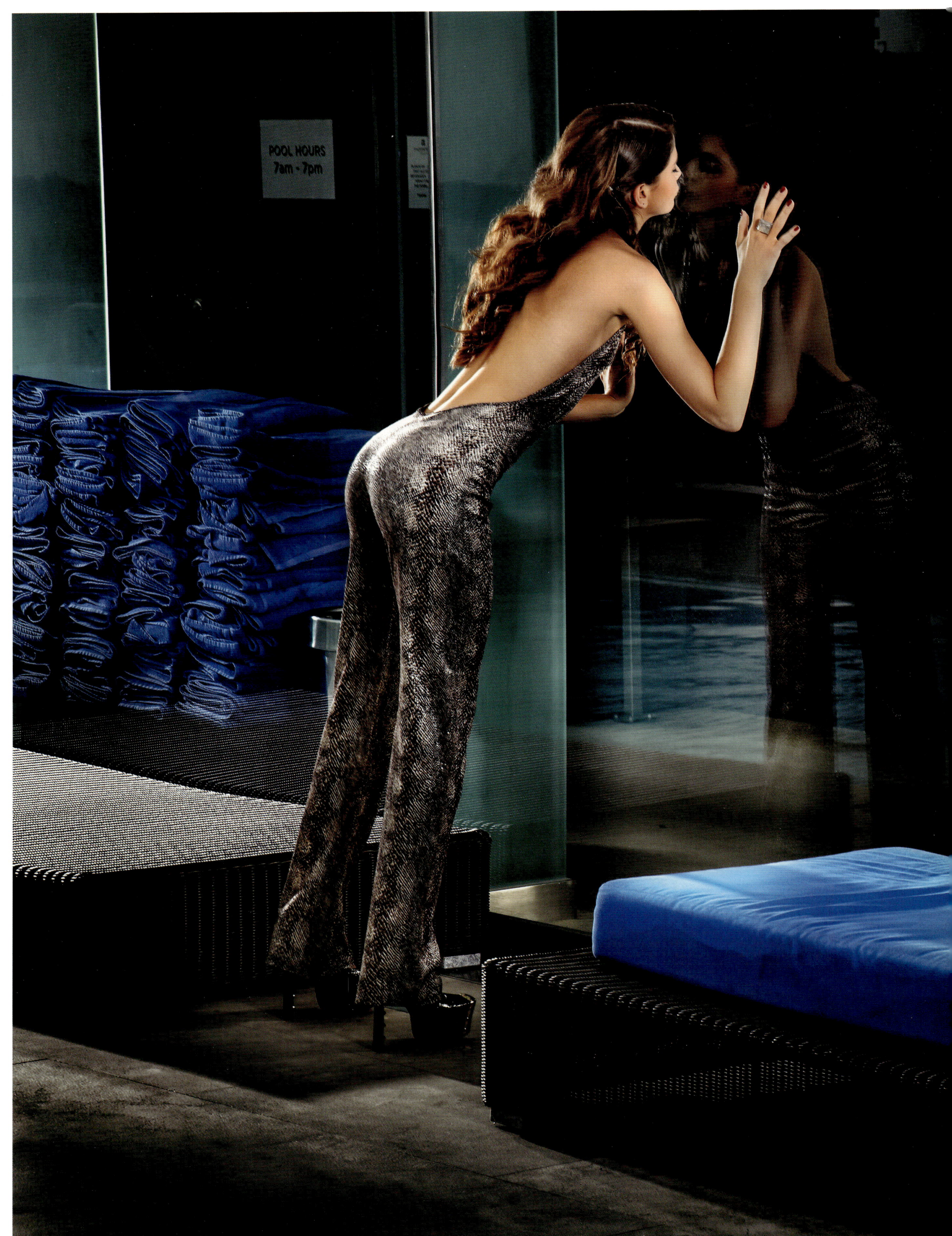

KISSING HERSELF | 2011

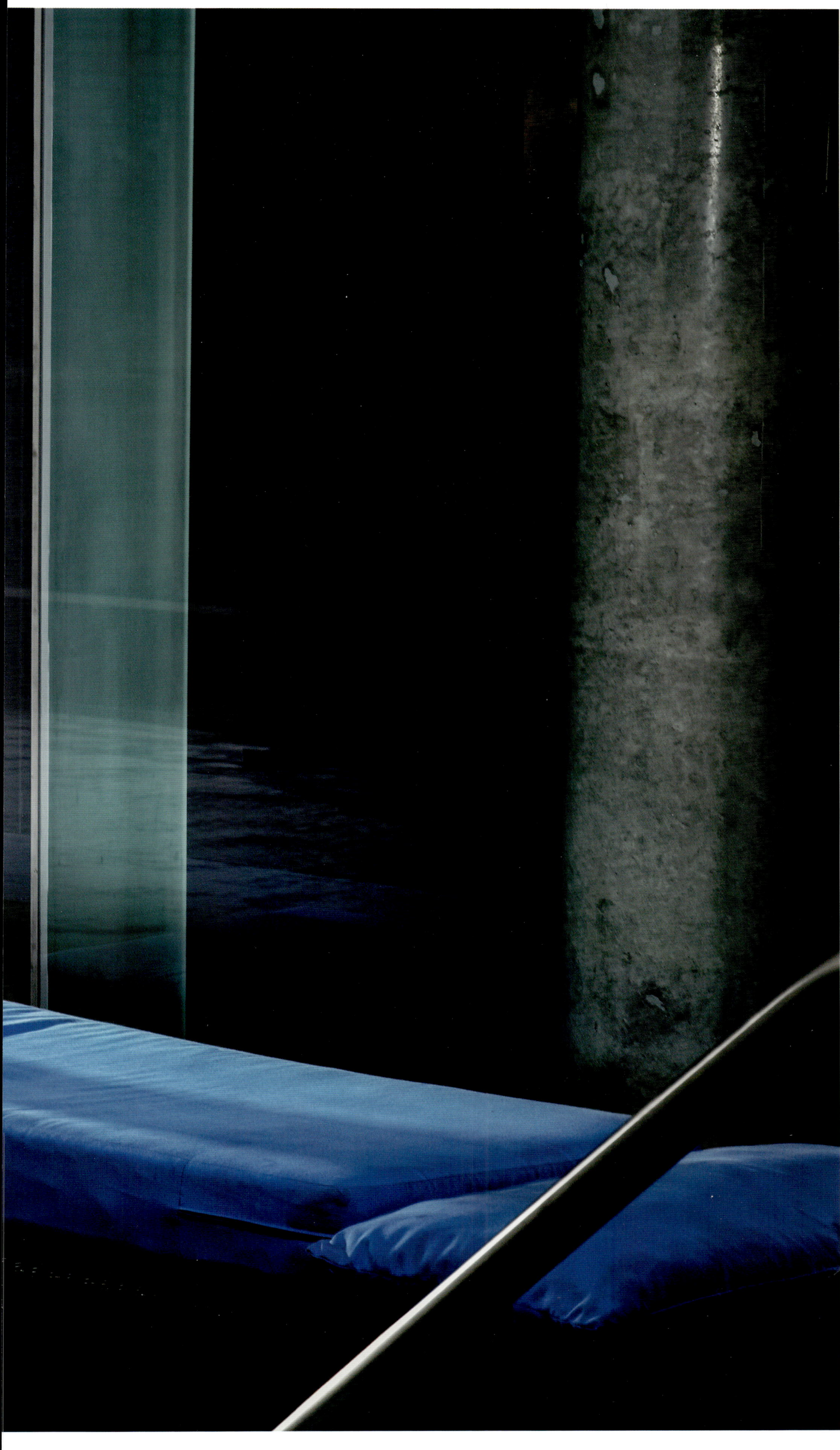

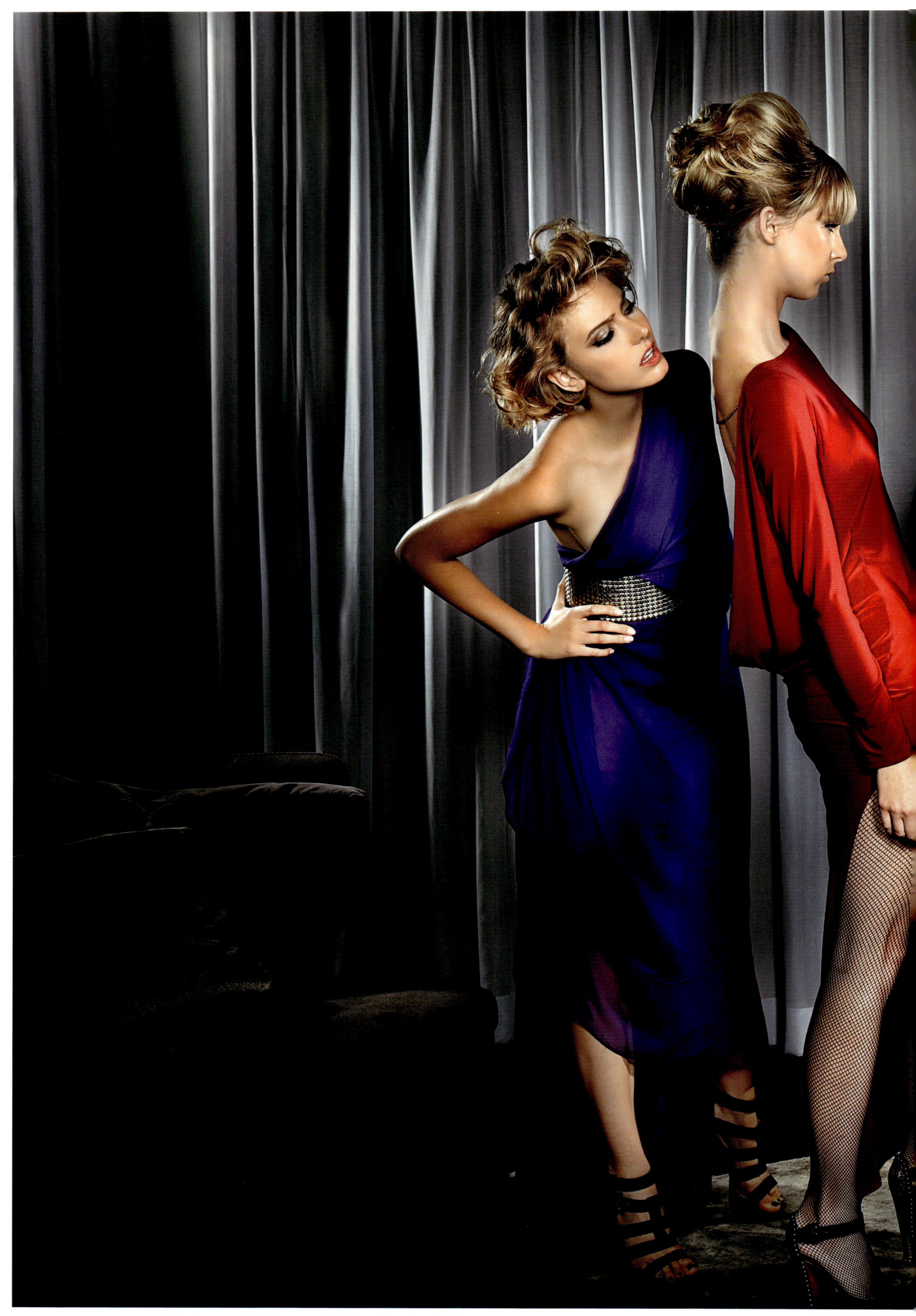

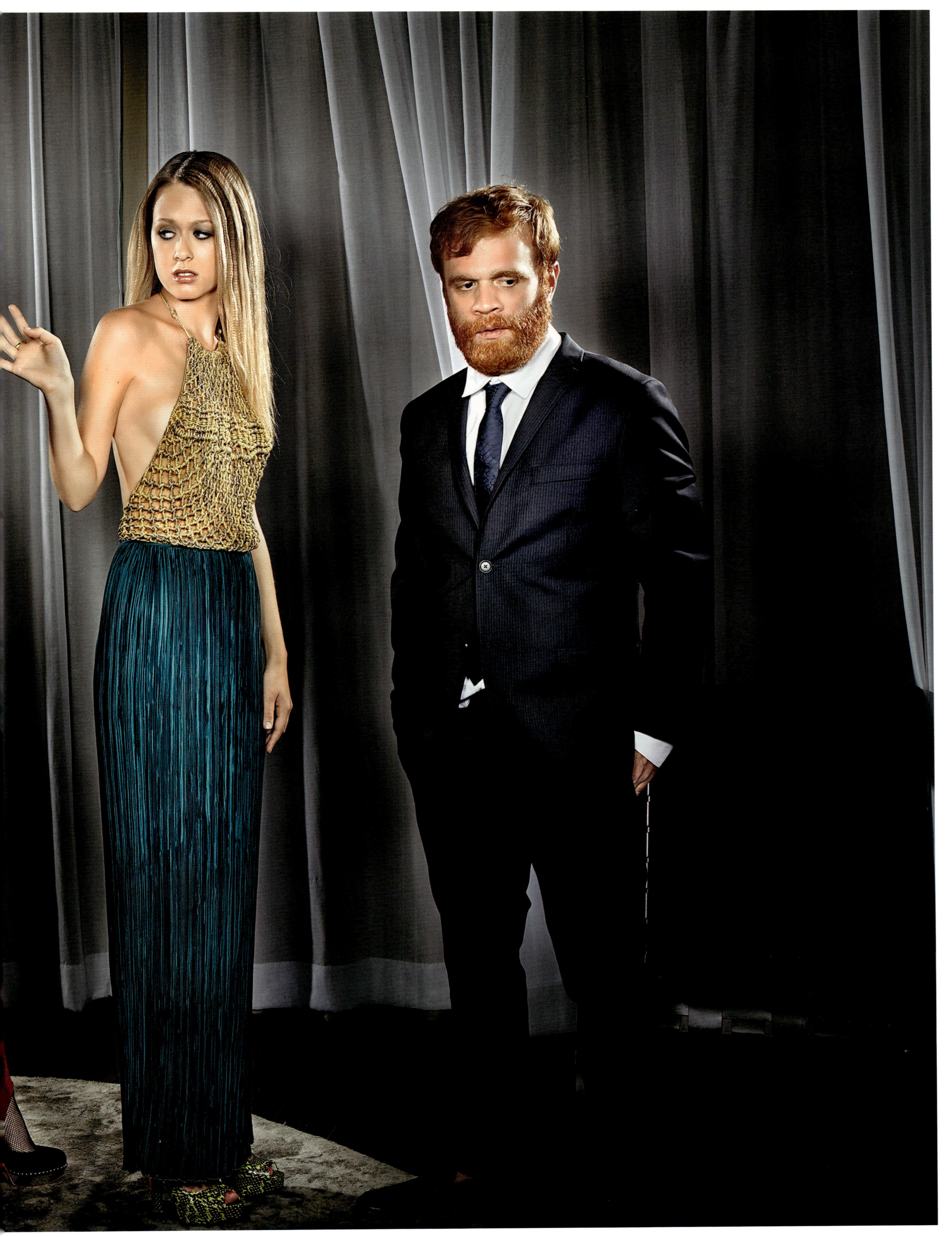

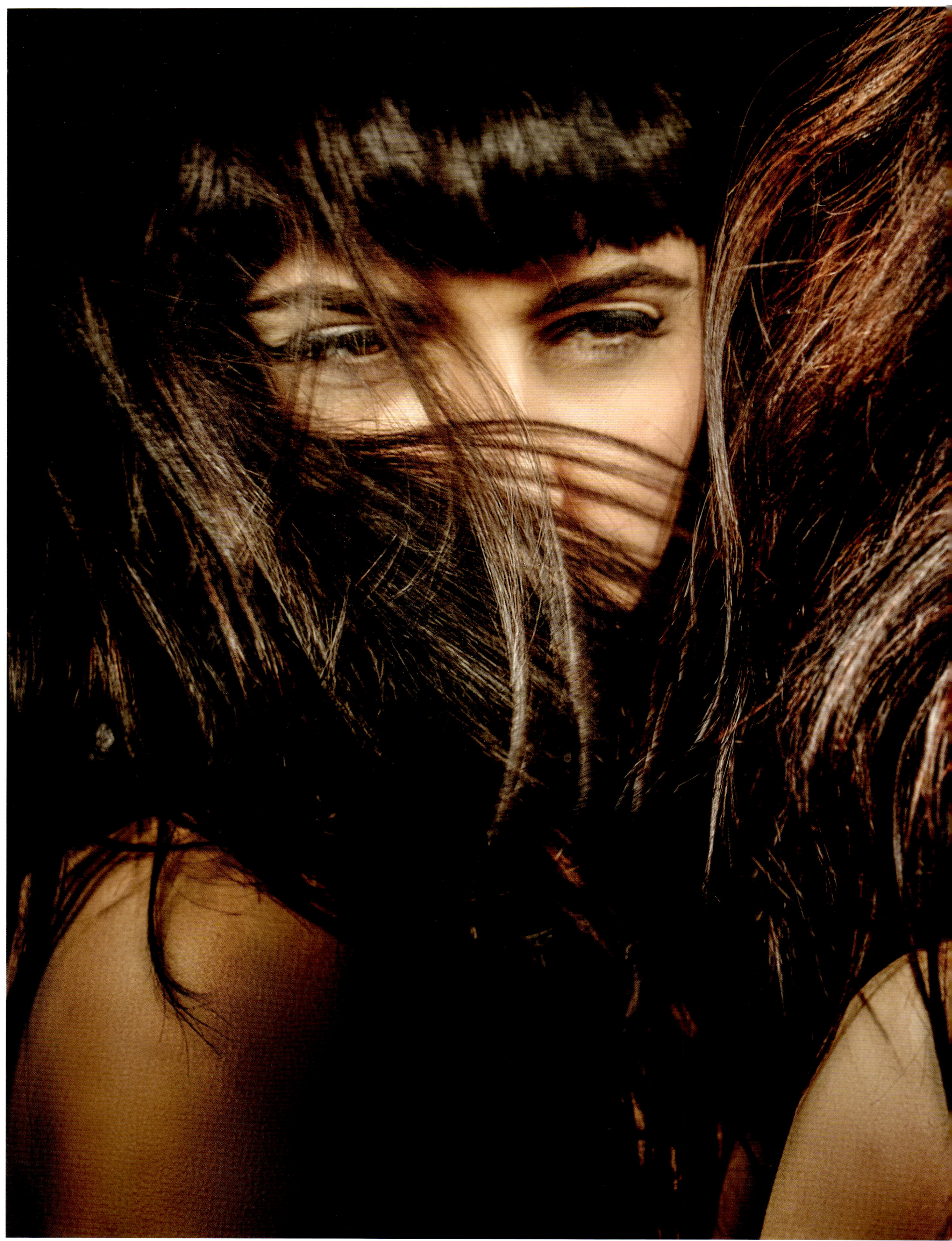

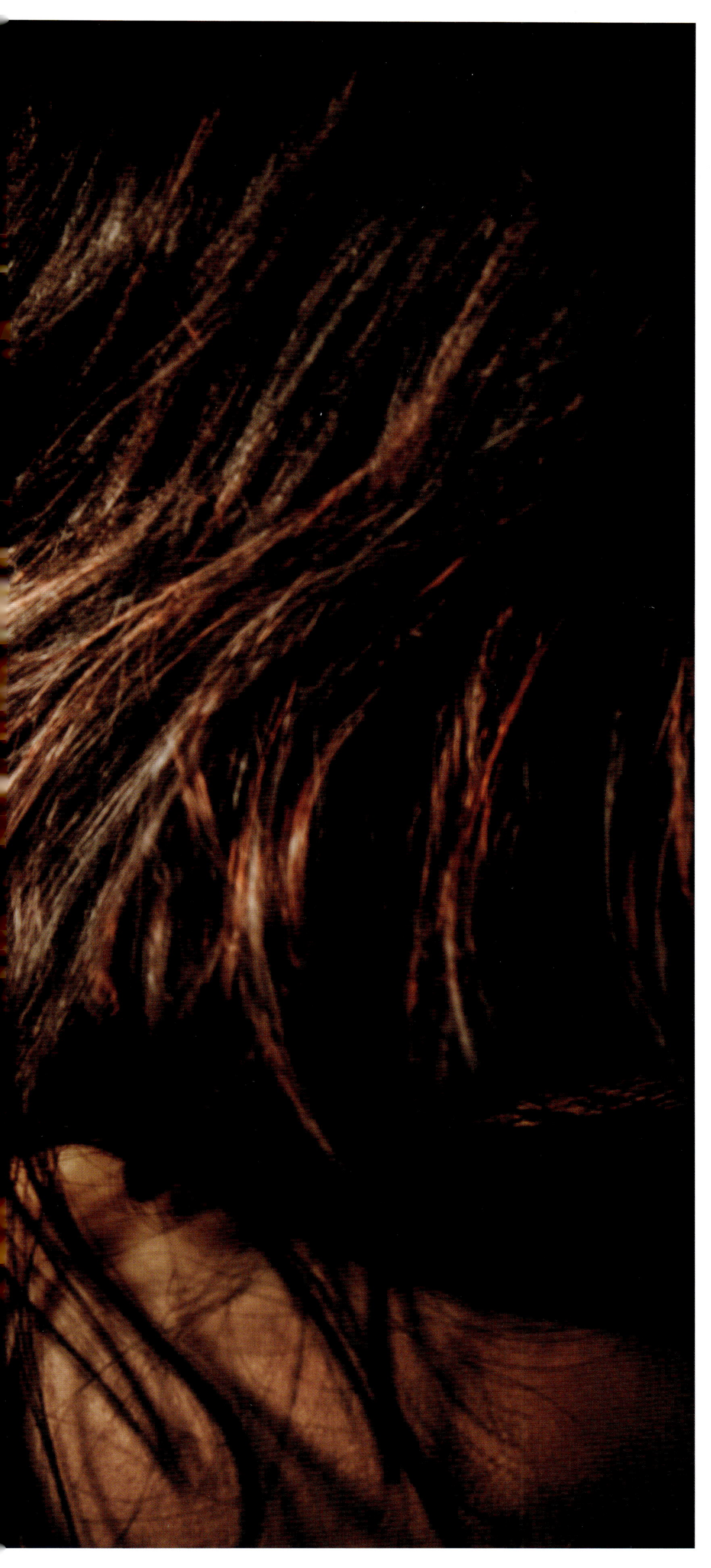

JUST ME | 2012

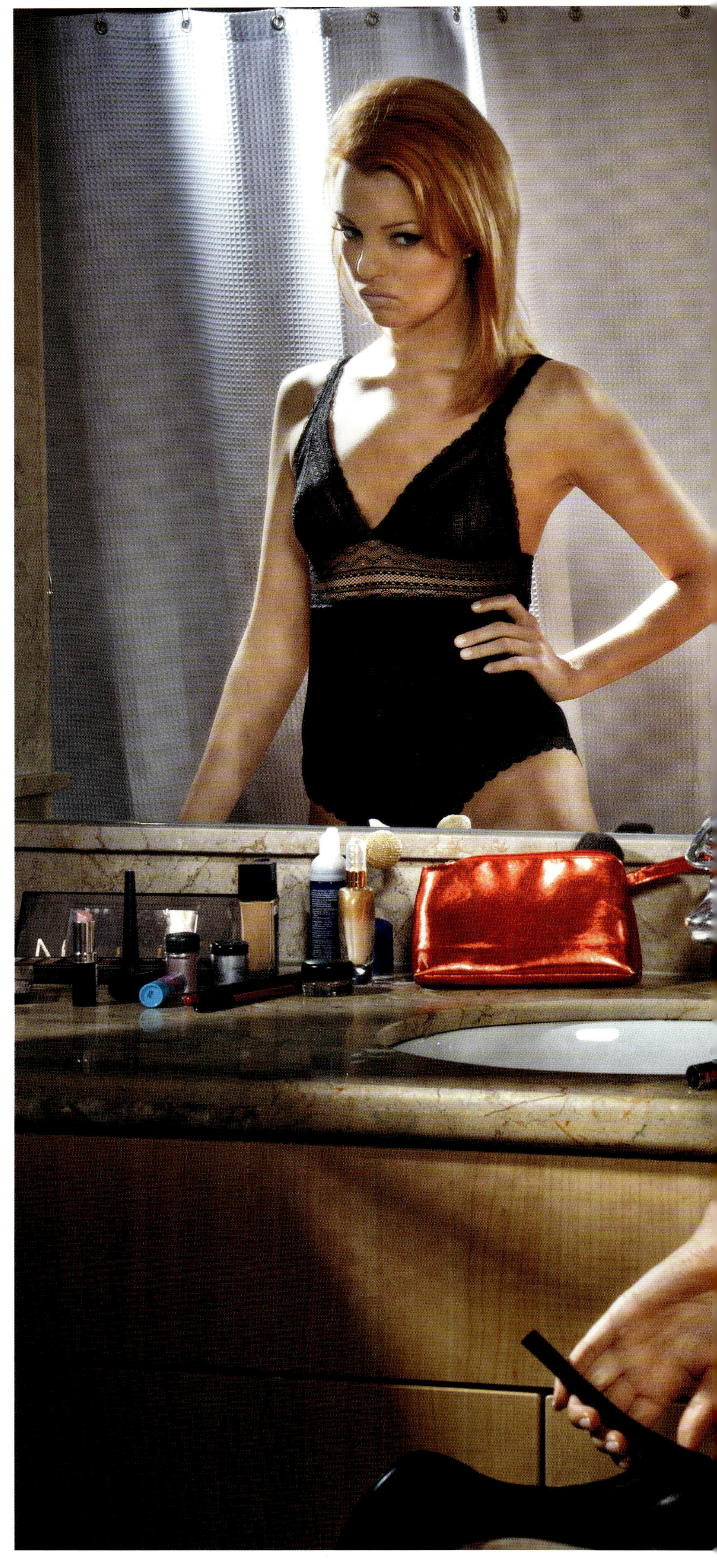

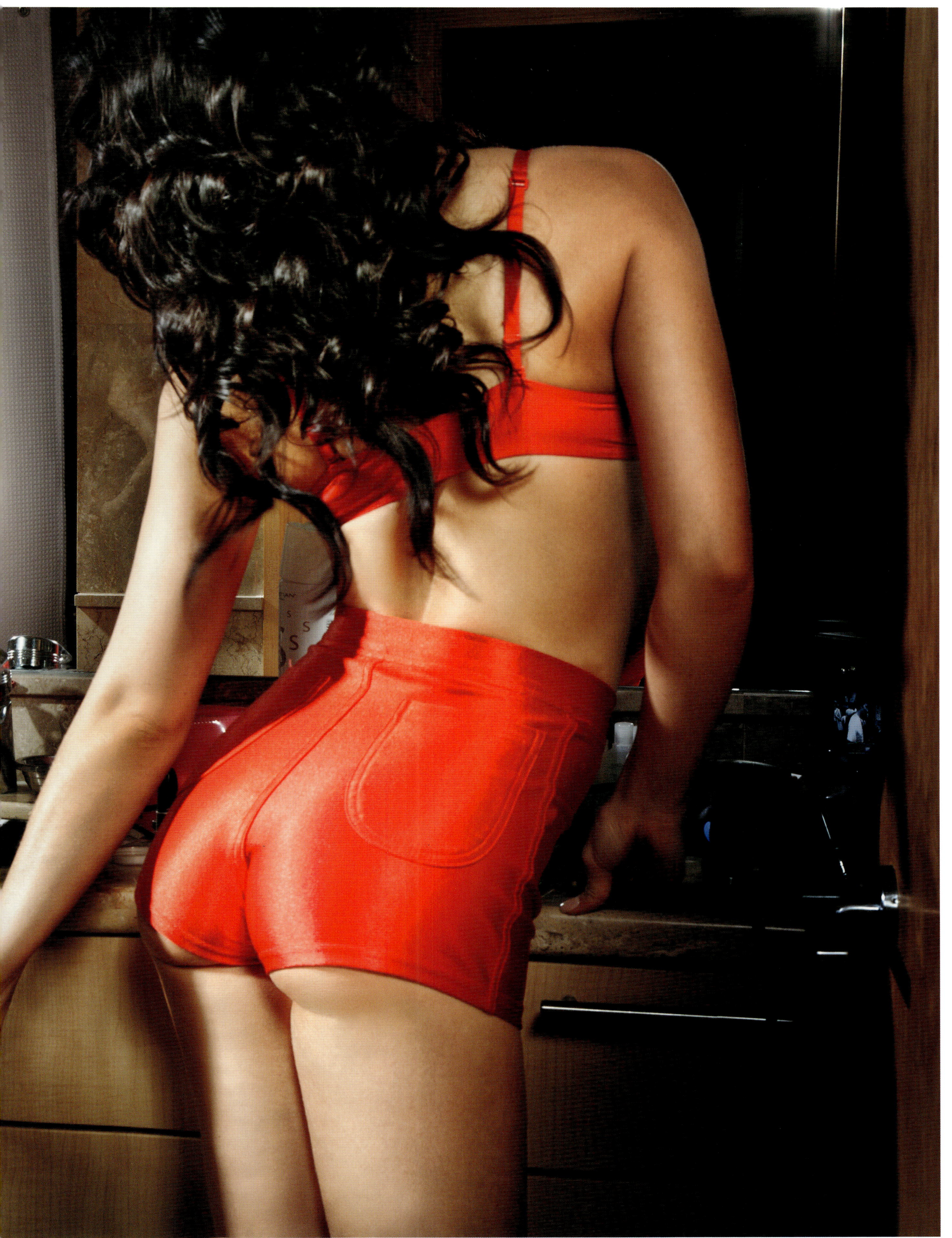

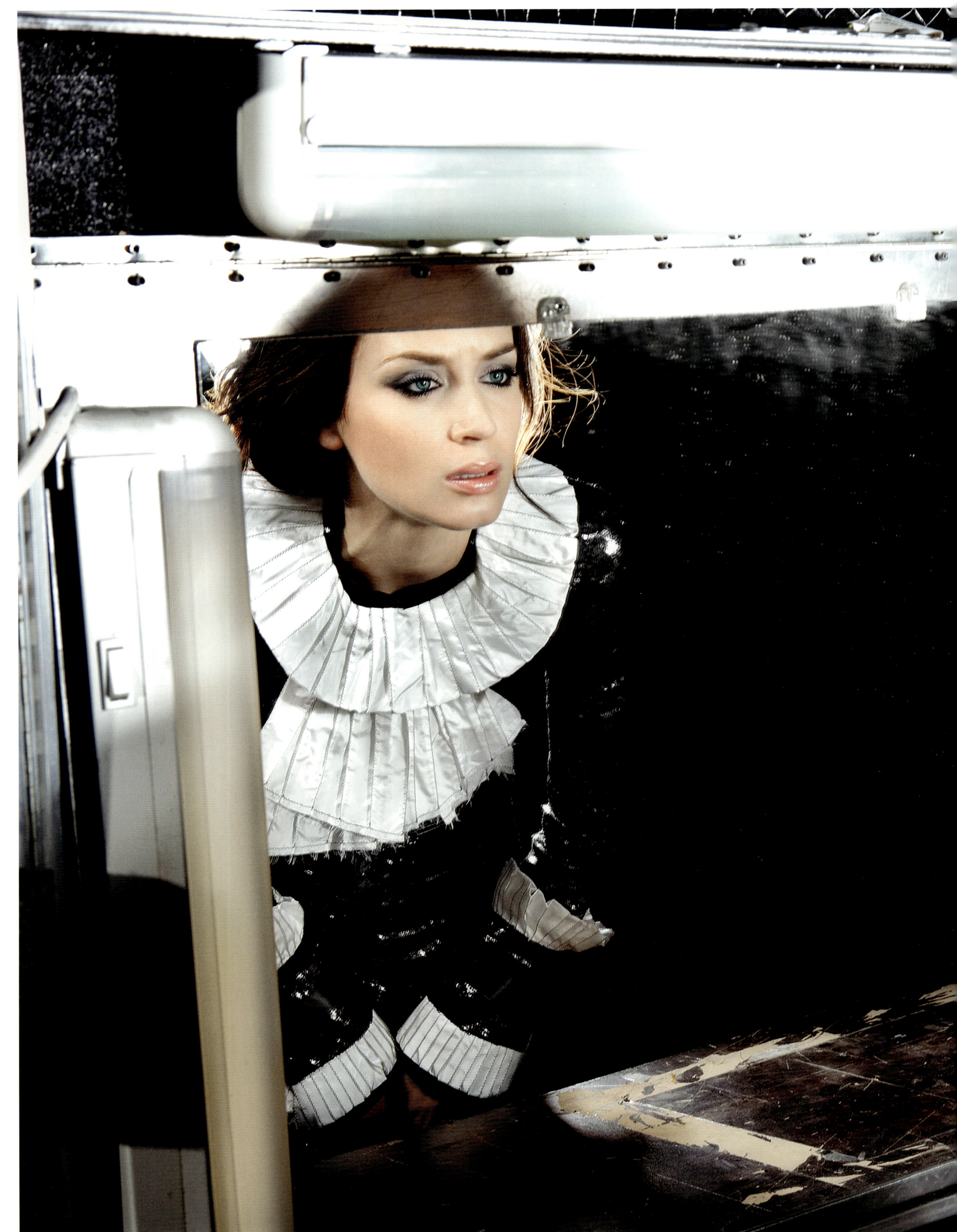

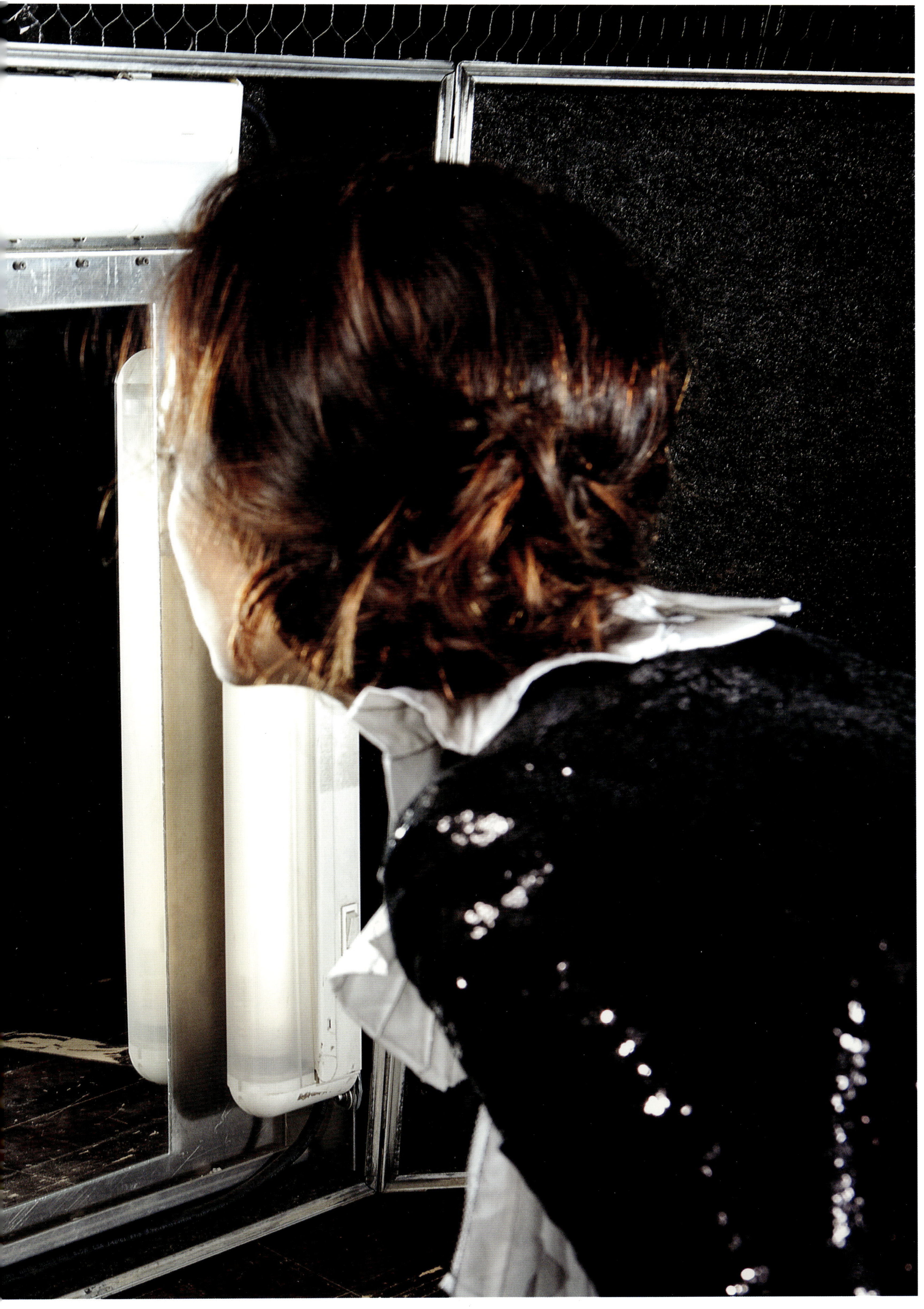

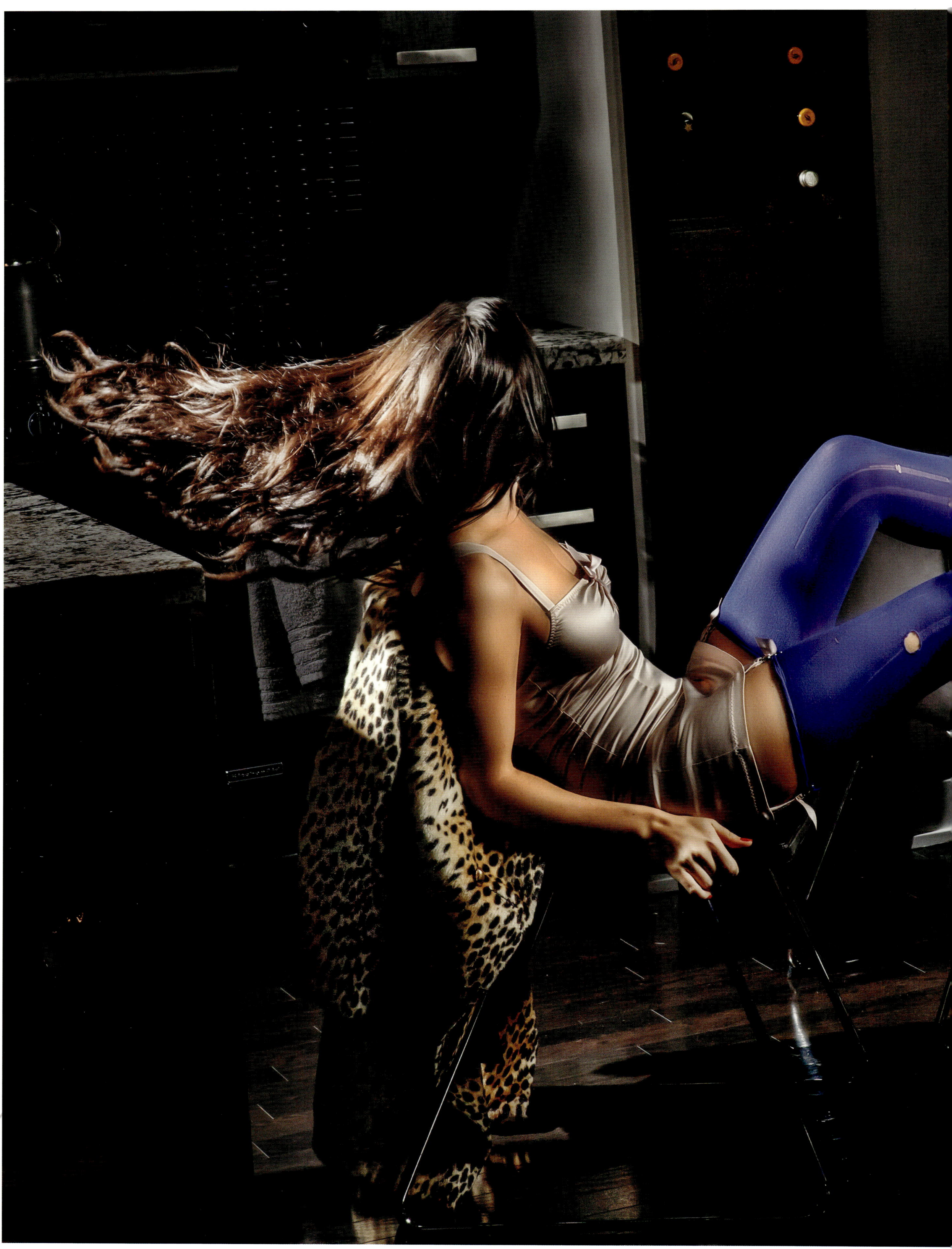

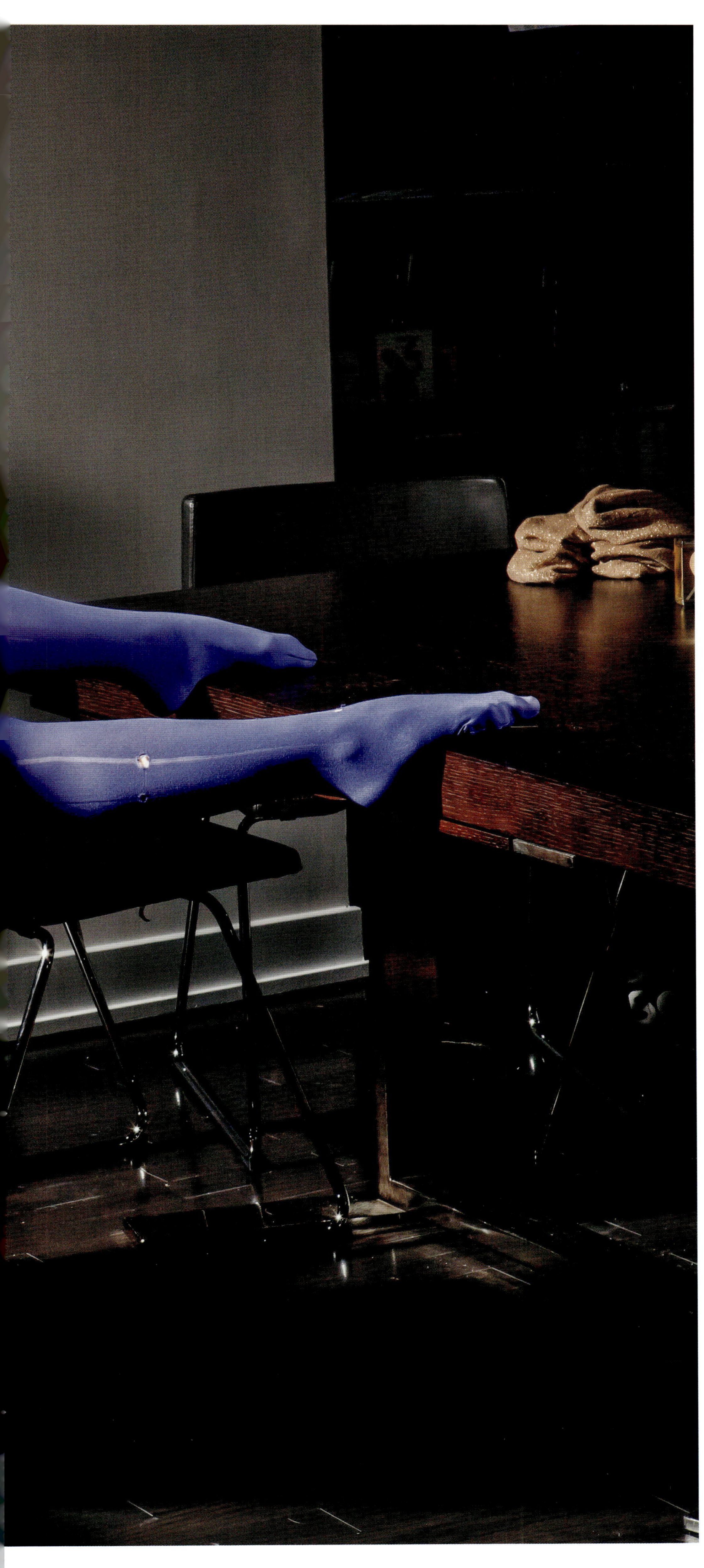

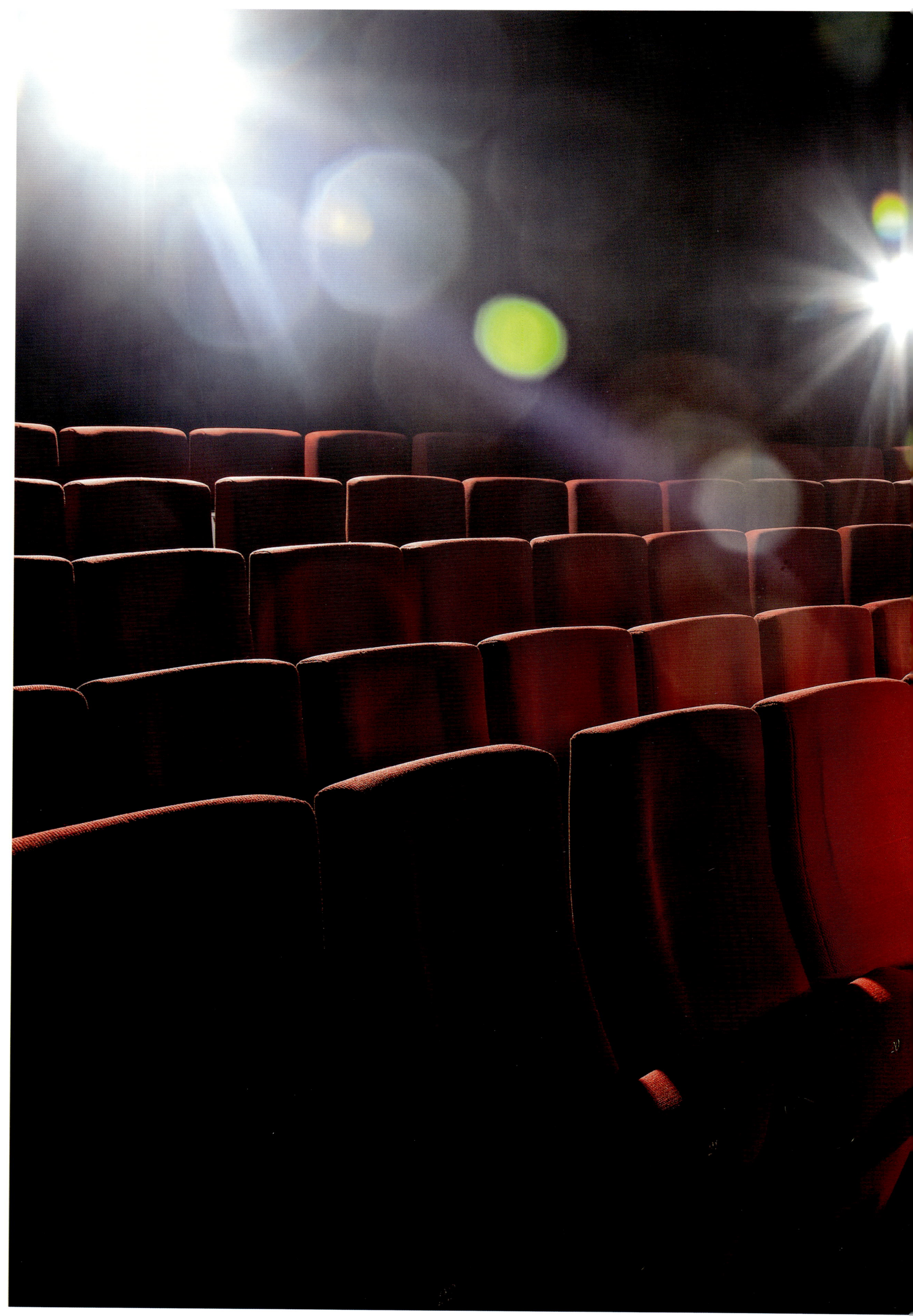

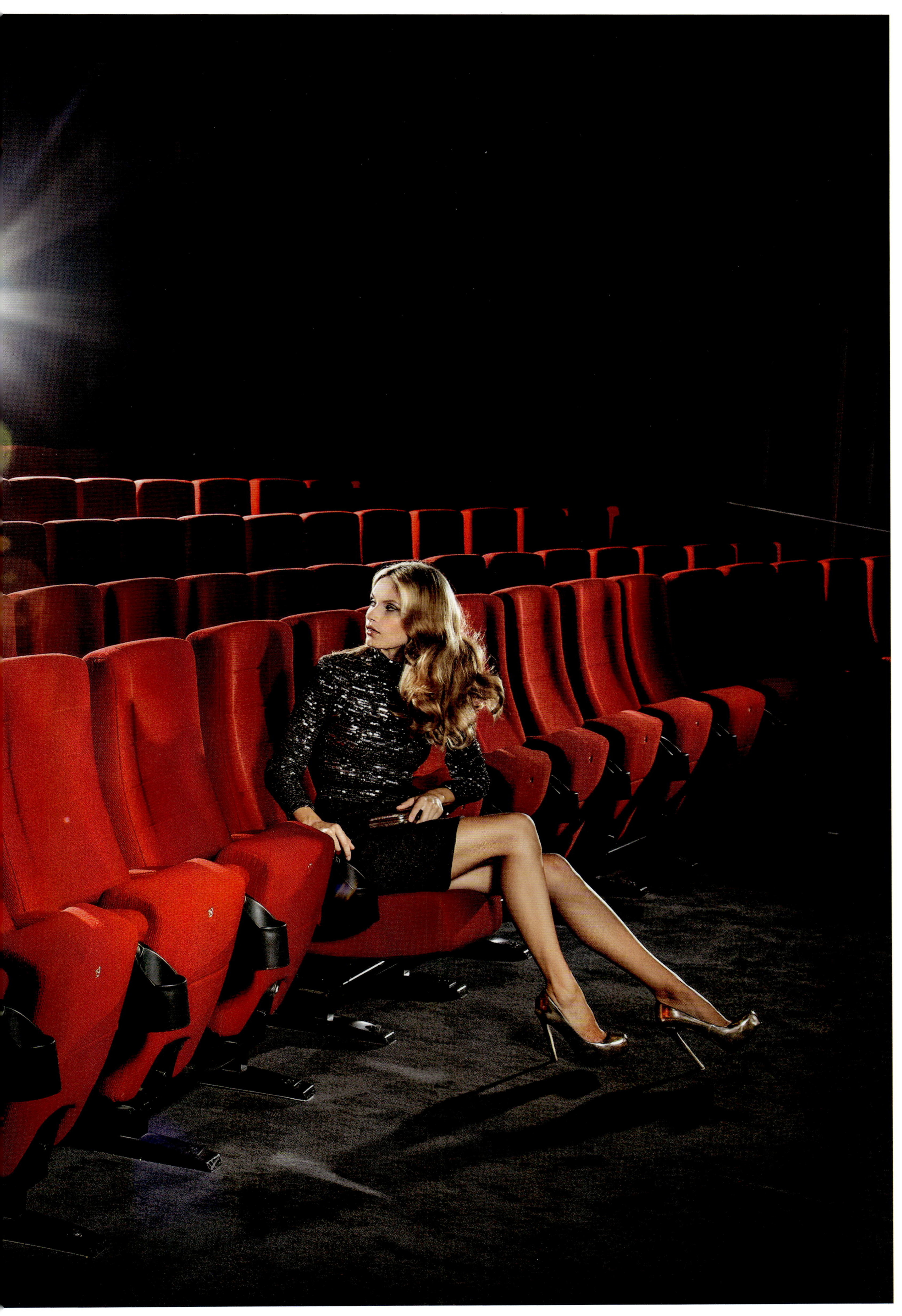

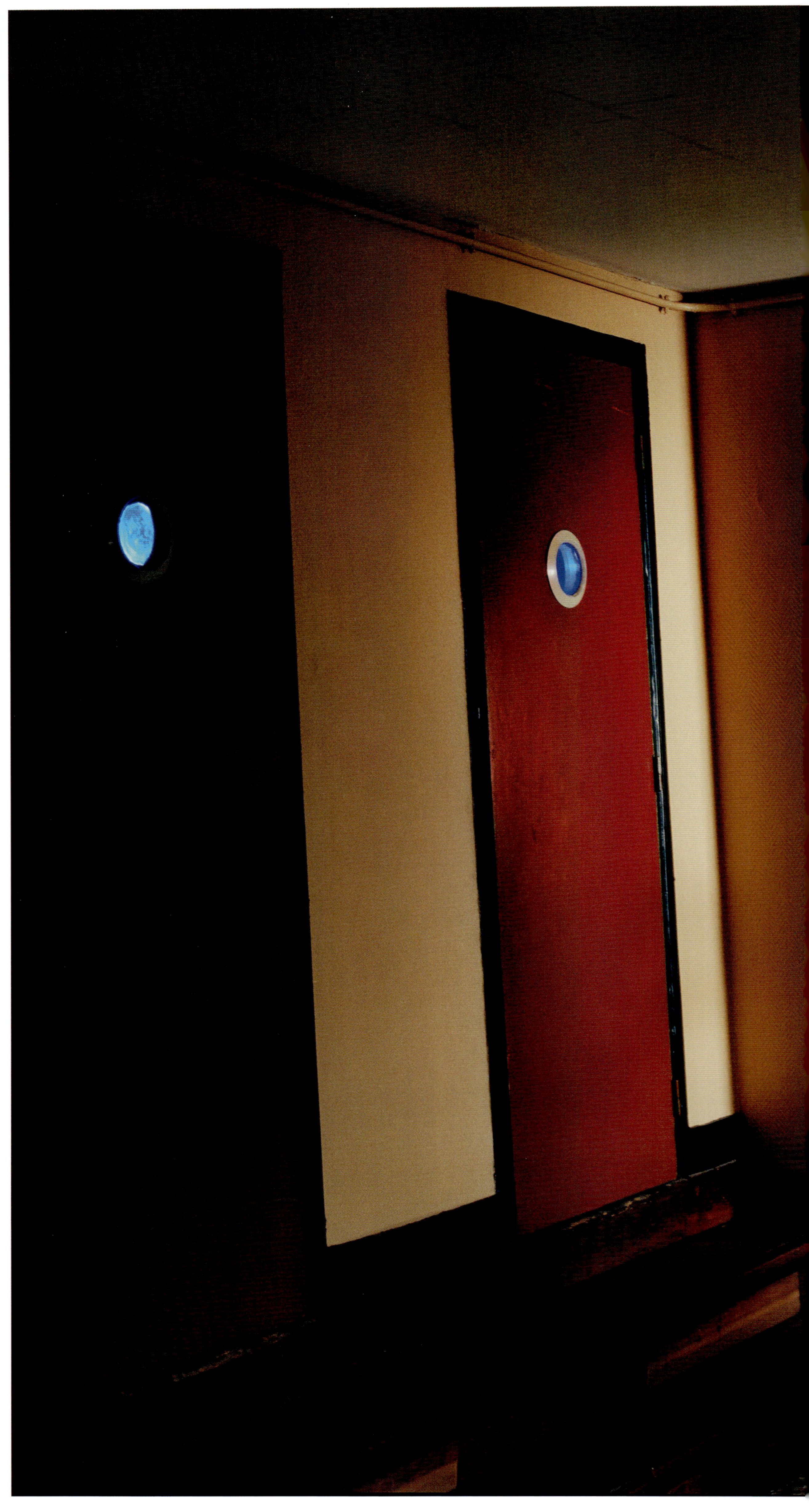

READY FOR ACTION | 2004

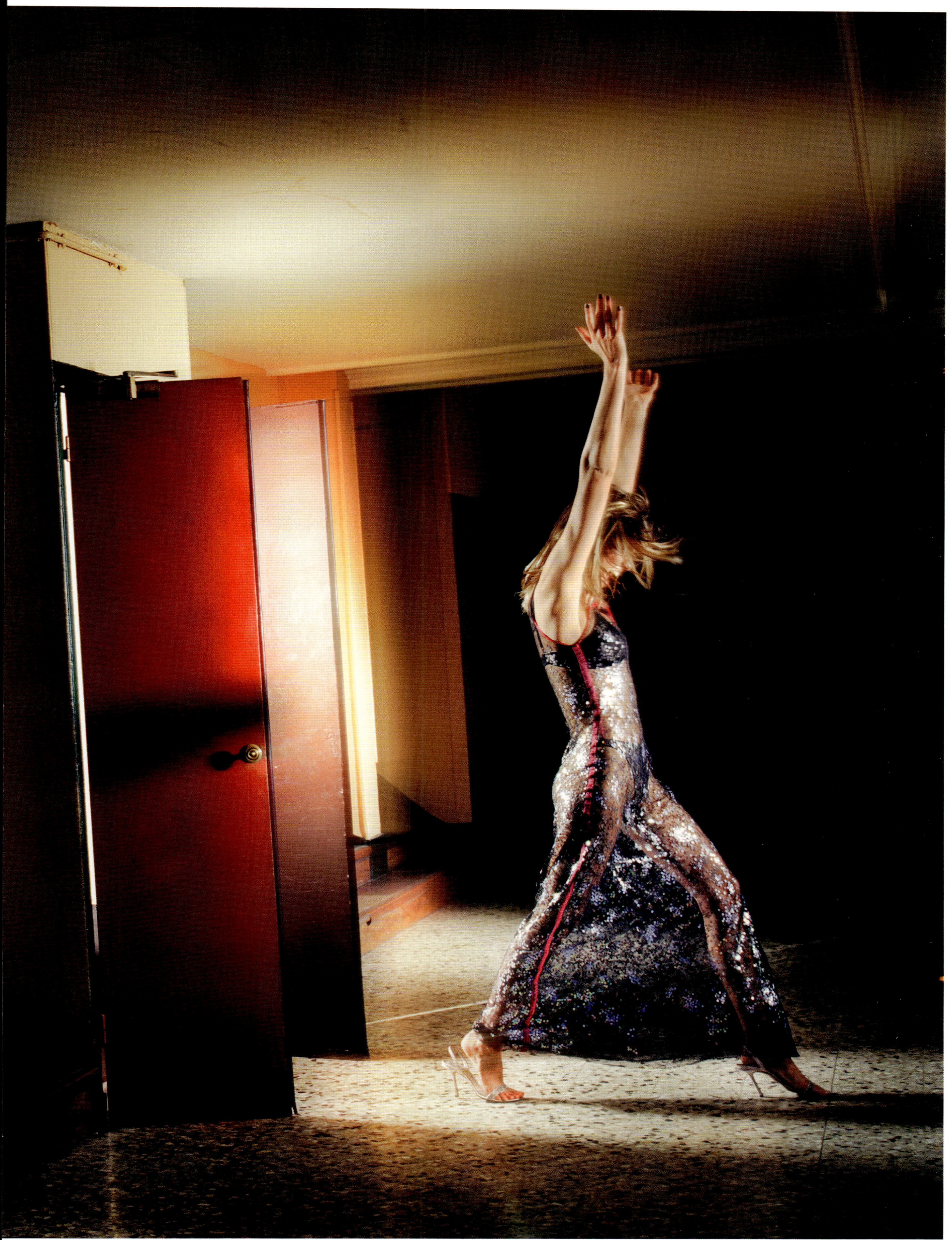

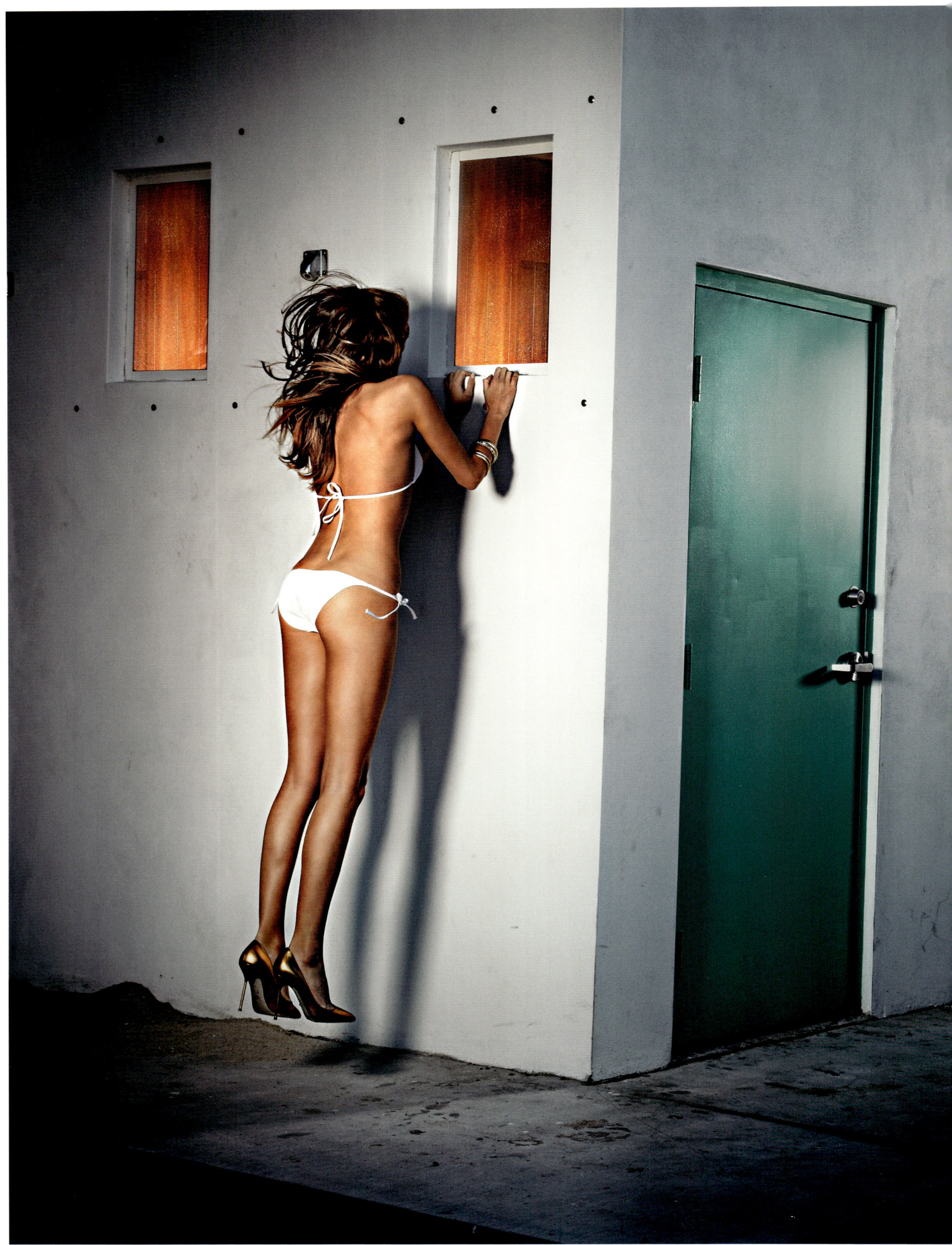

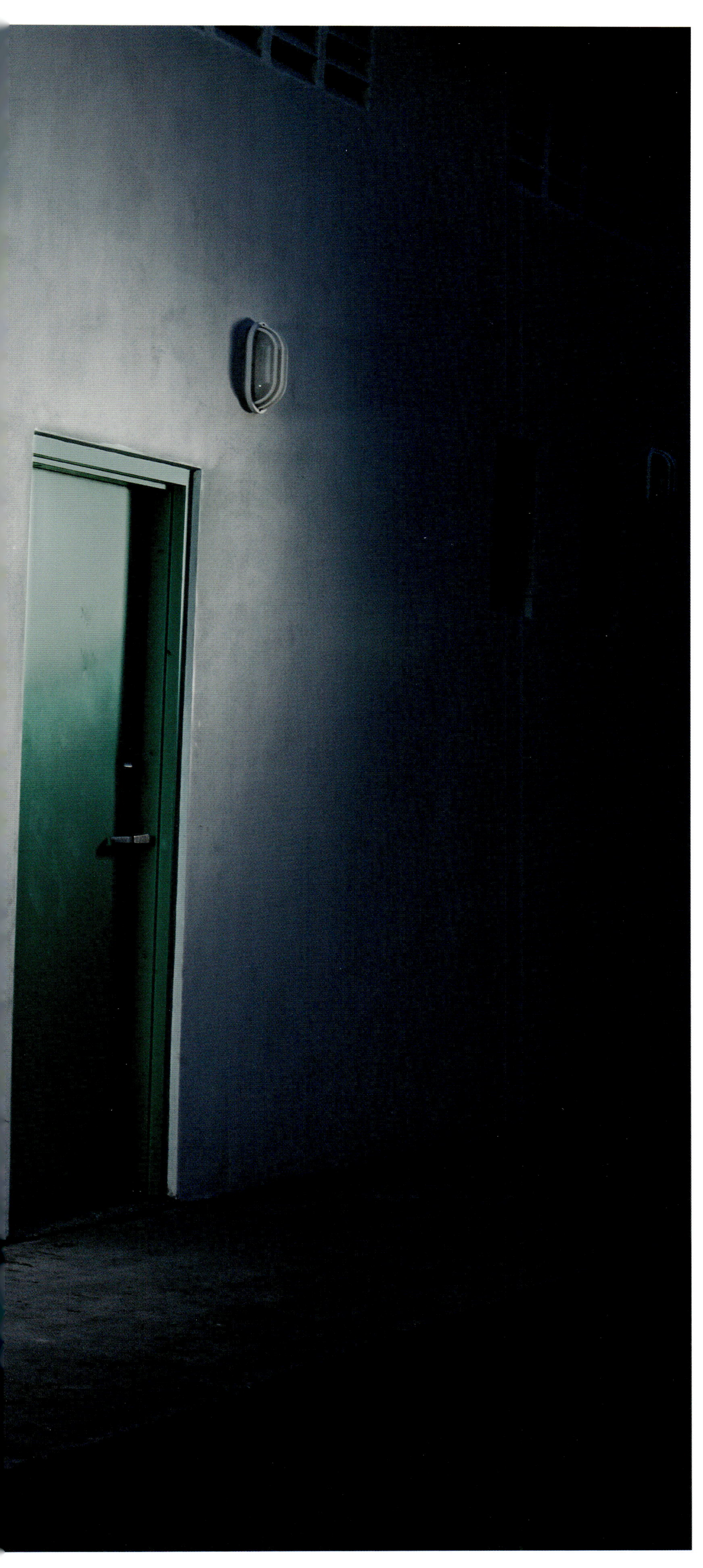

PEEPING | 2011

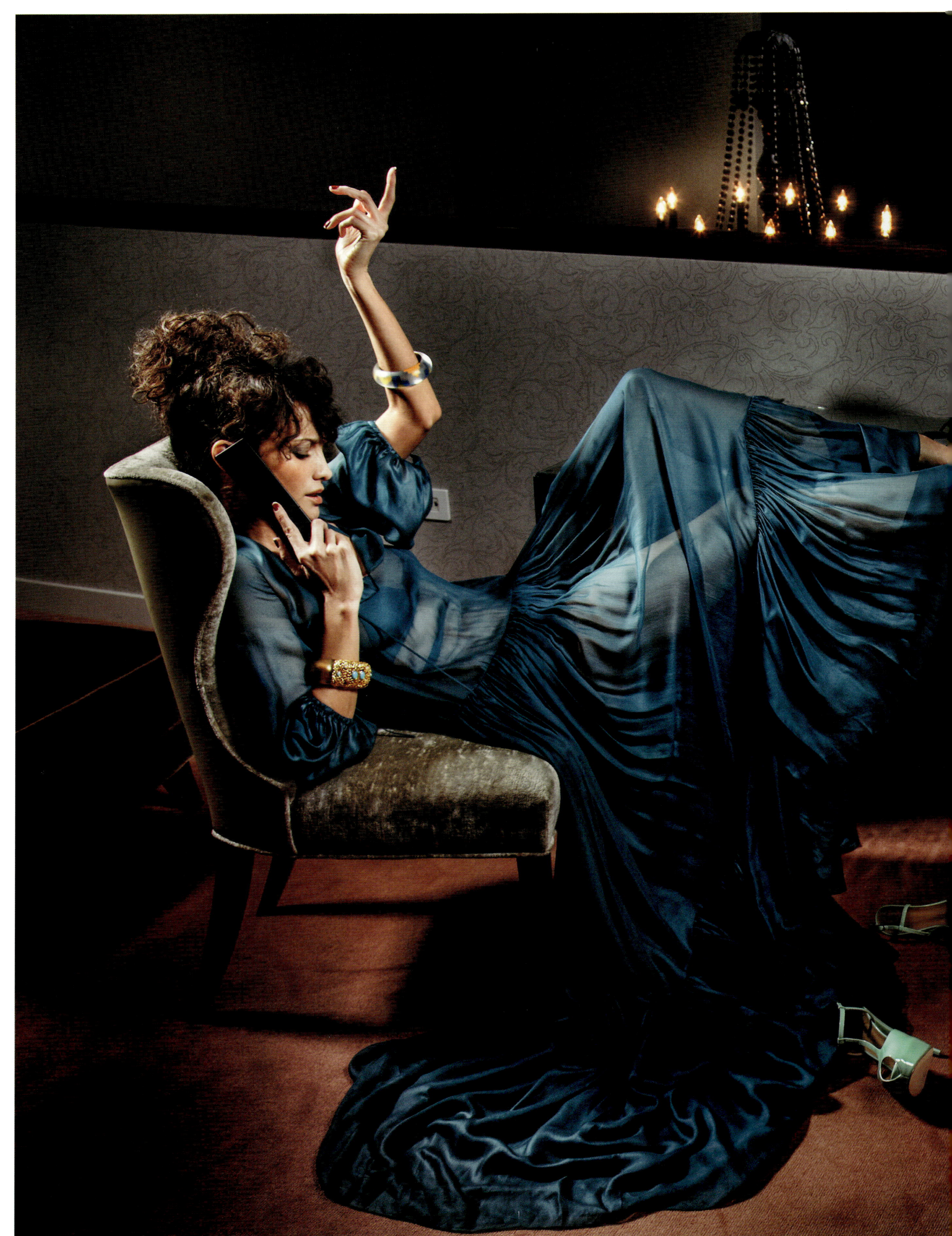

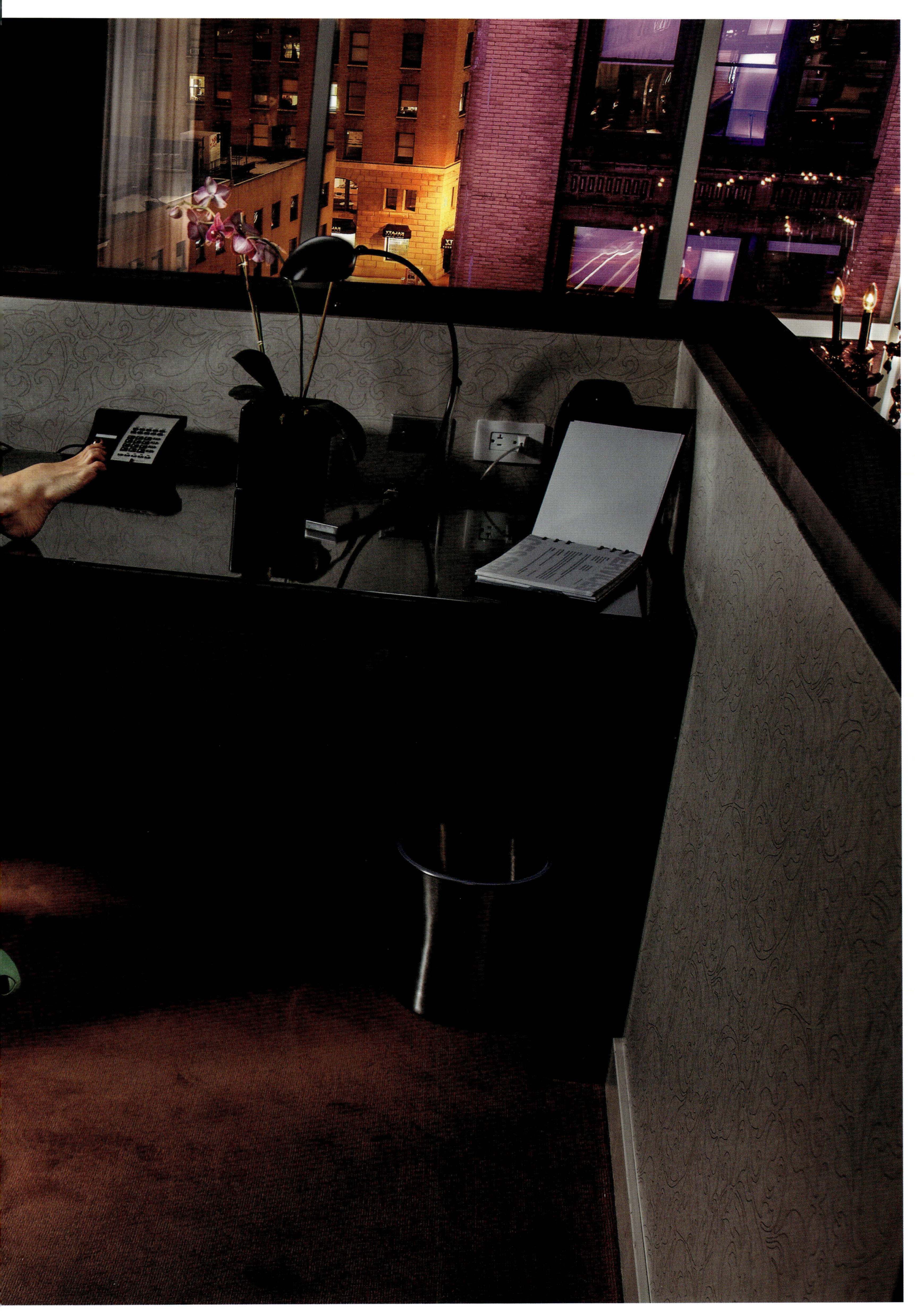

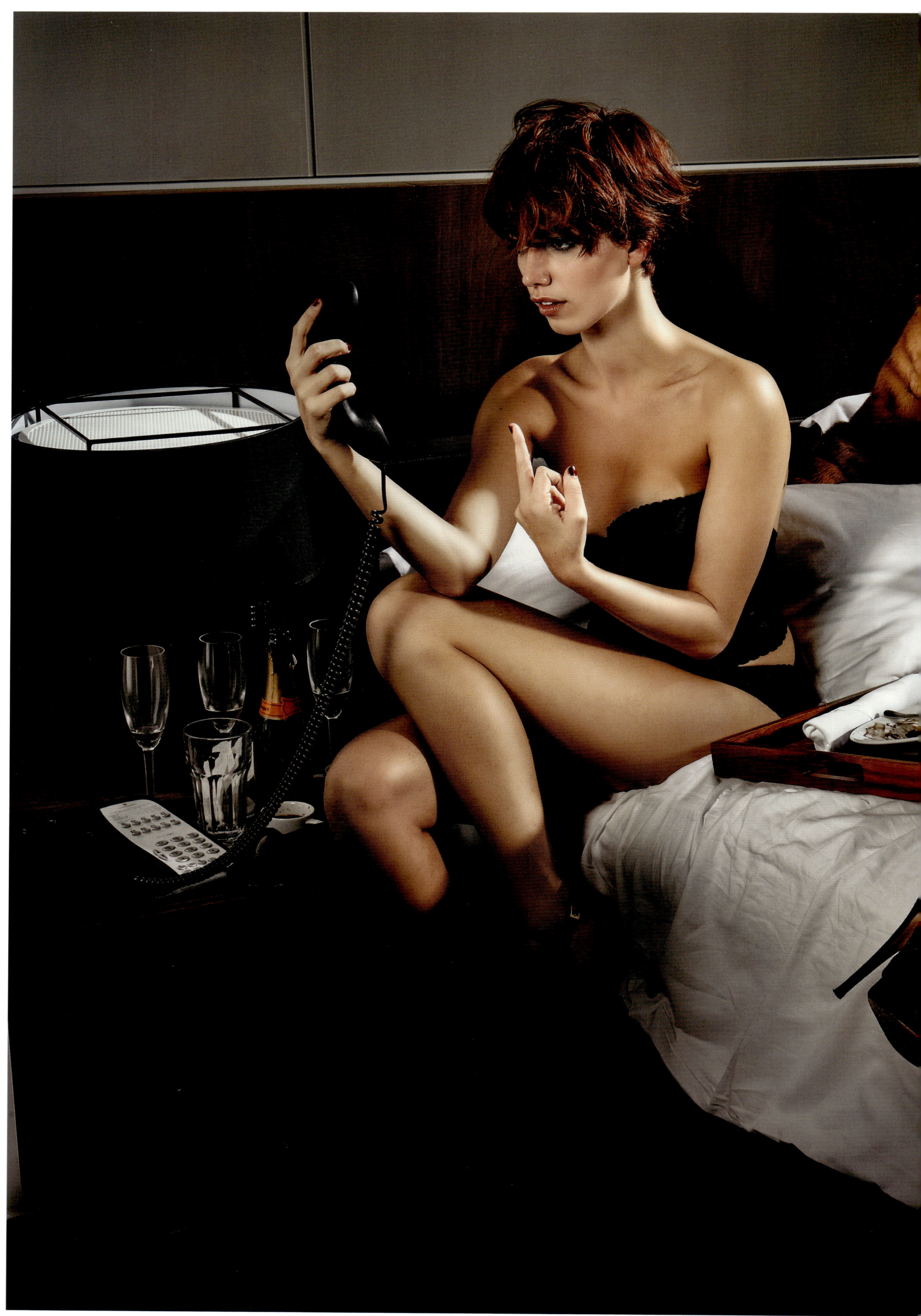

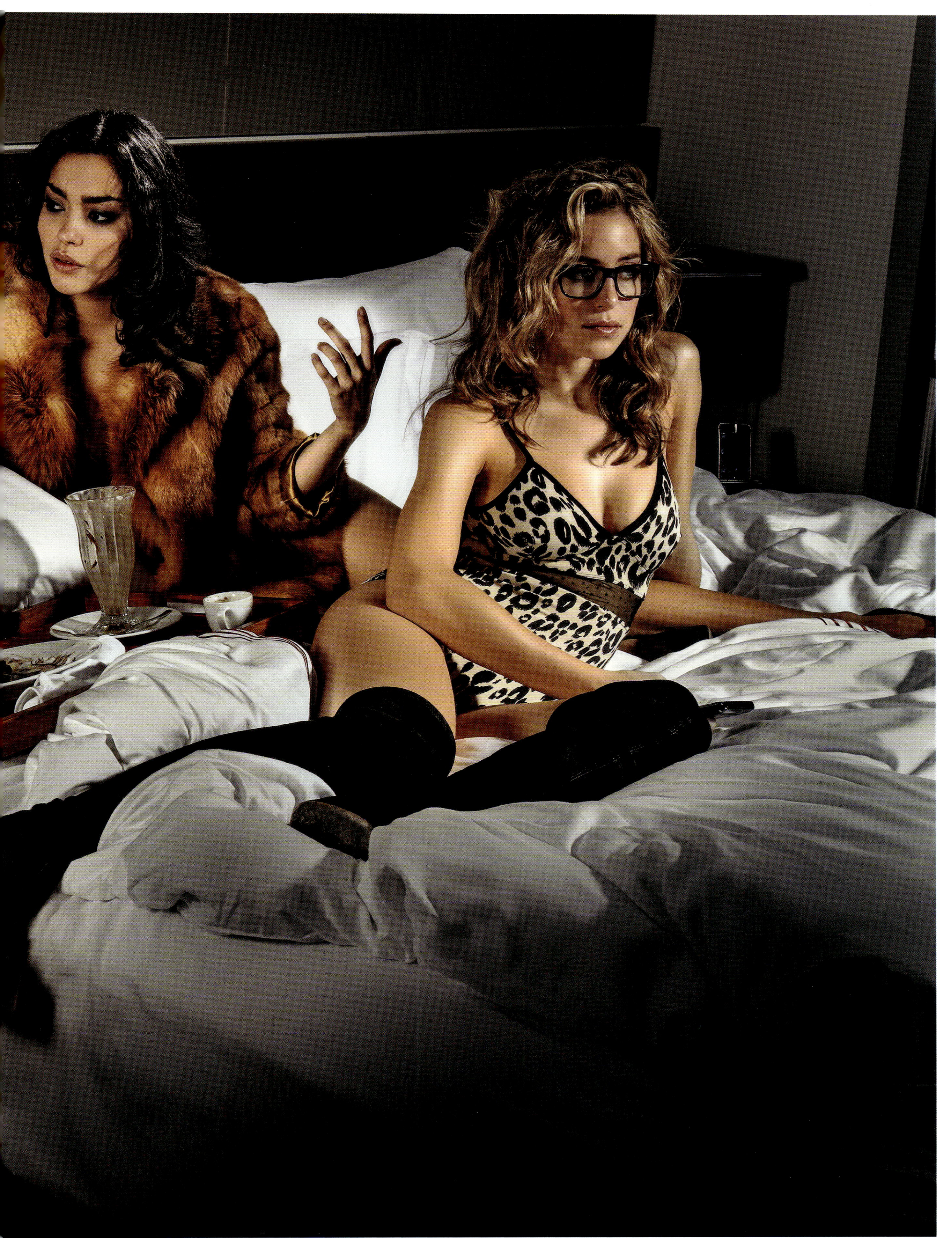

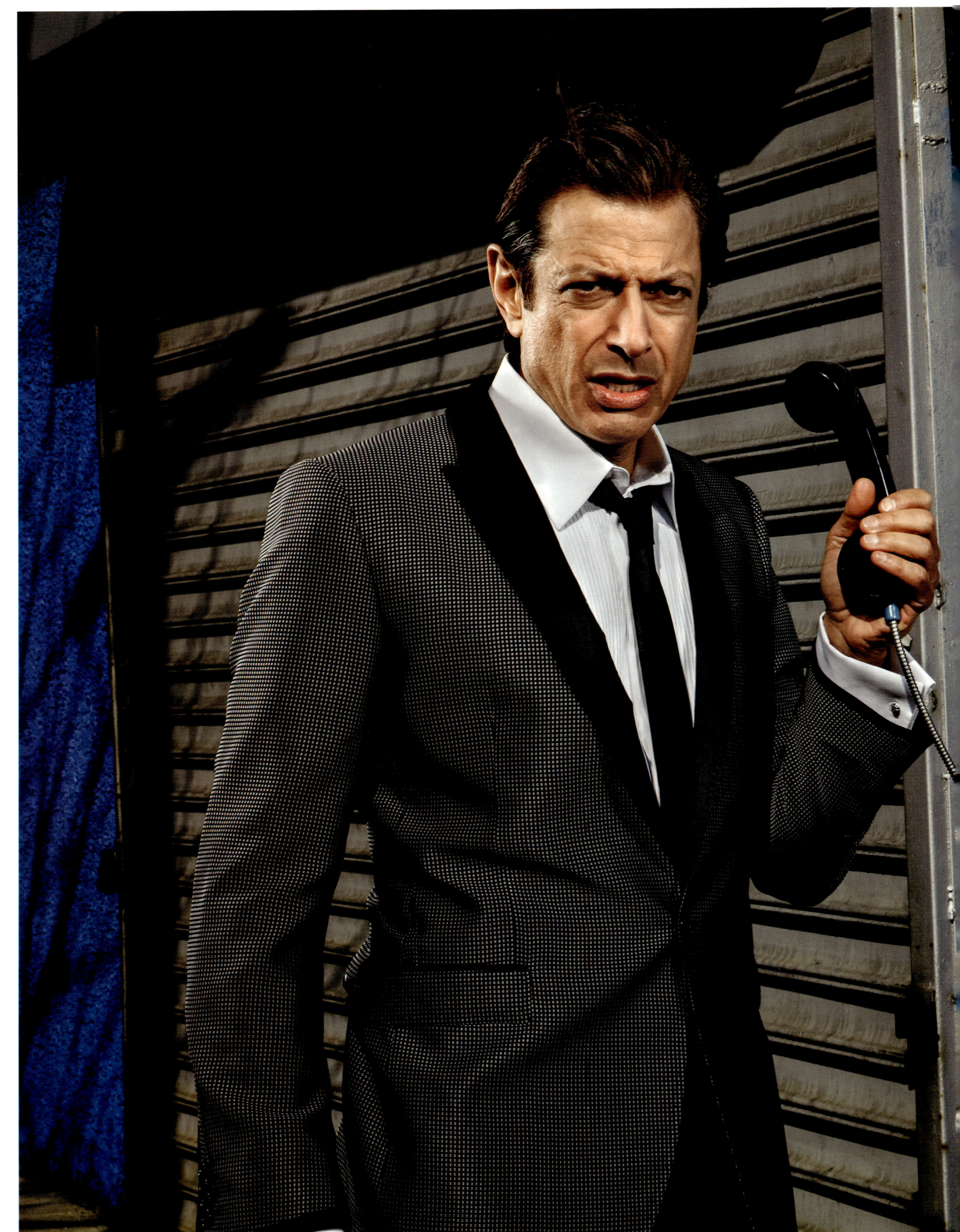

JEFF IS CALLING | 2010

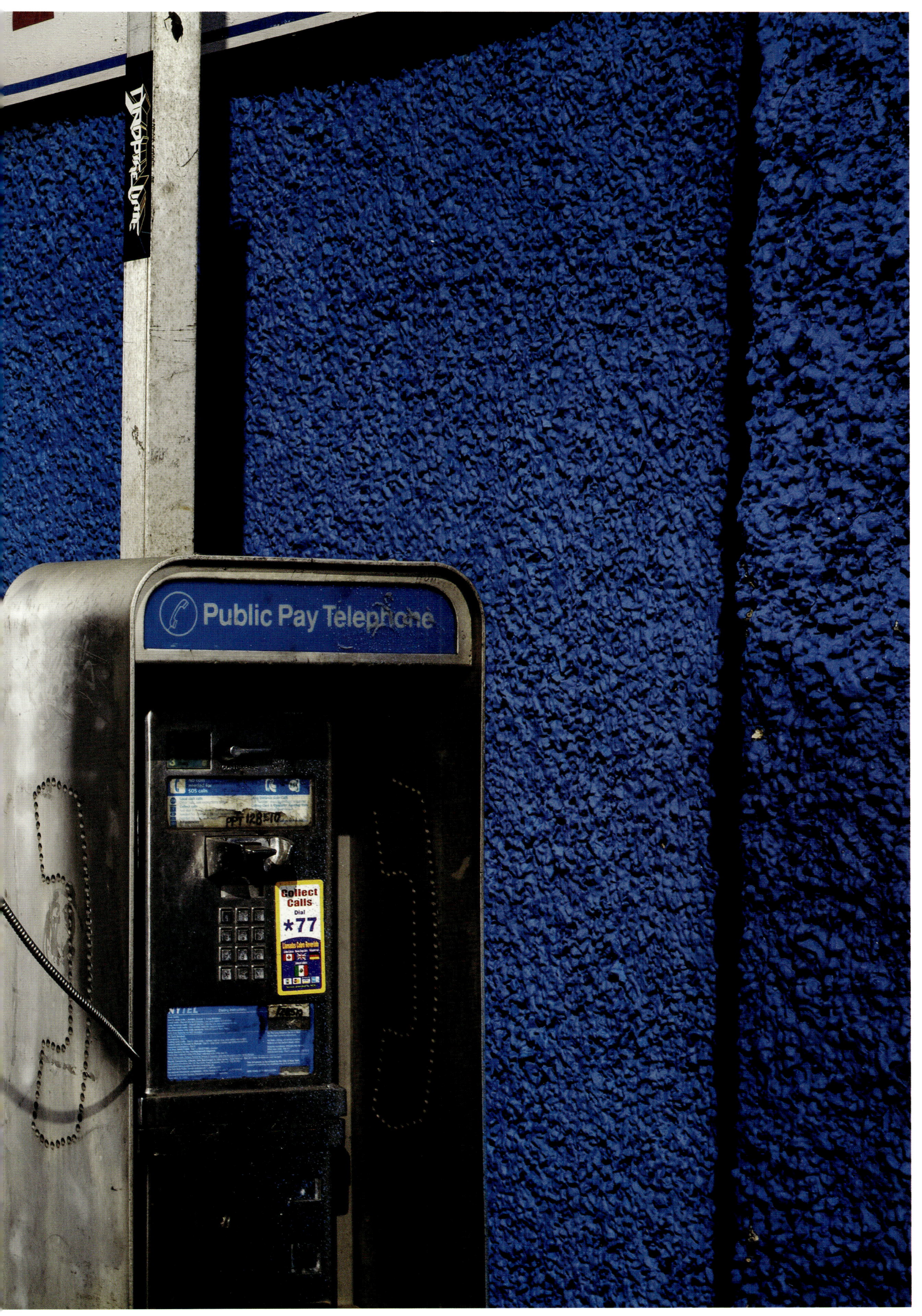
Public Pay Telephone
Collect Calls
Dial
*77

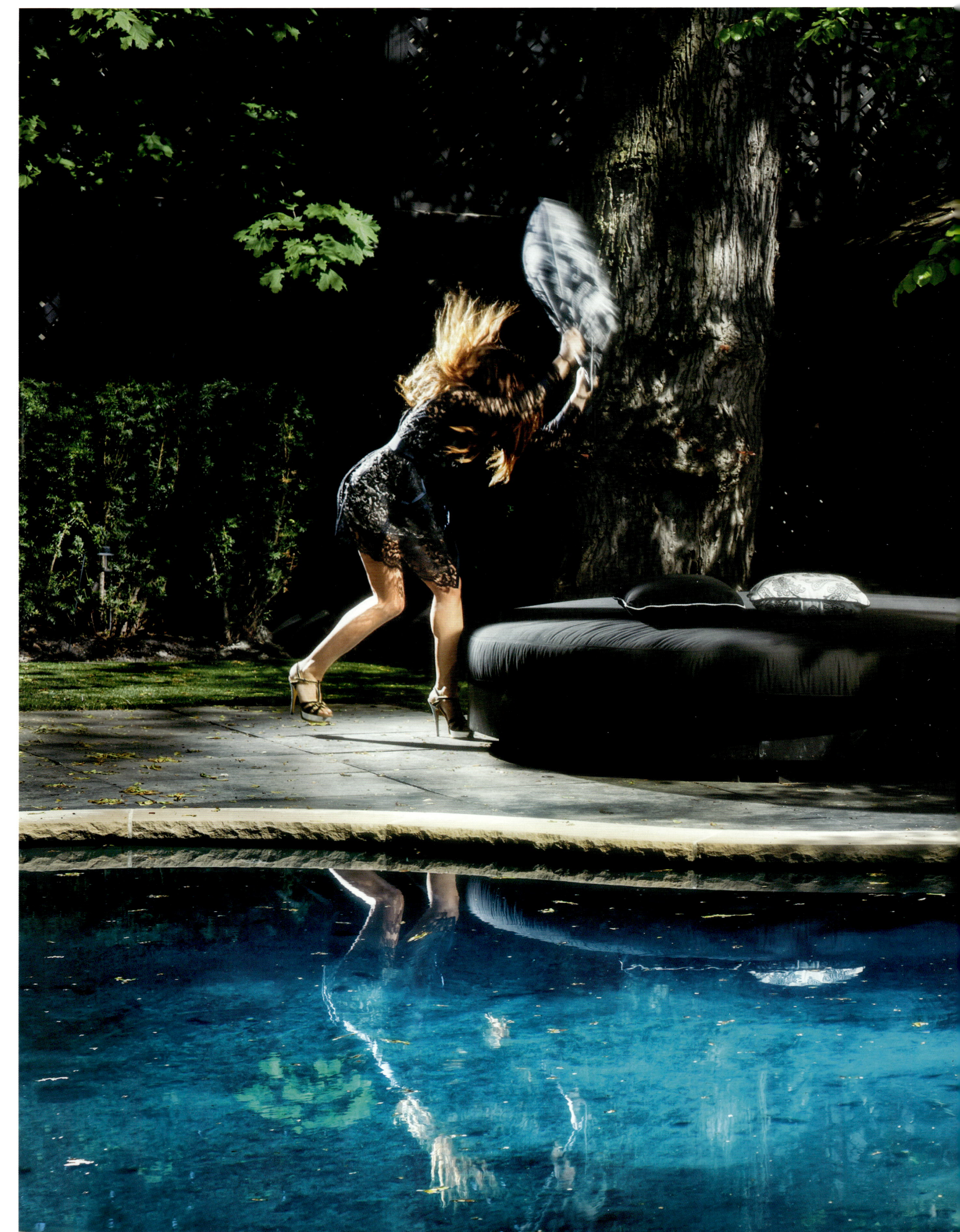

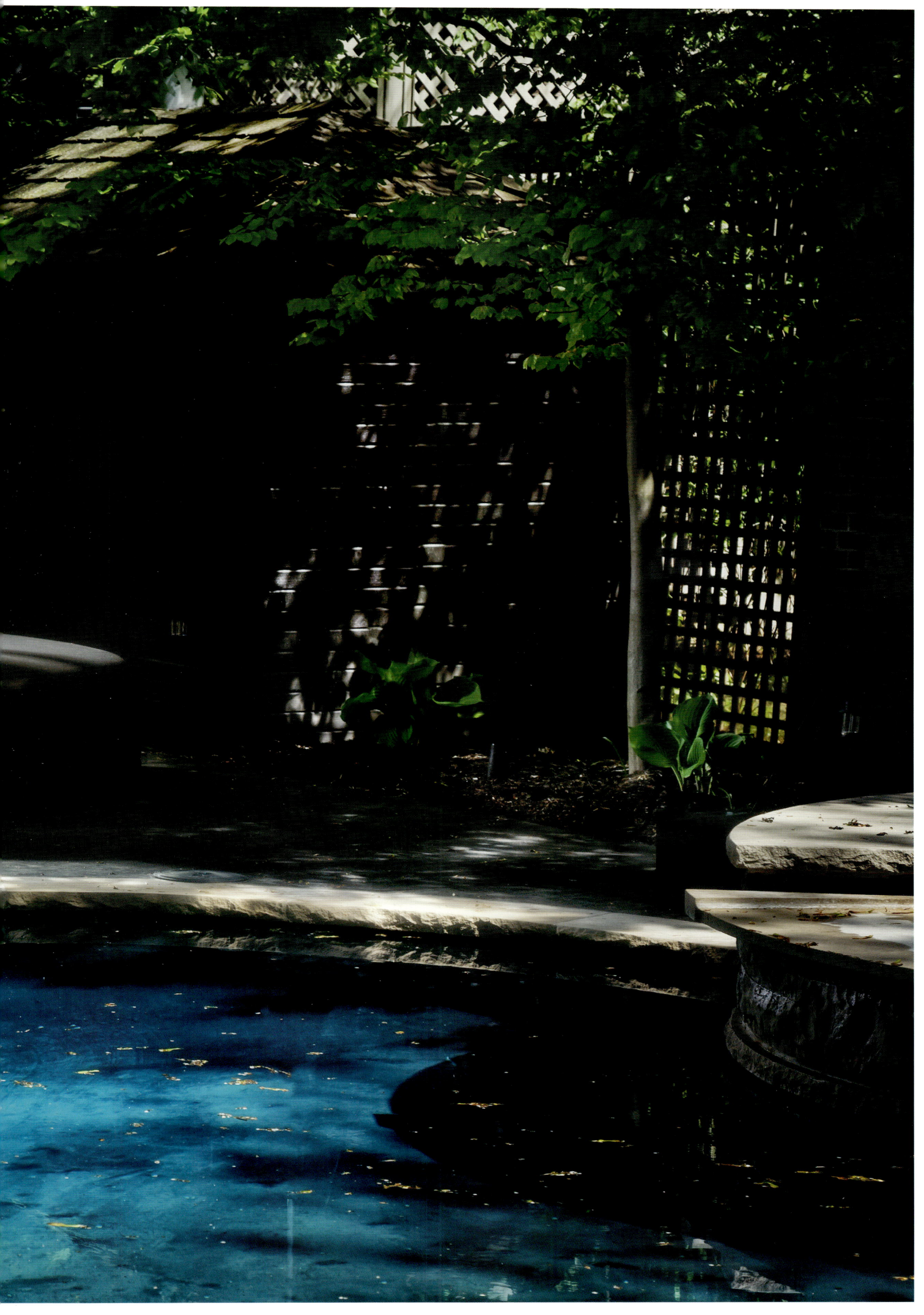

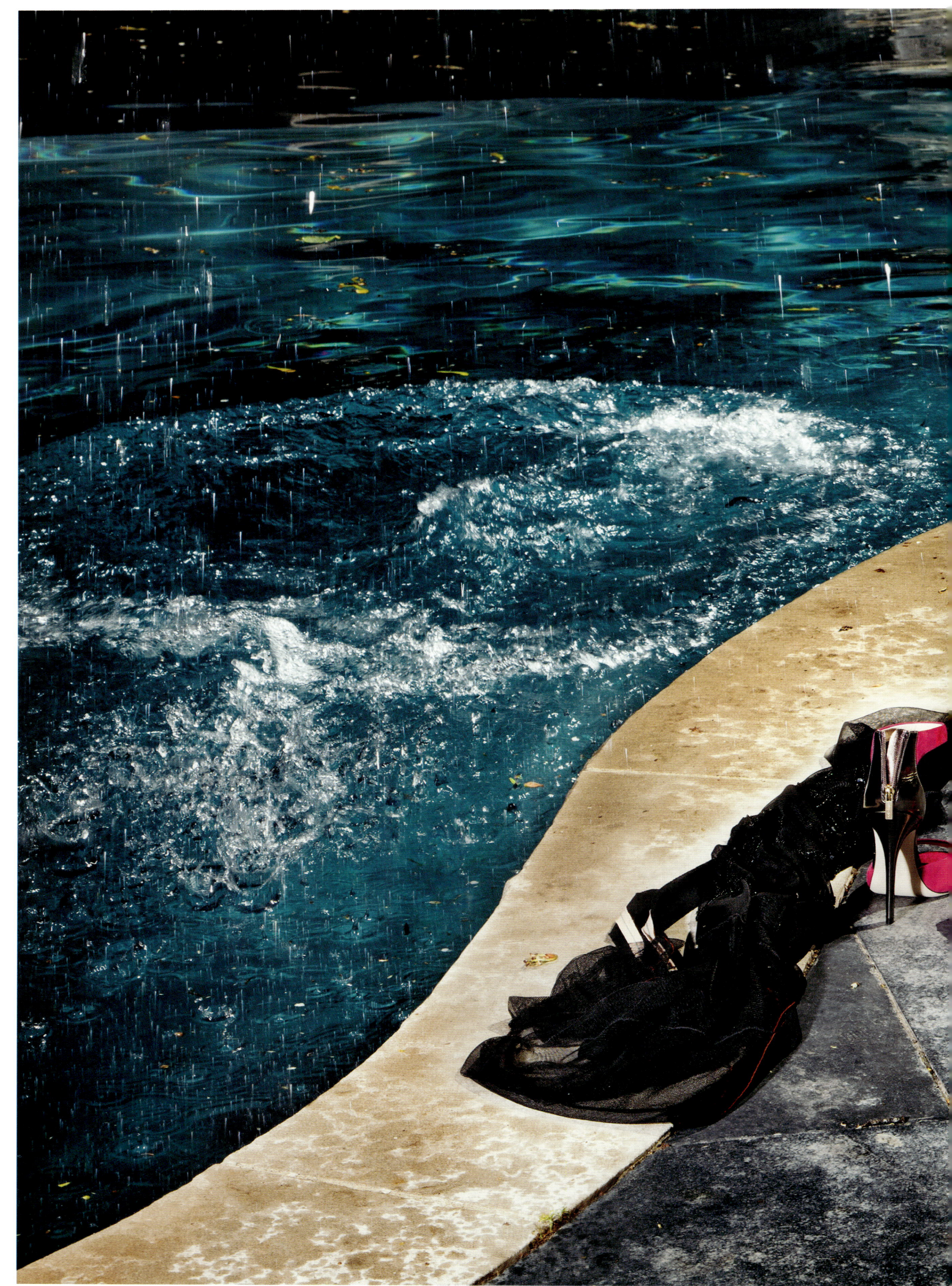

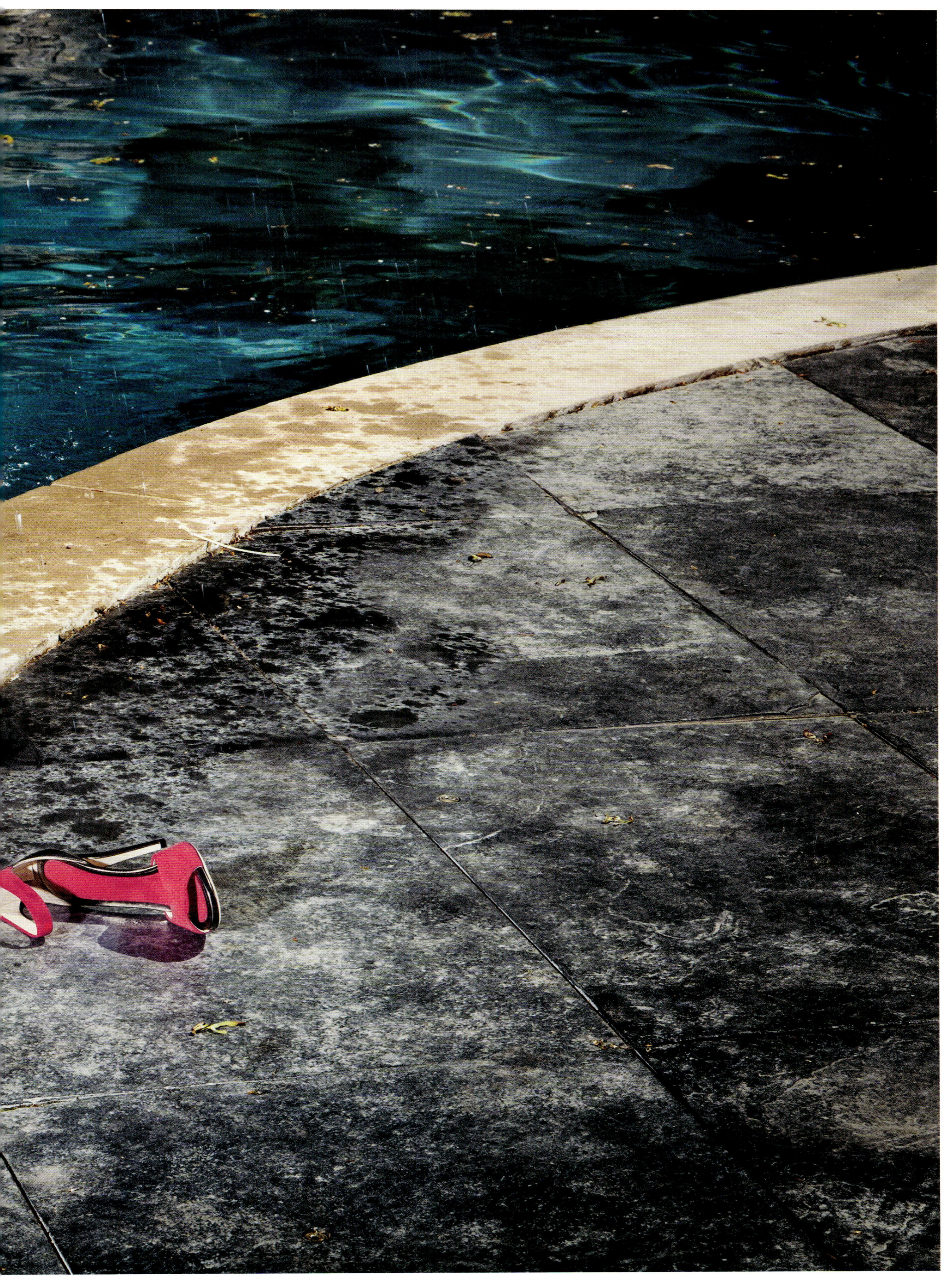

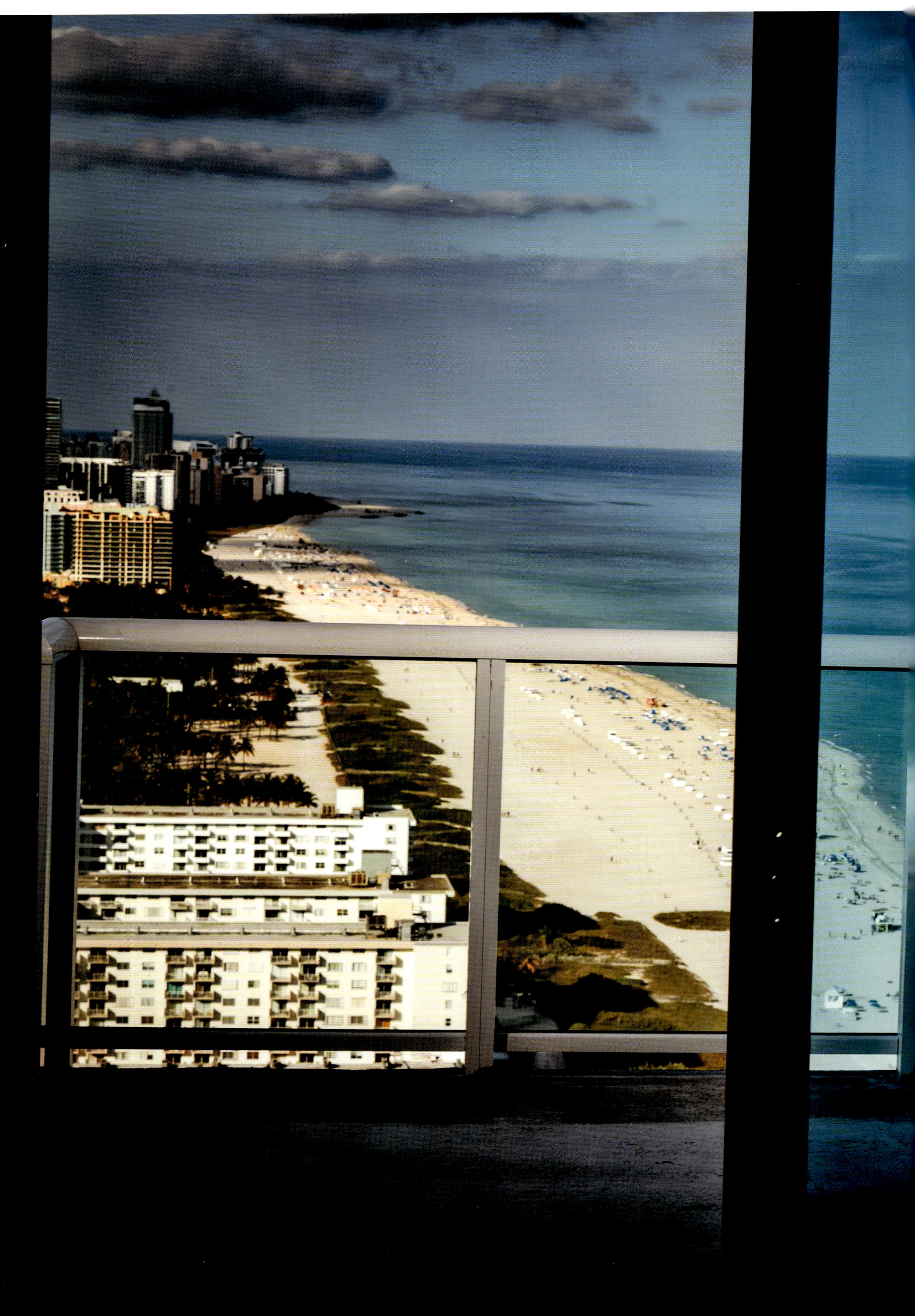

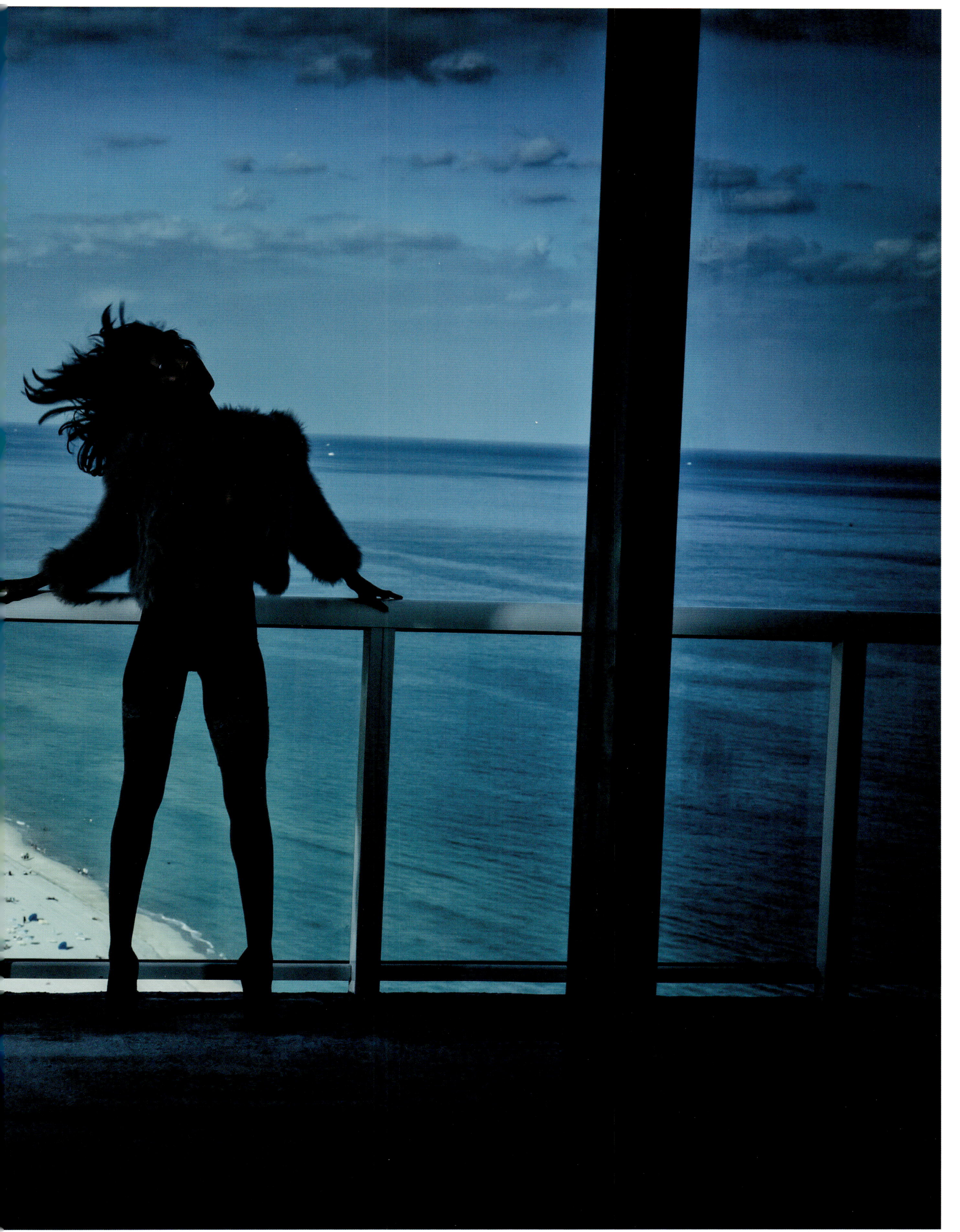

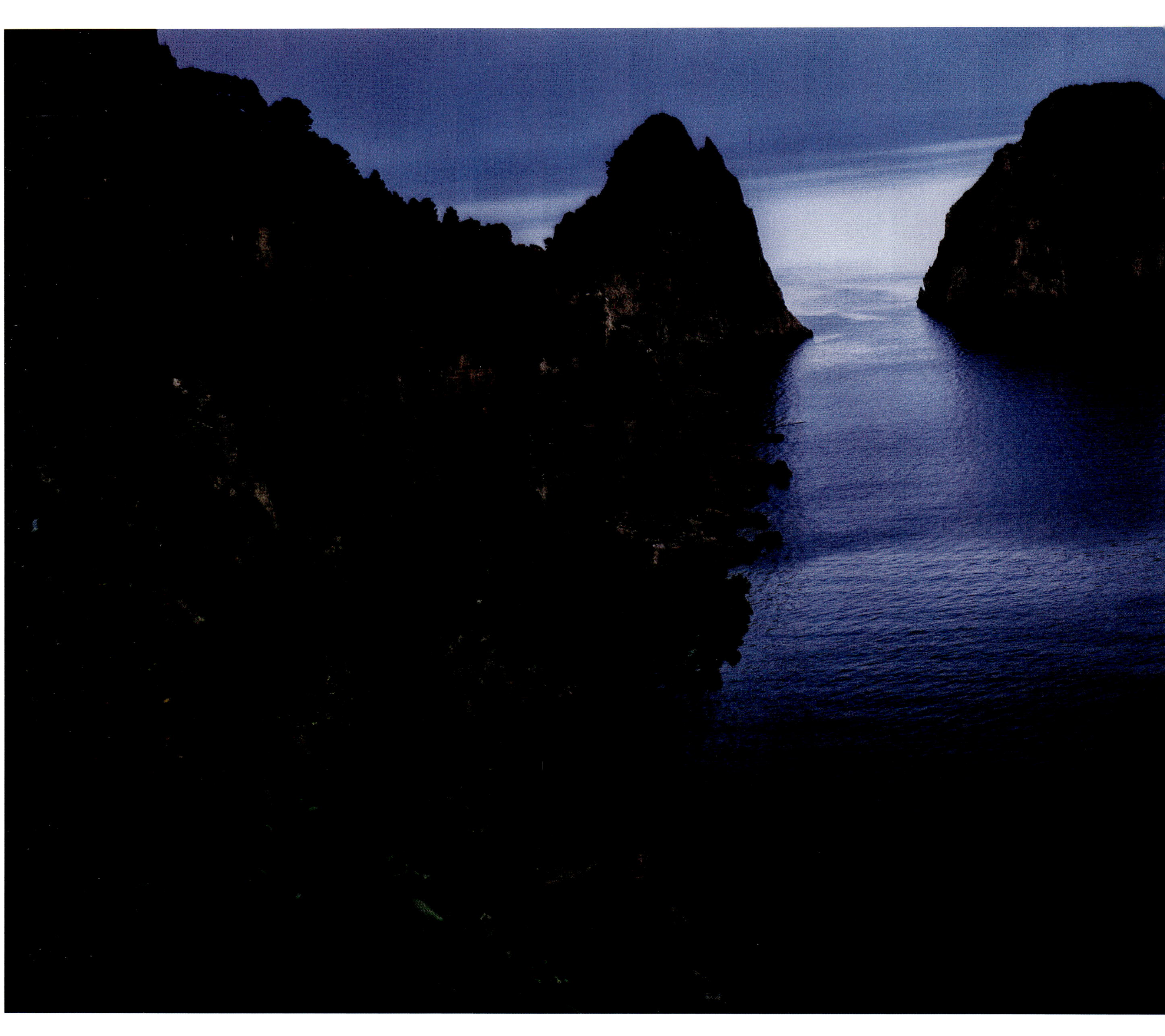

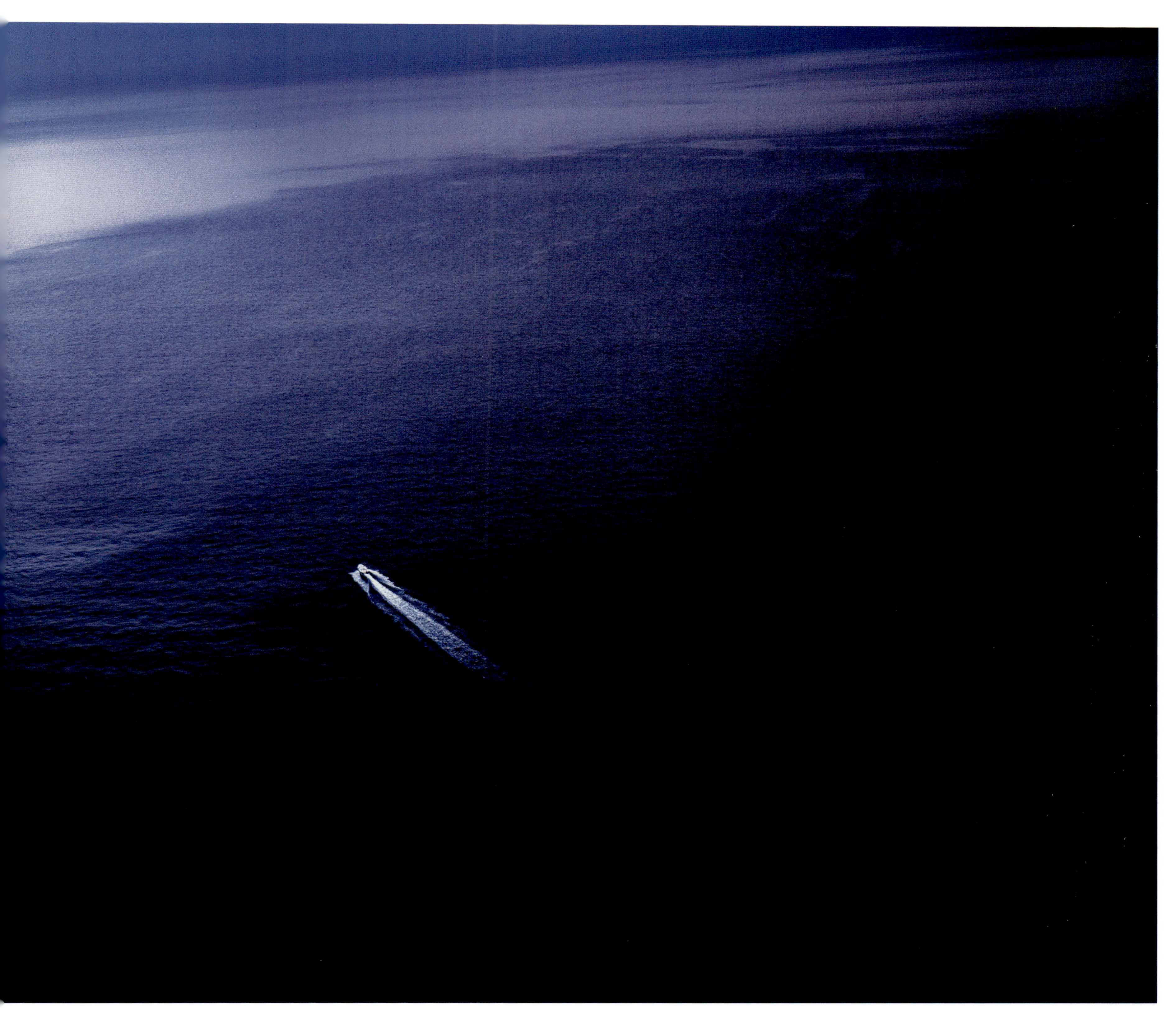

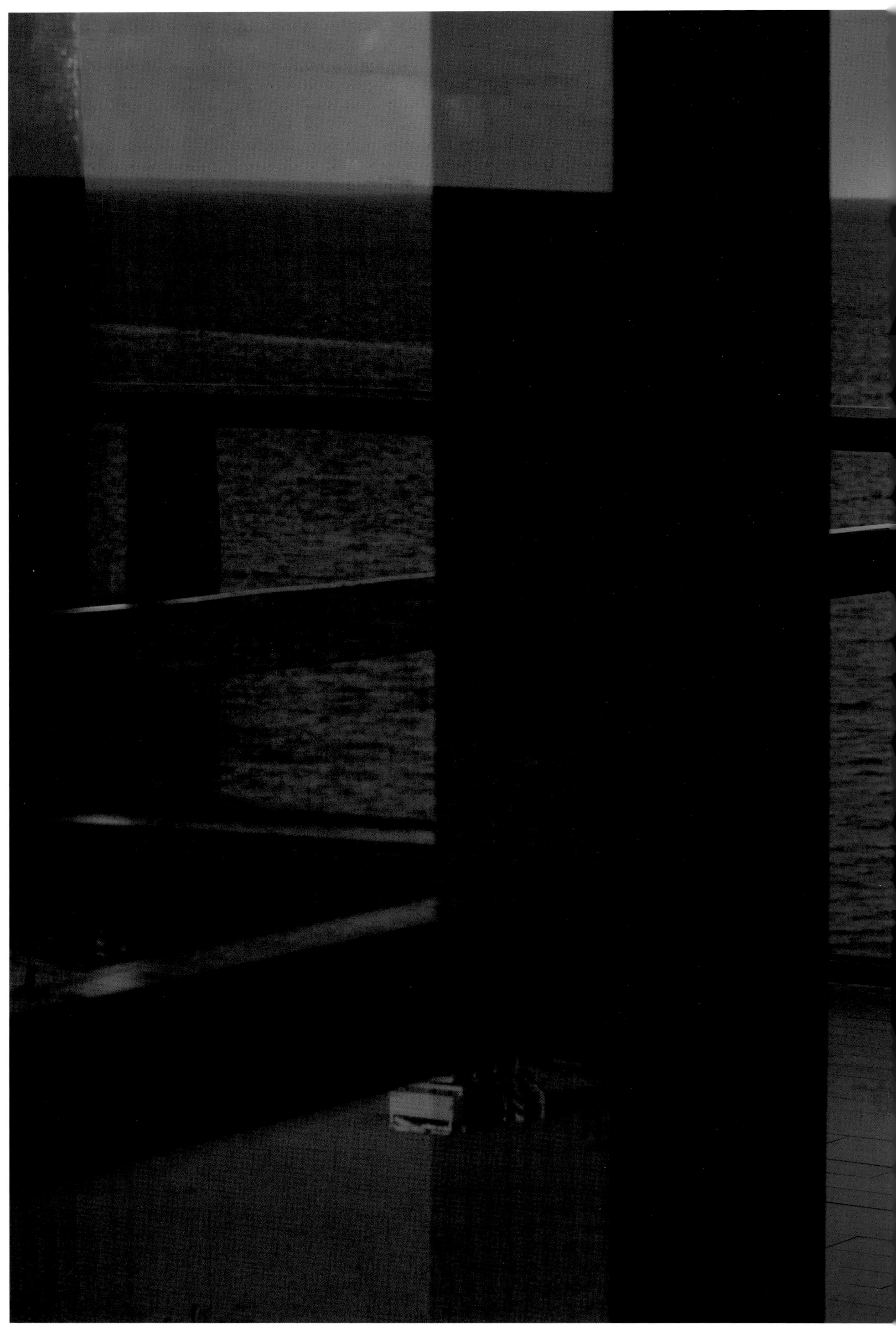

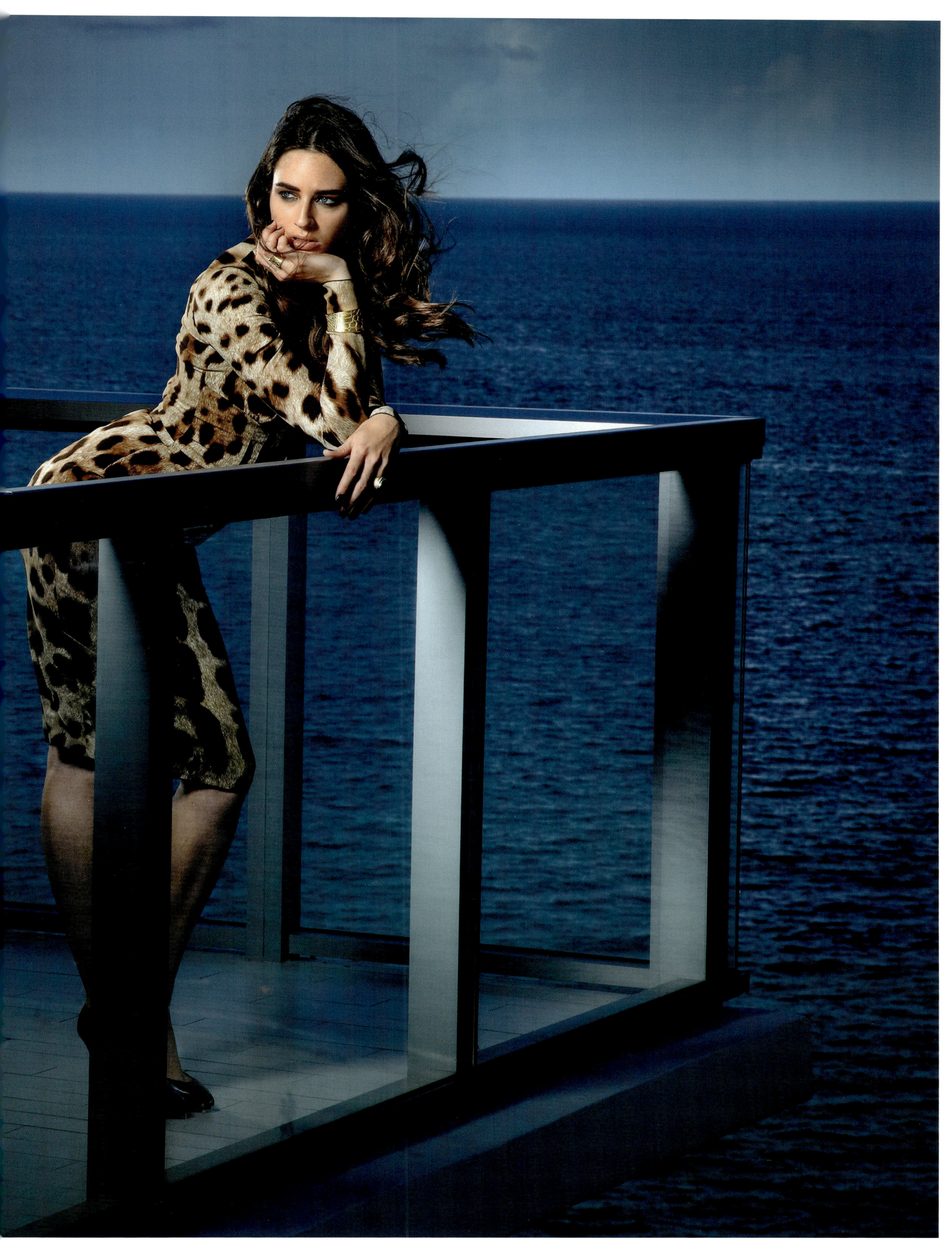

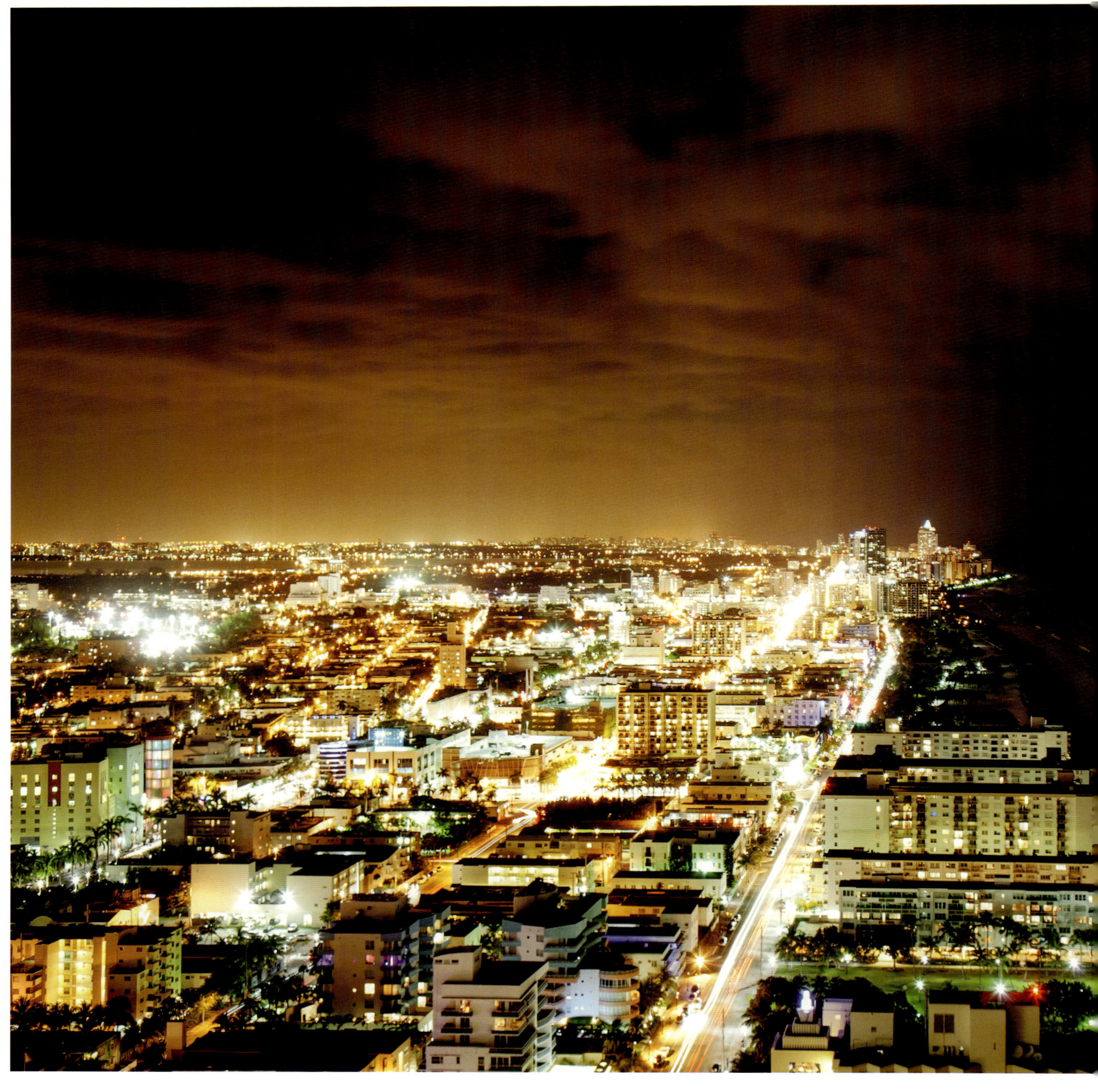

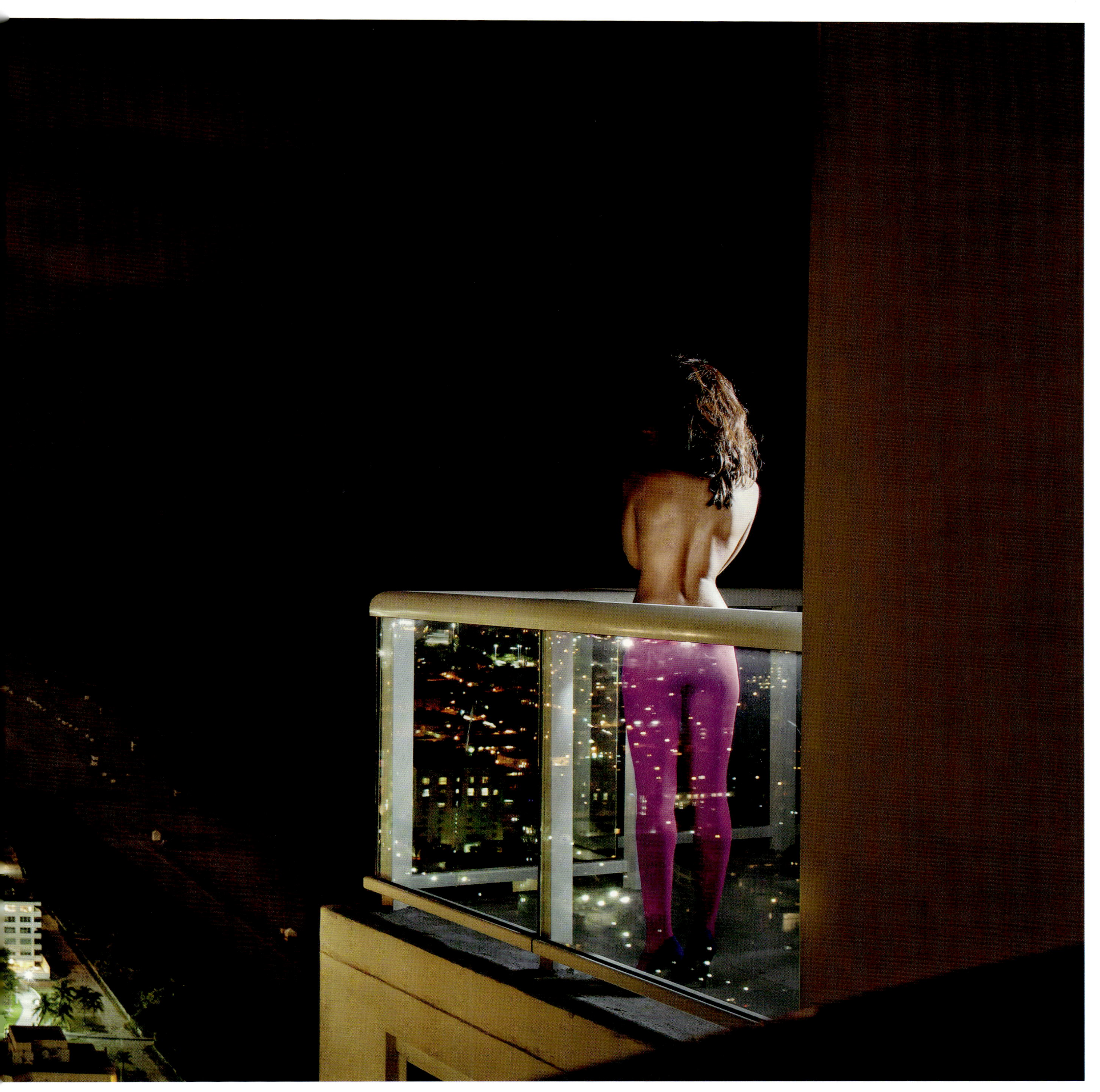

GLITTERING CITY | 2012

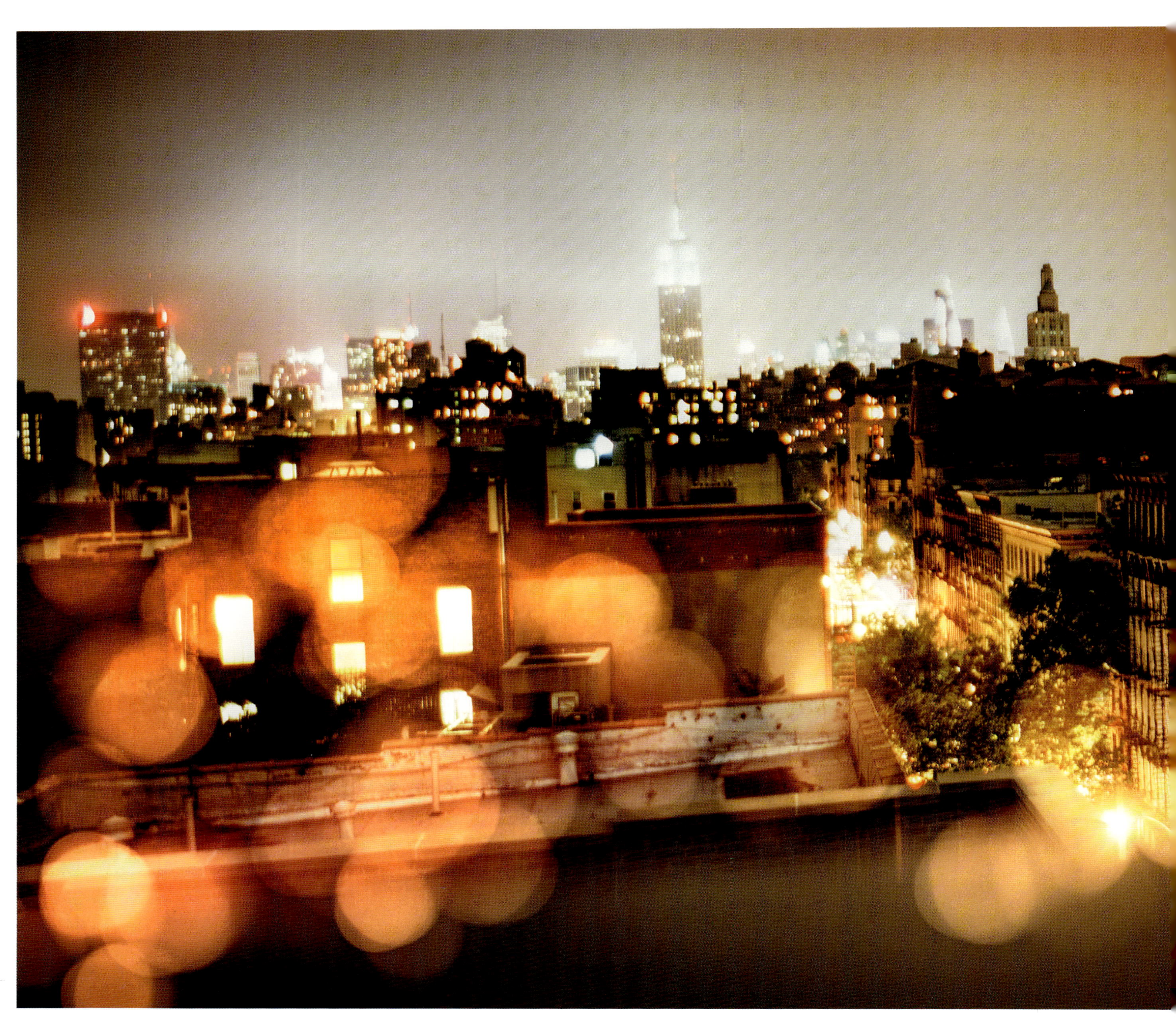

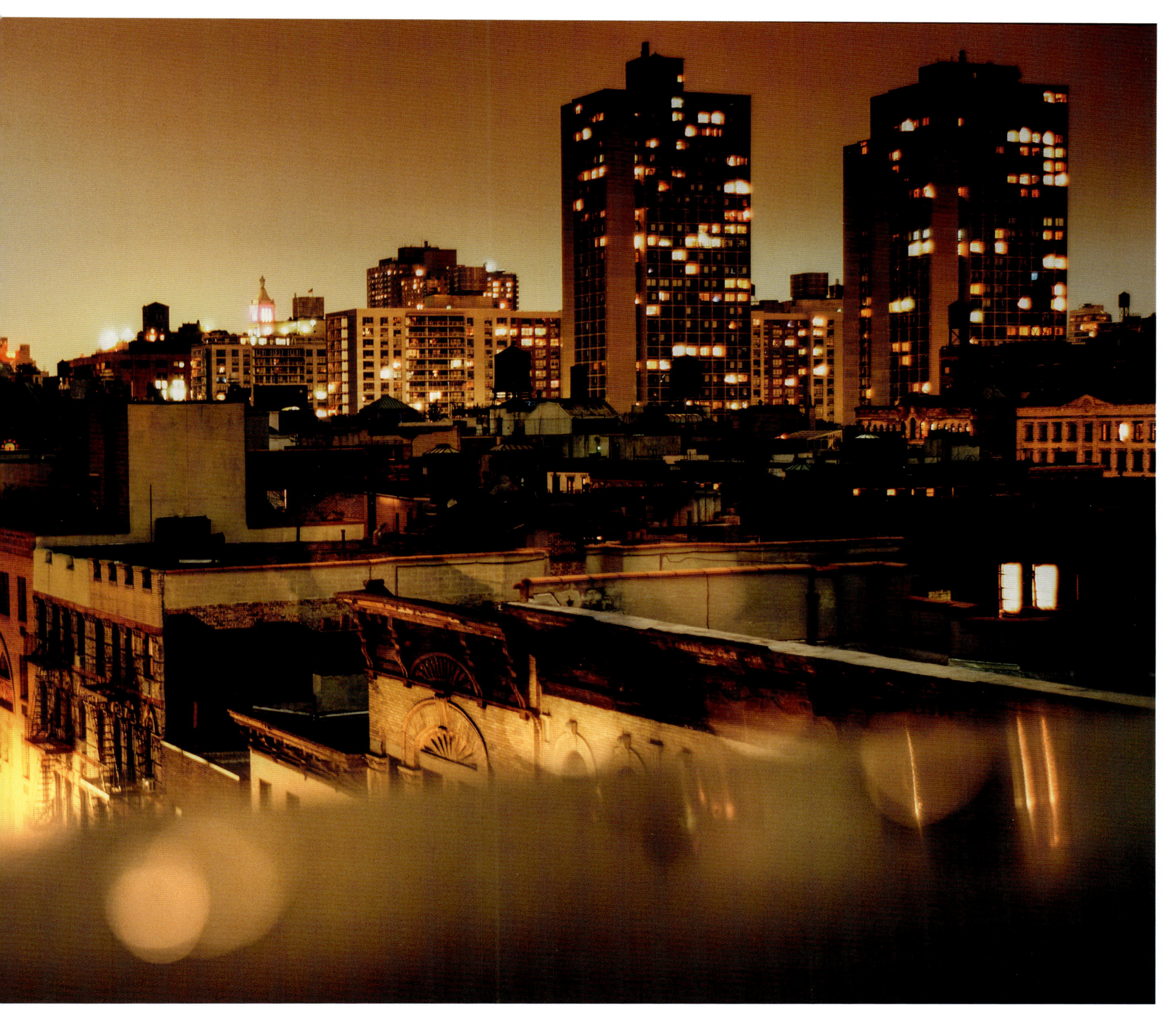

This view might be familiar to you :)

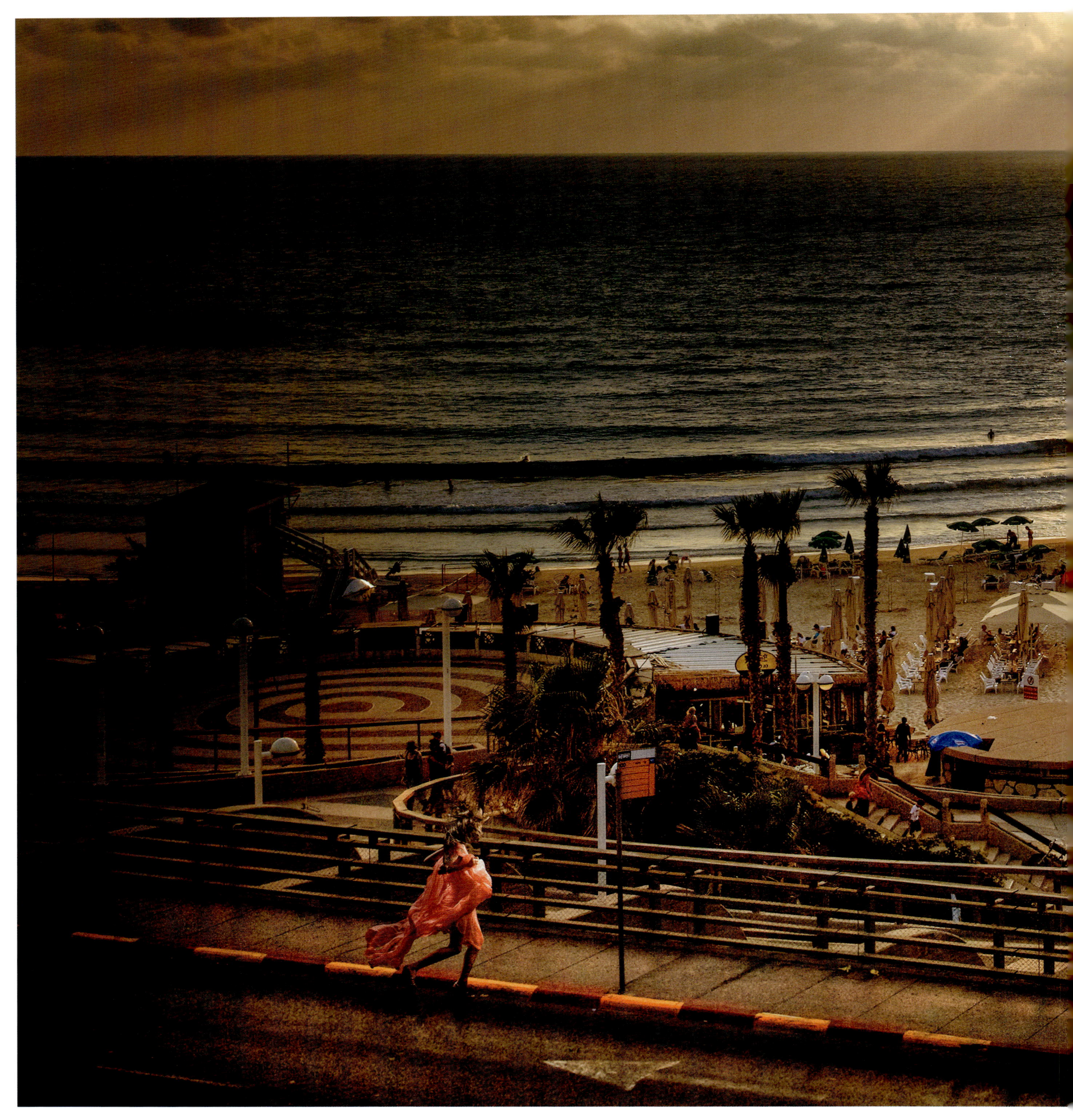

GIRL IN TEL AVIV | 2011

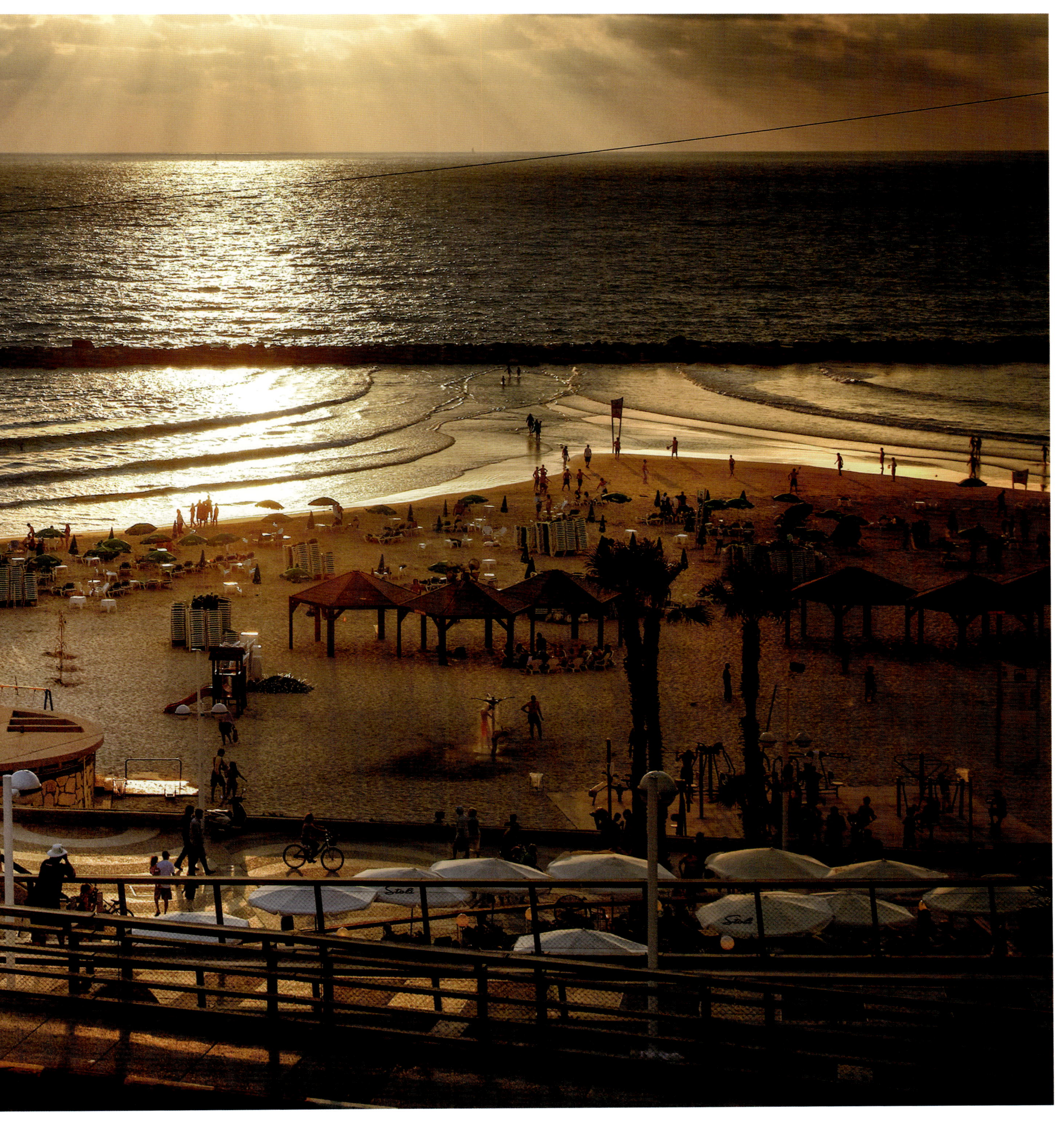

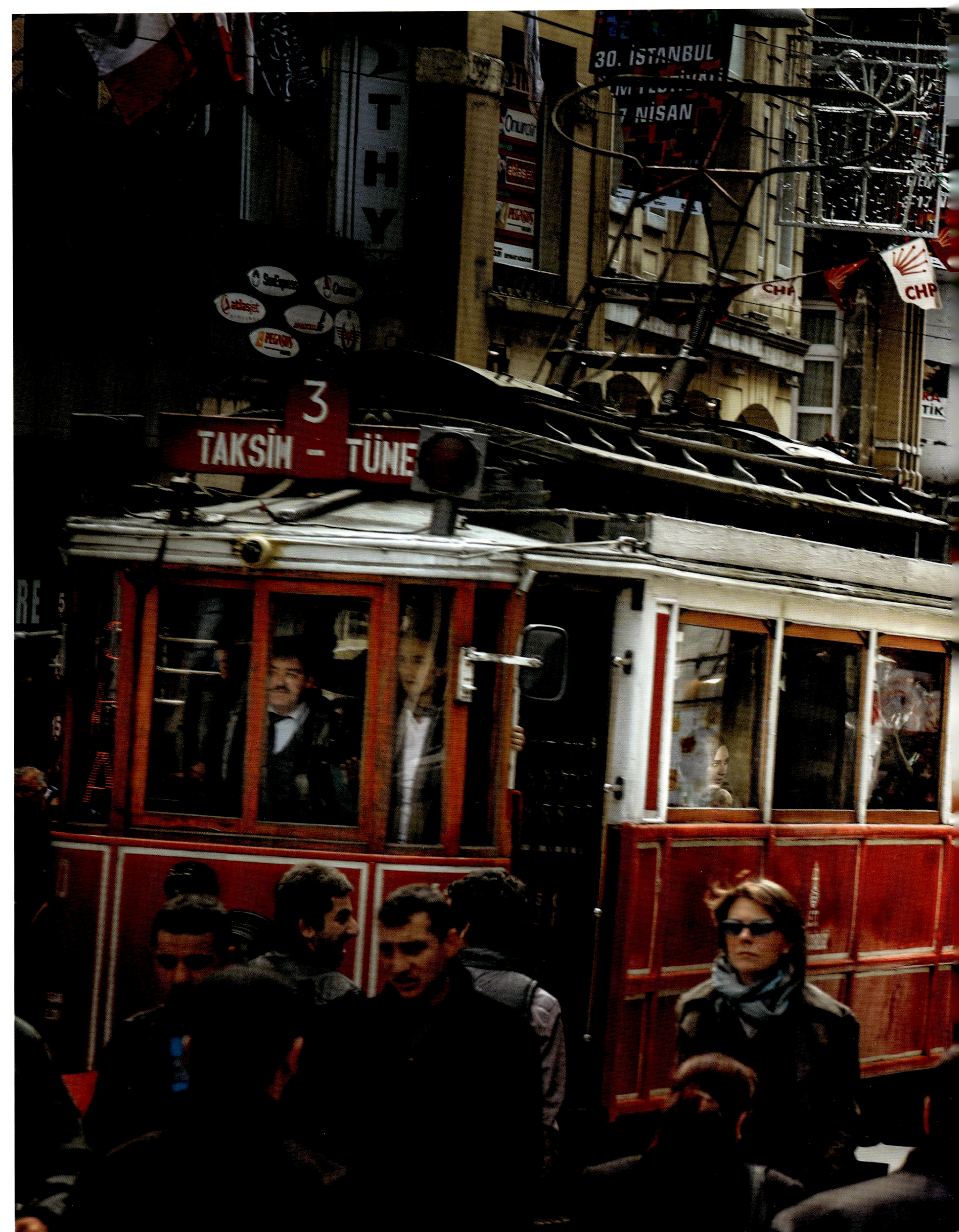
30. İSTANBUL
NİSAN
THY
CHP
3
TAKSİM - TÜNE

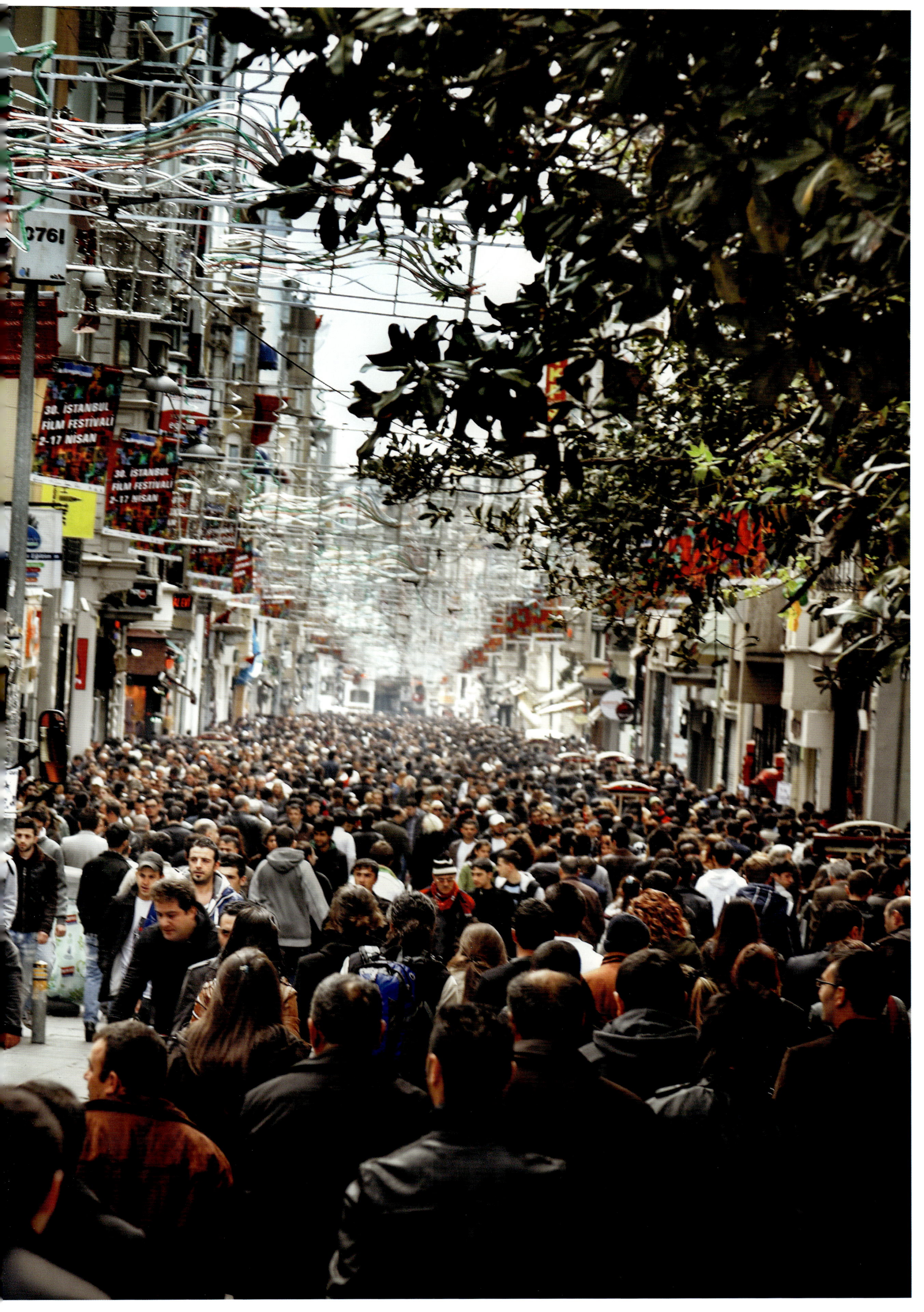
3761
30. İSTANBUL
FİLM FESTİVALİ
2-17 NİSAN
30. İSTANBUL
FİLM FESTİVALİ
2-17 NİSAN

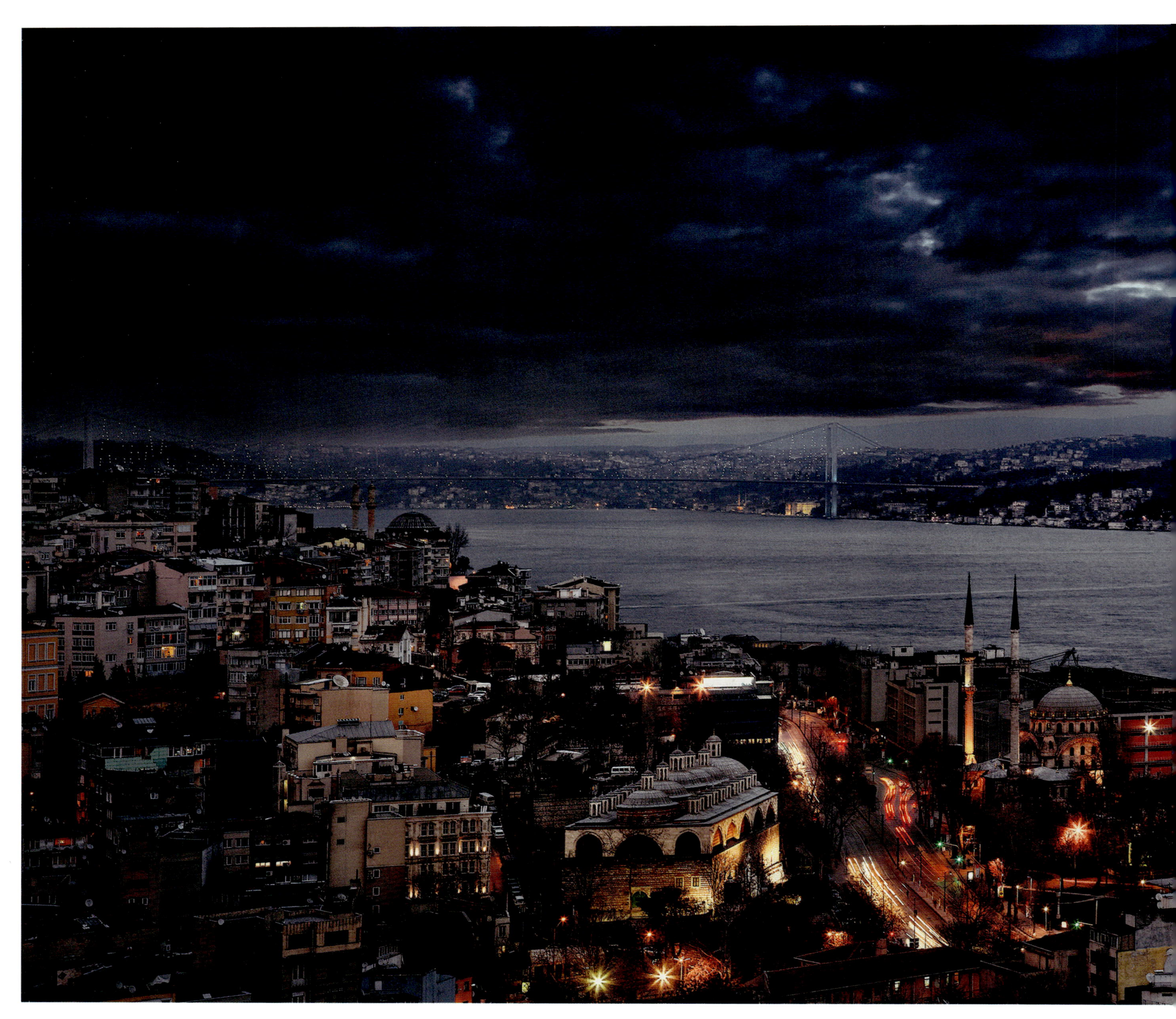

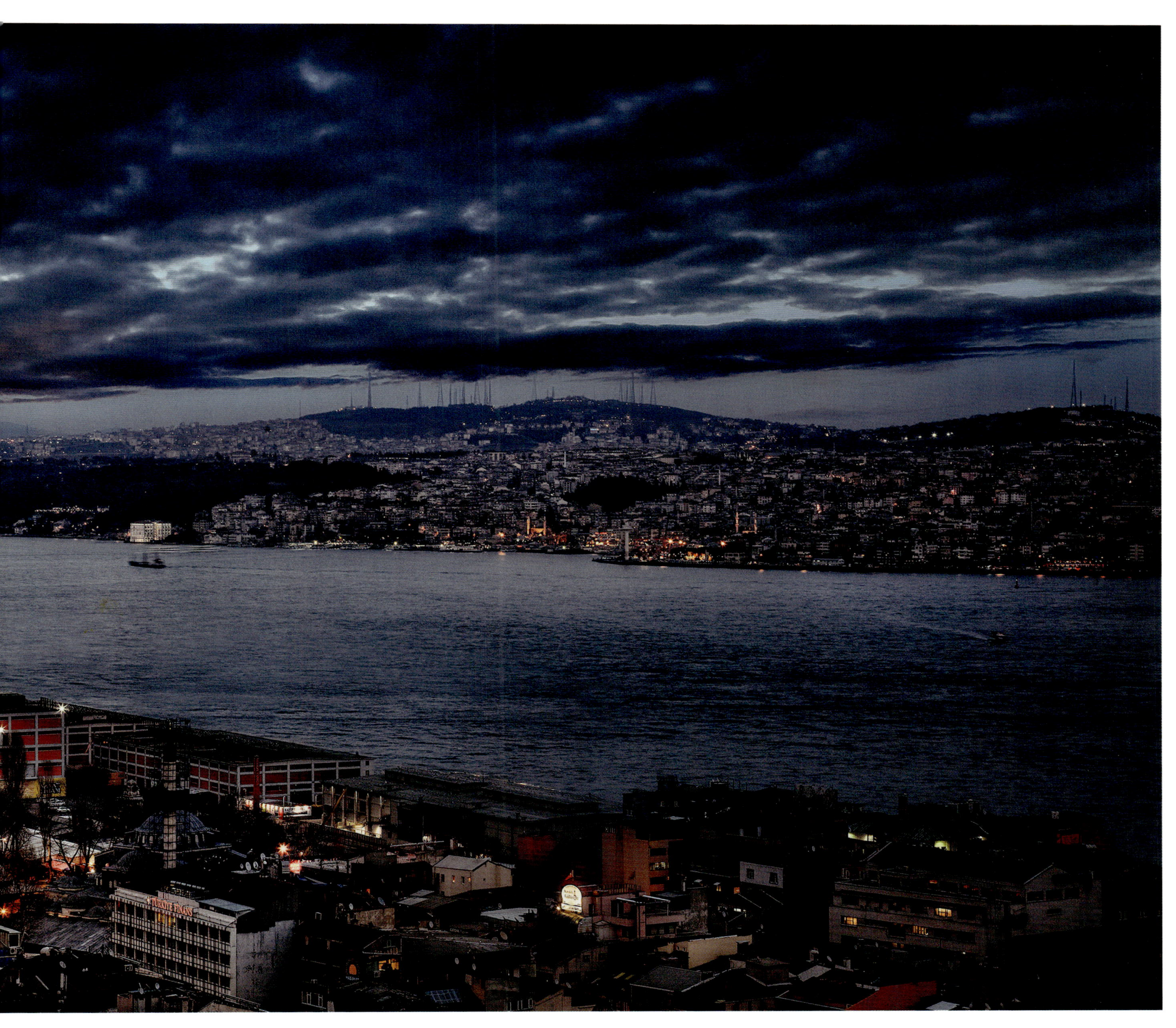
TÜRKİYE FİNANS

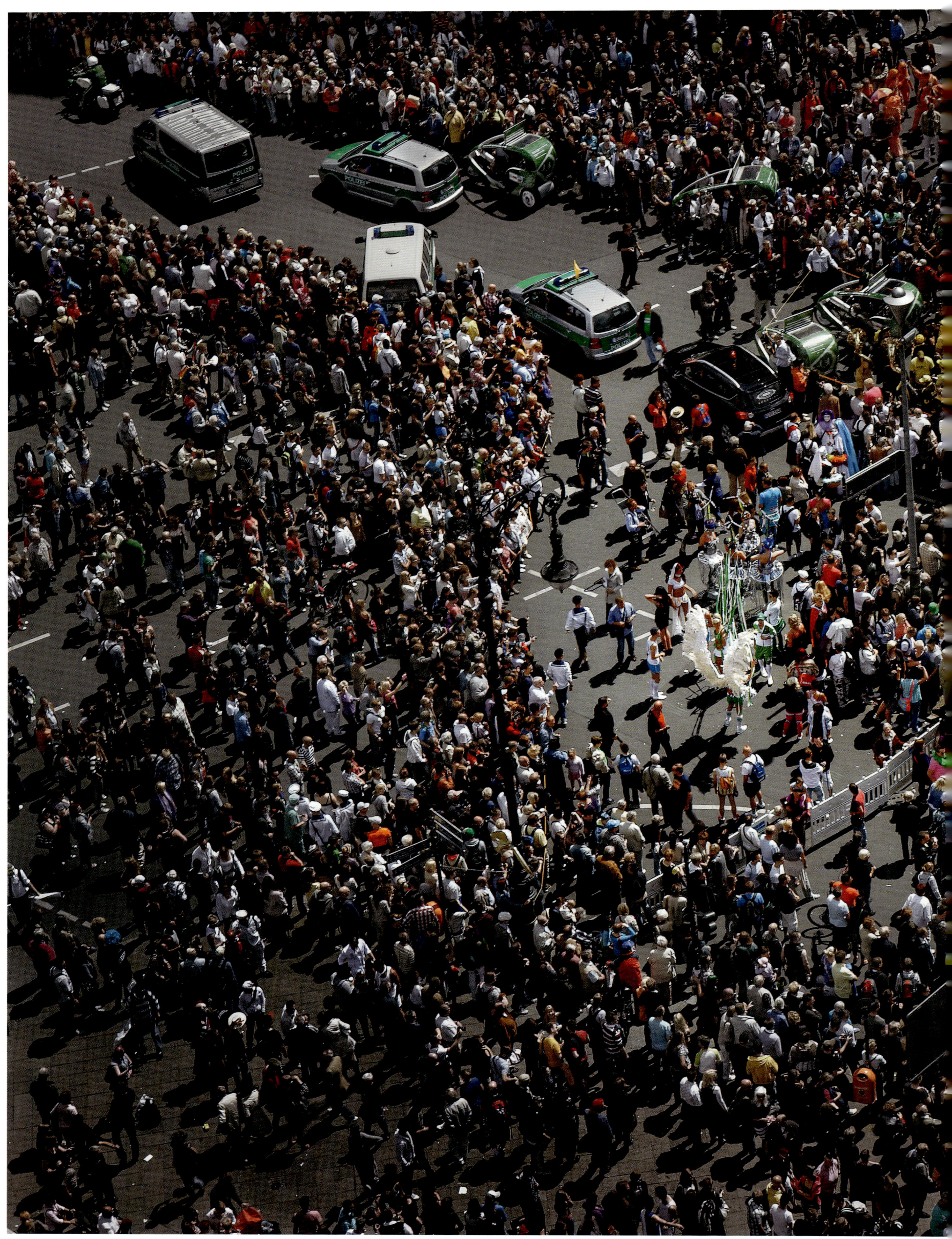

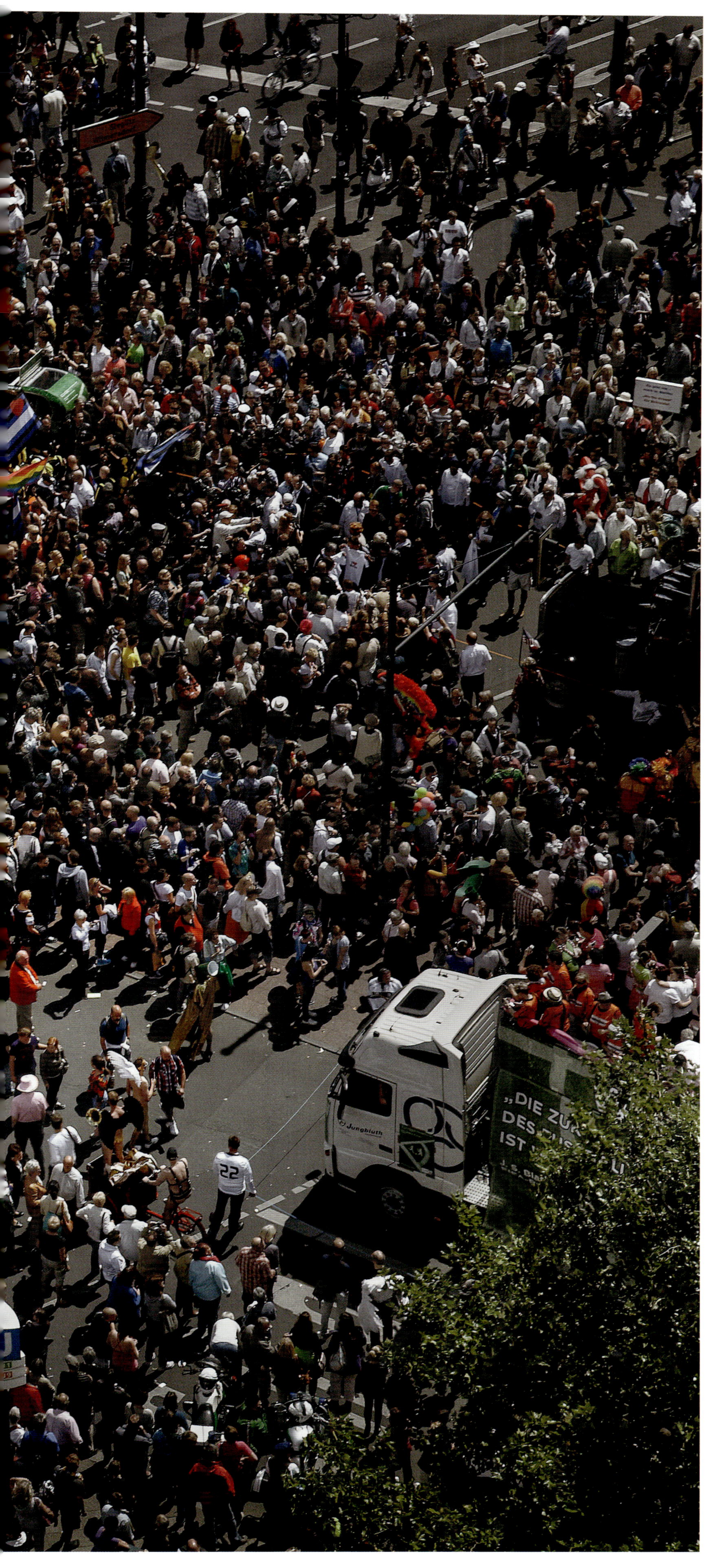

ANGEL IN BERLIN | 2011

FOLLOWING PAGE: BALLOON IN SKY | 2011

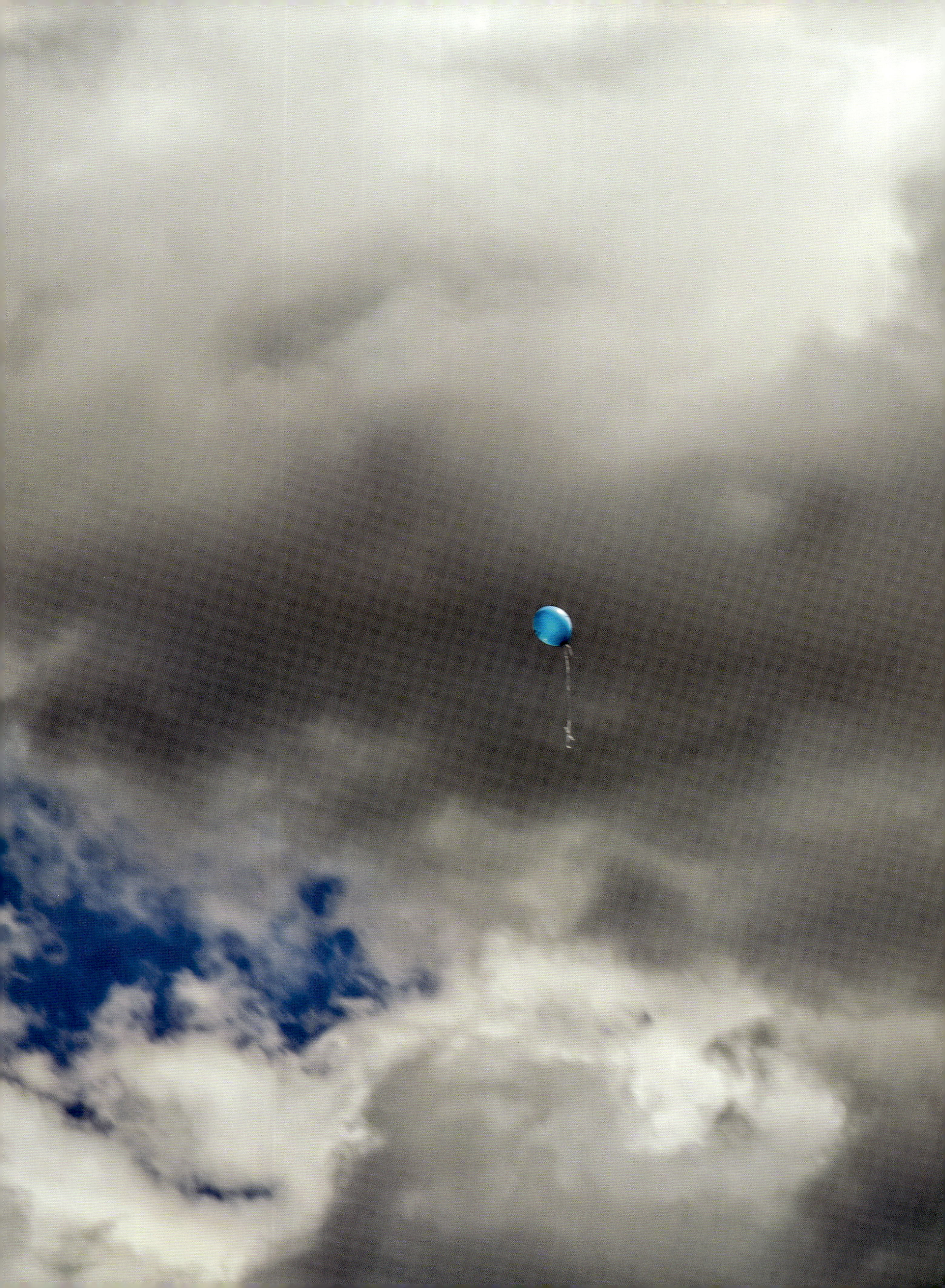

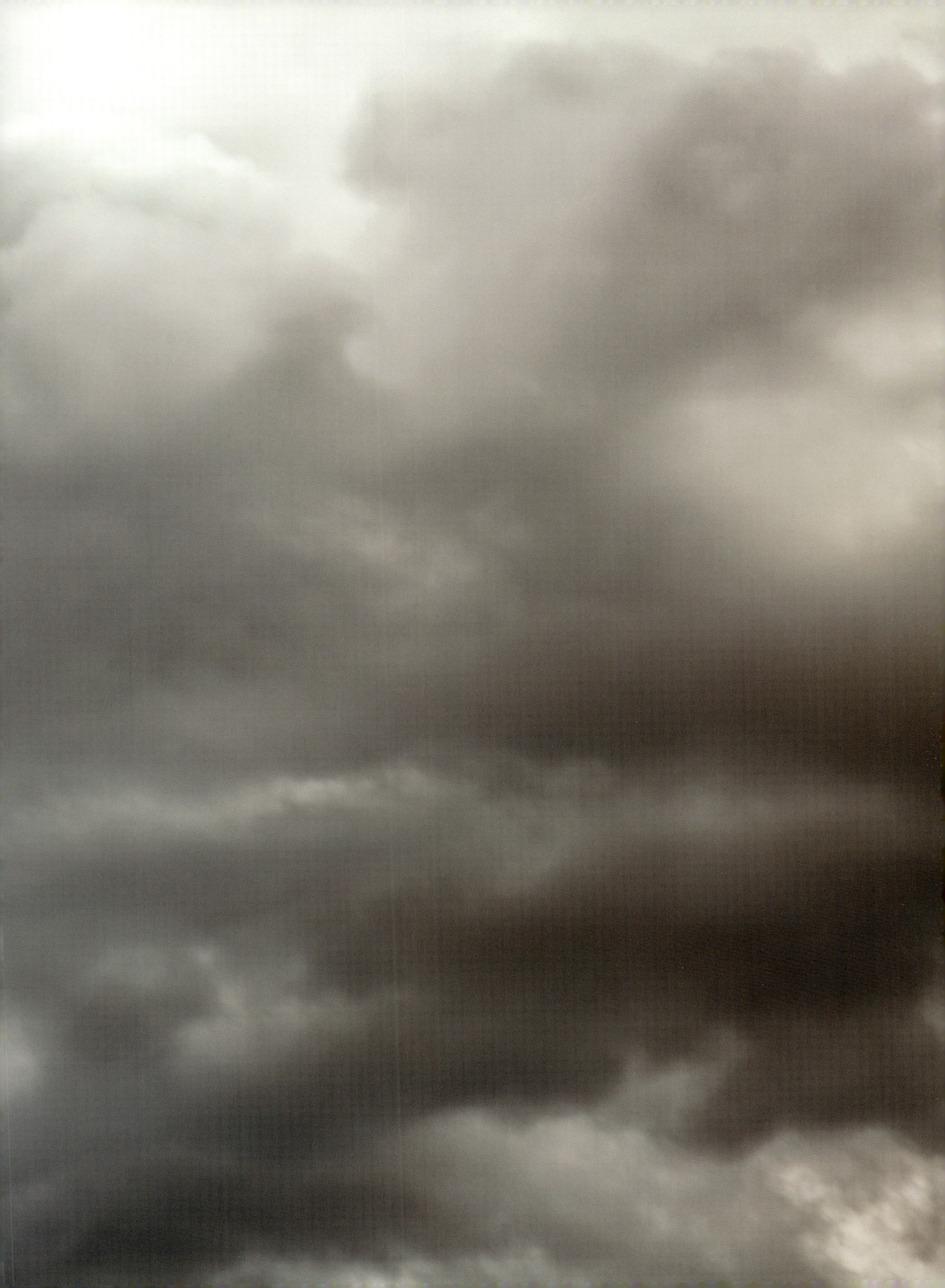

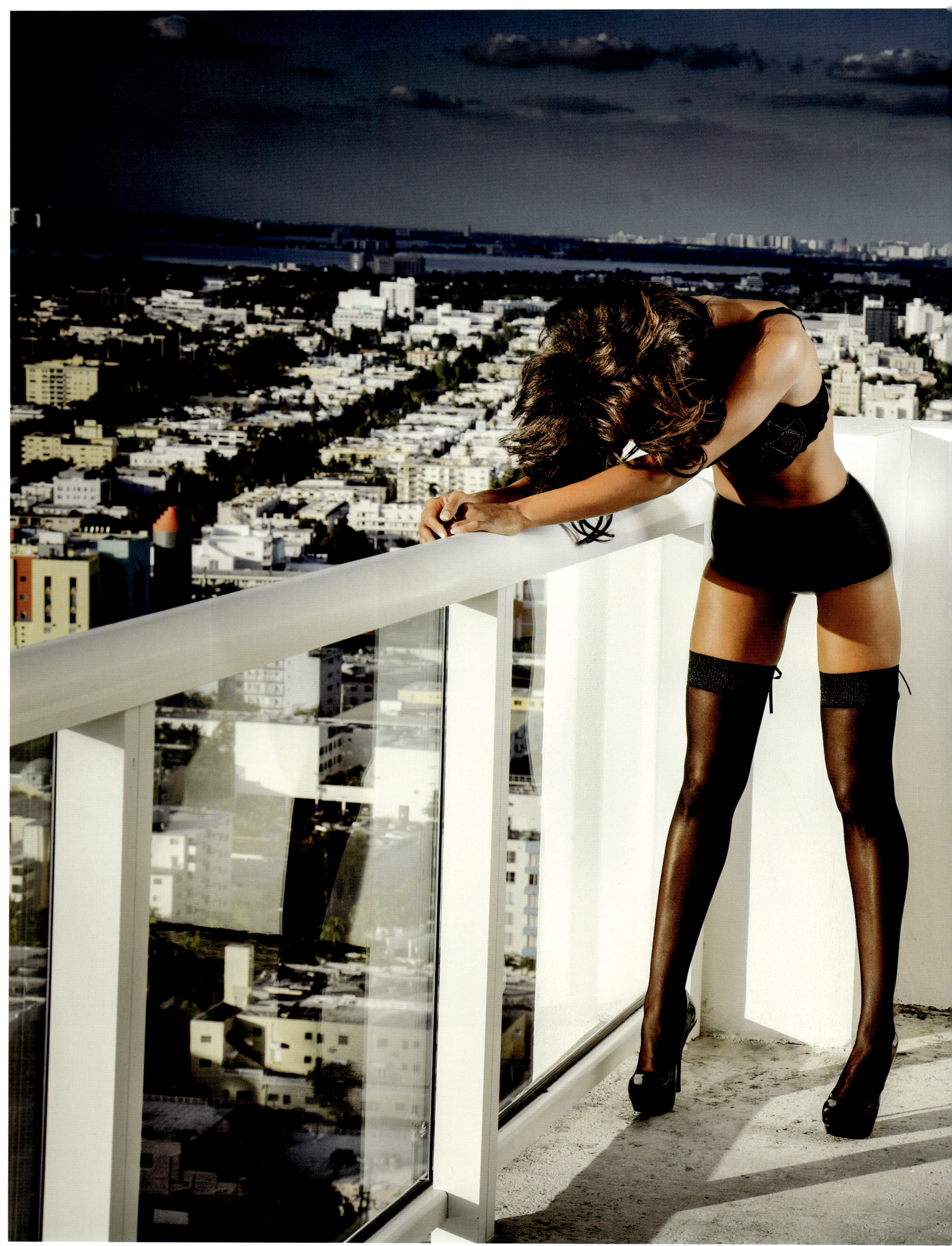

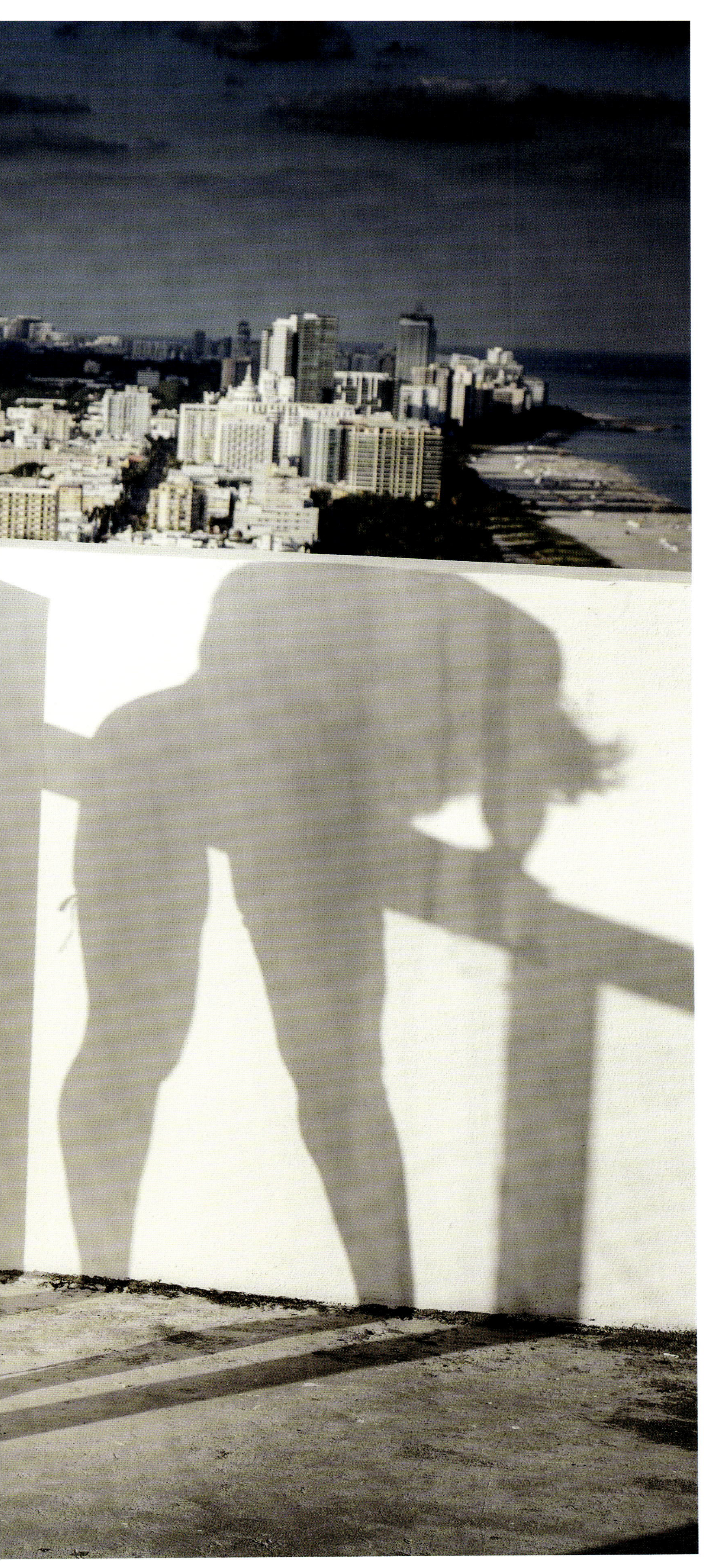

STORMY MOMENT | 2012

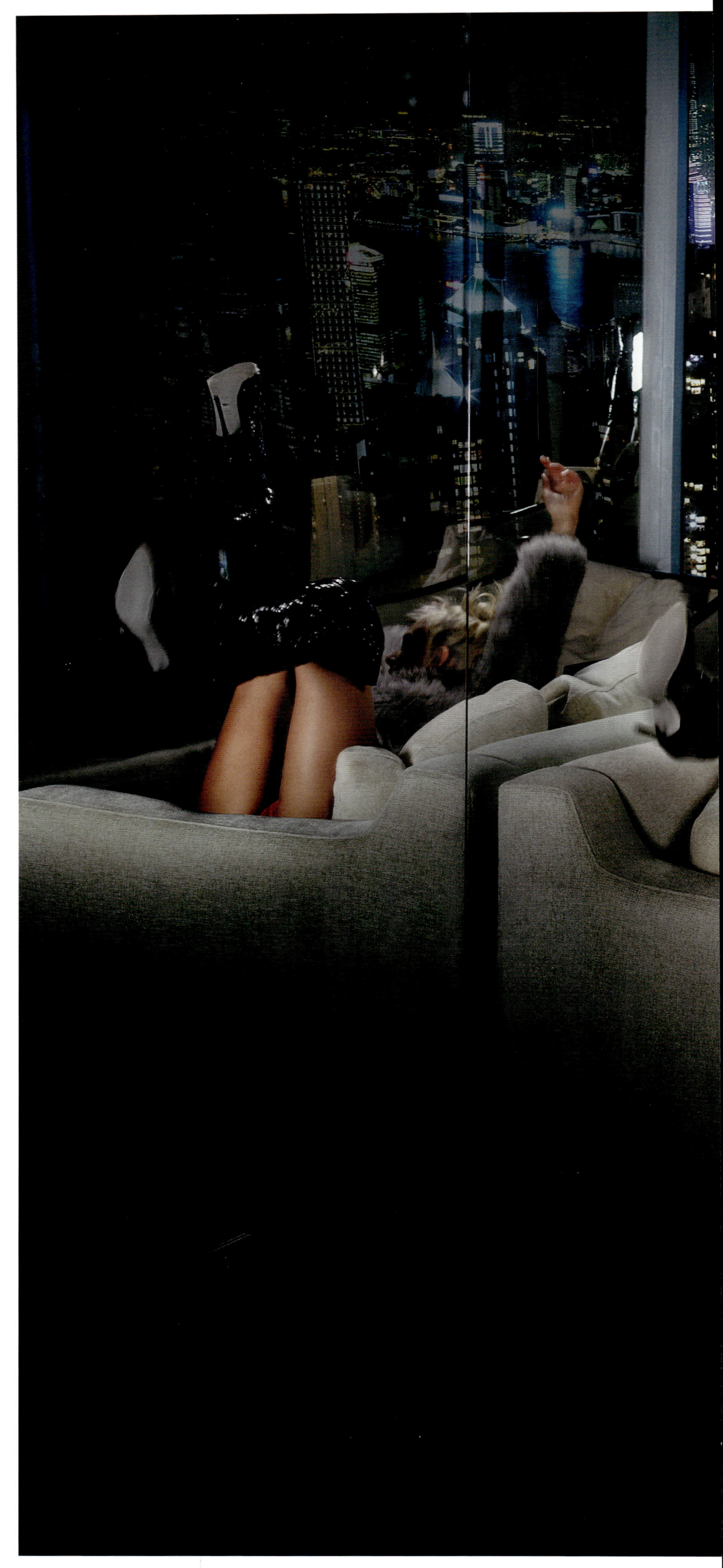

FALLING BACK | 2011

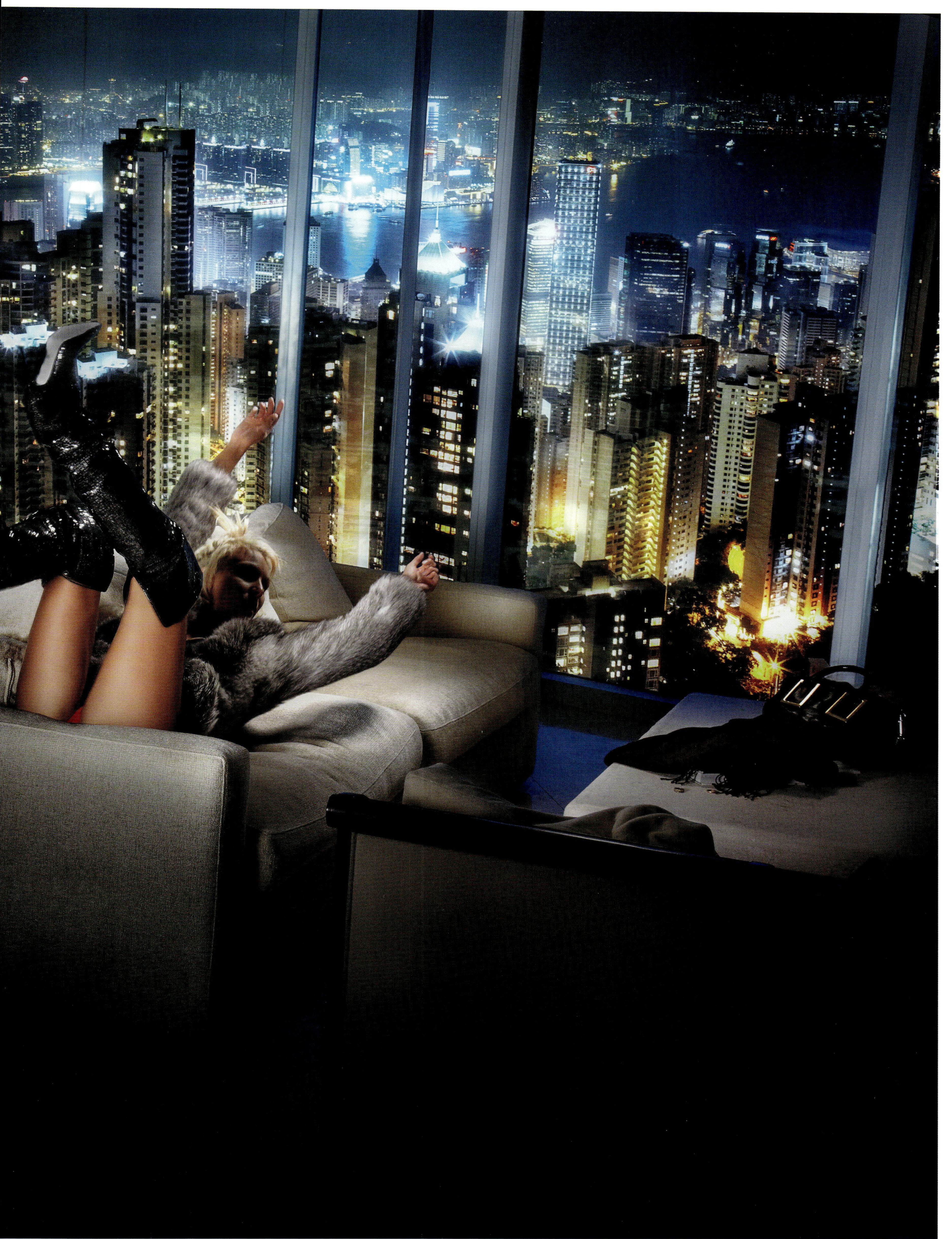

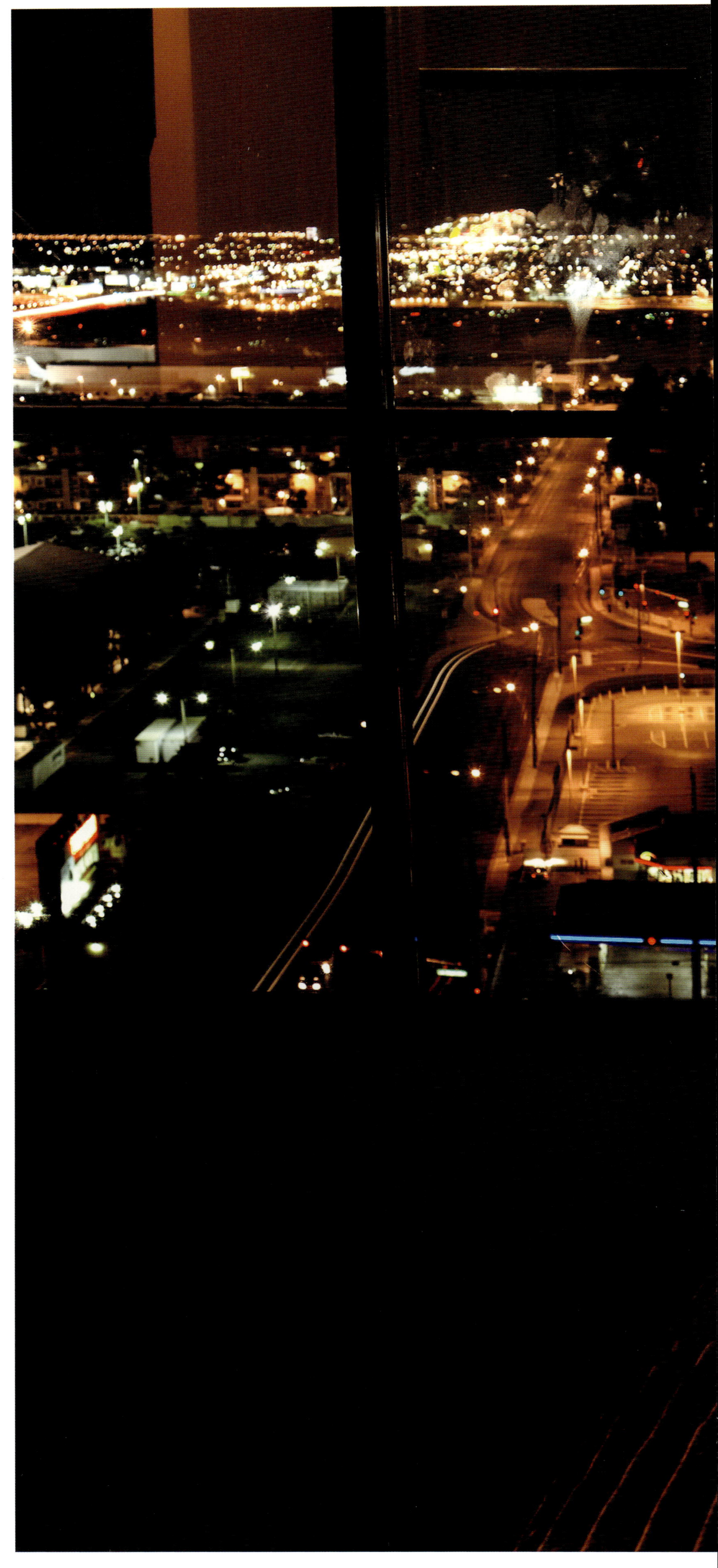

TIME FOR BLUES | 2010

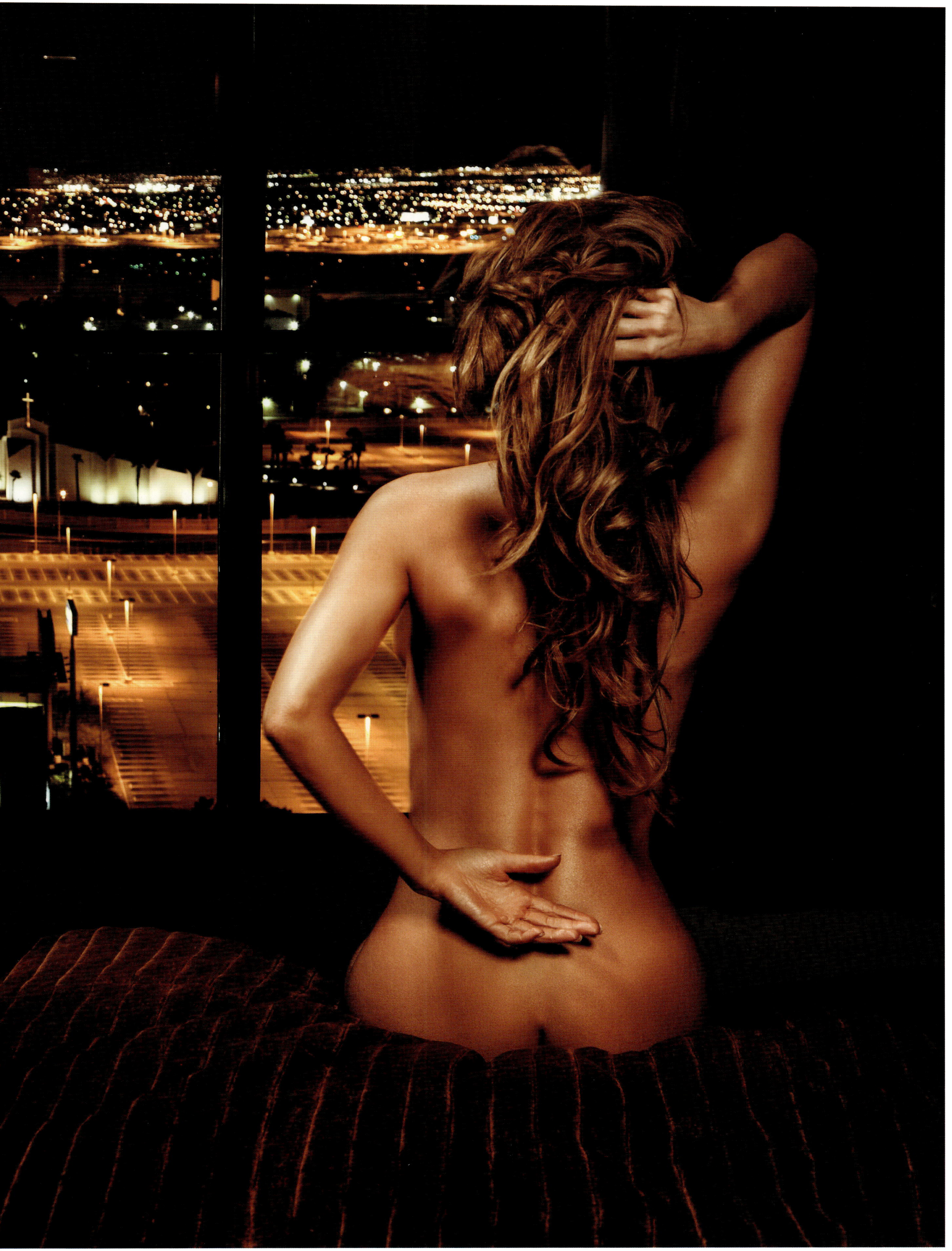

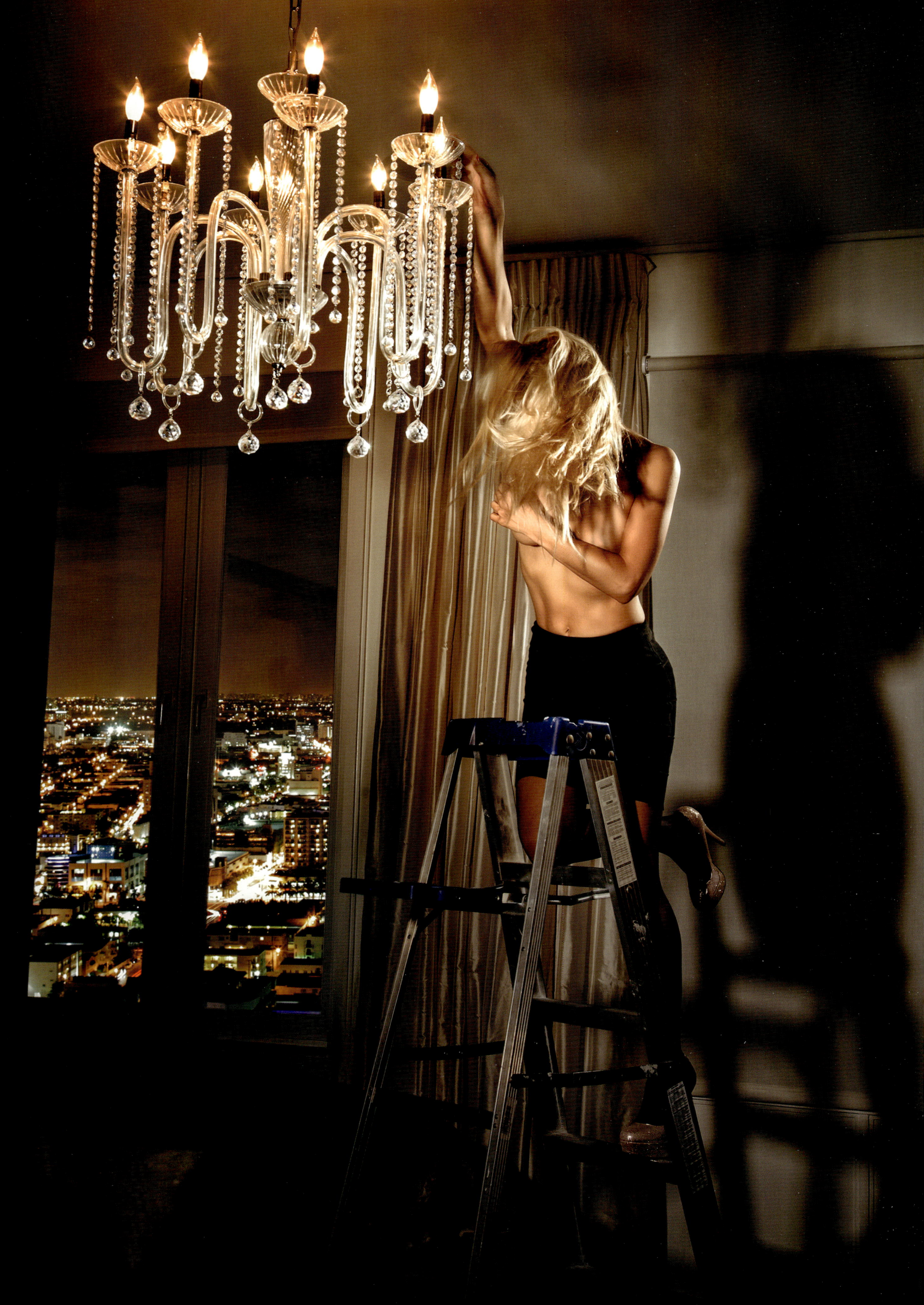

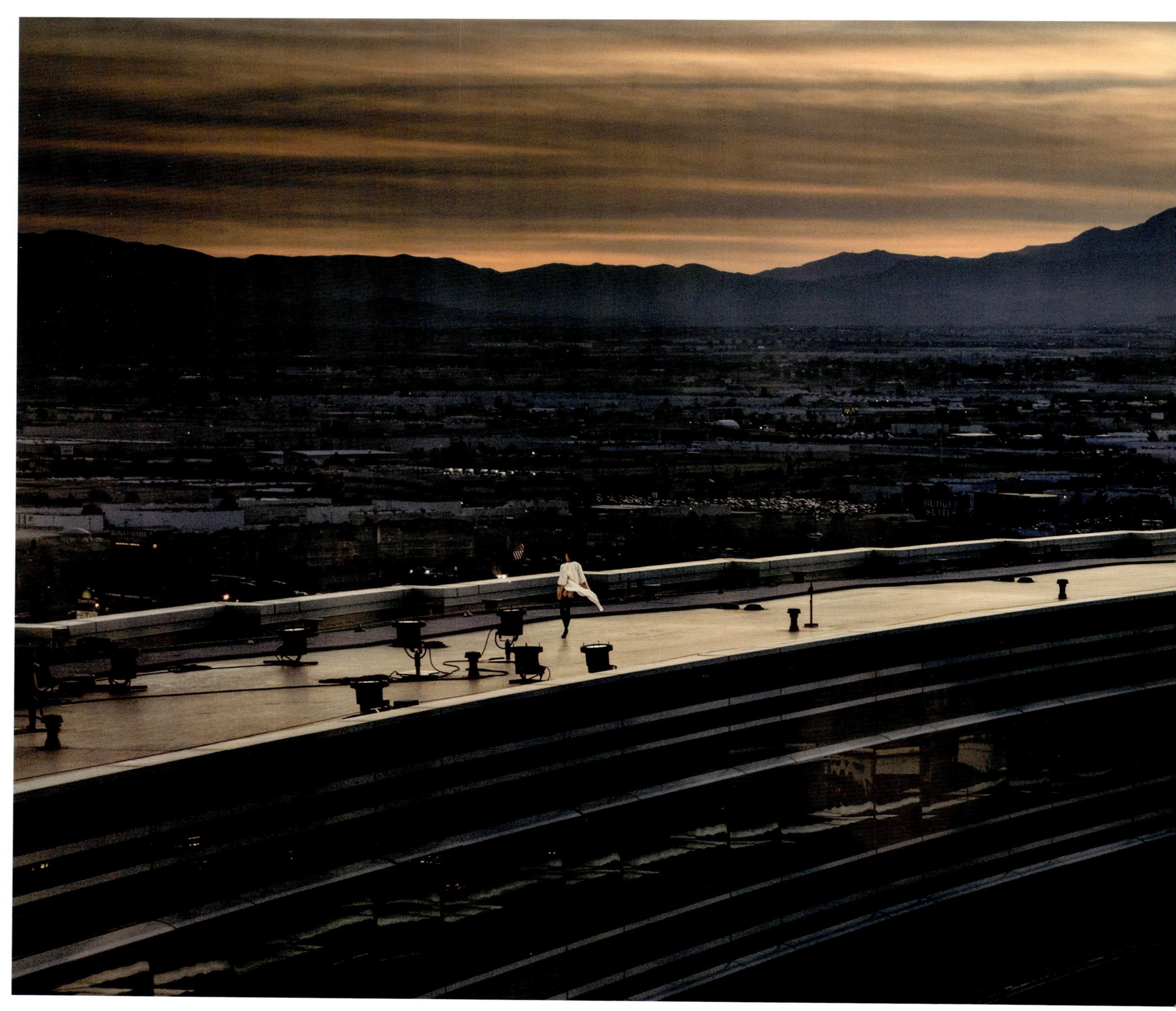

WALKING AWAY | 2012

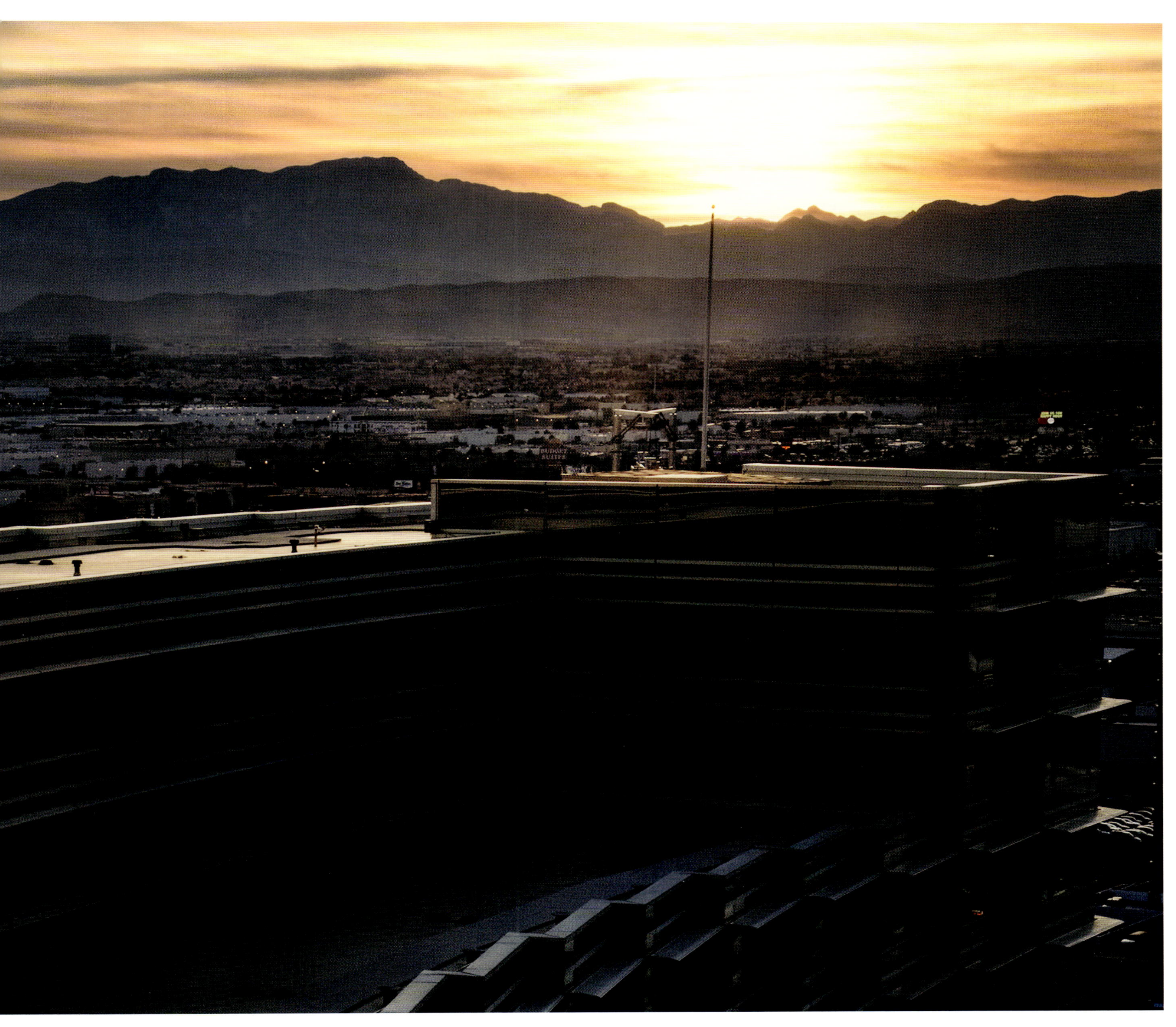

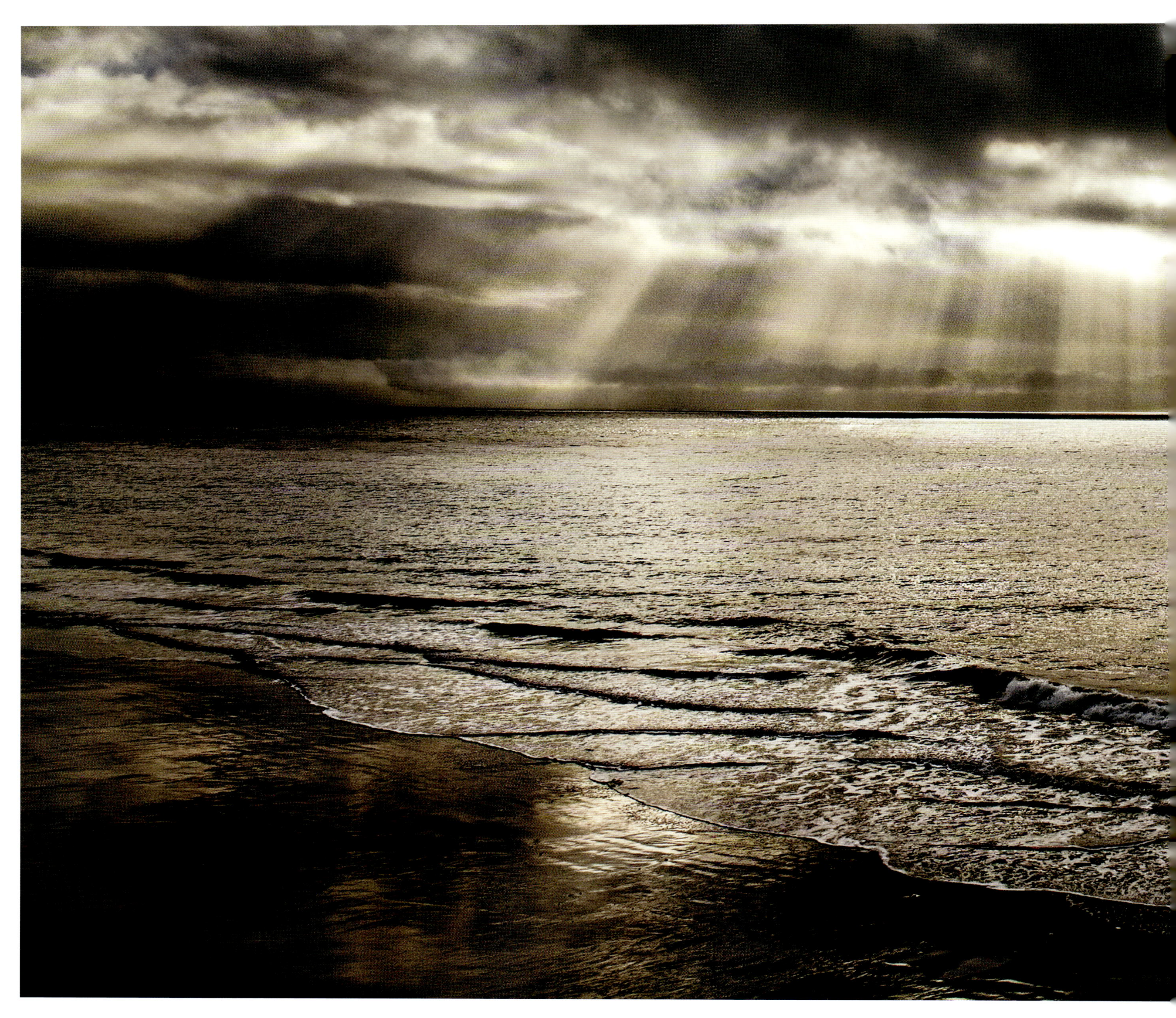

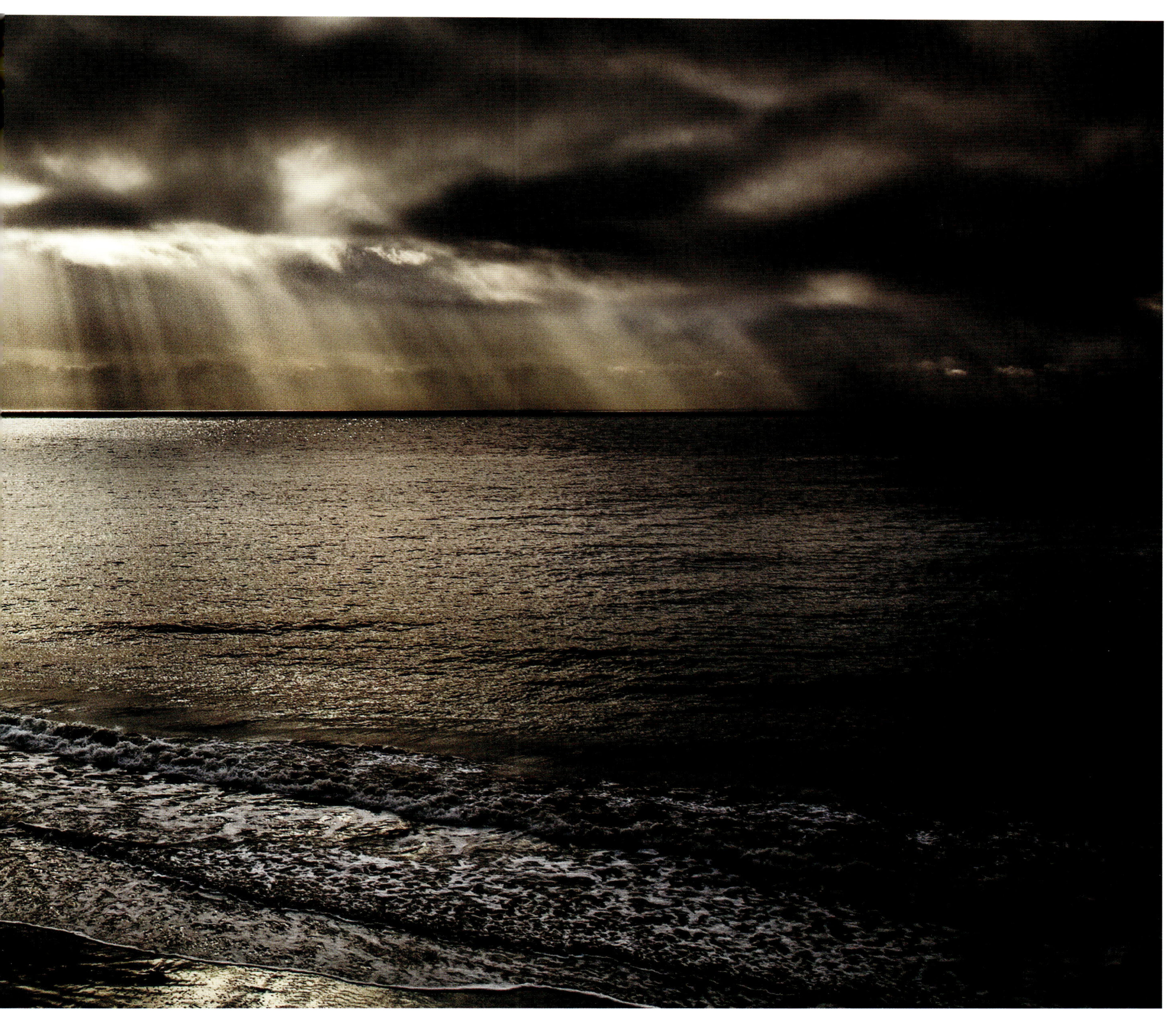

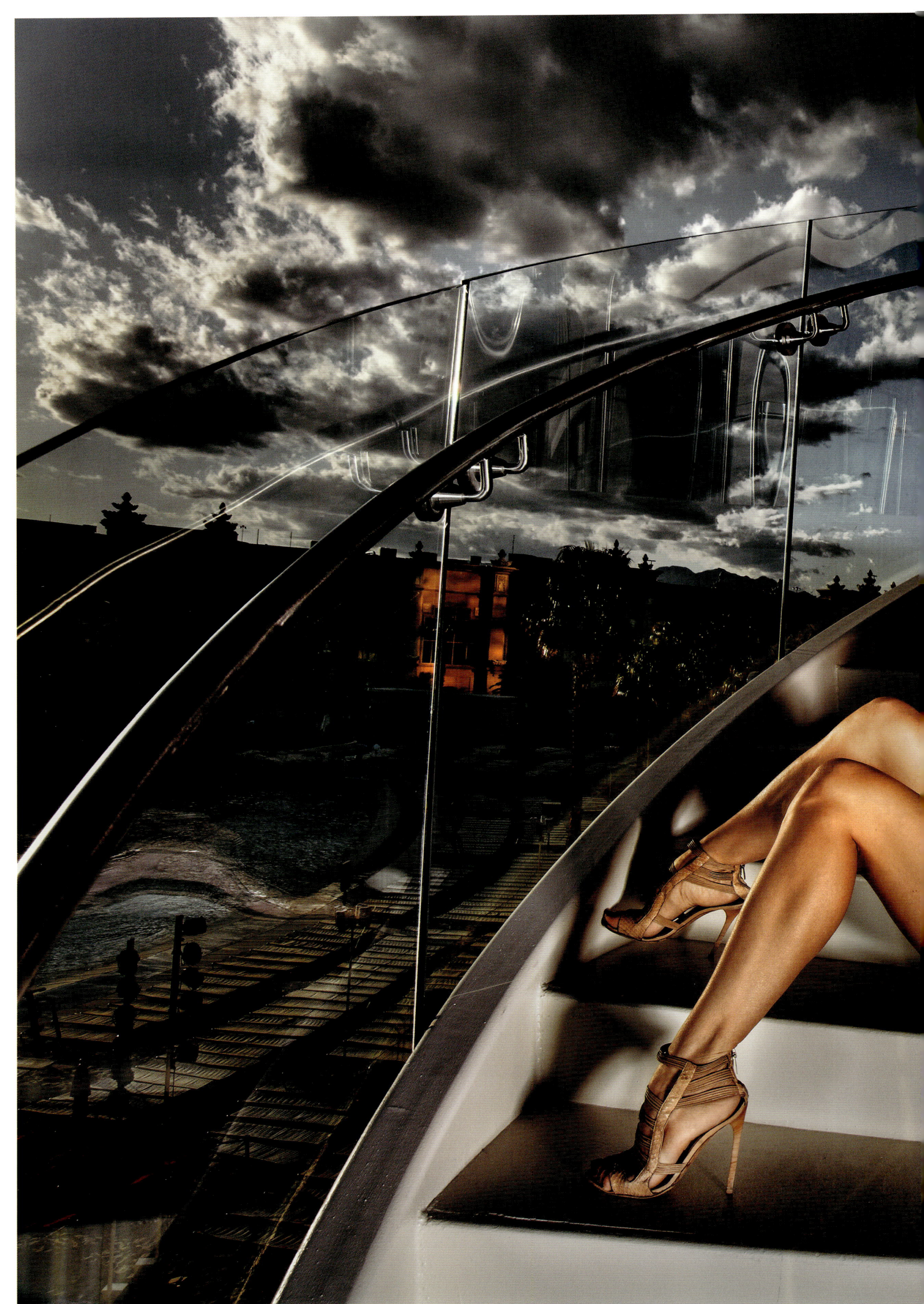

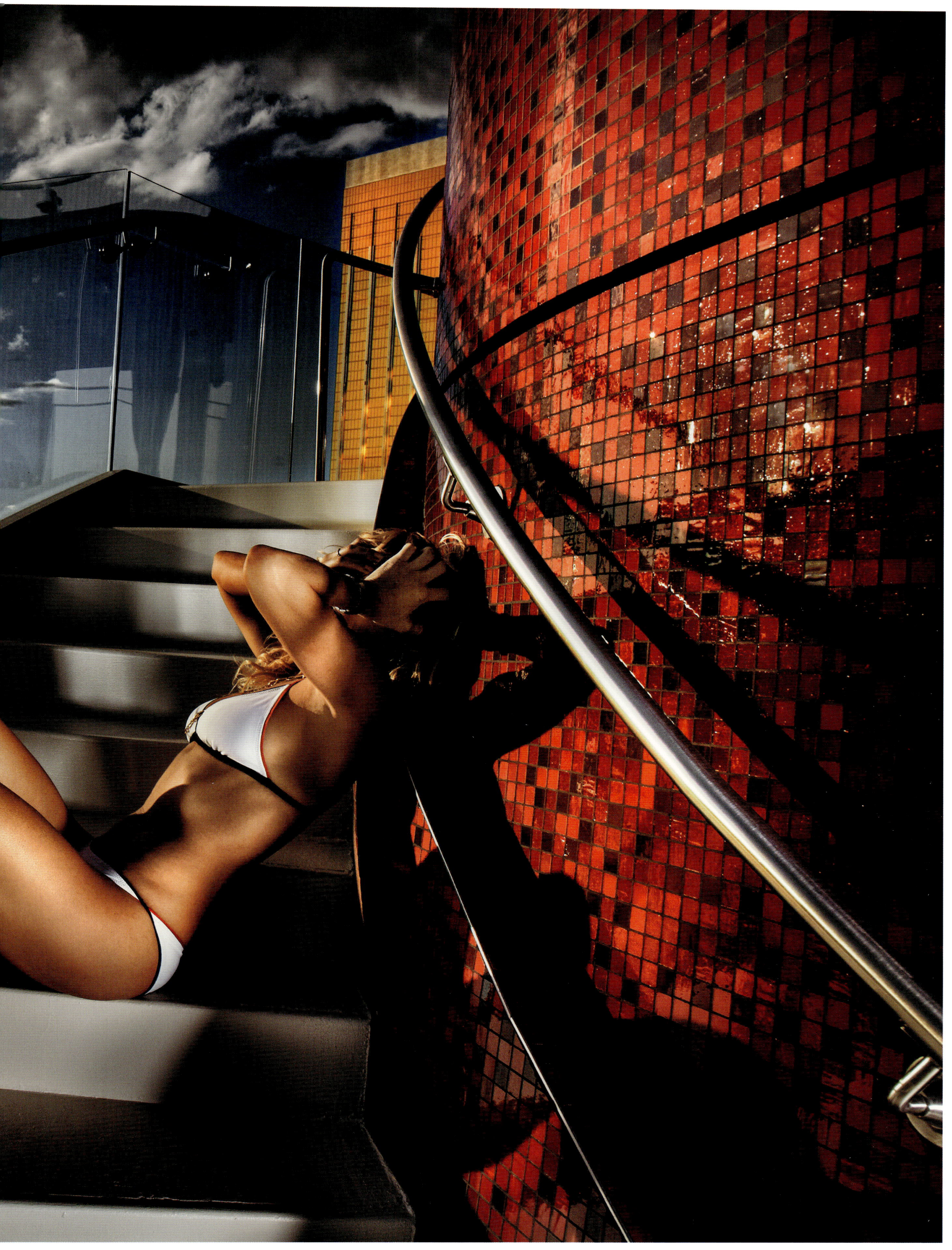

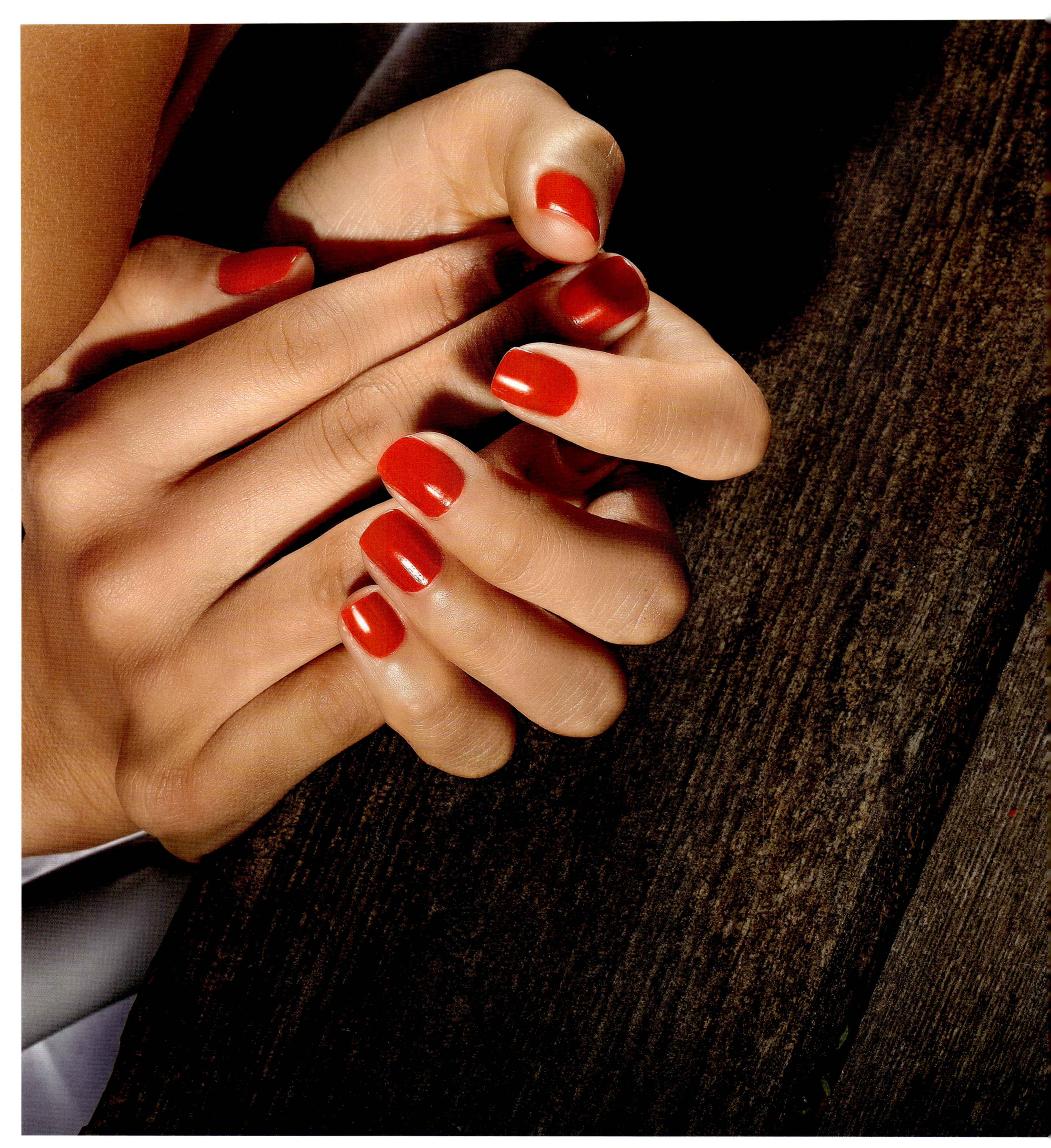

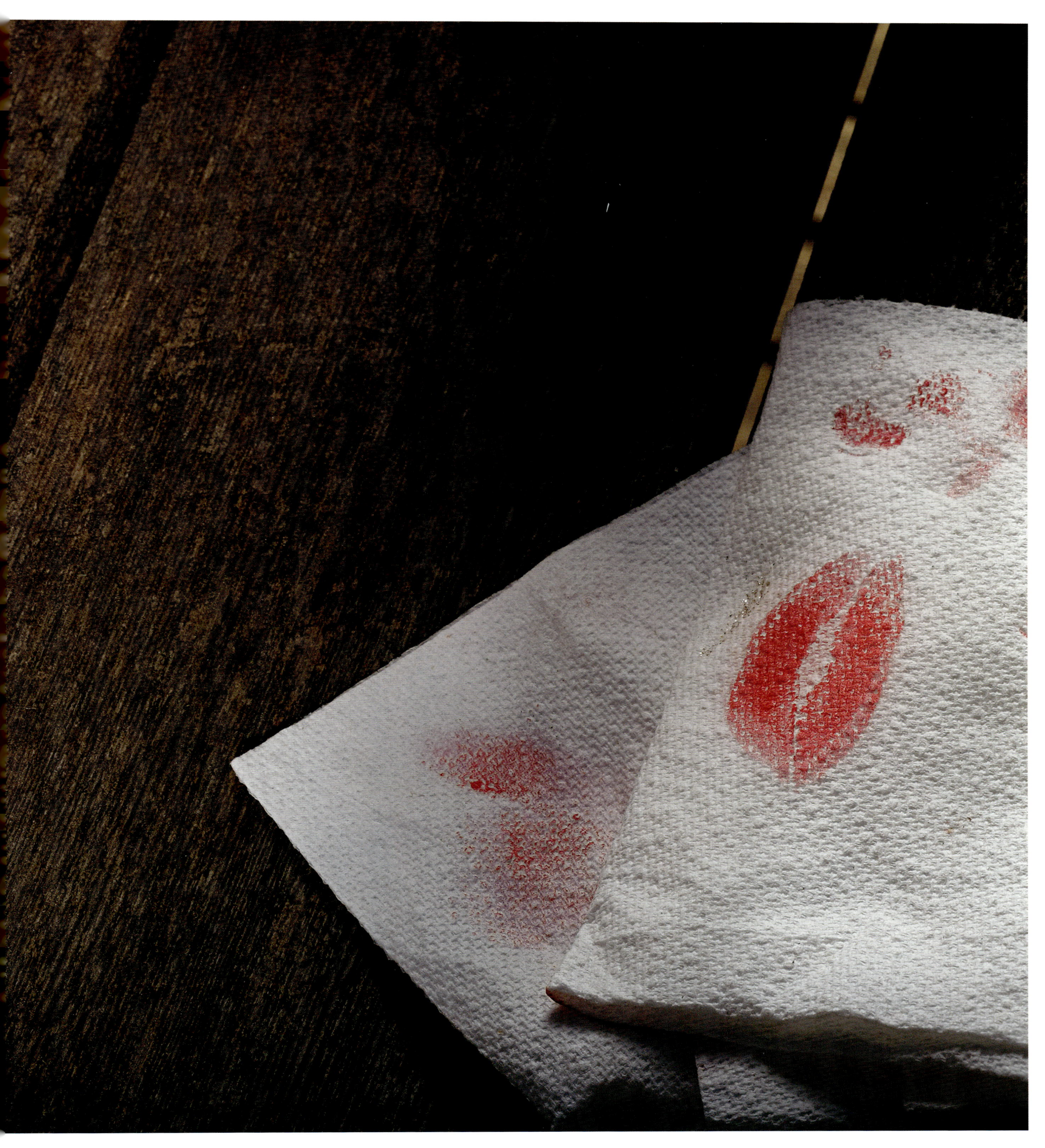

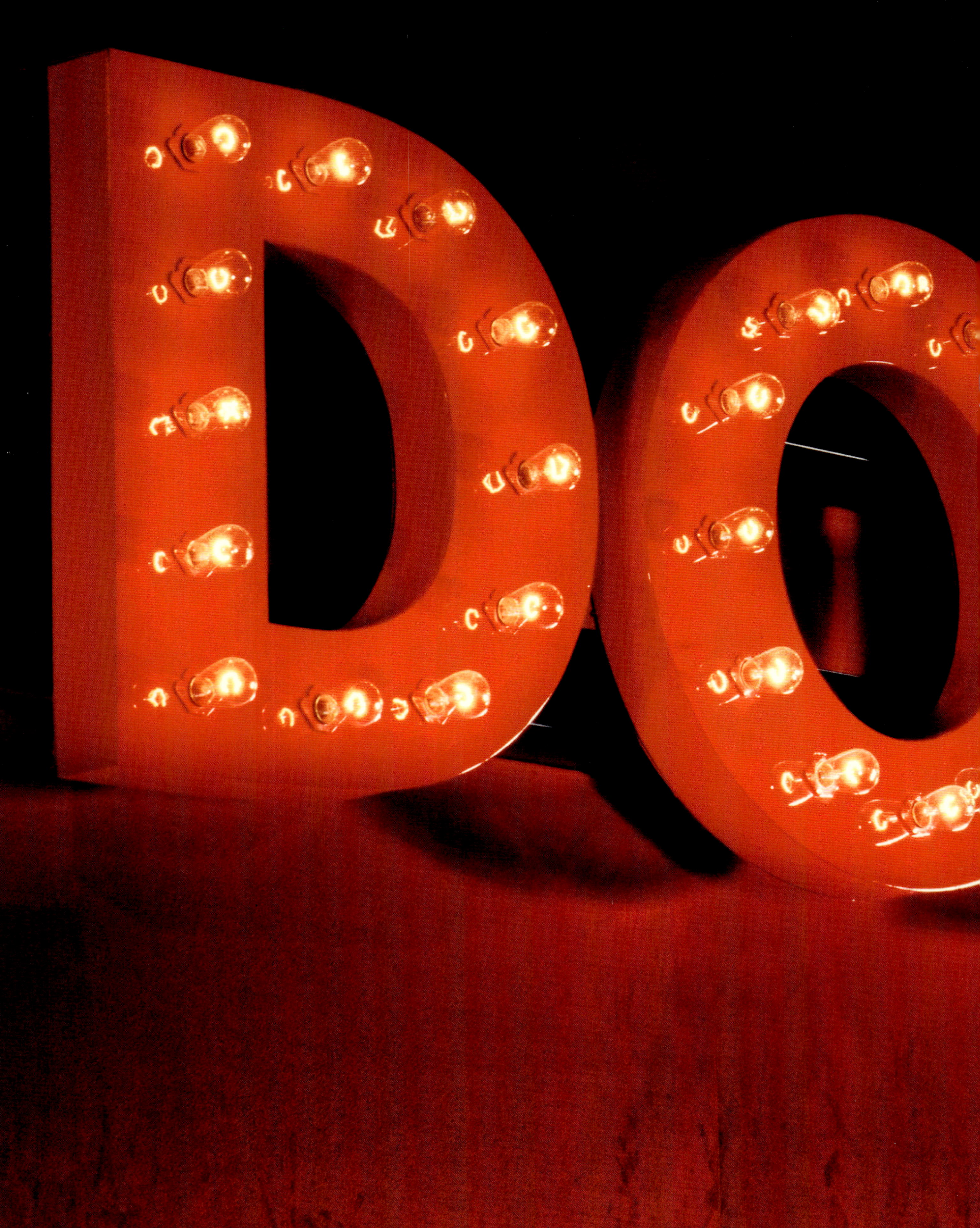

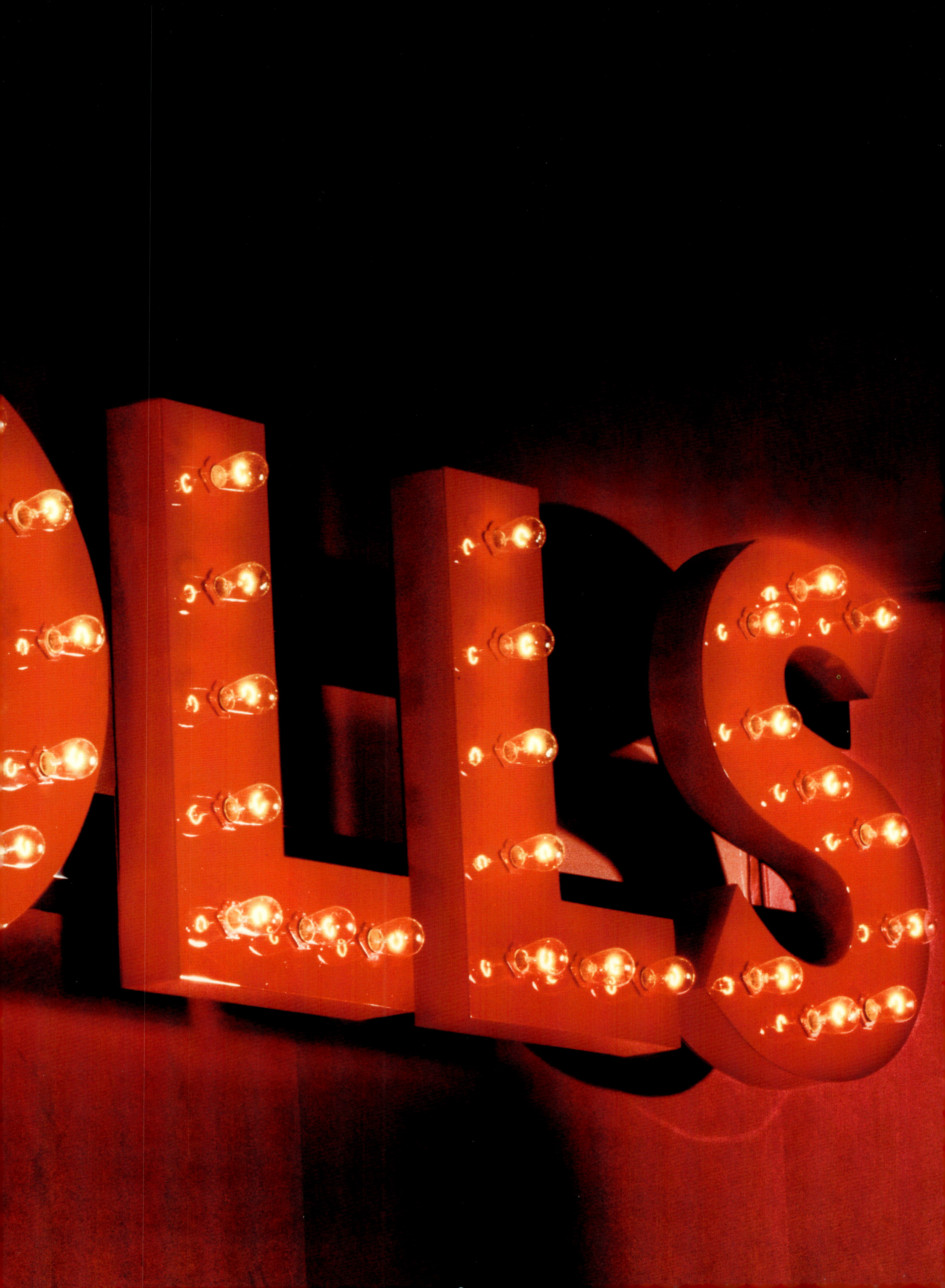
LLS

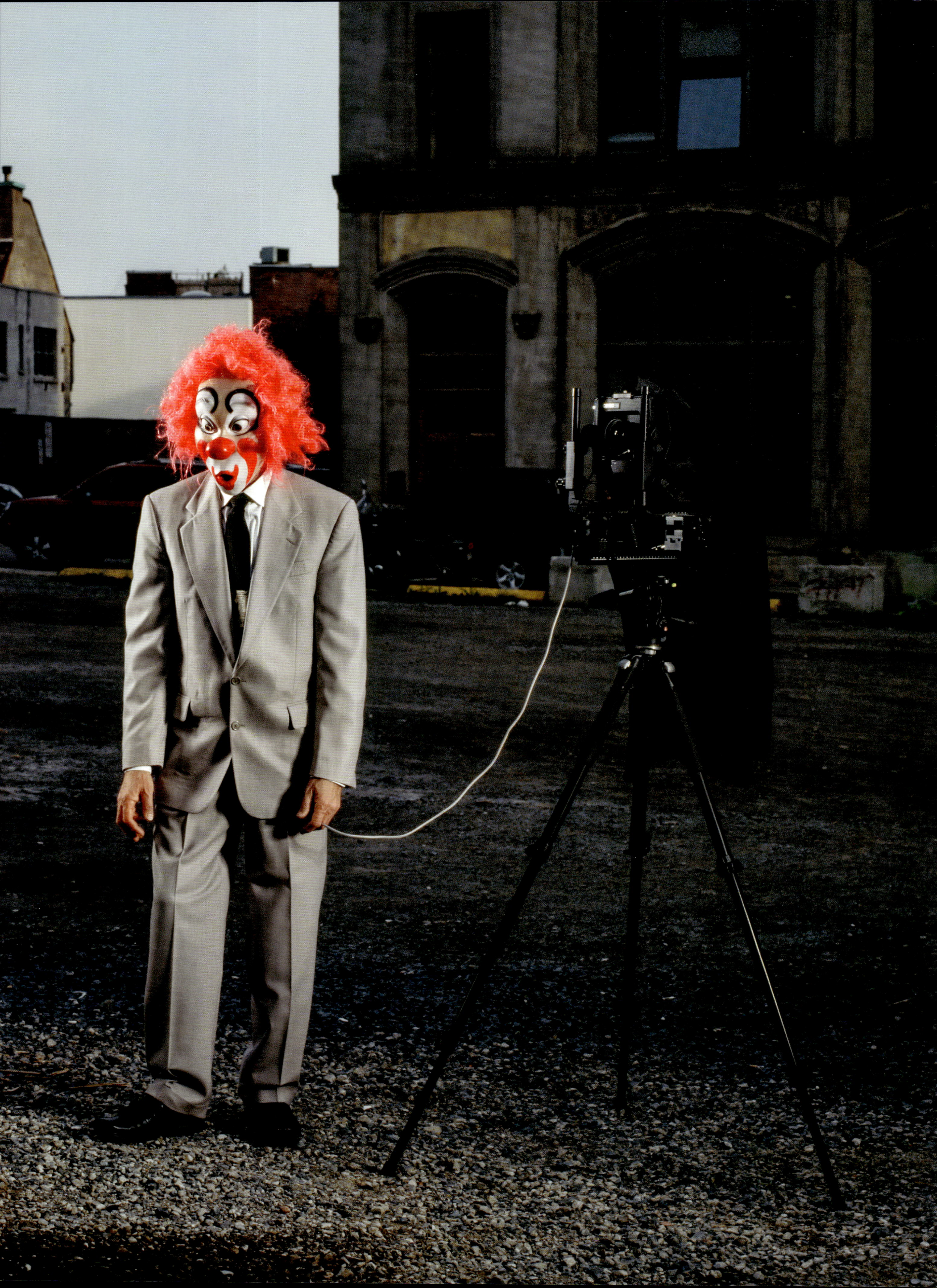

ENTERTAINING HIMSELF I 2008
PREVIOUS PAGE: DOLLS I 2008

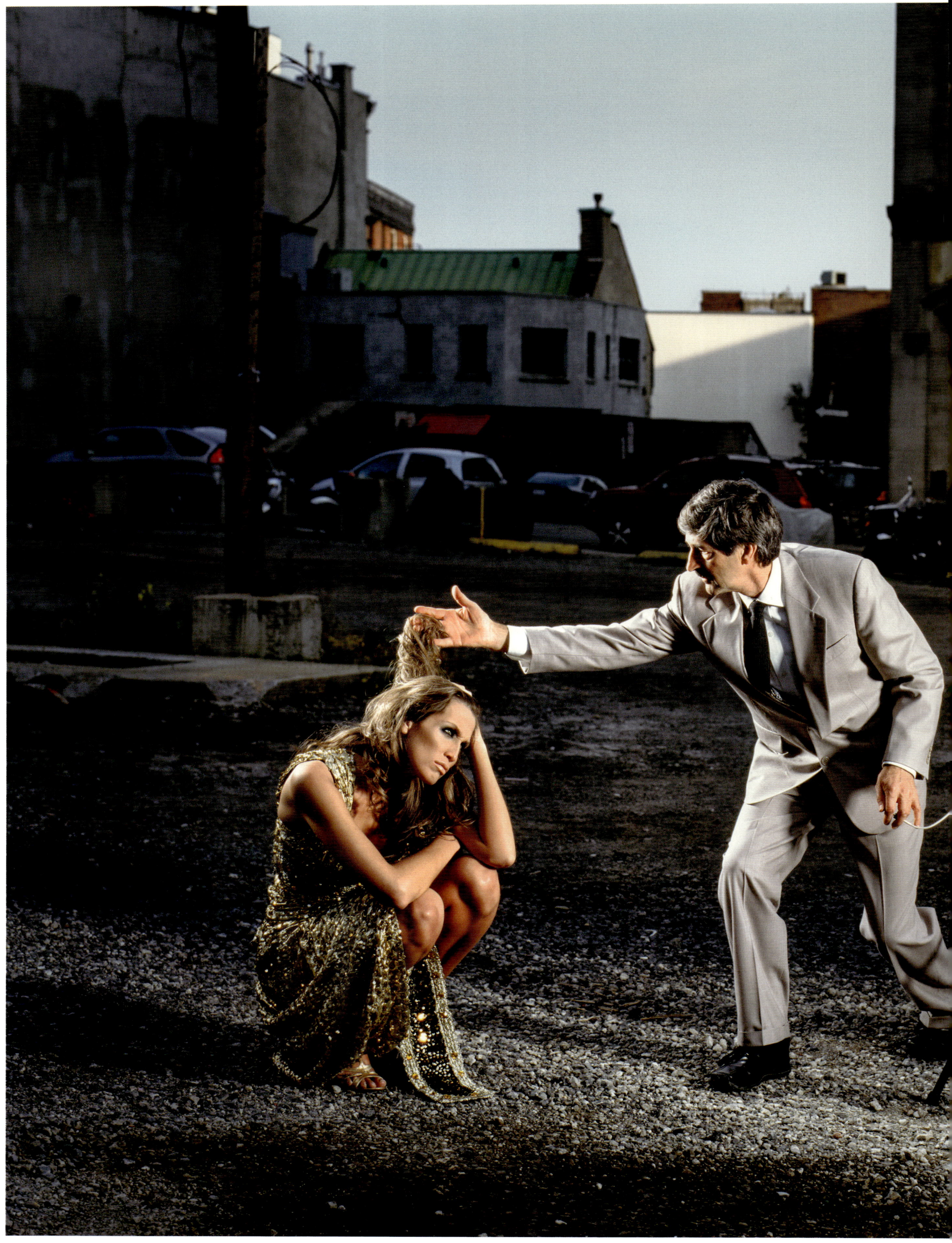

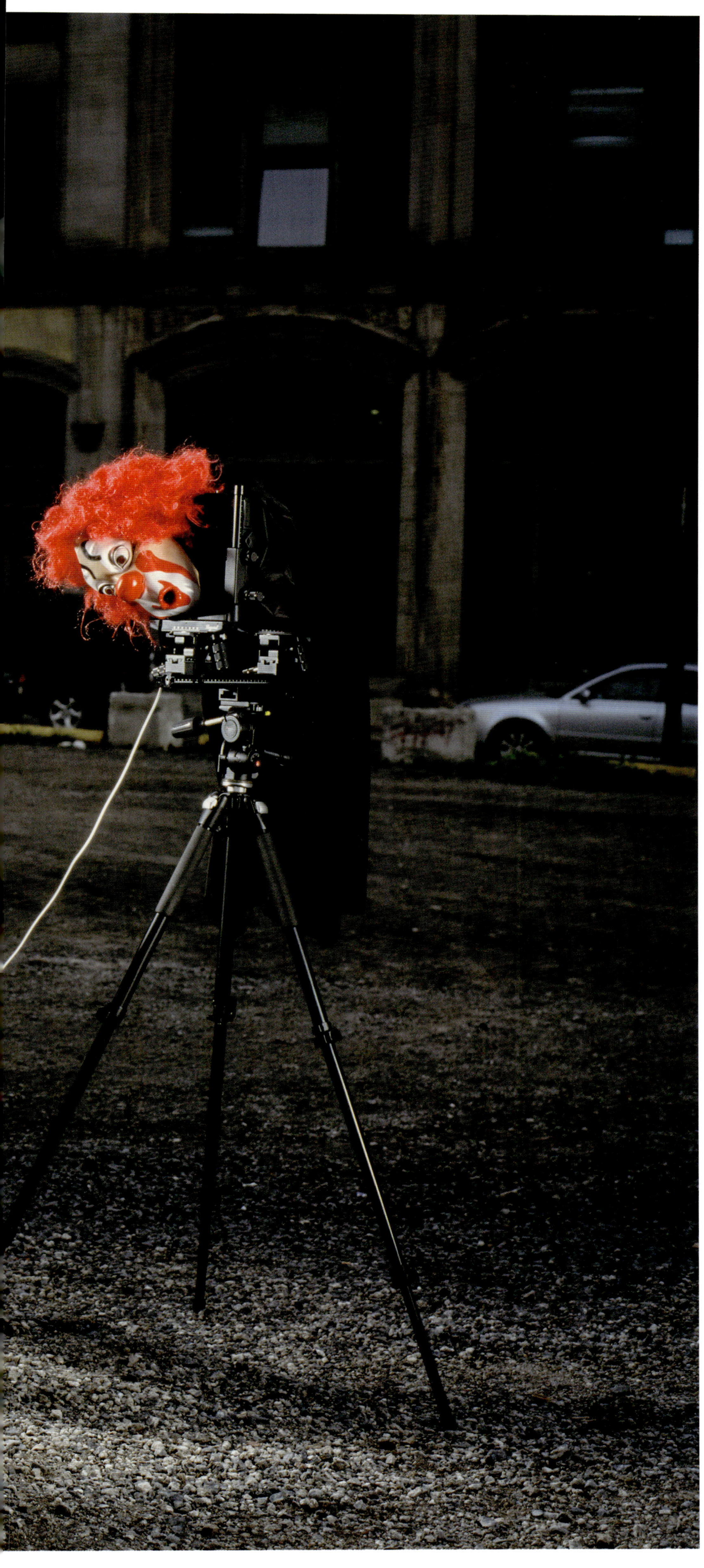

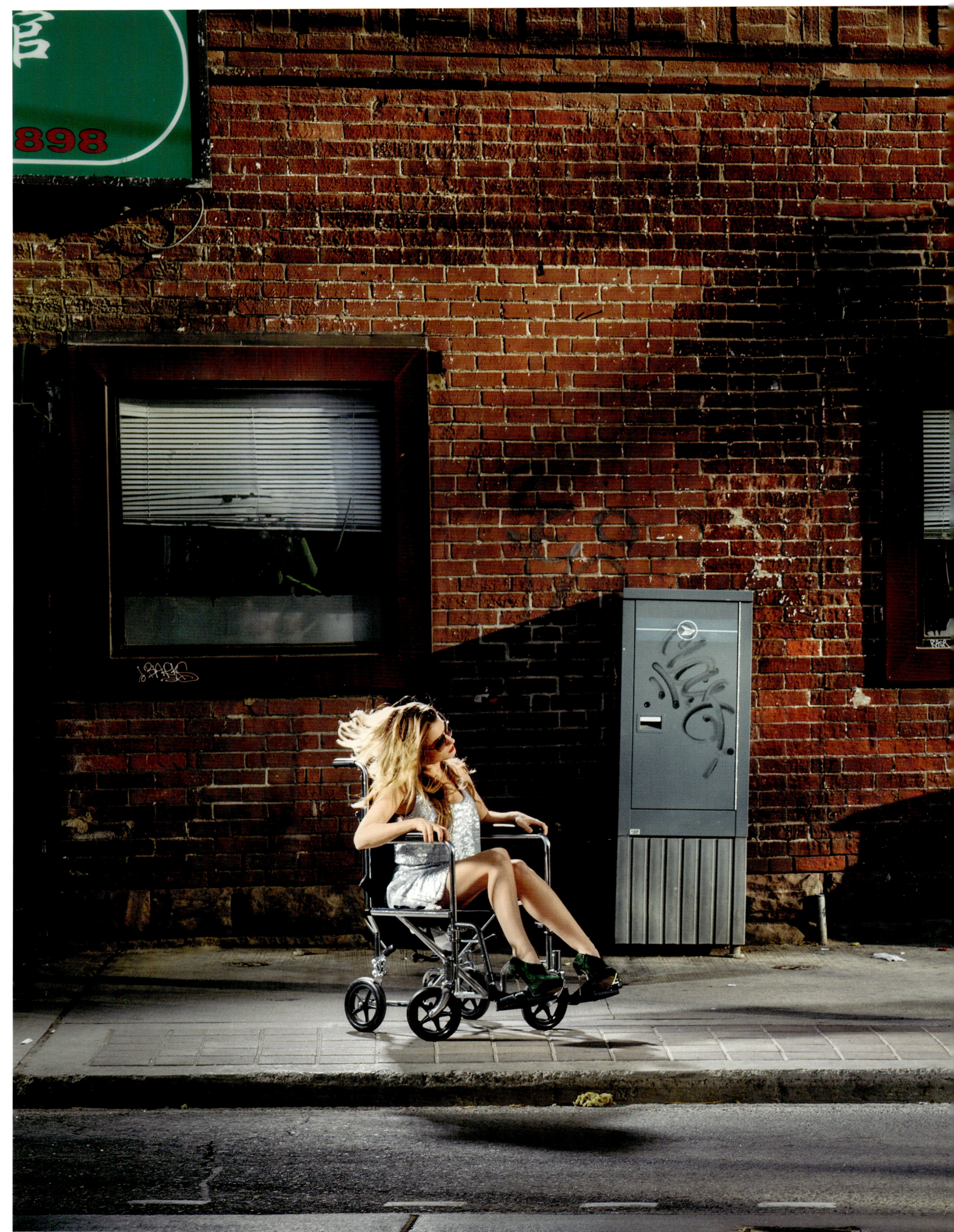
898

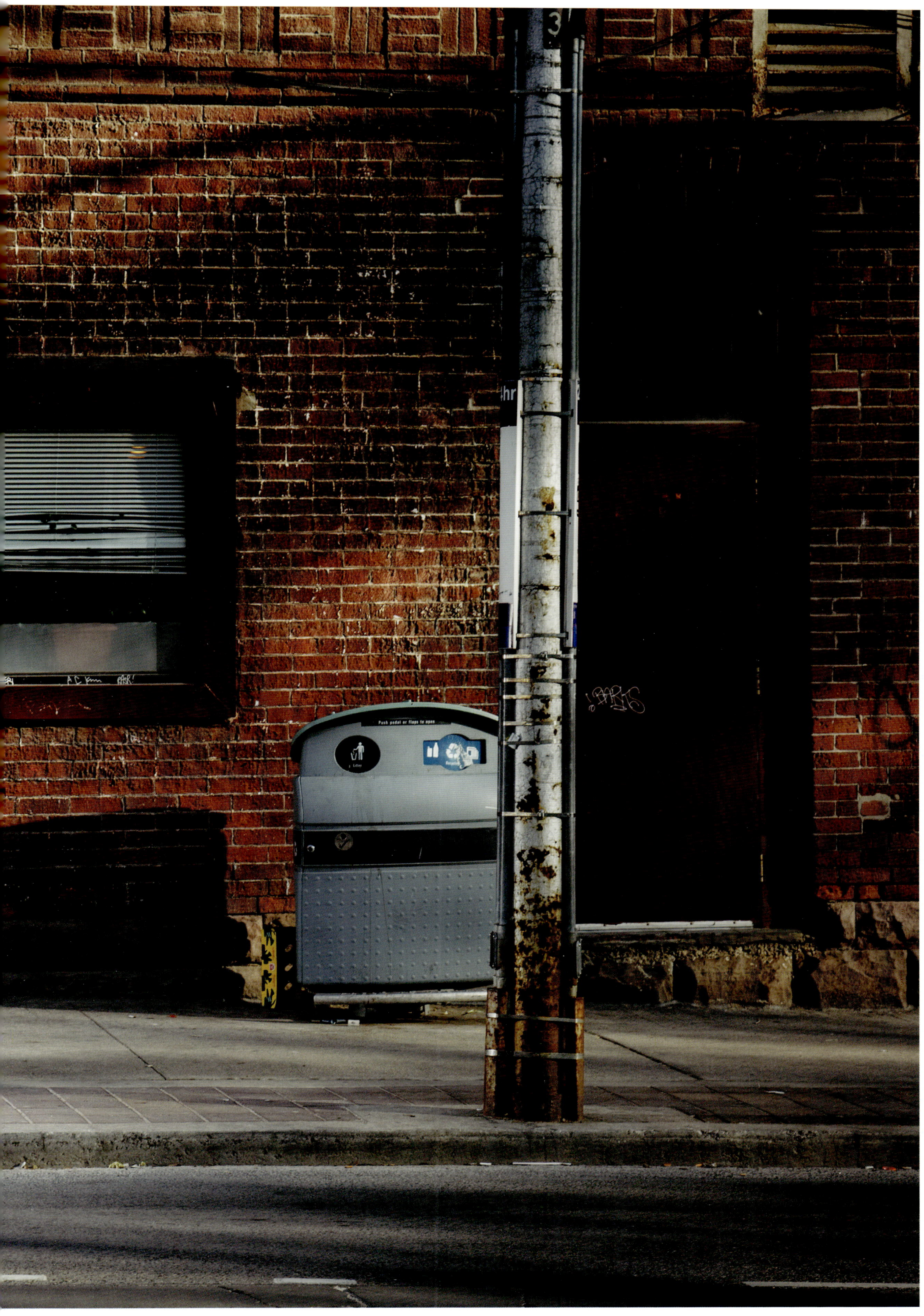

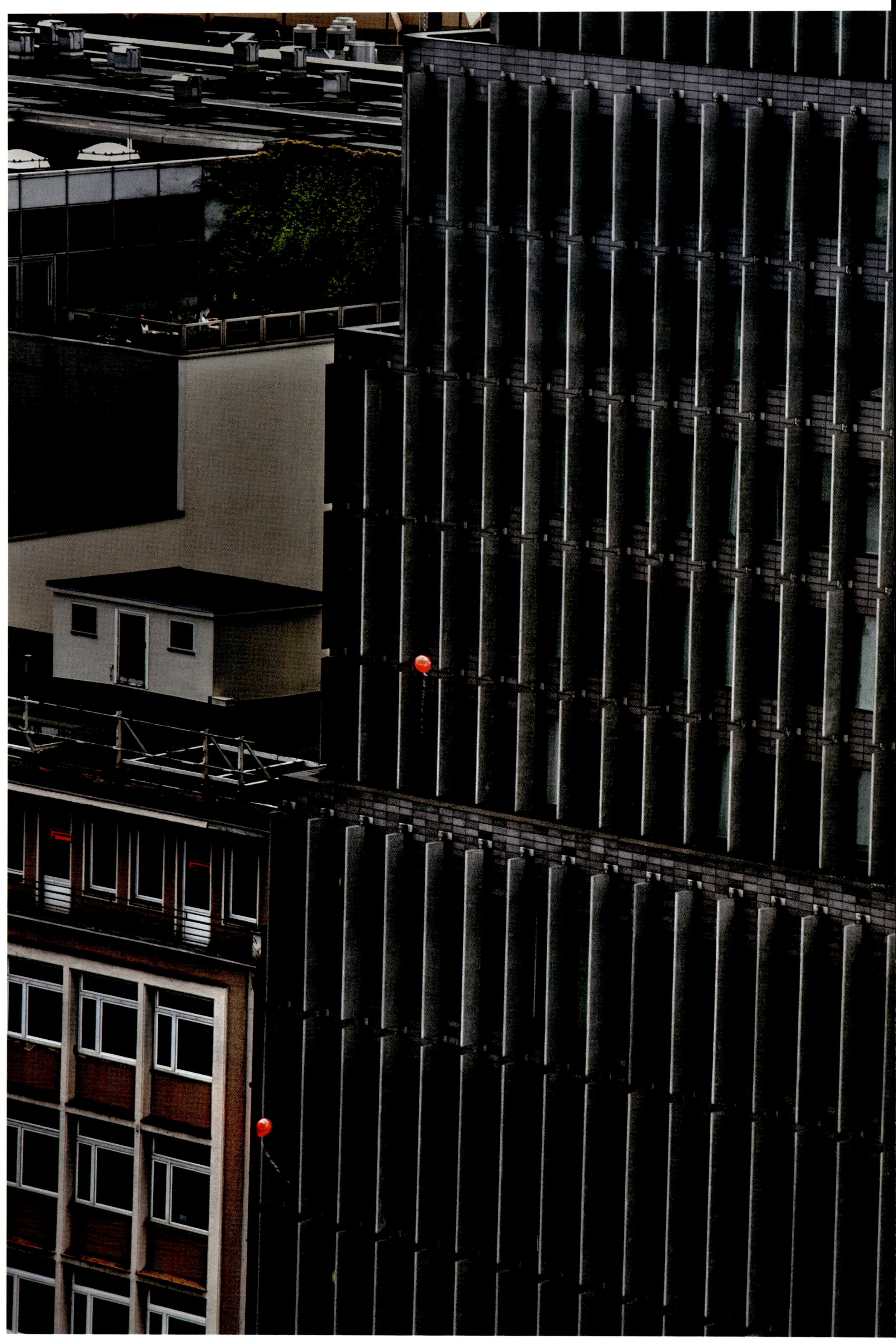

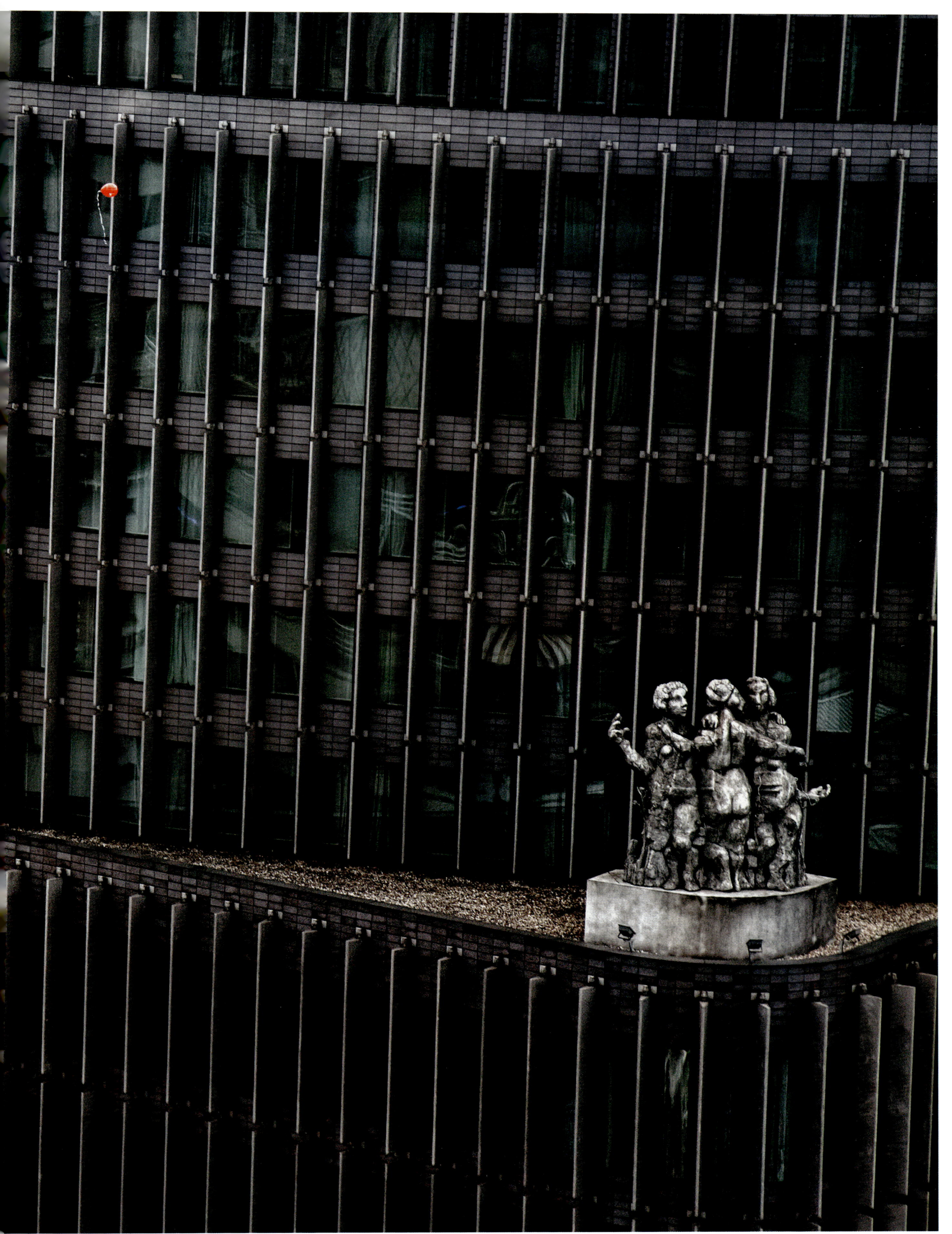

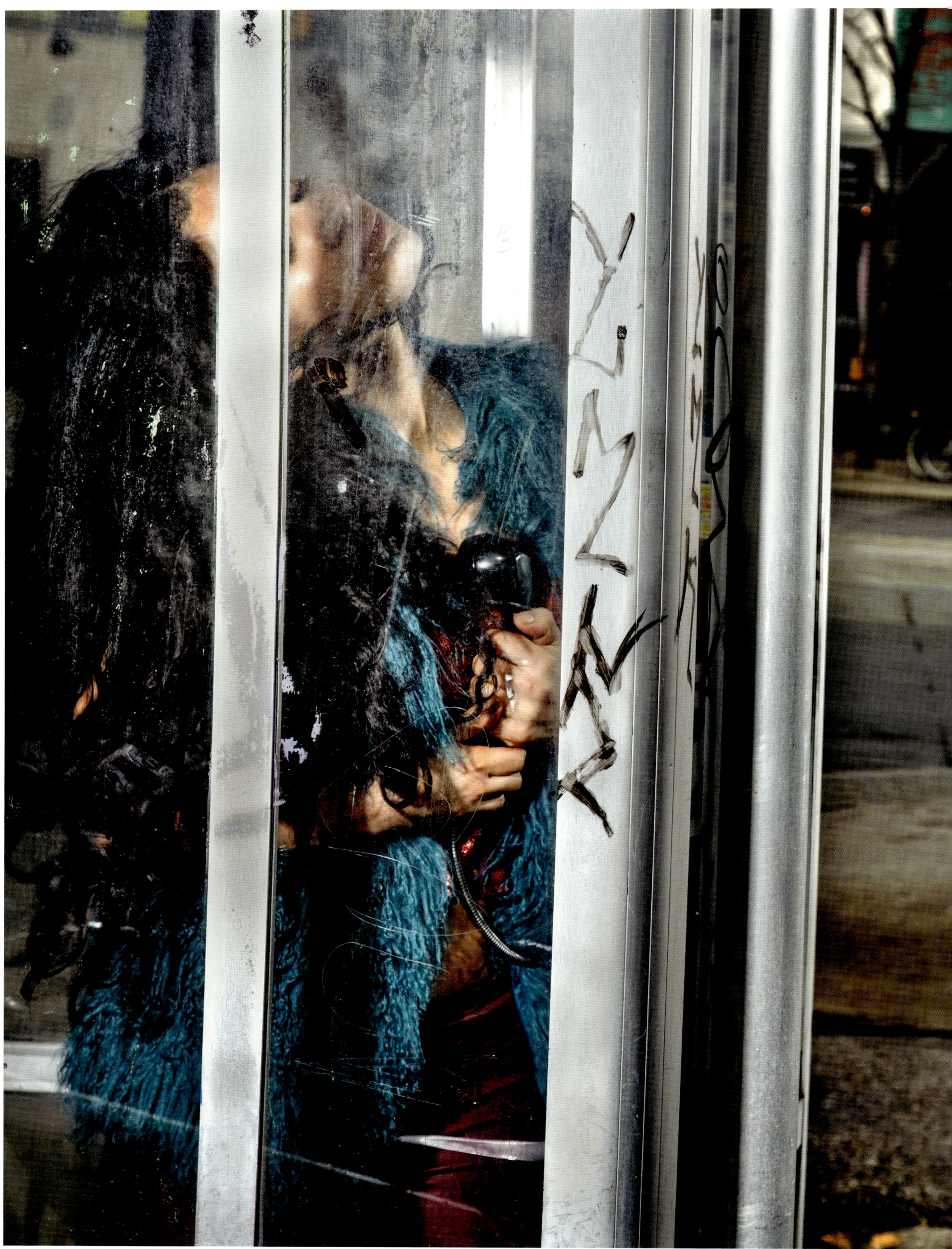

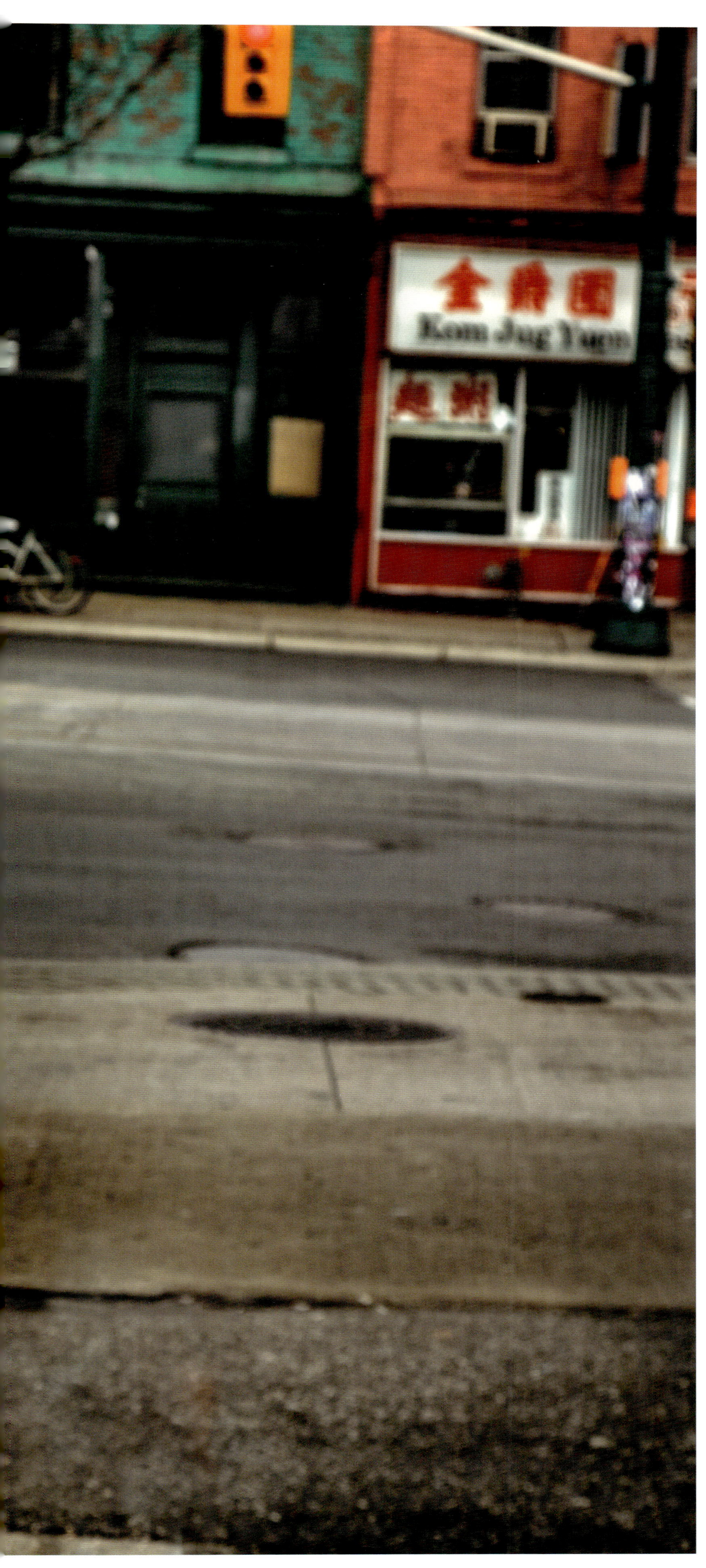

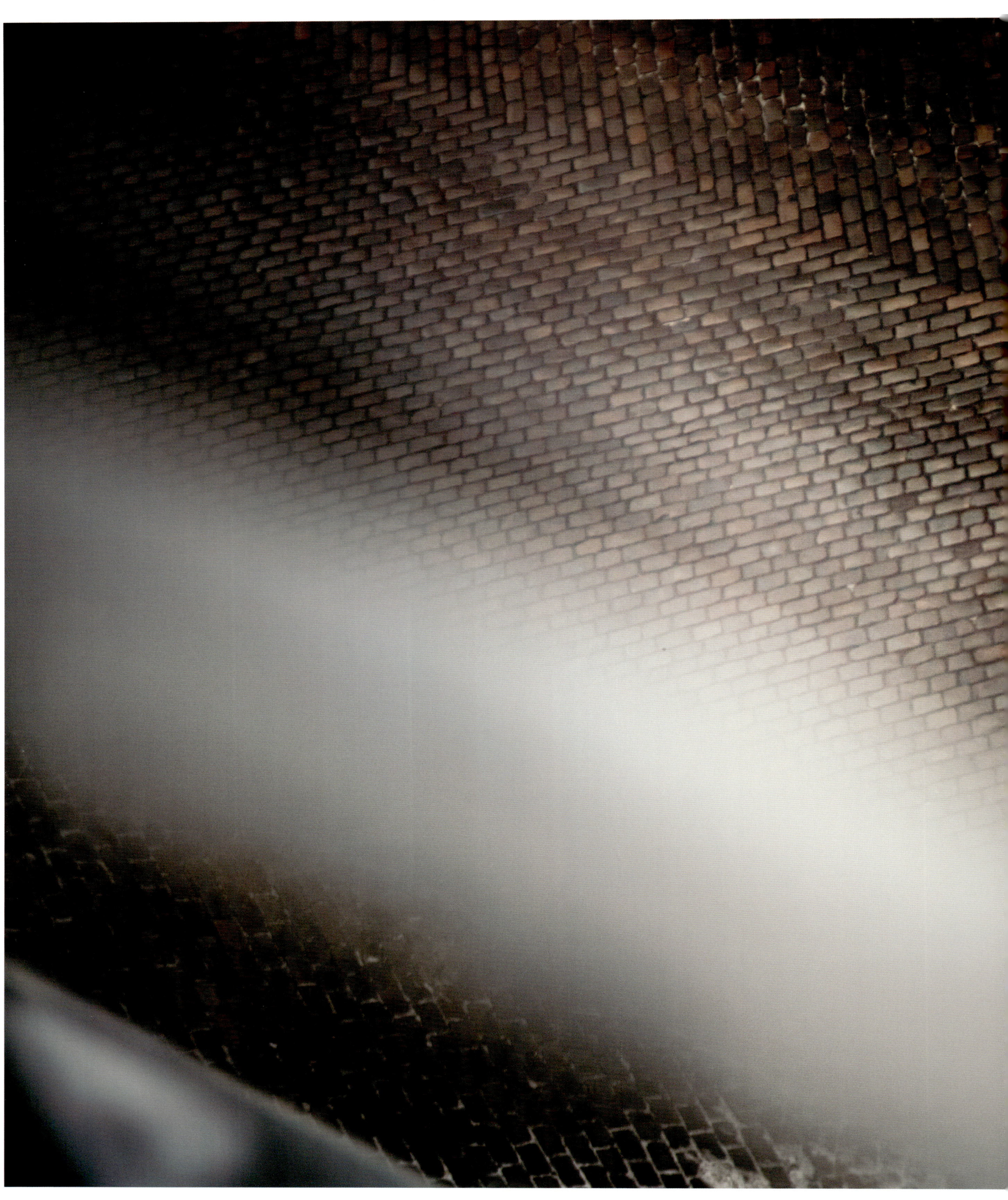

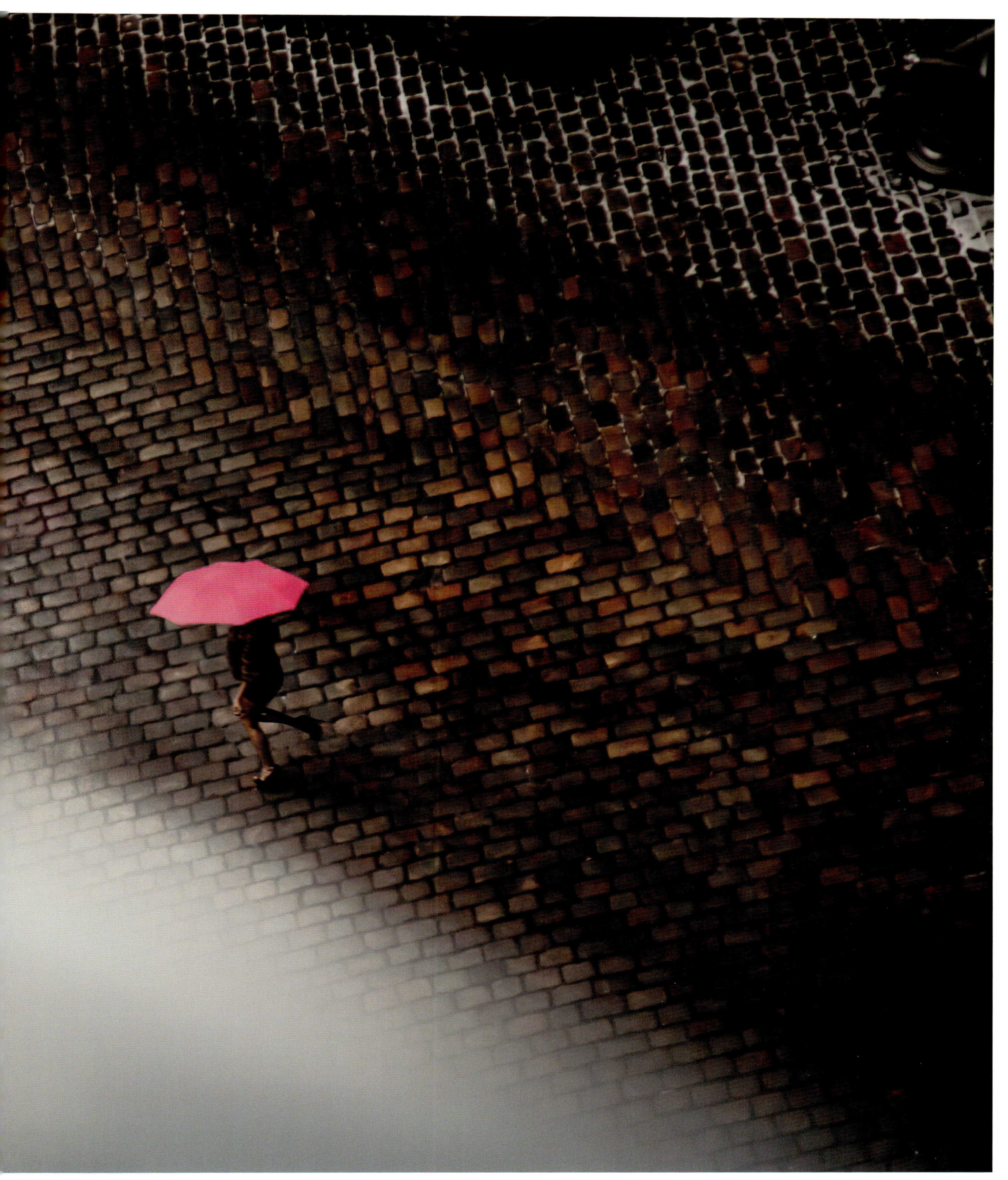

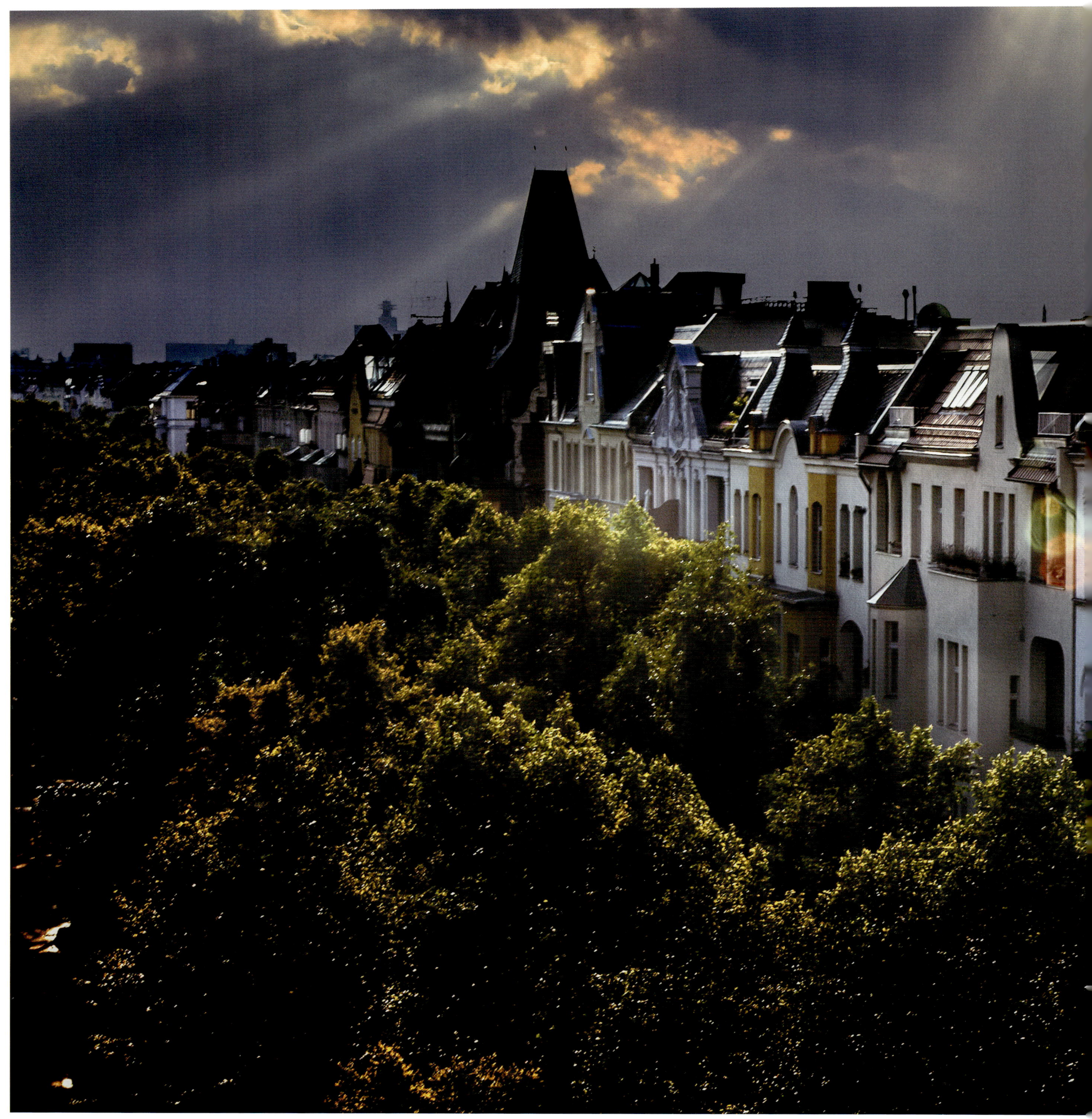

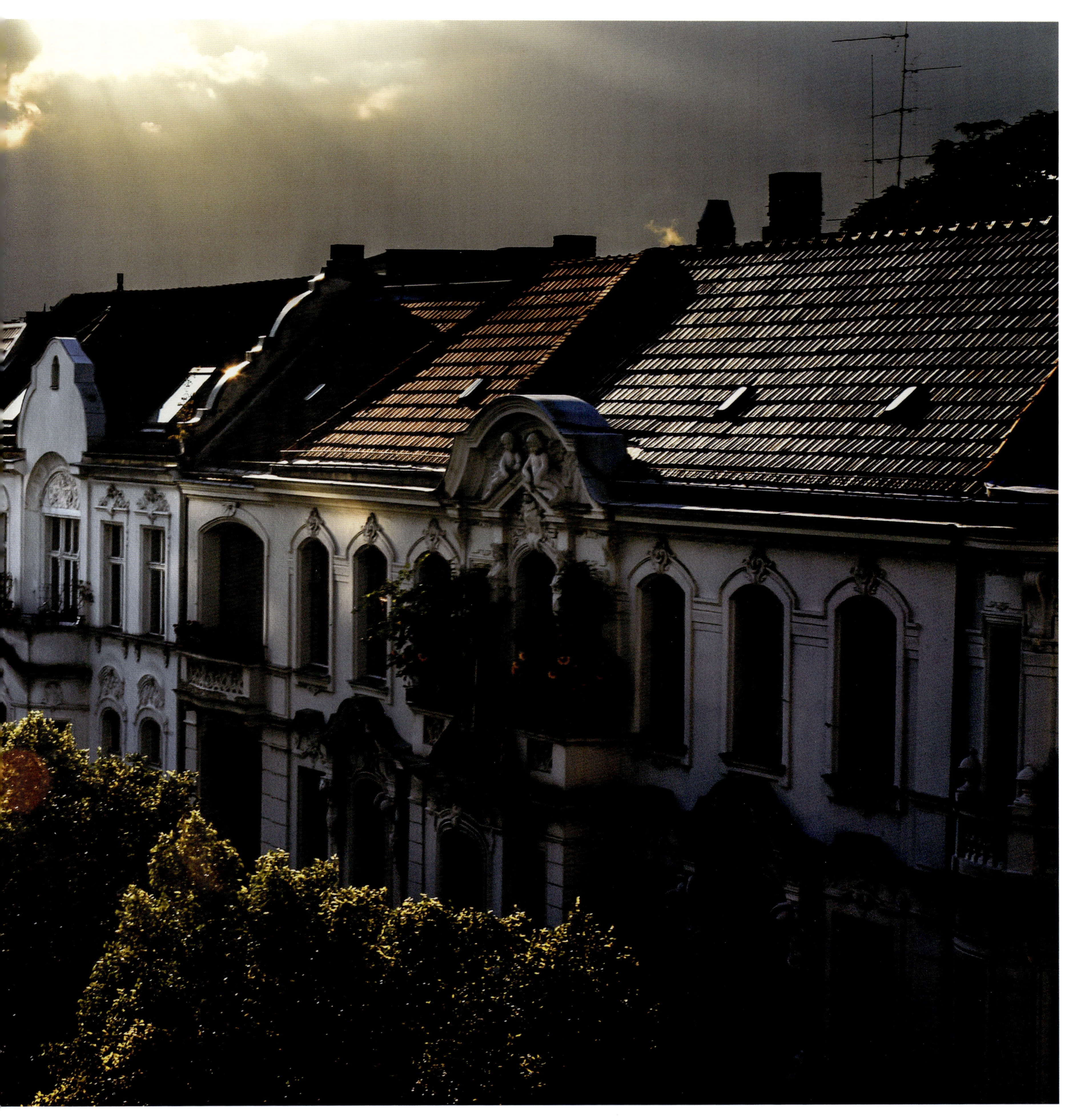

DUSK IN BERLIN | 2011

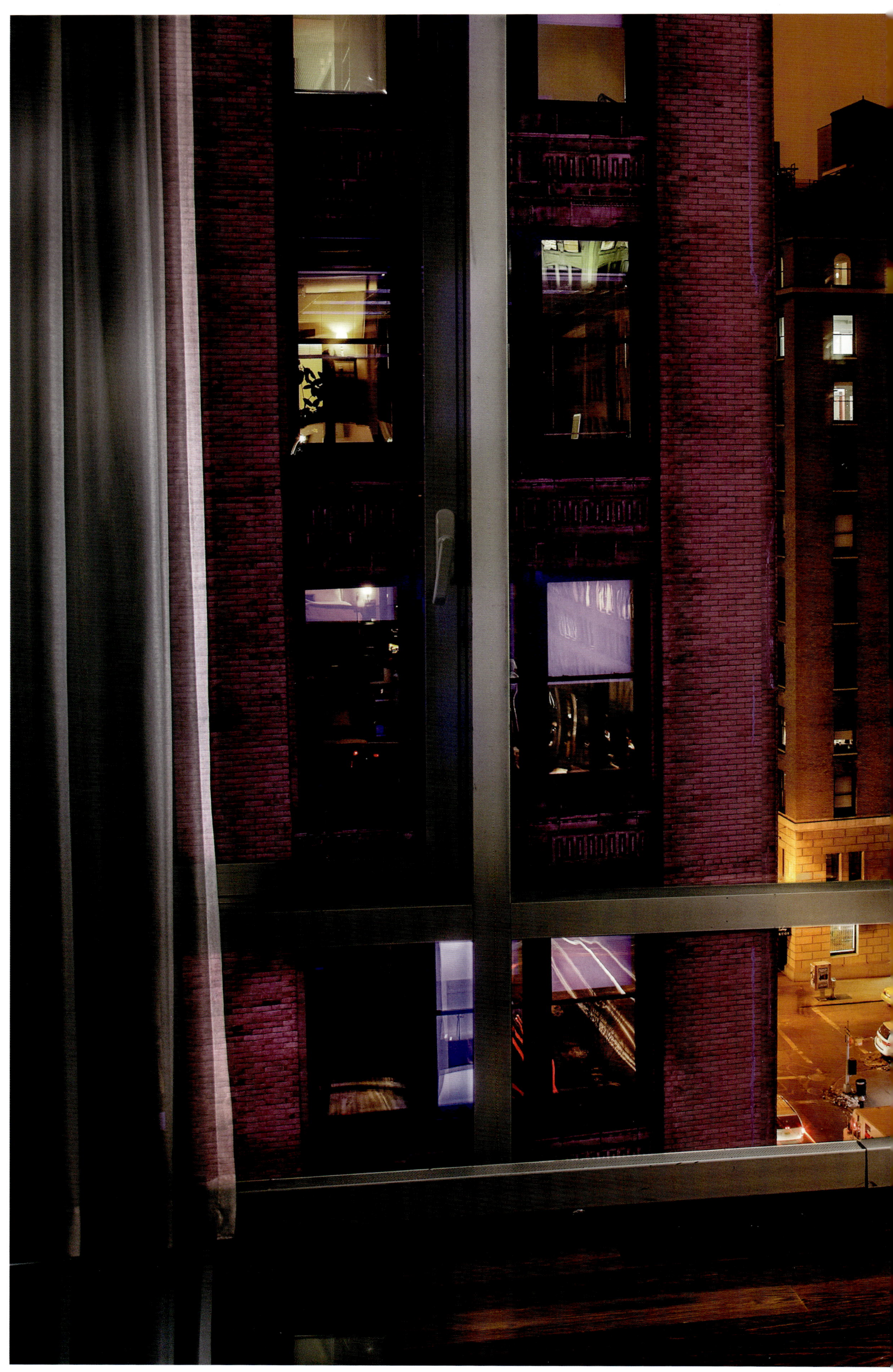

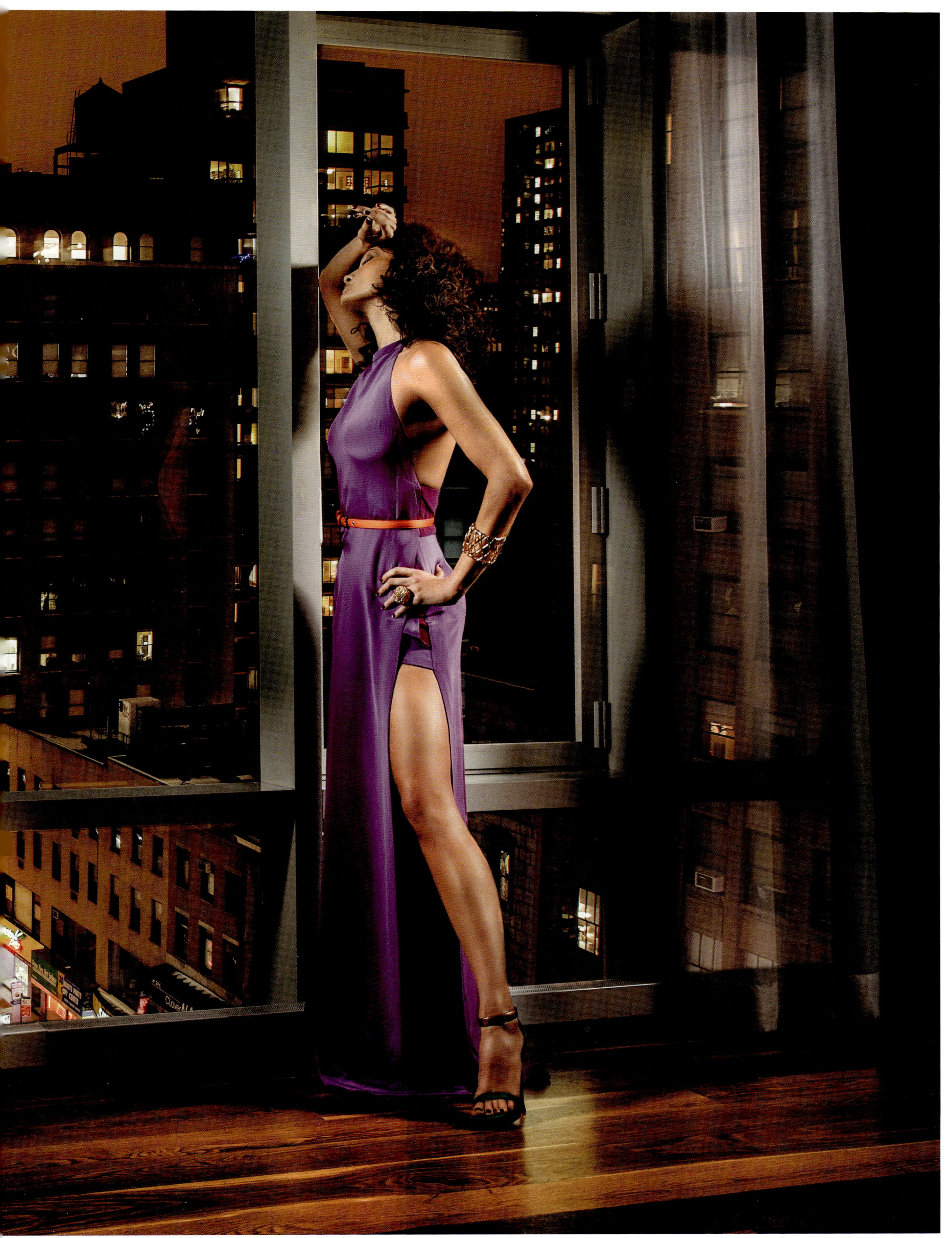

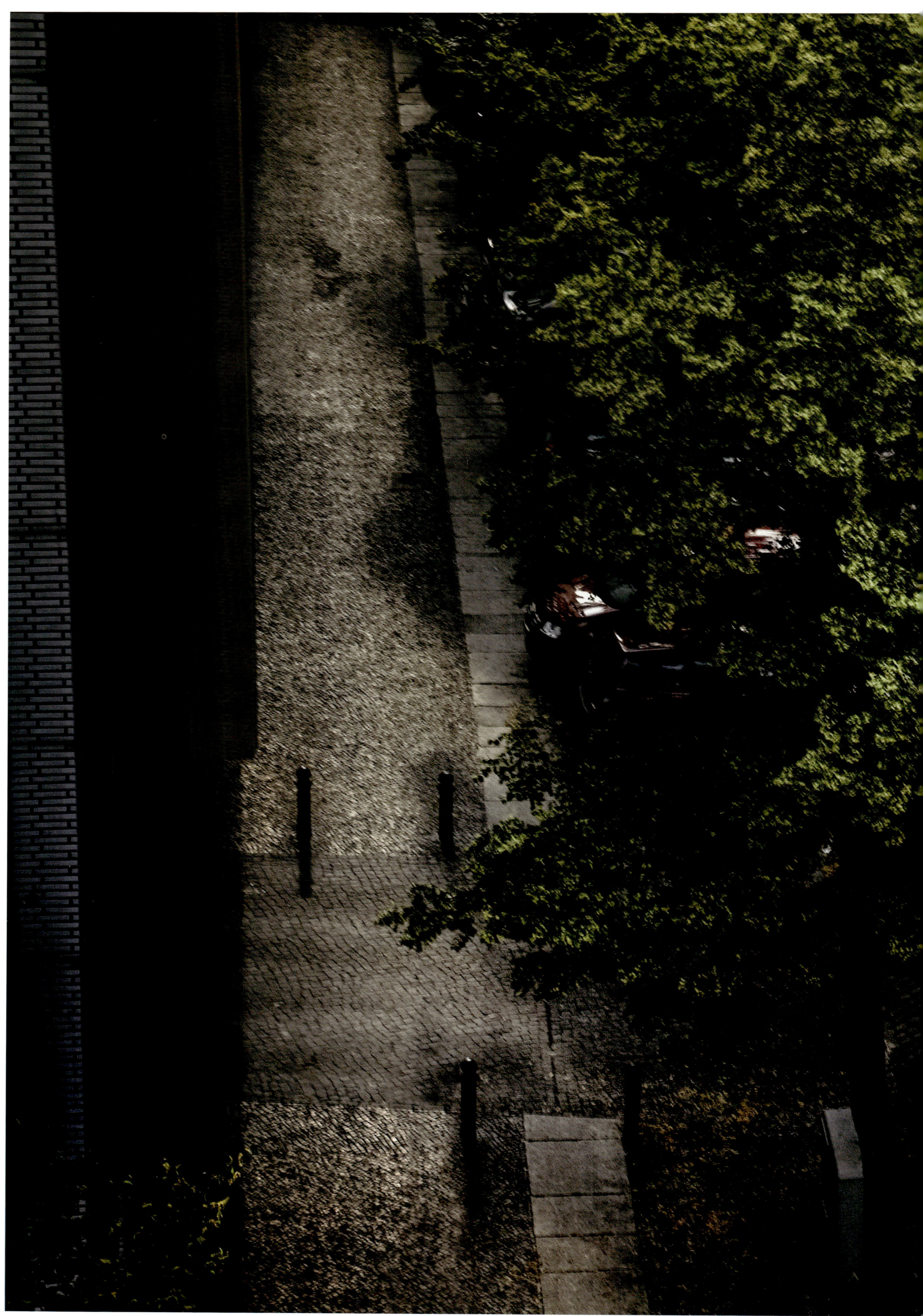

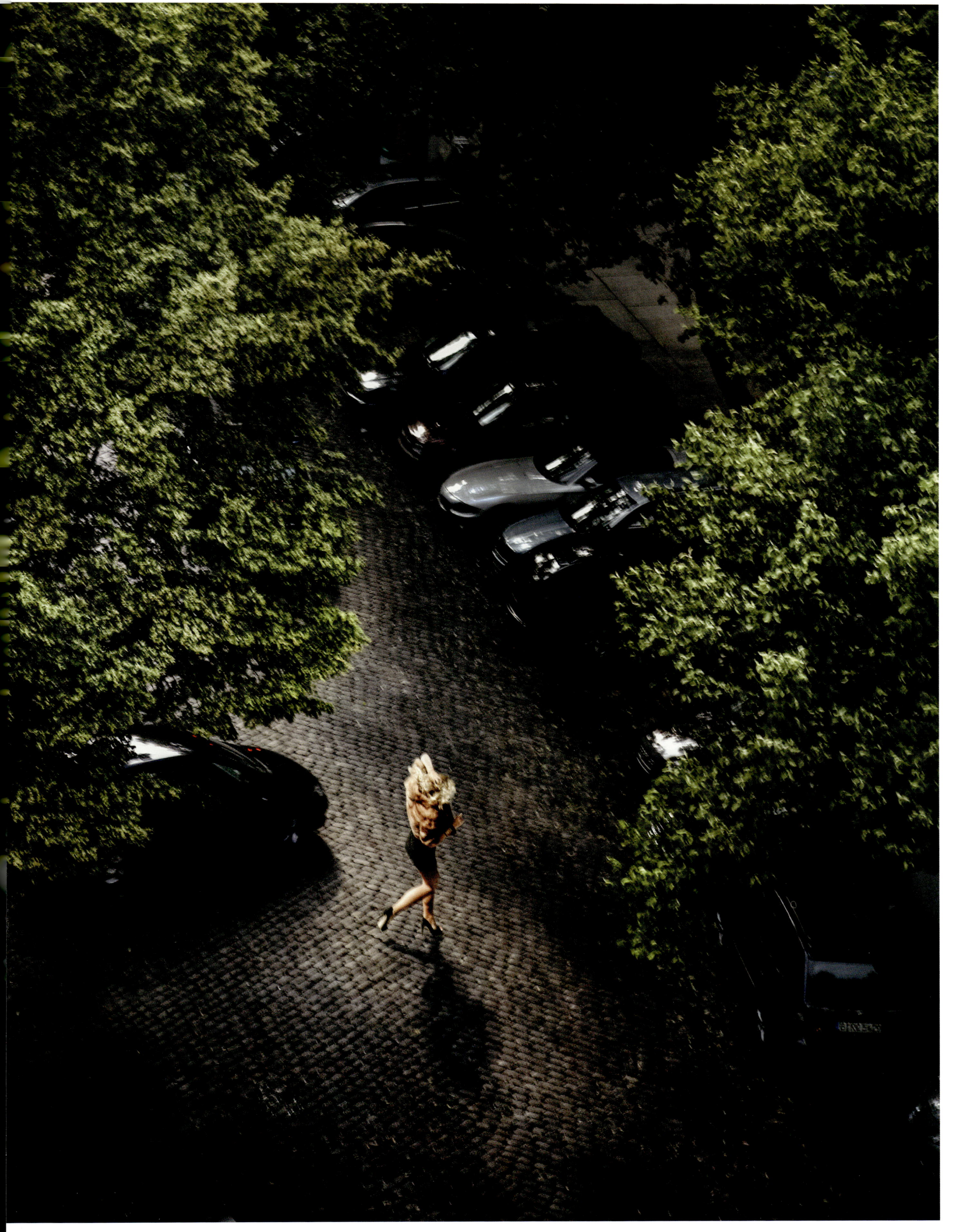

GIRL IN BERLIN | 2011

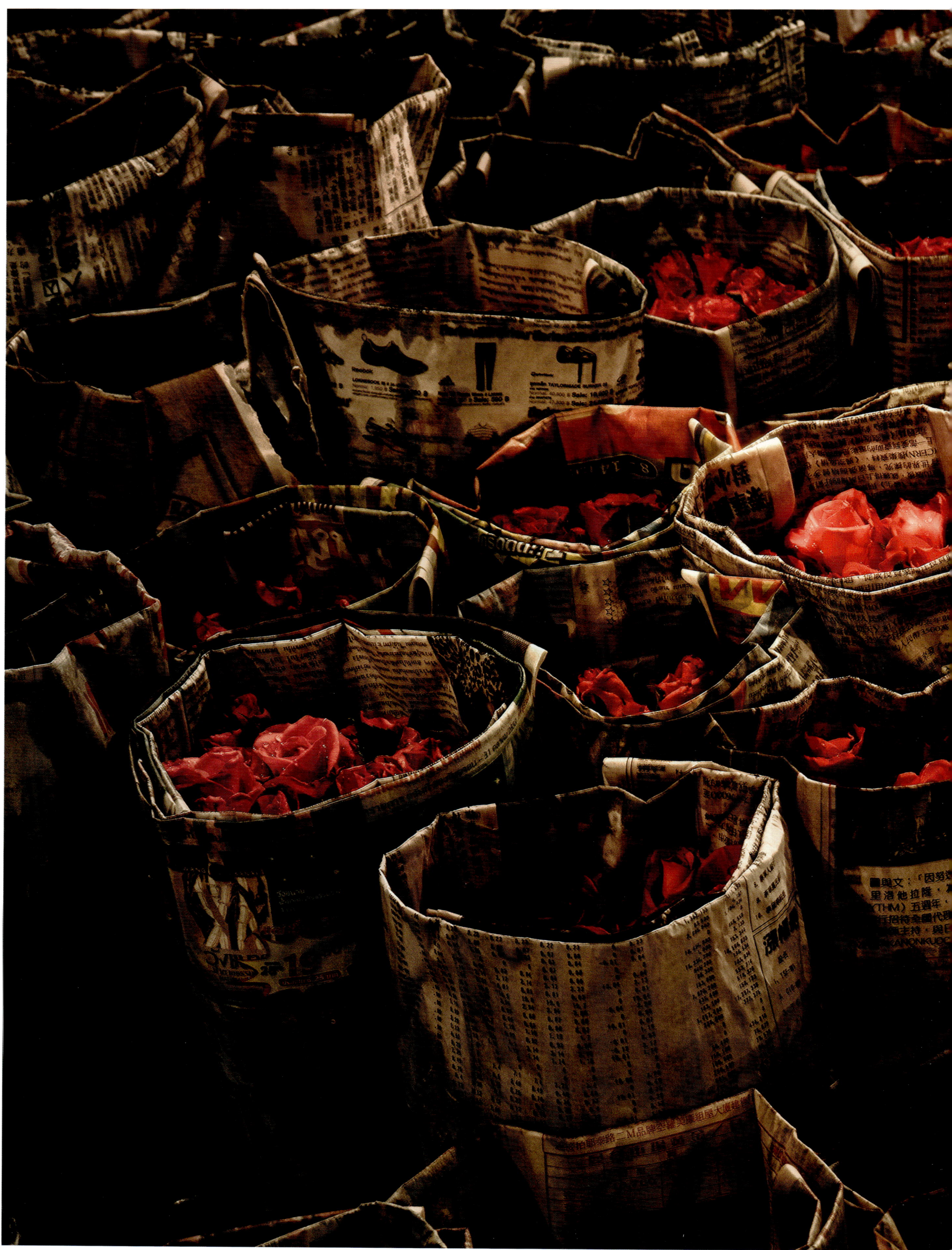

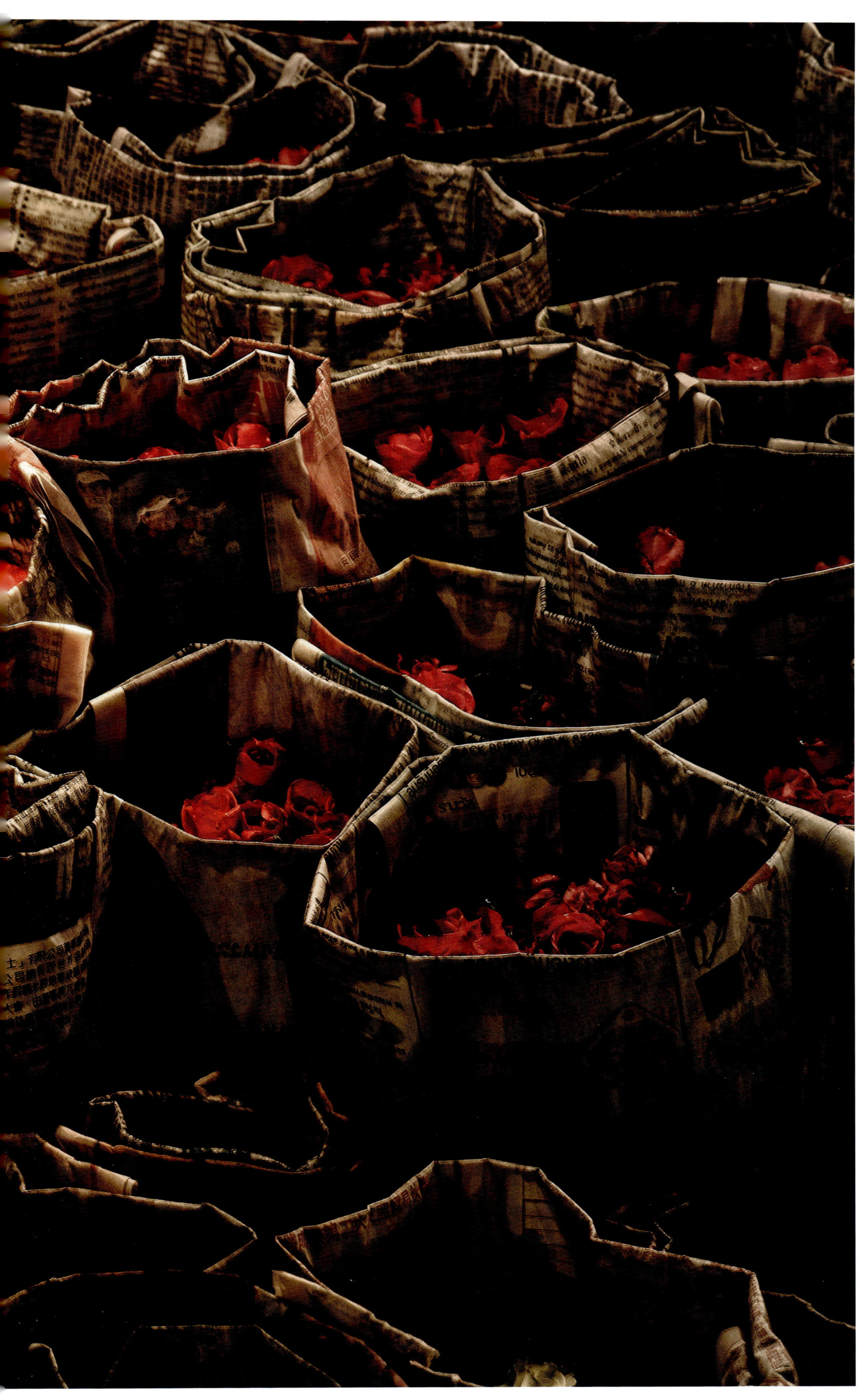

WAITING FOR LOVERS | 2012

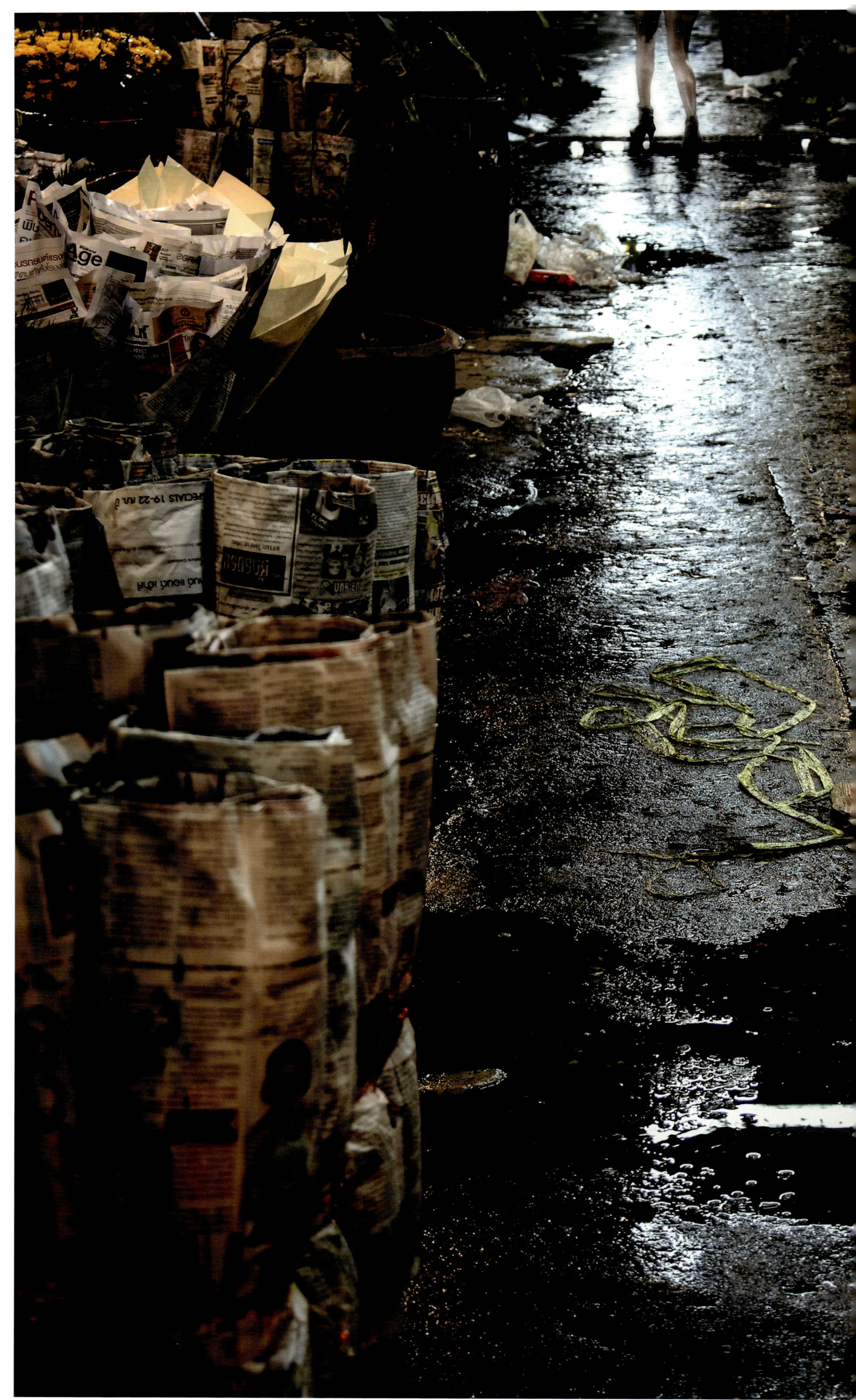

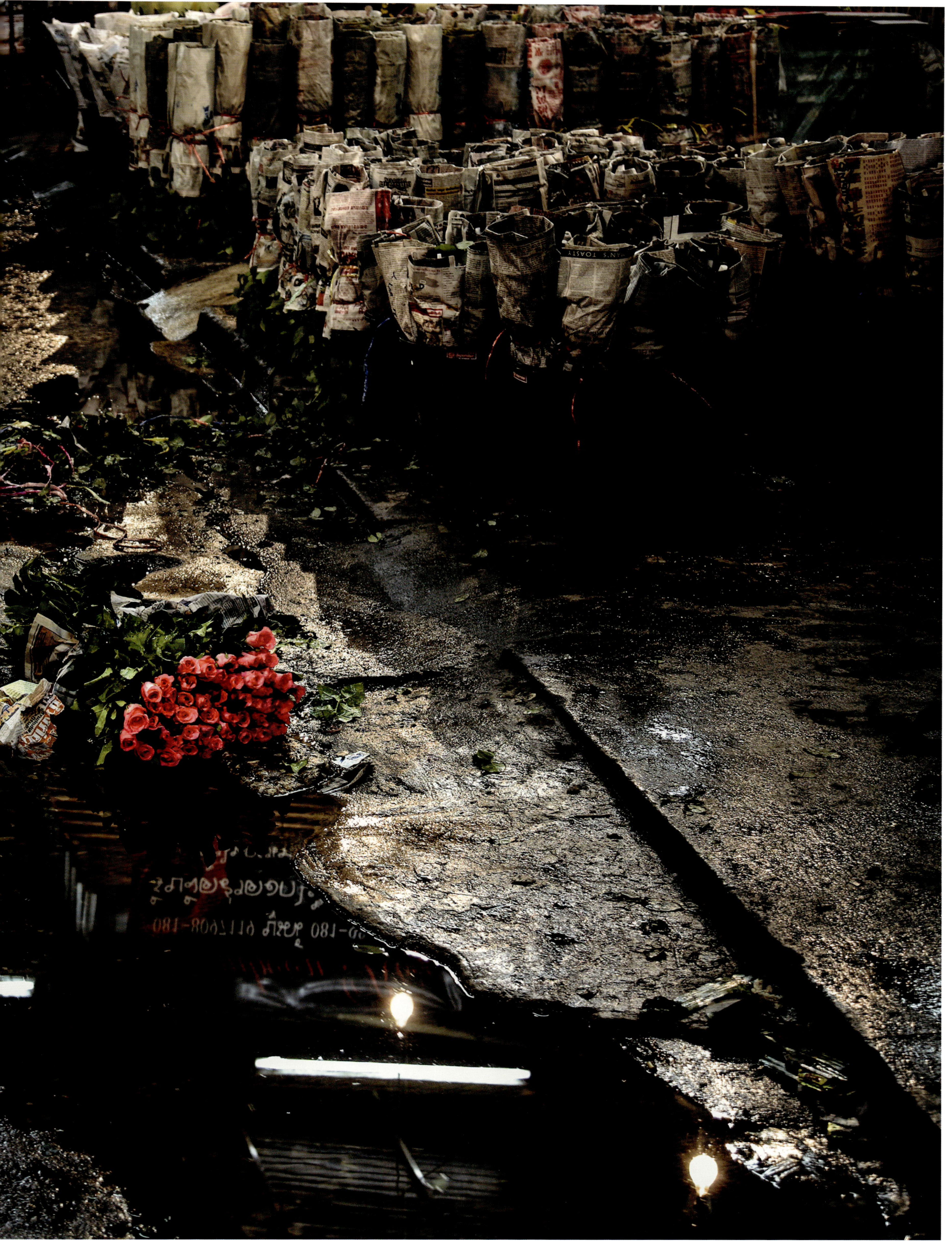

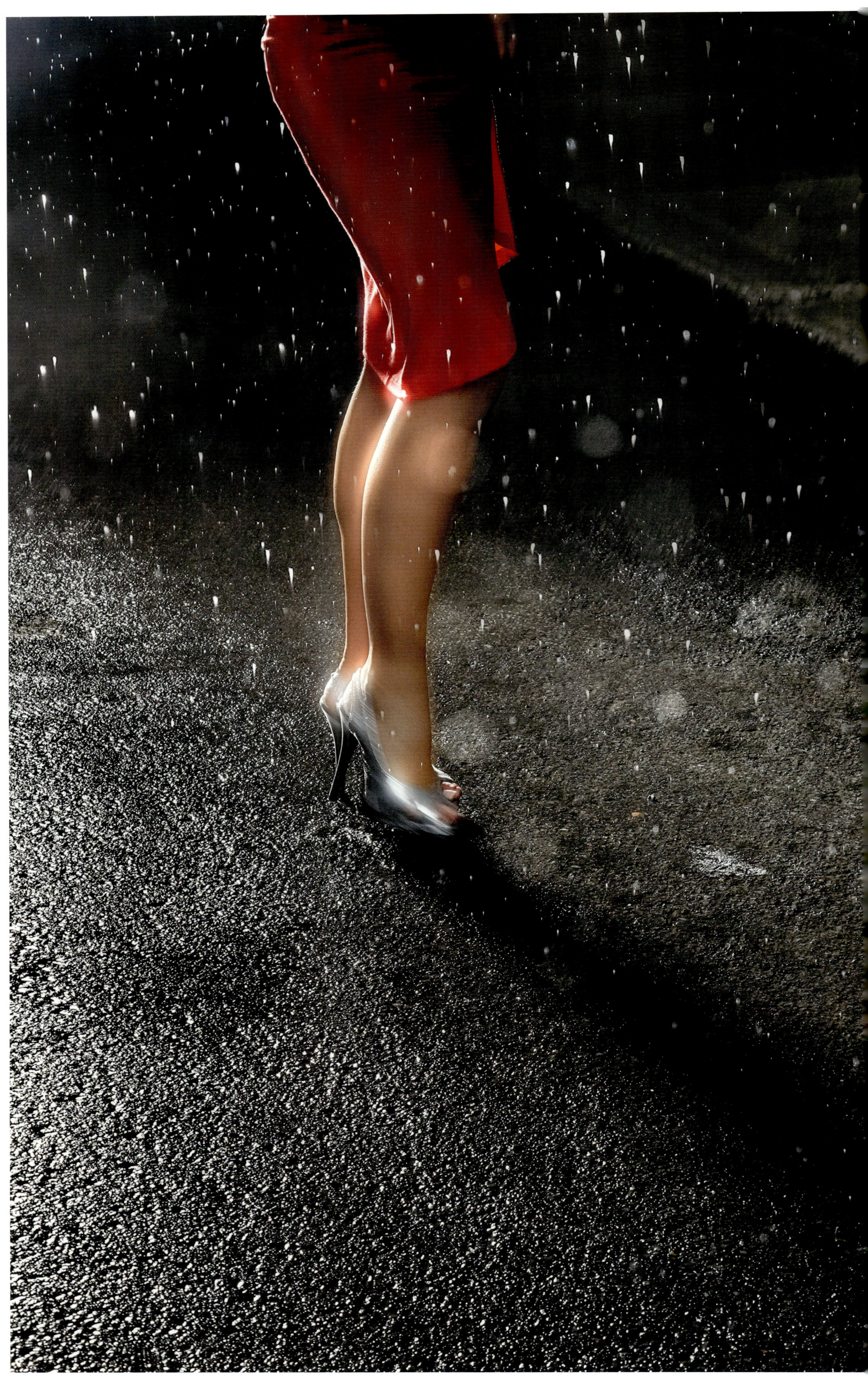

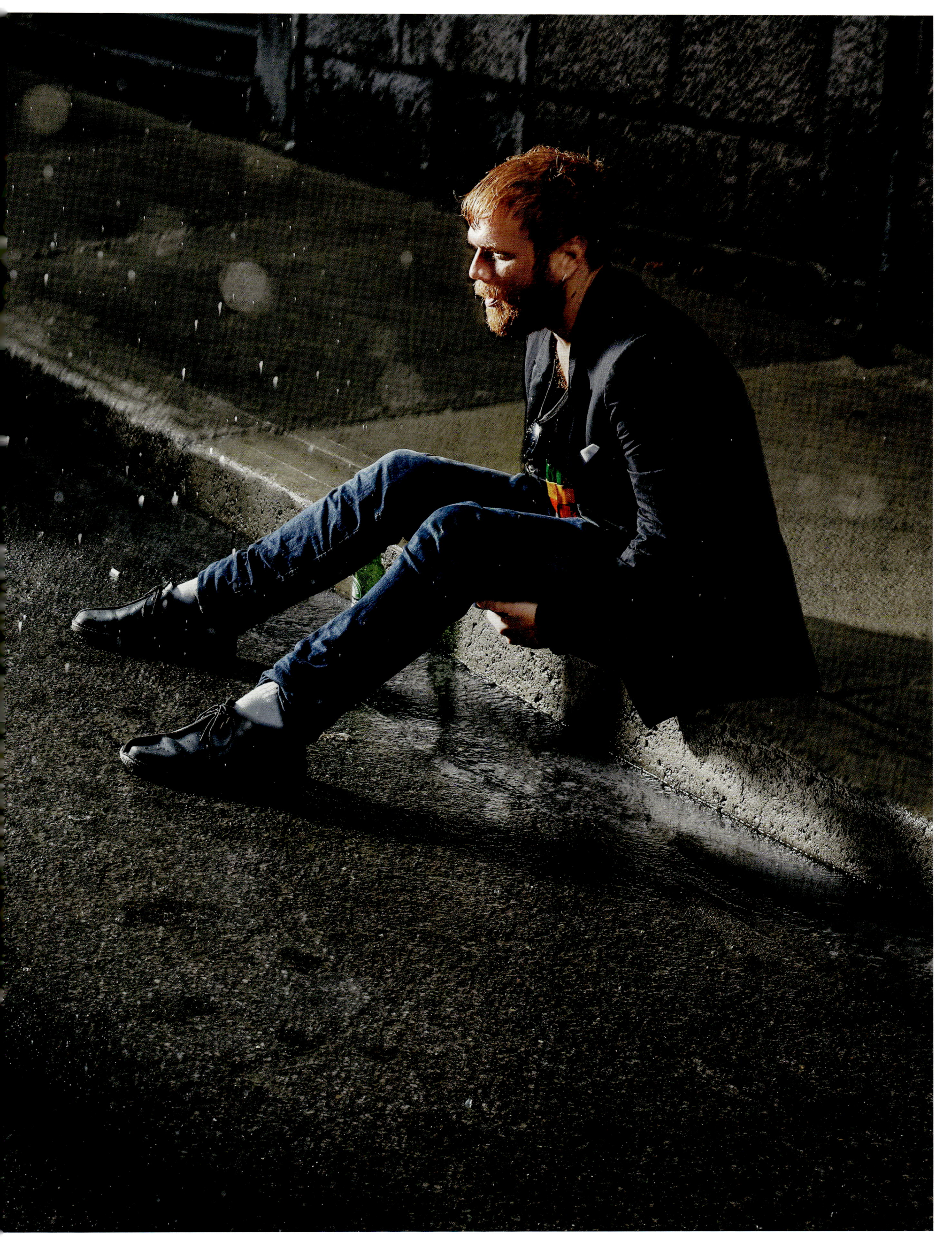

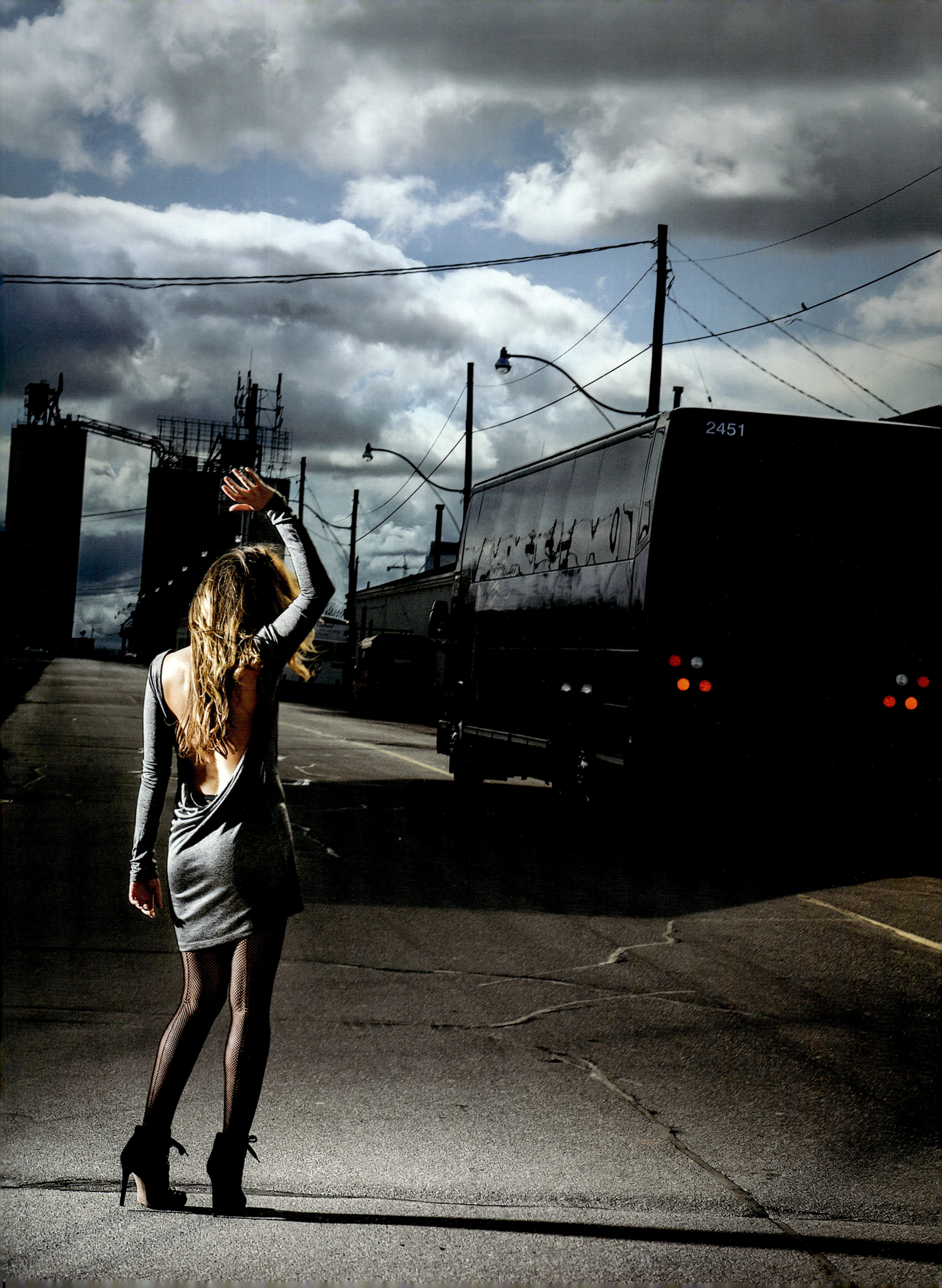
2451

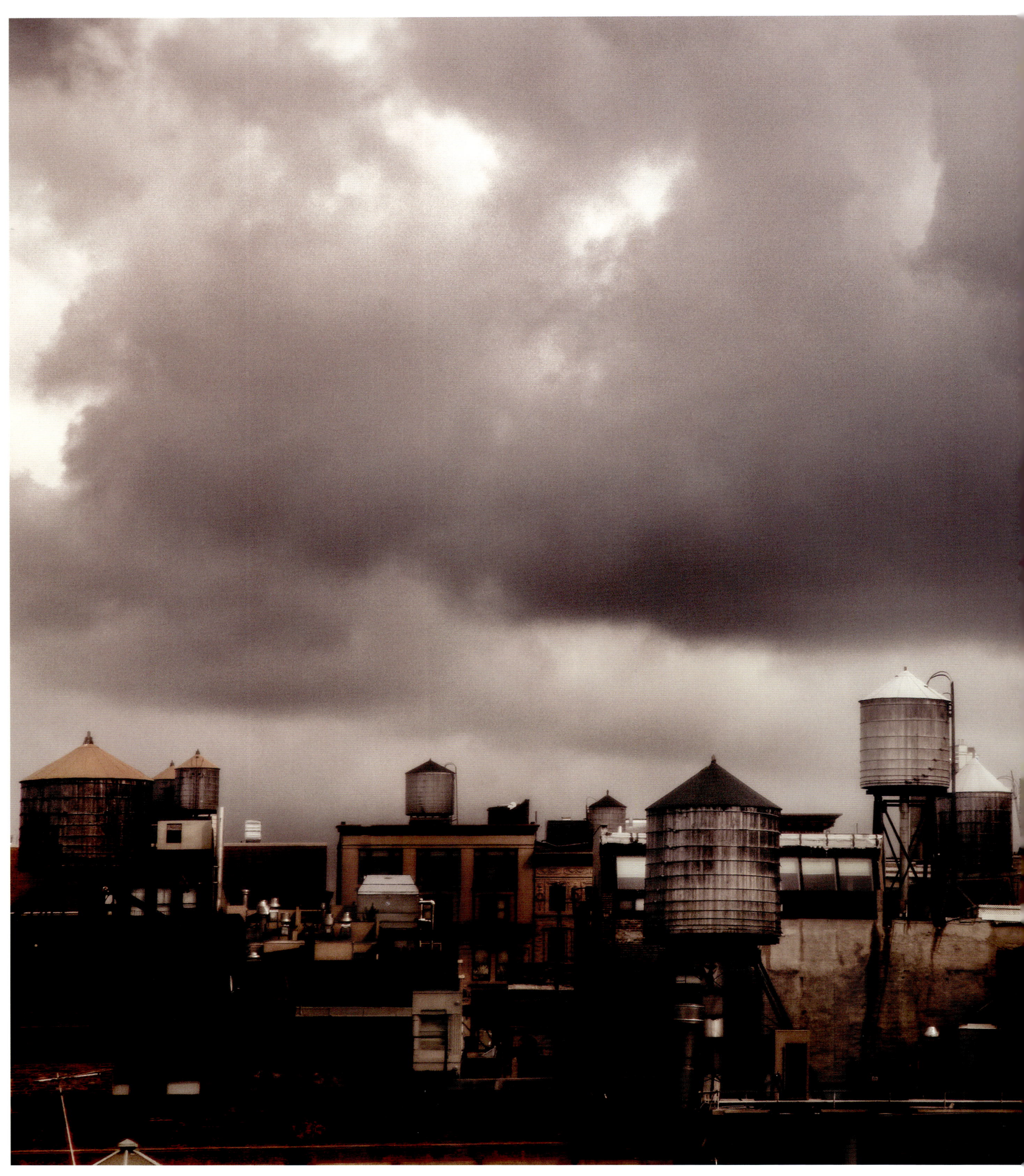

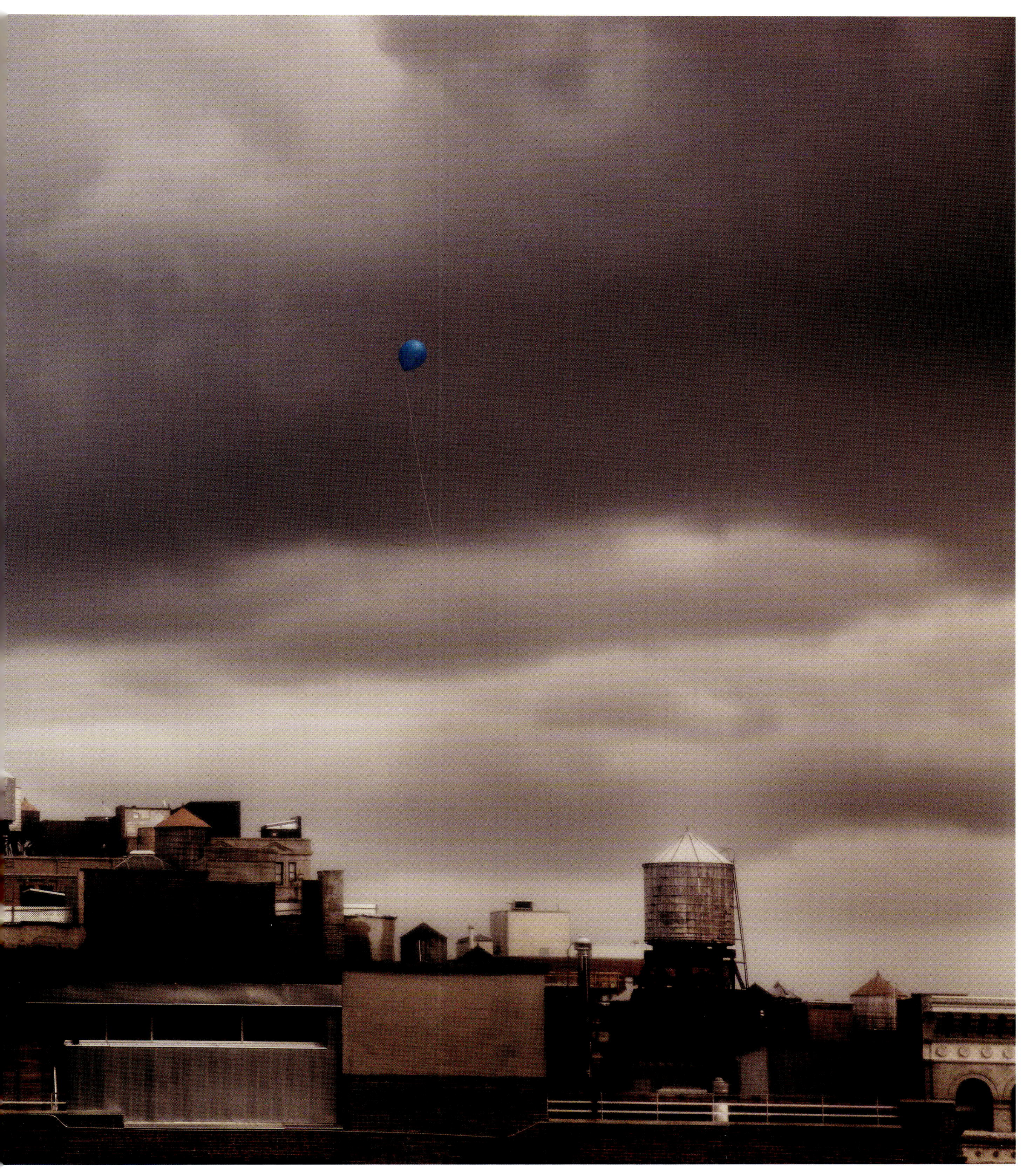

BALLOON OVER NYC | 2010

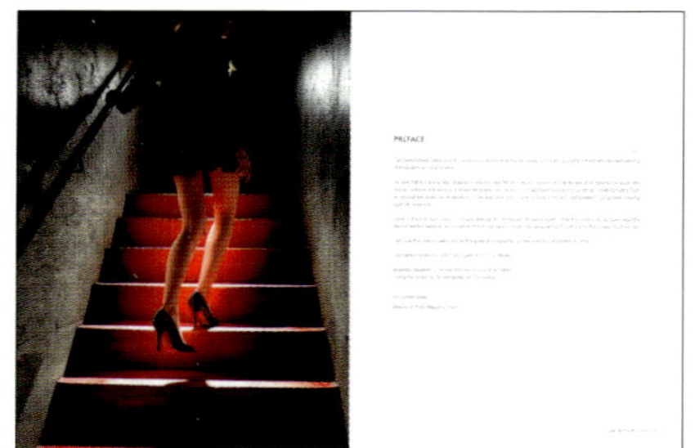
4 GIRL ON THE RED STEPS I 2012

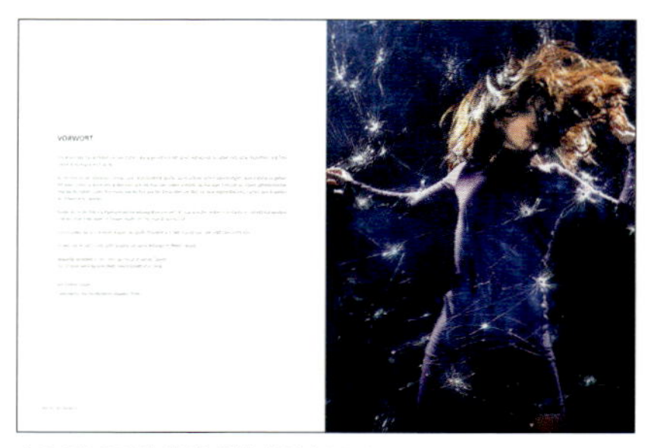
6 DODGING THE BULLET I 2012

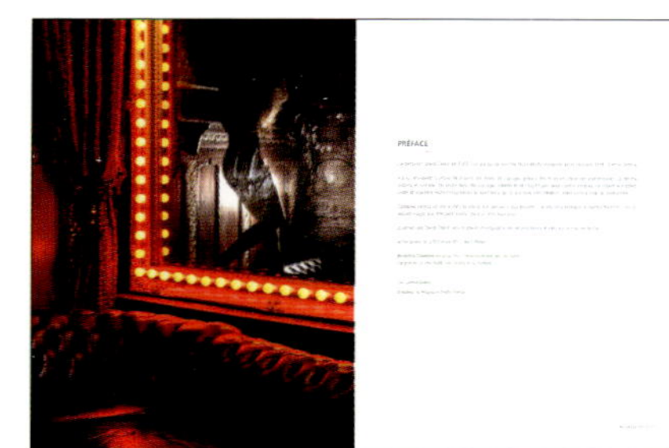
8 PHANTOM GIRL I 2012

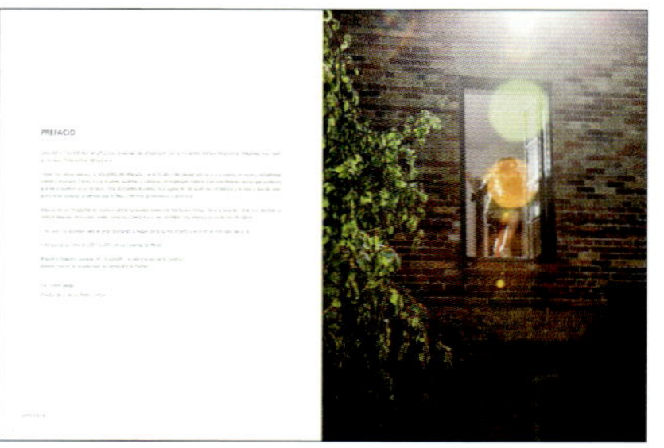
10 DANGER ZONE I 2012

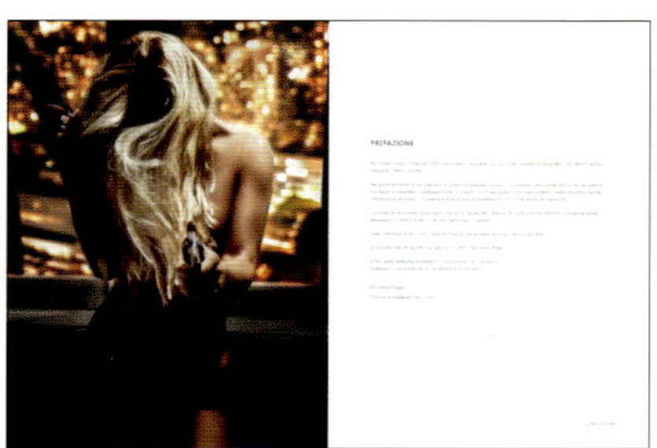
12 GLORIOUS DANGER I 2012

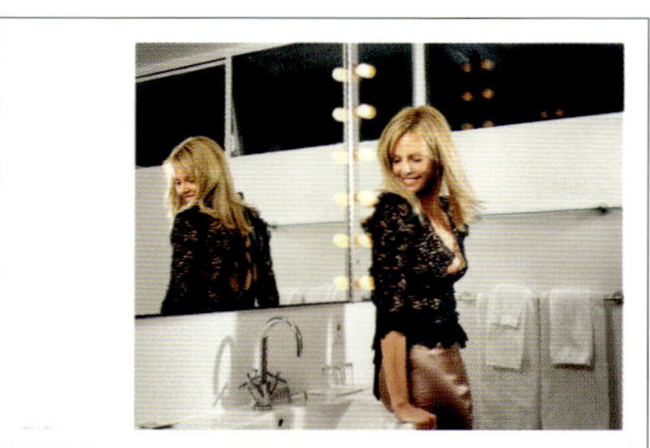
14 CHARLIZE IN MIRROR I 2003

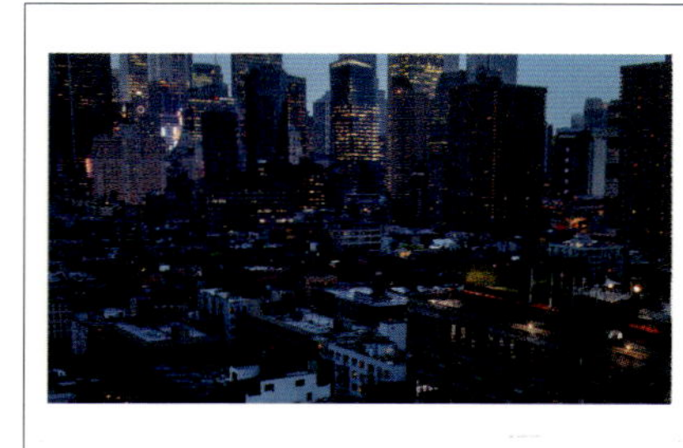
16 GIRL IN NEW YORK I 2011

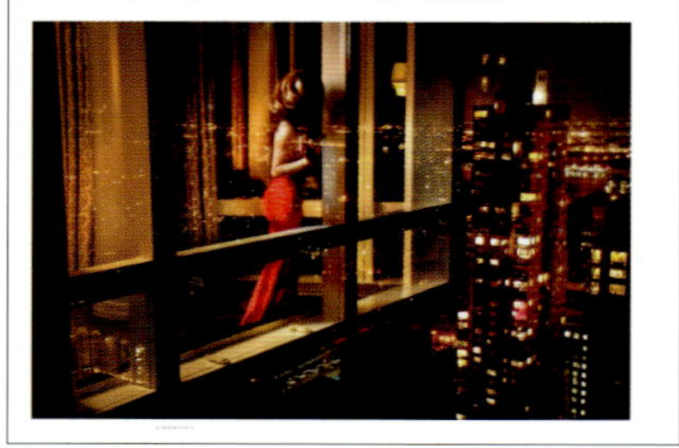
18 ULTIMATUM CITY I 2012

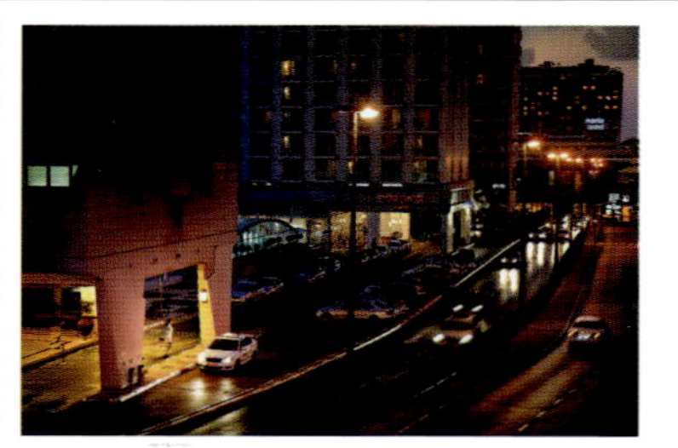
20 HEELS IN TEL AVIV I 2011

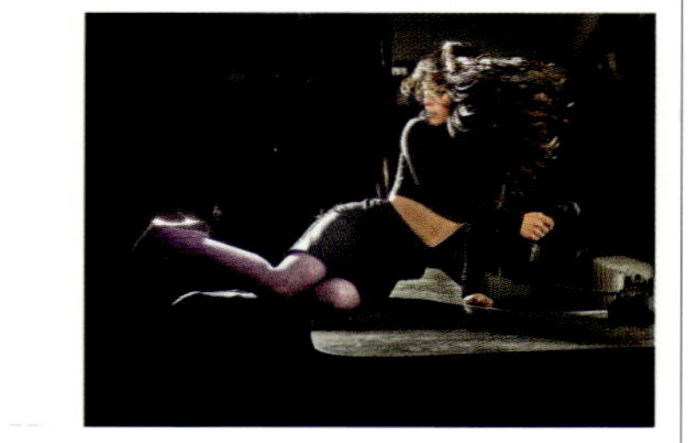
22 LONDON CALLING I 2012

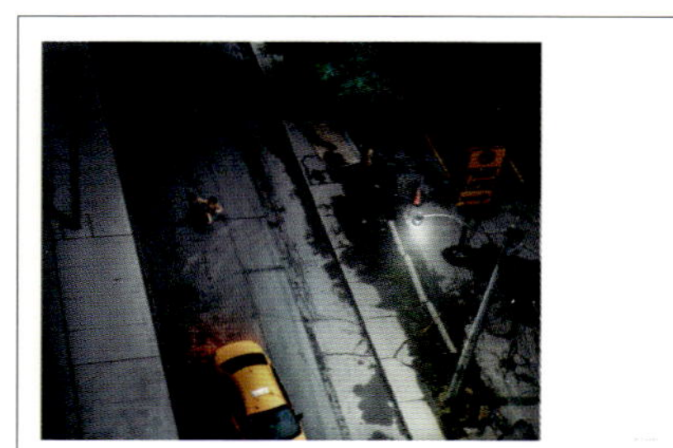
24 LOST CHANCE I 2011

26 DAWN IN NEW YORK I 2012

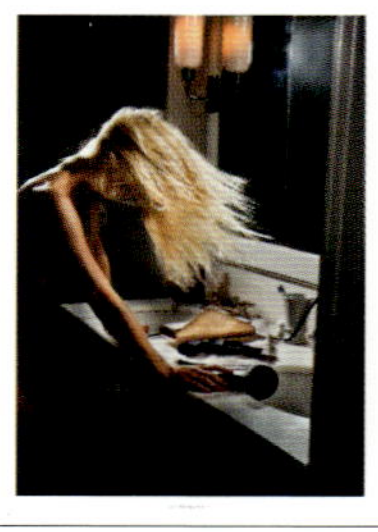
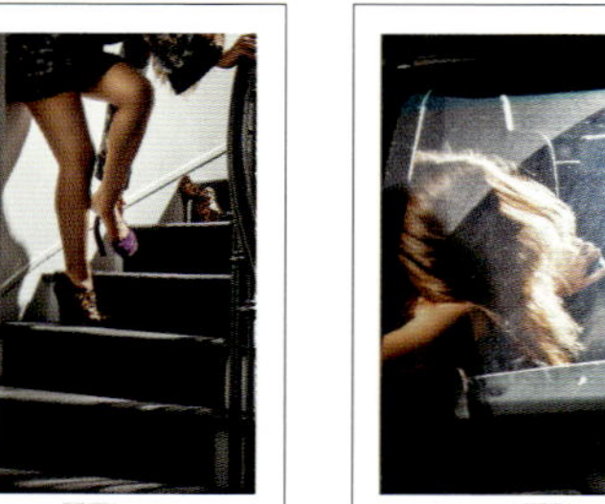
28 GETTING READY I 2012
29 INDECISIVE MOMENT I 2012

30 IN THE SPOTLIGHT I 2012

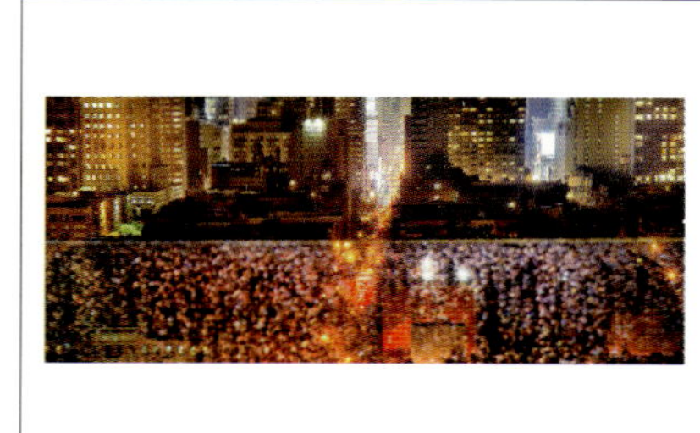
32 DREAMS OF NEW YORK I 2012

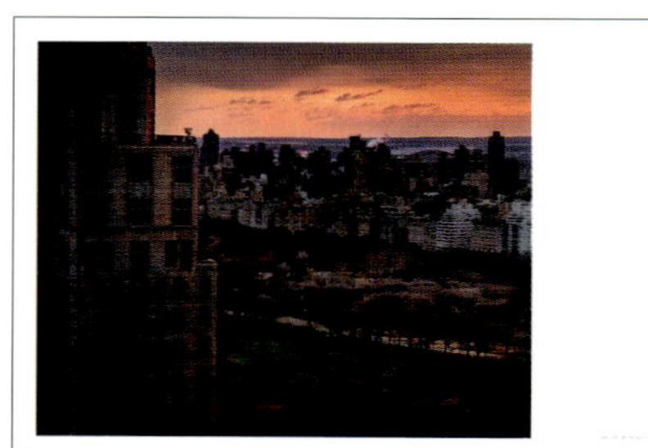
34 GIRL OVER CENTRAL PARK I 2012

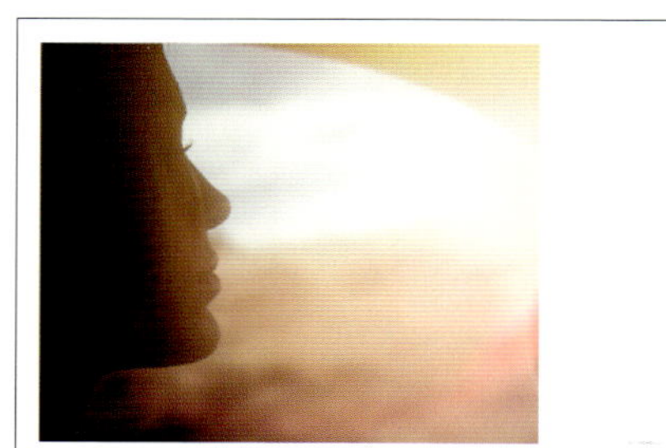
36 HAZY DREAMS I 2012

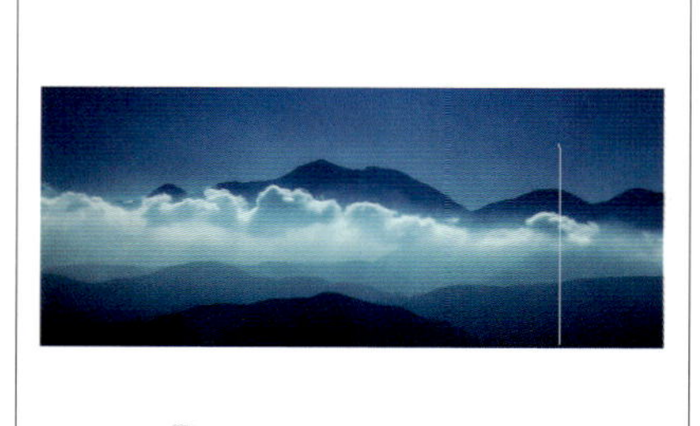
38 HEAVEN I 2012

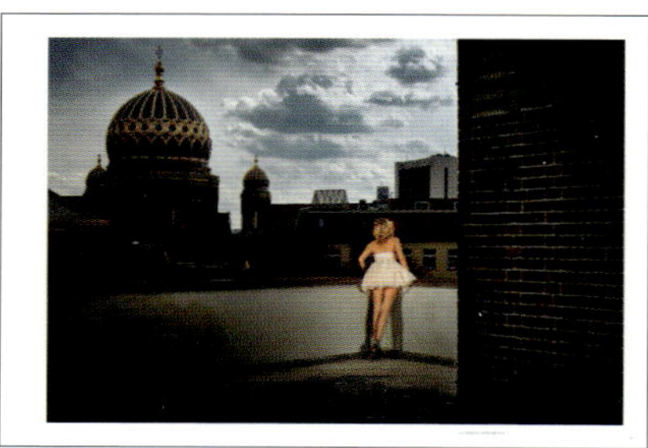
40 AFTERNOON FROM BERLIN I 2011

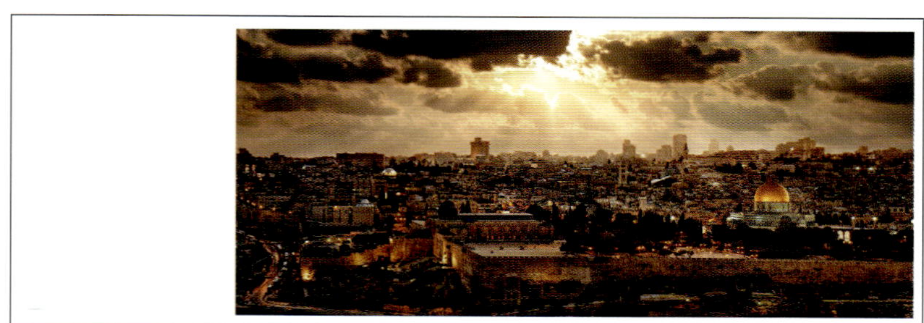
43 JERUSALEM I 2011

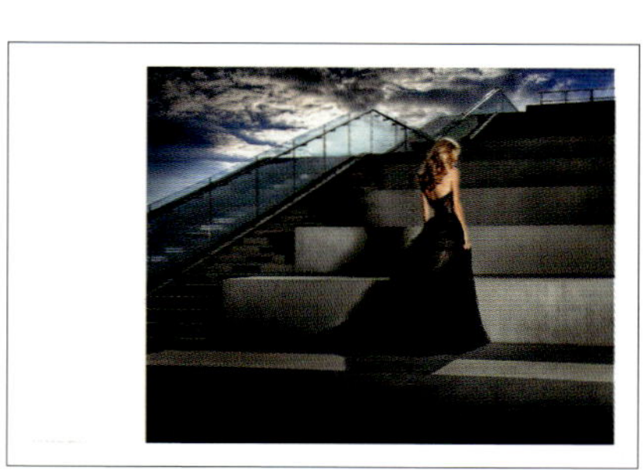
48 THE GIRL IN THE BLACK DRESS I 2011

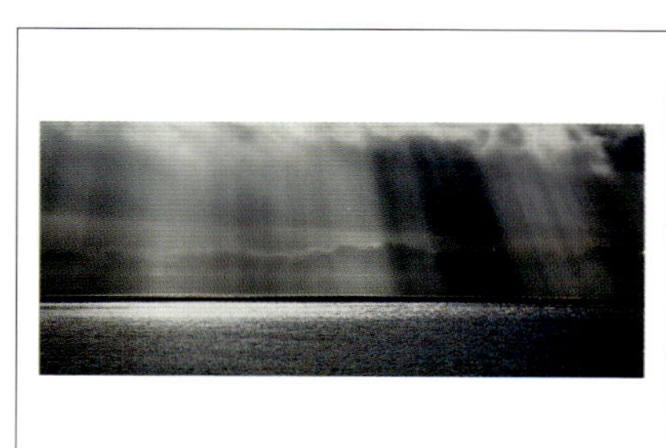
50 HEAVEN CAN WAIT I 2011

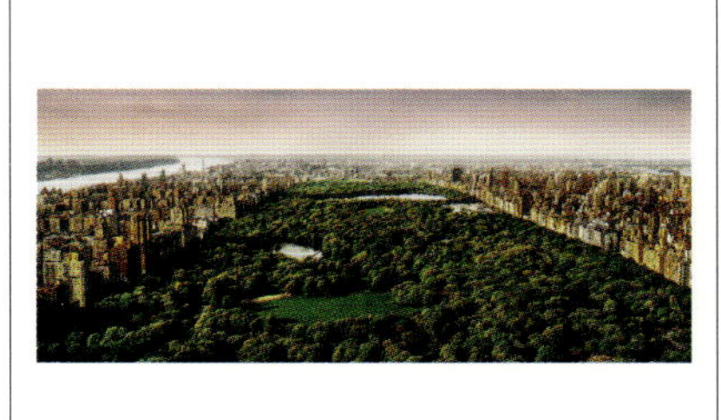
52 DREAMS OF CENTRAL PARK I 2006

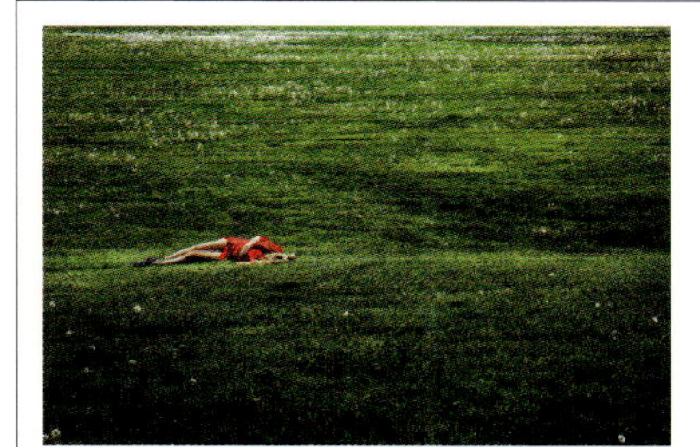
54 FIELD OF DREAMS I 2012

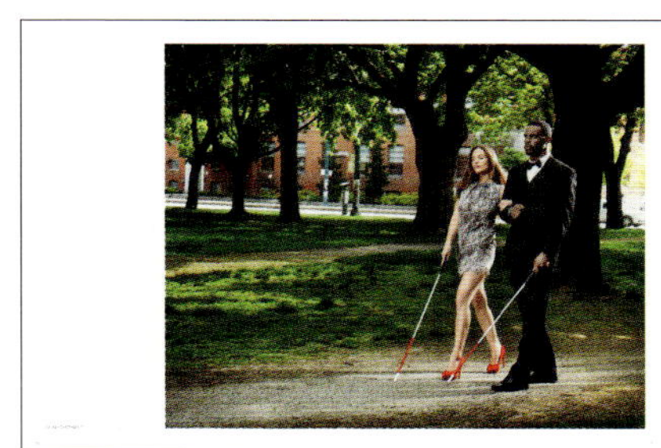
56 STICKED TOGETHER I 2012

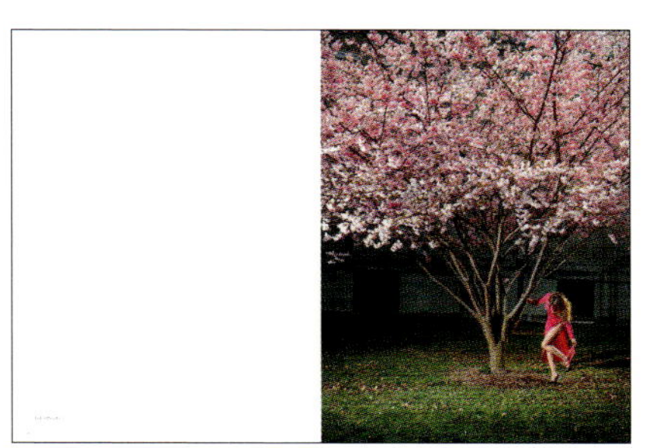
58 PINK MOMENT I 2012

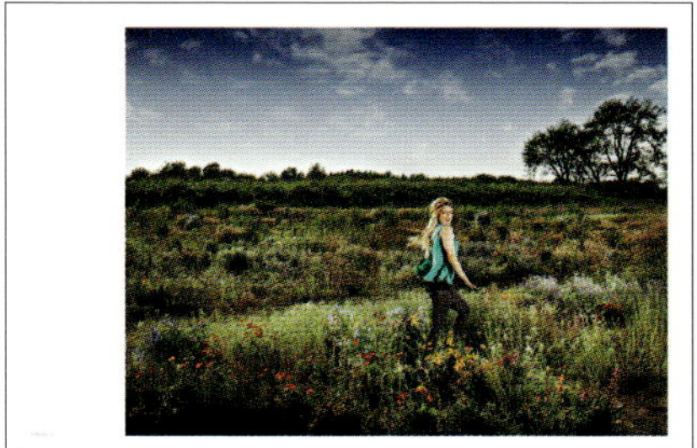
60 FERGIE I 2007

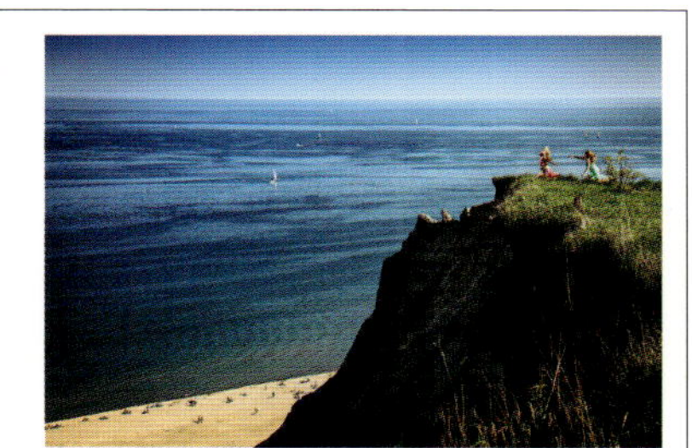
62 BEAUTIFUL DISASTERS I 2012

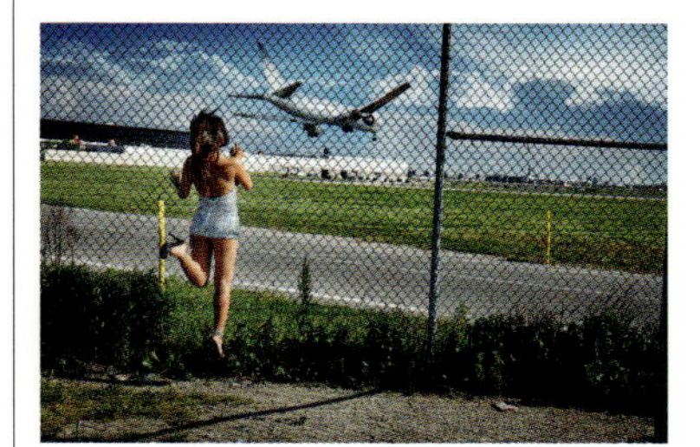
64 COMING HOME I 2012

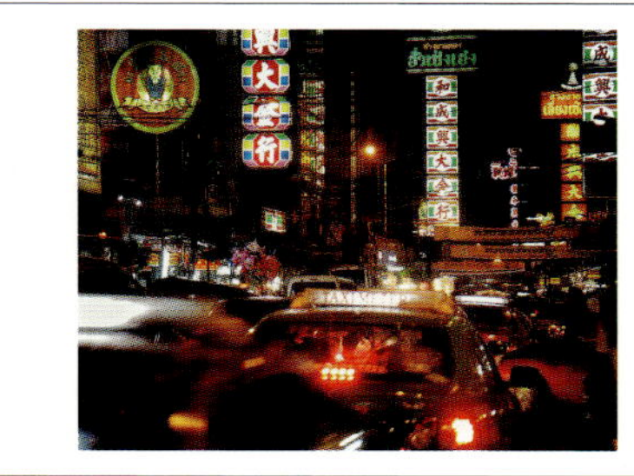
66 TAXI LOVERS I 2011

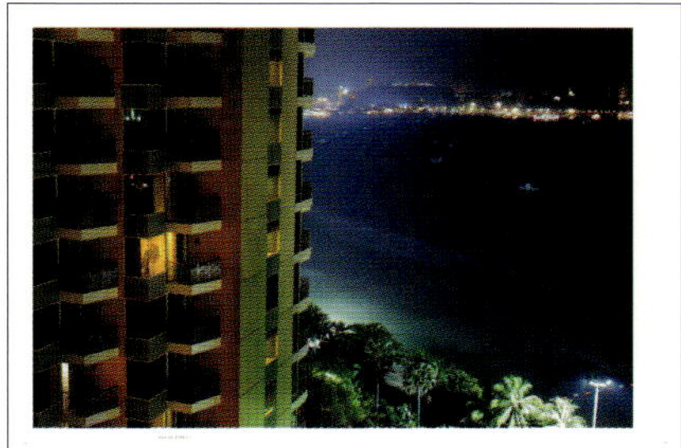
68 NOW OR NEVER I 2011

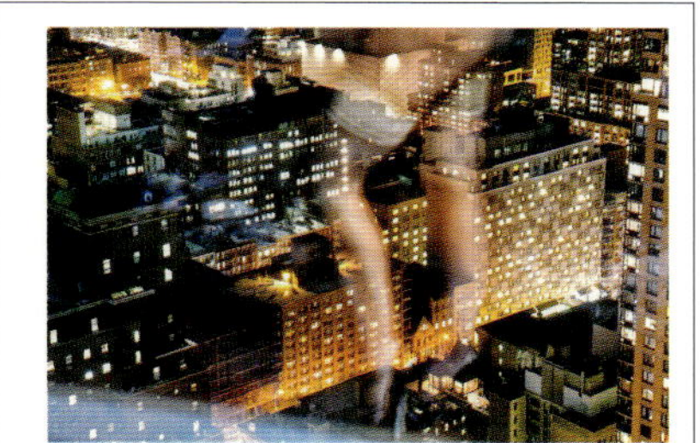
70 FLASHING THE CITY I 2012

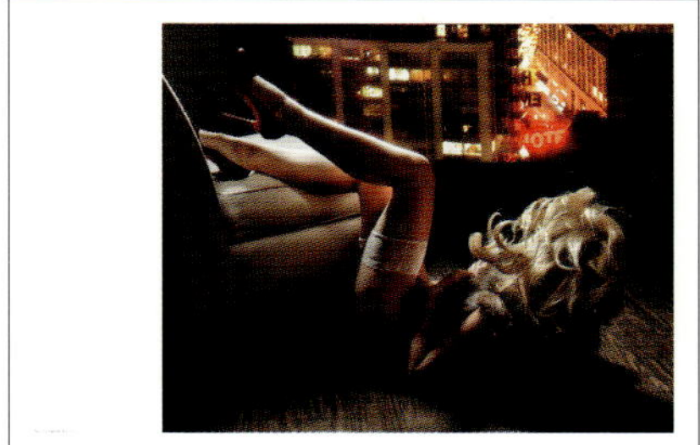
72 BIG CITY BLONDE I 2012

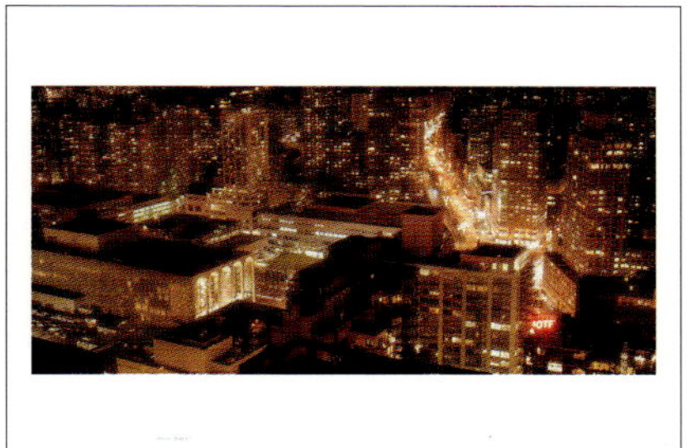
74 LINCOLN CENTER I 2012

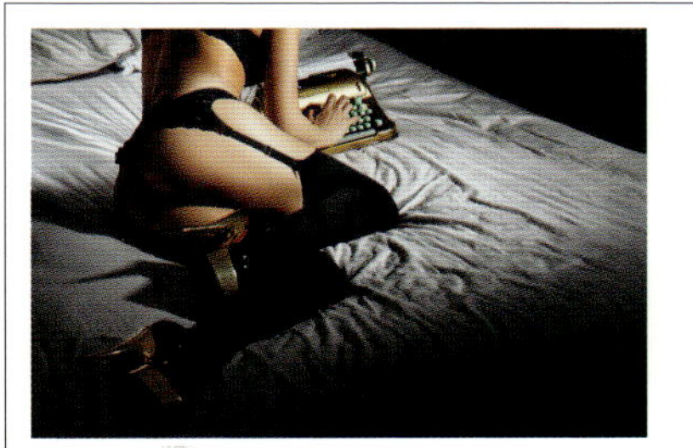
76 LOVE LETTER I 2012

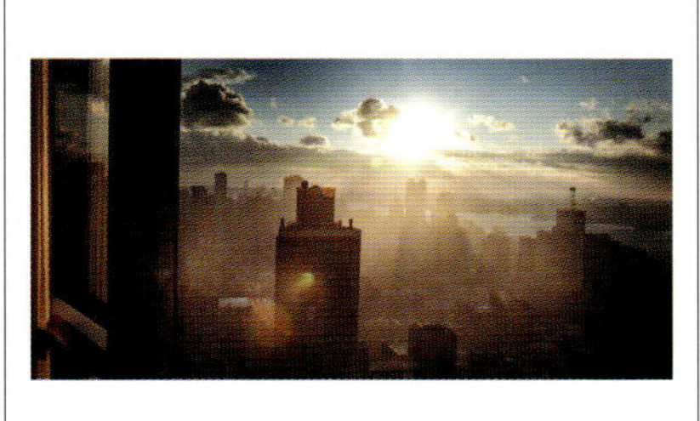
78 AWAKENING CITY I 2012

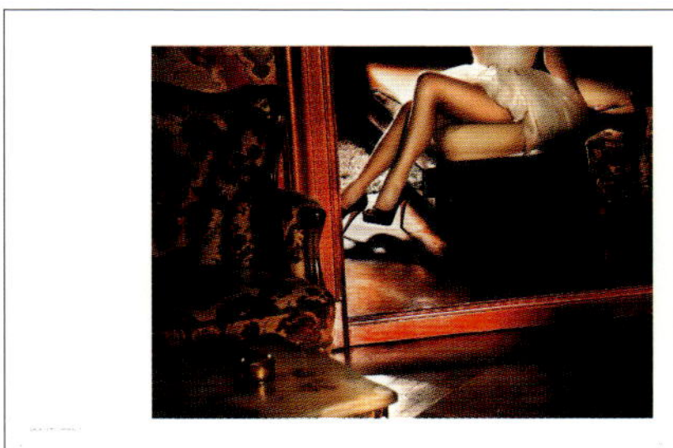
80 GIRL IN THE RED MIRROR I 2011

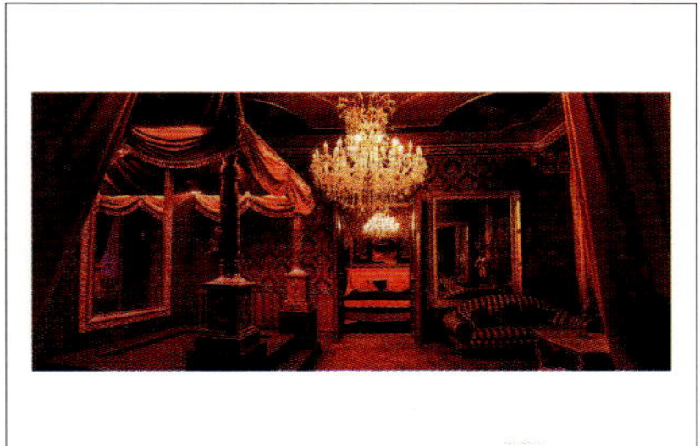
82 PLACE D'AMOUR I 2012

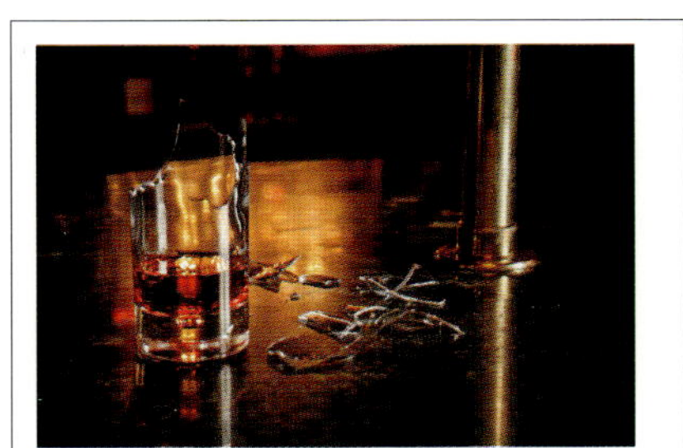
84 GAME OVER I 2012

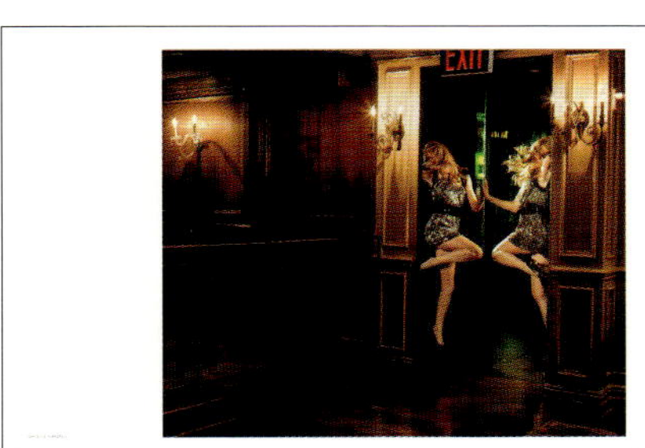

86 DANCING IN MIRROR I 2012

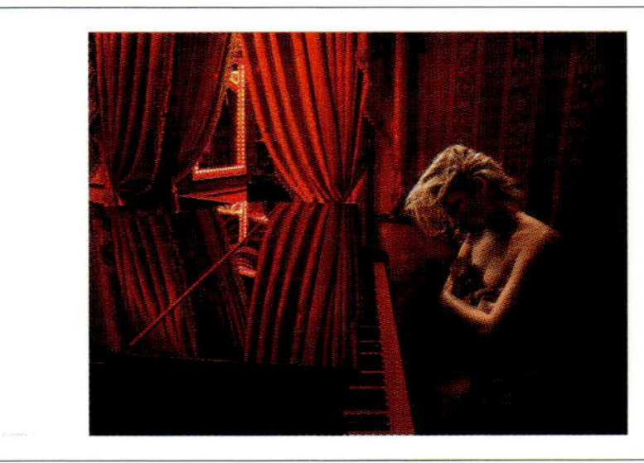
88 GOOD NIGHT I 2012

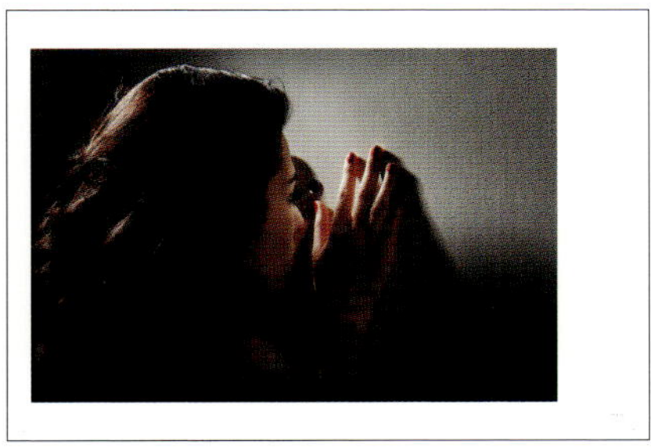
90 SPY I 2011

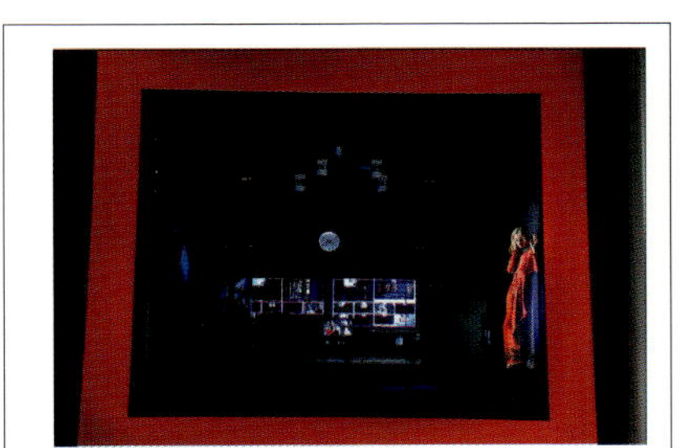
92 ALL IN RED I 2012

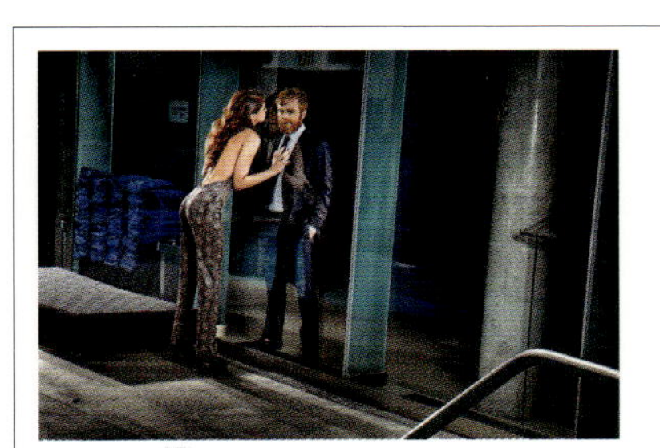
94 LADIES MAN I 2011

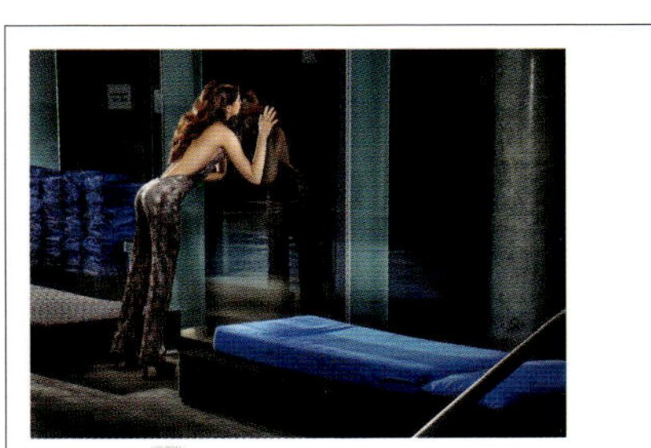
96 KISSING HERSELF I 2011

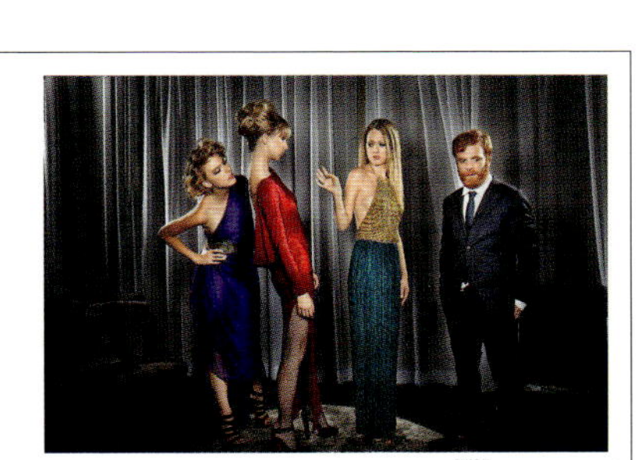
98 WHO'S THE ONE? I 2011

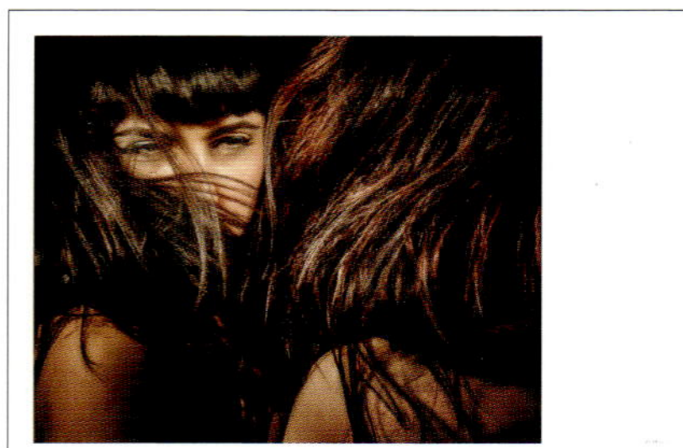
100 JUST ME I 2012

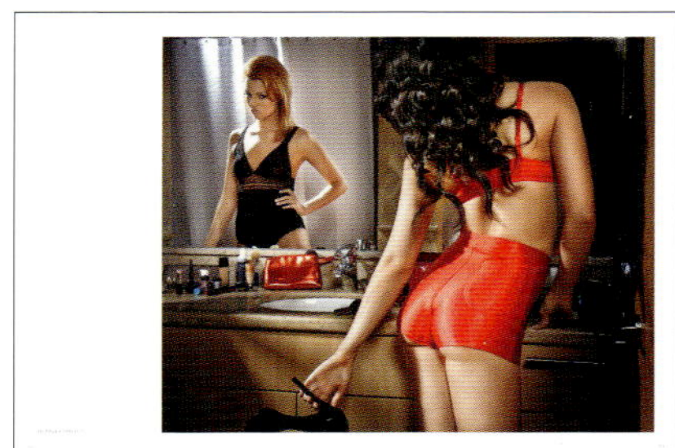
102 FACING EACH OTHER I 2012

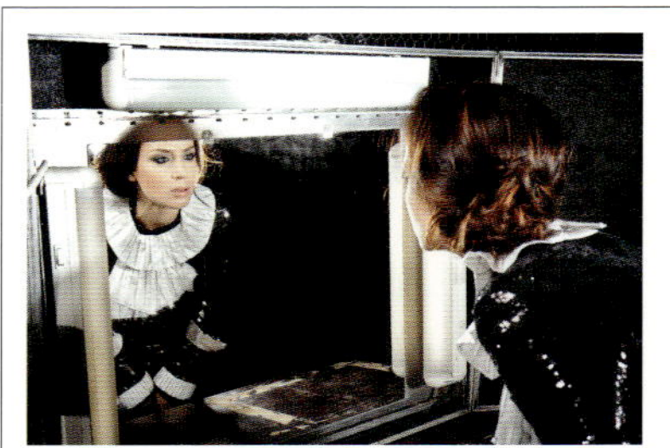
104 EMILY BLUNT I 2010

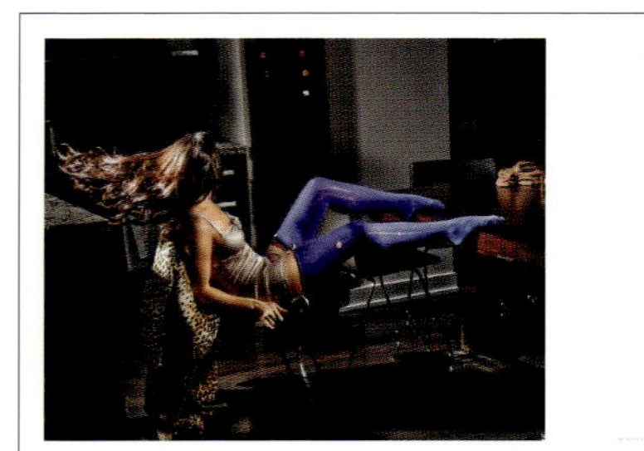
106 FOLLOWING NO RULES II I 2012

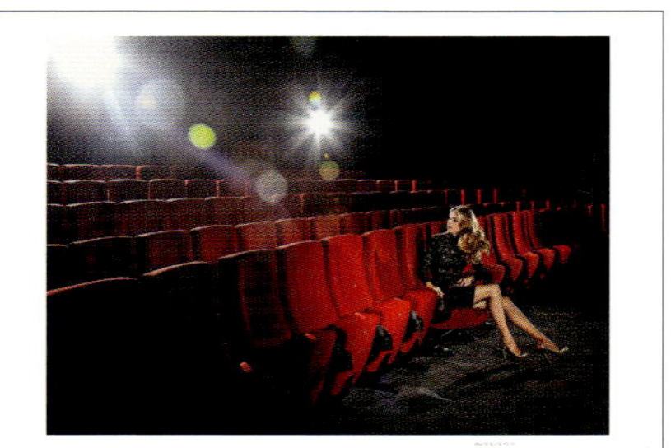
108 PRIVATE AUDITION I 2011

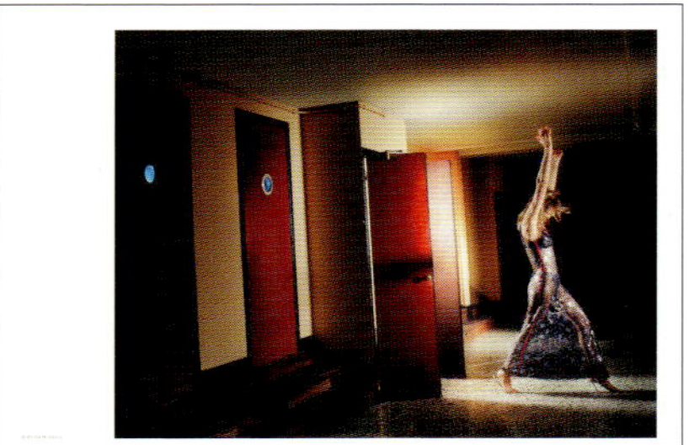
110 READY FOR ACTION I 2004

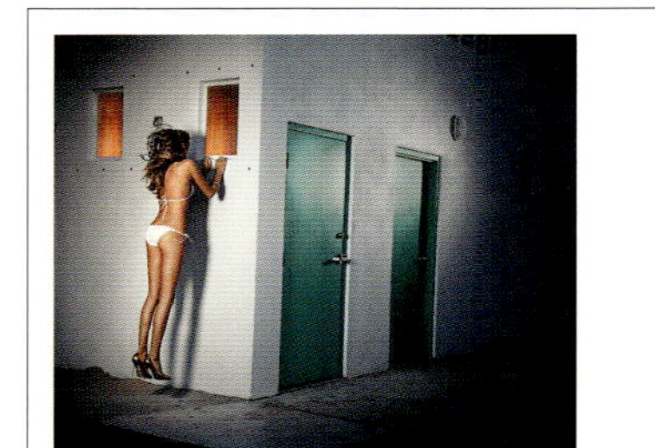
112 PEEPING I 2011

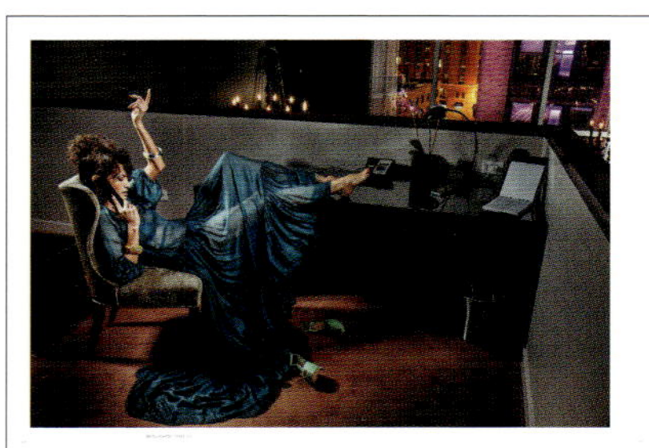
114 ENOUGH ABOUT YOU I 2011

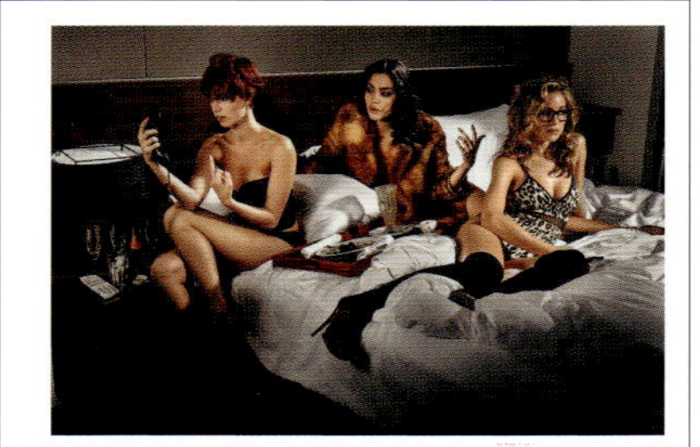
116 THE THREE OF US I 2011

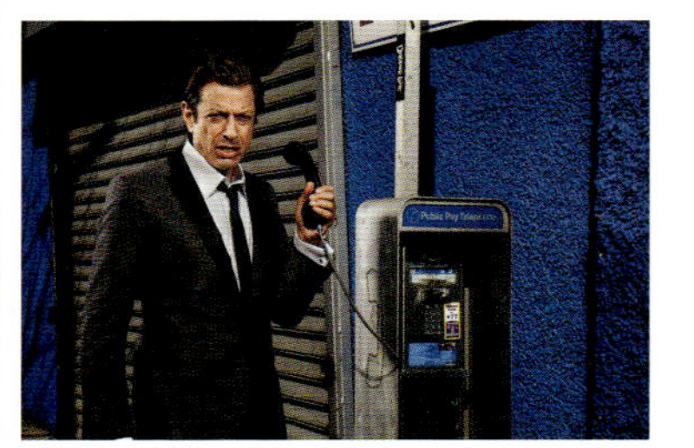
118 JEFF IS CALLING I 2010

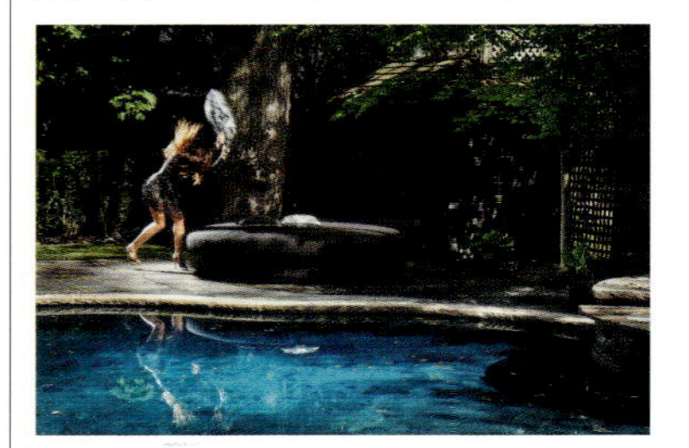
120 FREAKING OUT I 2012

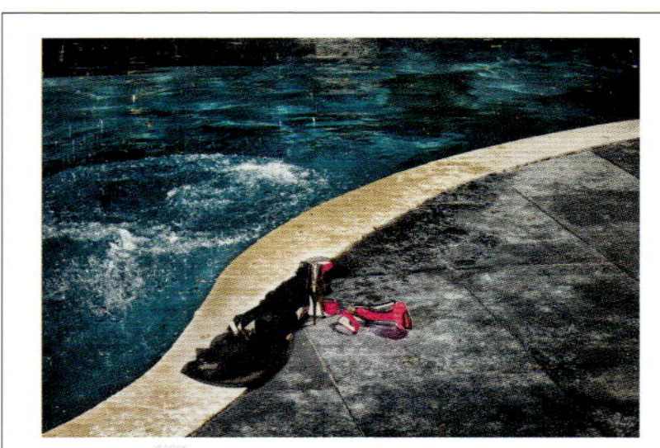
122 SPLASH & HEELS I 2012

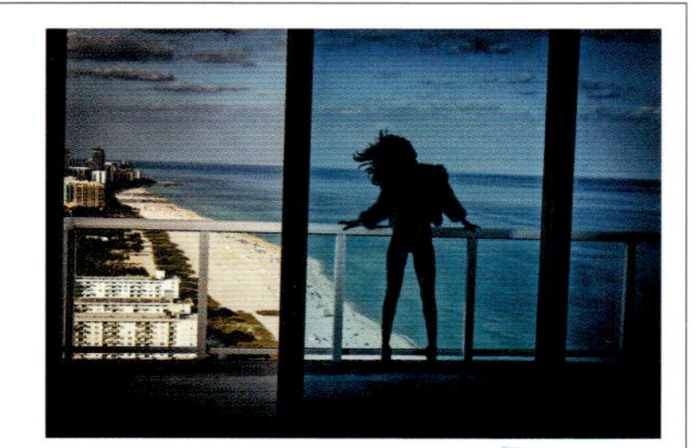
124 RECAP I 2012

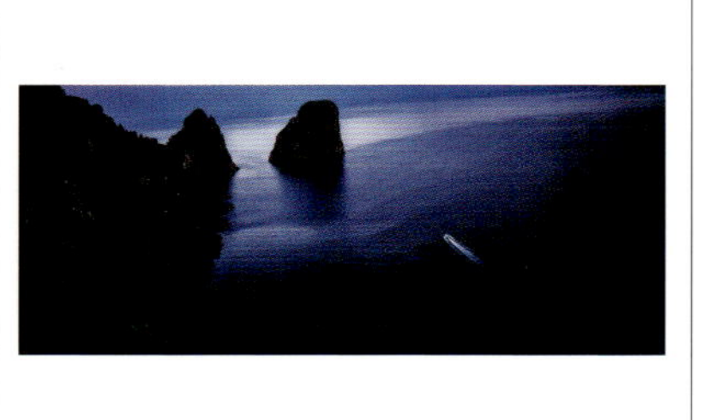
126 CAPRI DREAMS I 2008

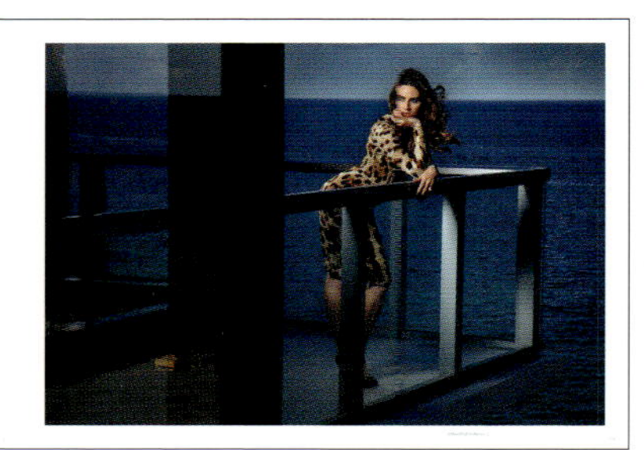
128 DANGEROUS MIND I 2010

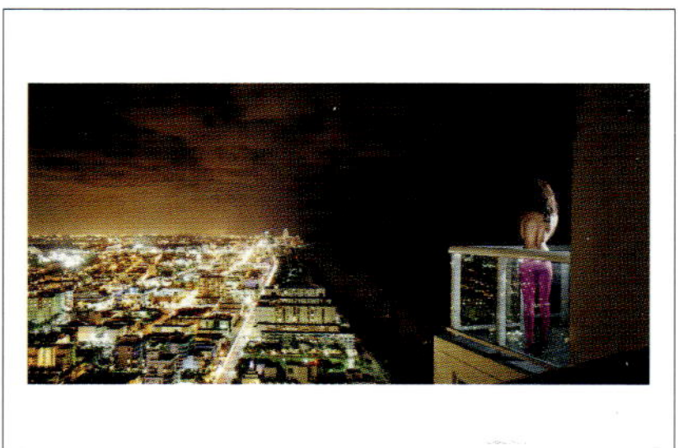
130 GLITTERING CITY I 2012

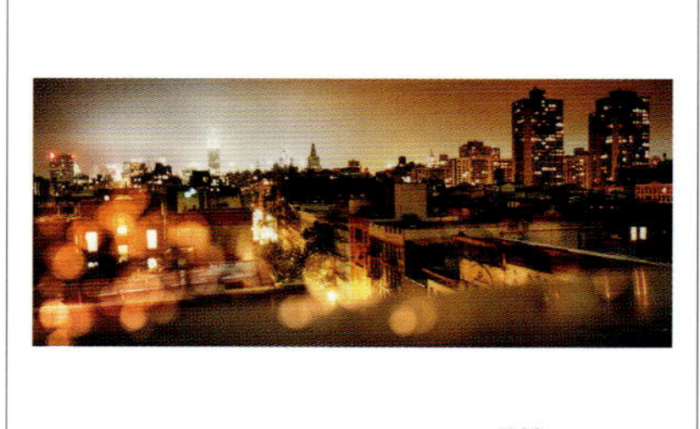
132 NEW YORK, NEW YORK I 2011

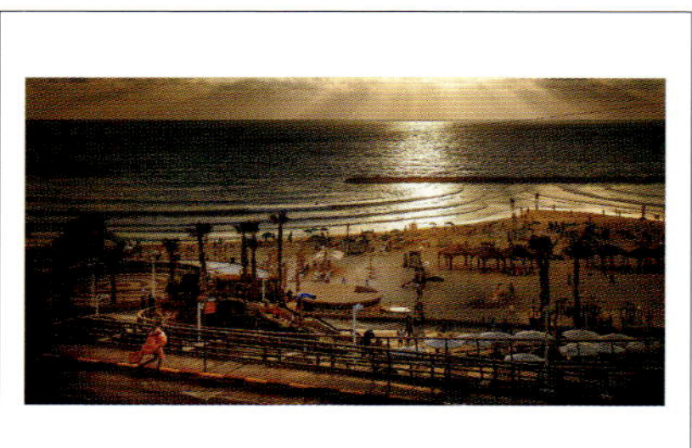
134 GIRL IN TEL AVIV I 2011

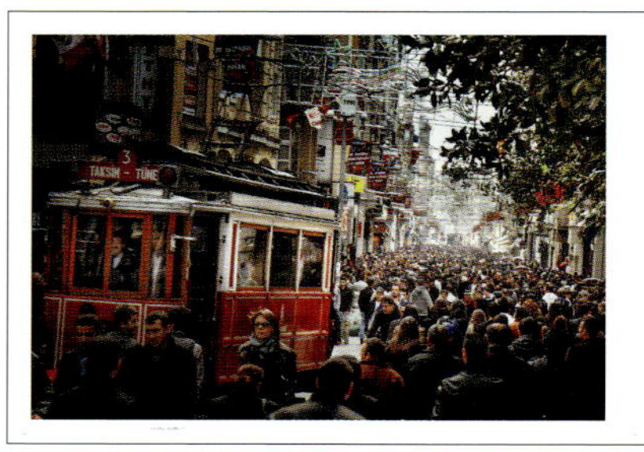
136 ISTANBUL LOVERS I 2011

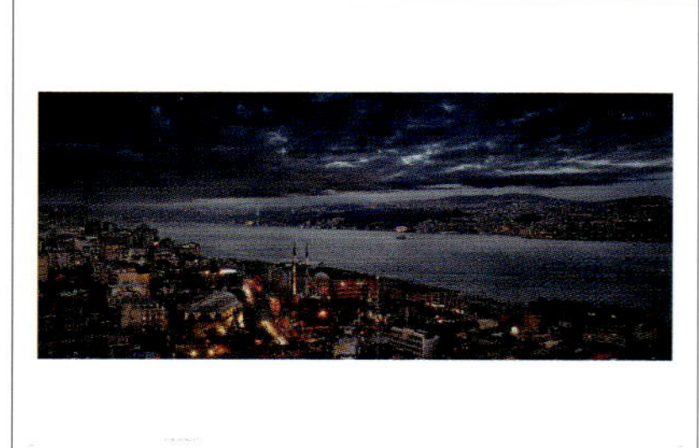
138 THE BOSPHORUS I 2011

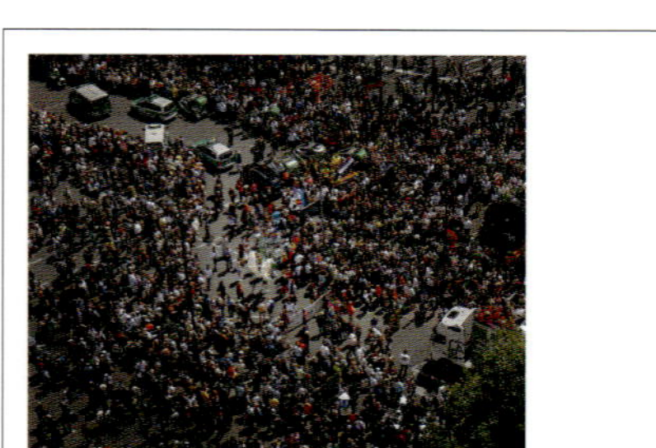
140 ANGEL IN BERLIN I 2011

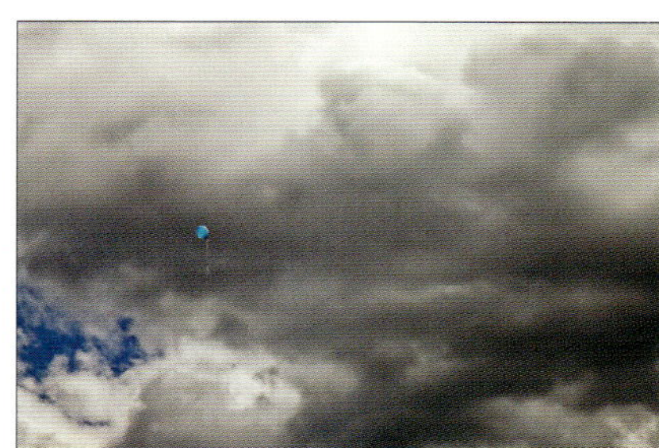
142 BALLOON IN SKY I 2011

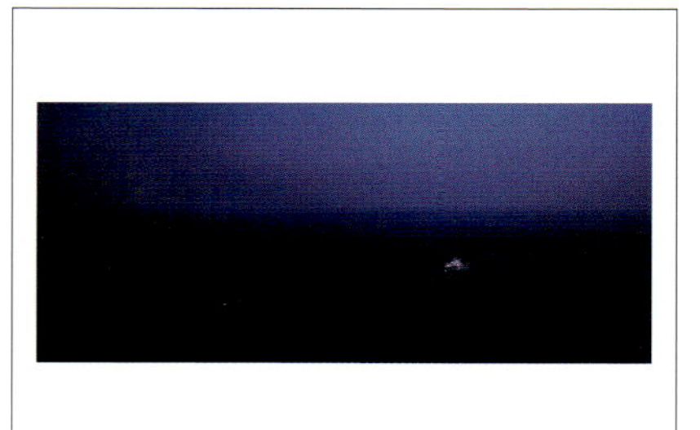
144 THE ESCAPE I 2008

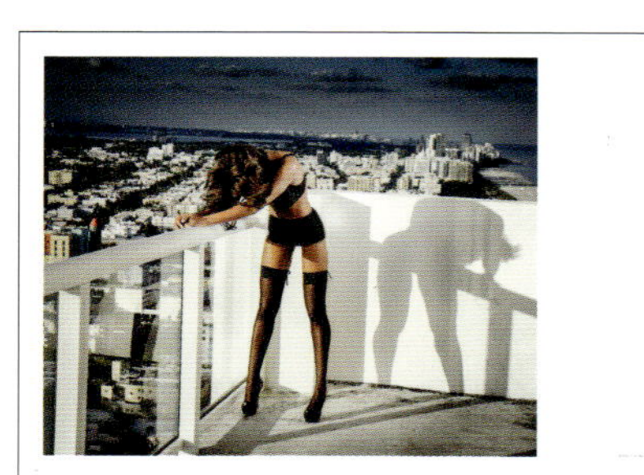
146 STORMY MOMENT I 2012

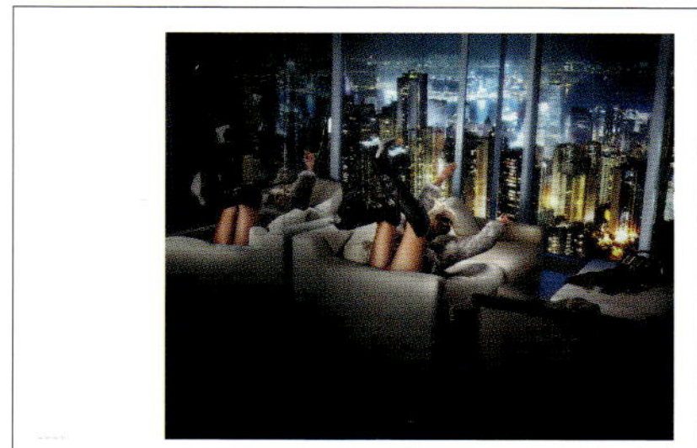
148 FALLING BACK I 2011

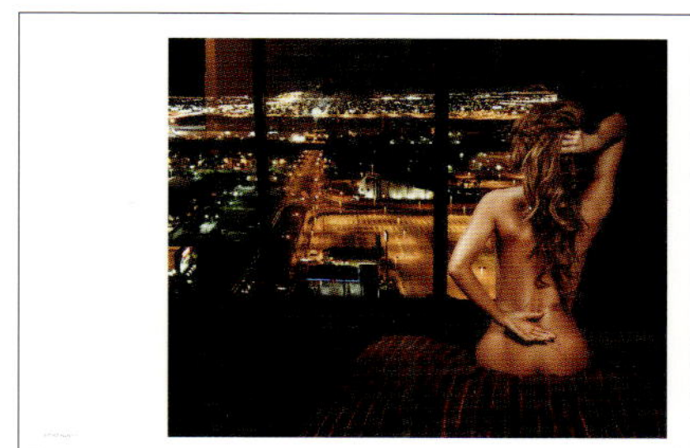
150 TIME FOR BLUES I 2010

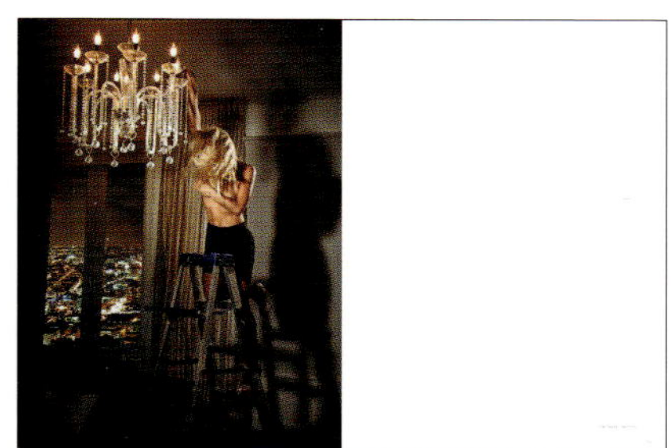
152 HIGH MAINTENANCE I 2012

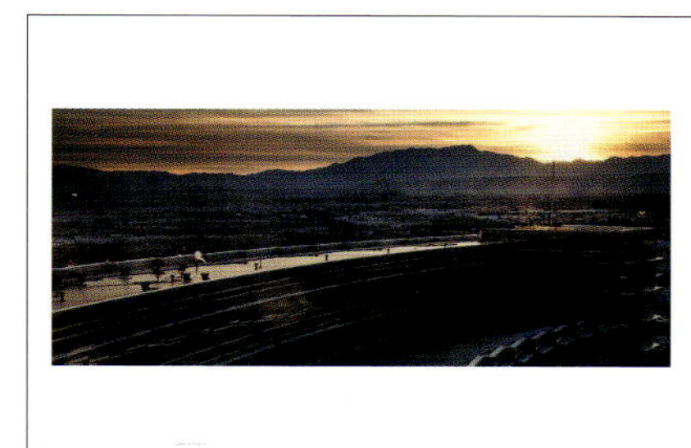
154 WALKING AWAY I 2012

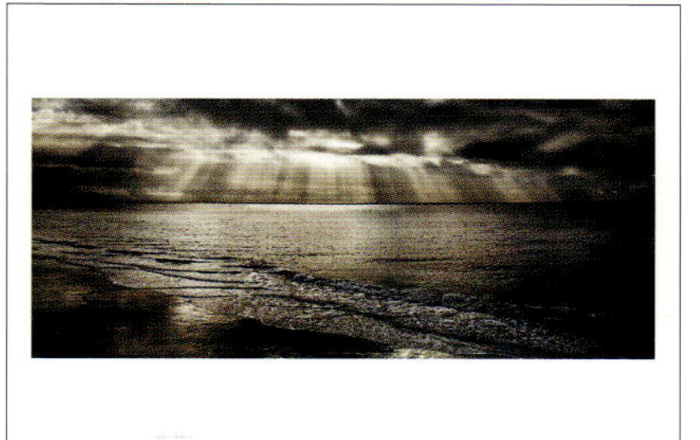
156 ALL OF A SUDDEN I 2011

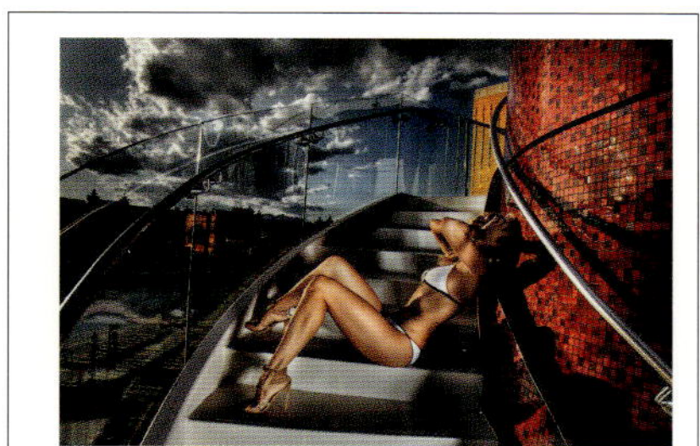
158 PERFECT STORM I 2011

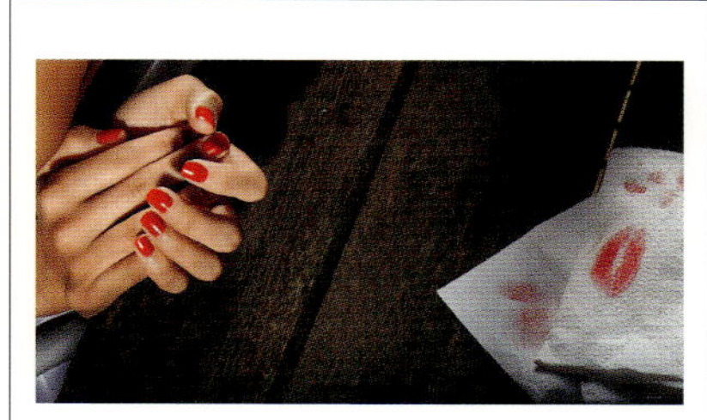
160 DRY RUN I 2011

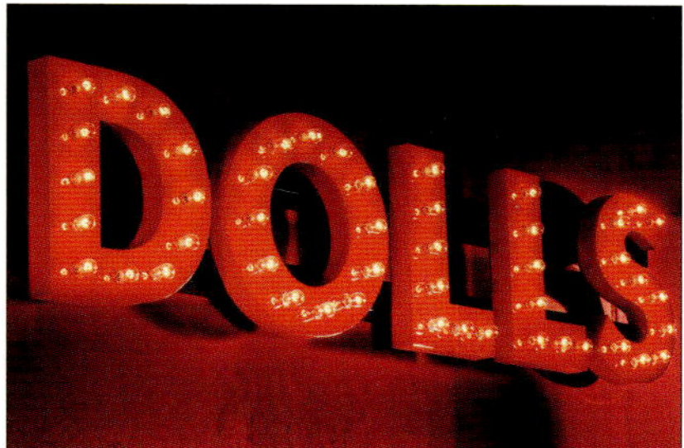

162 DOLLS I 2008

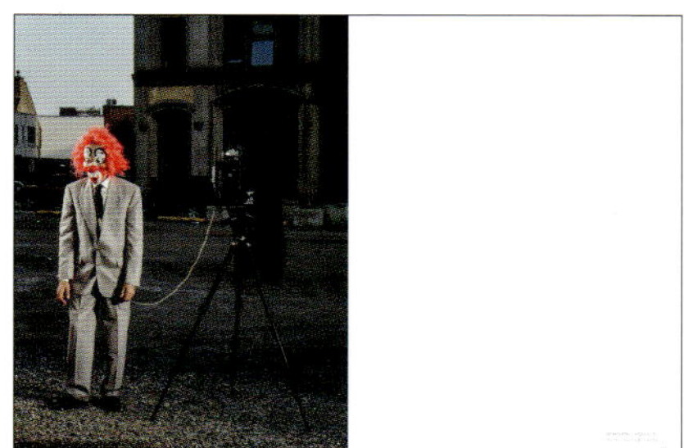
164 ENTERTAINING HIMSELF I 2008

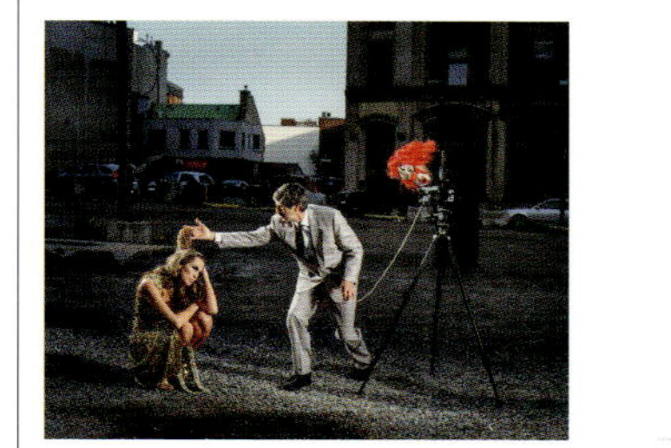
166 TOUCH OF MAGIC I 2008

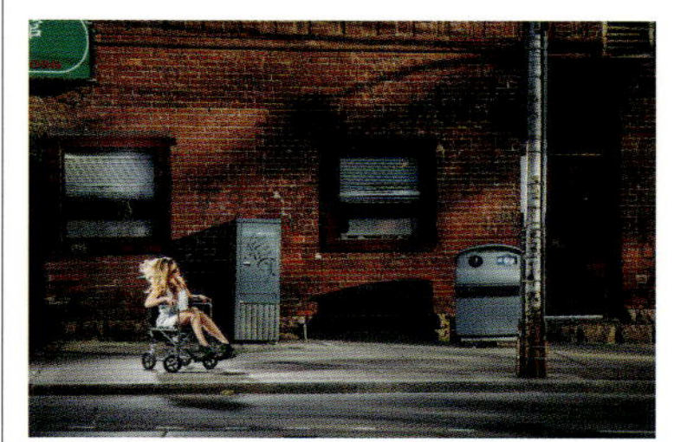
168 HEELS ON WHEELS I 2012

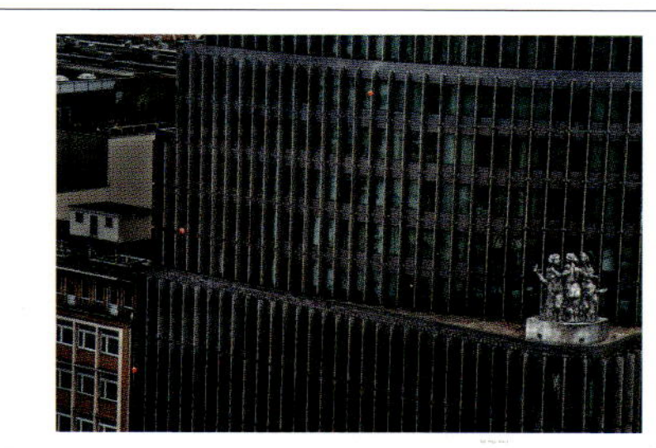
170 RED BALLONS I 2011

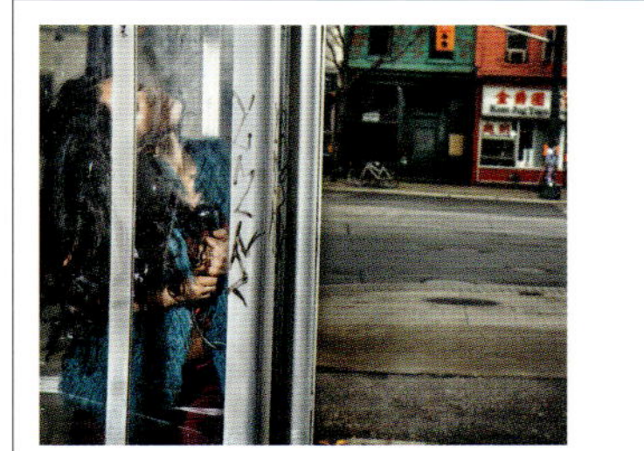
172 HEARTBREAKER I 2012

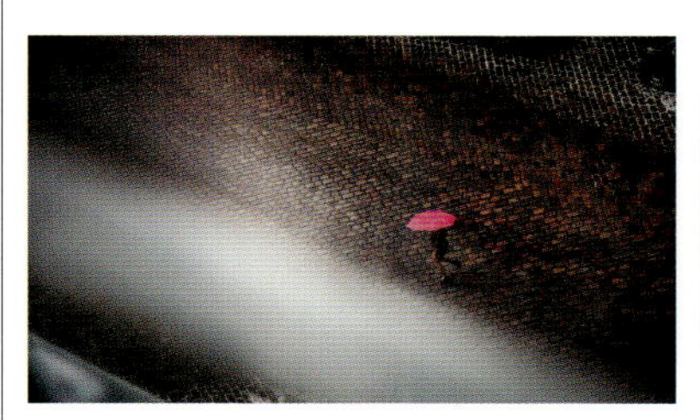
174 UNDERCOVER I 2012

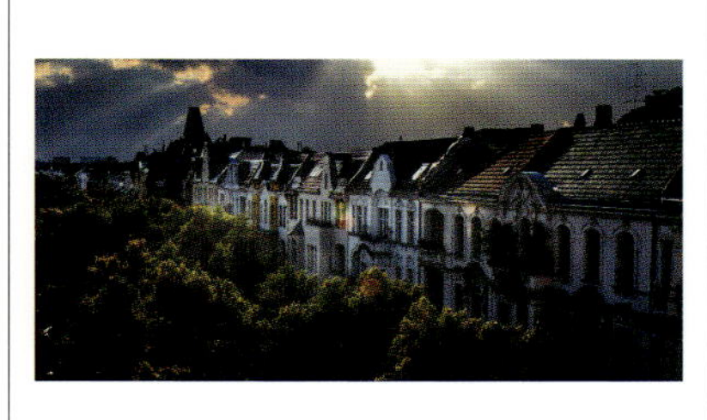
176 DUSK IN BERLIN I 2011

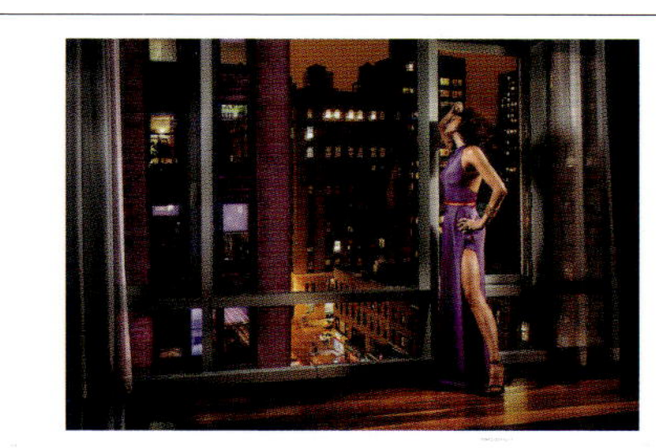
178 PURPLE LOVE I 2011

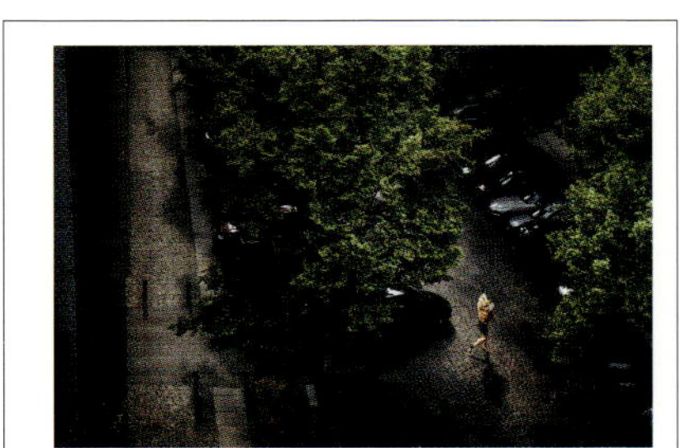
180 GIRL IN BERLIN I 2011

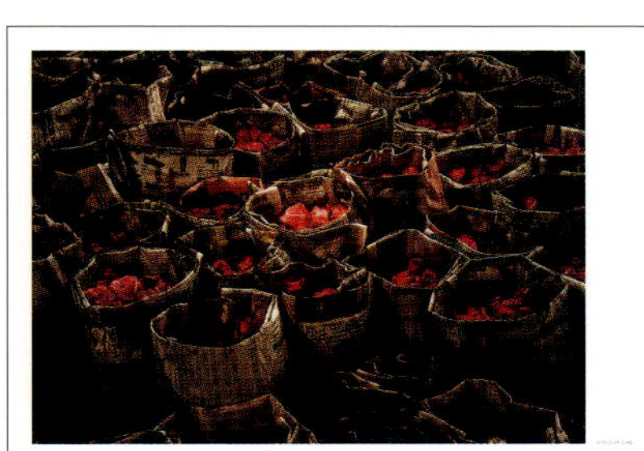
182 WAITING FOR LOVERS I 2012

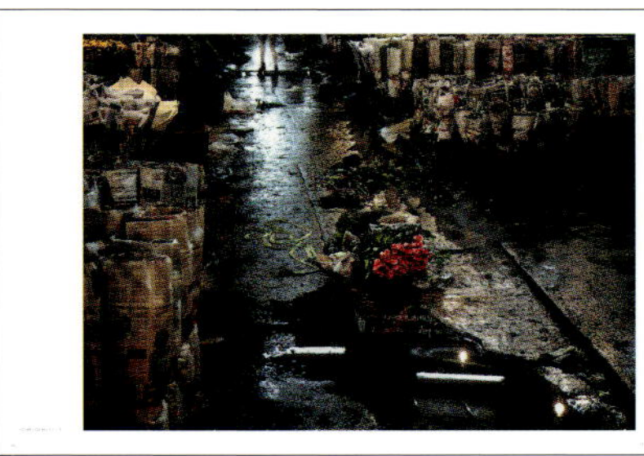
184 NEVER LOOK BACK I 2011

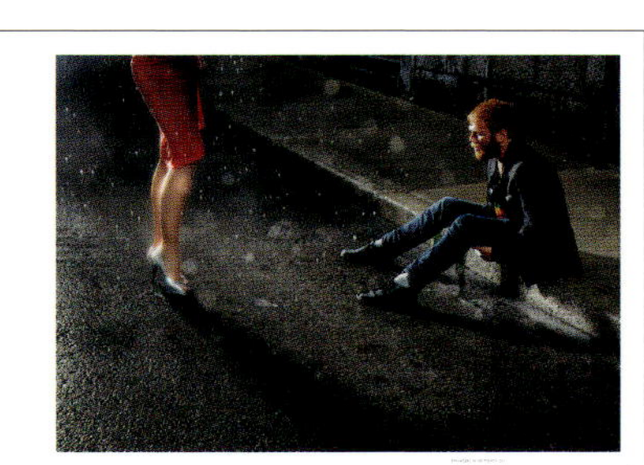
186 STRANGERS IN THE NIGHT I 2011

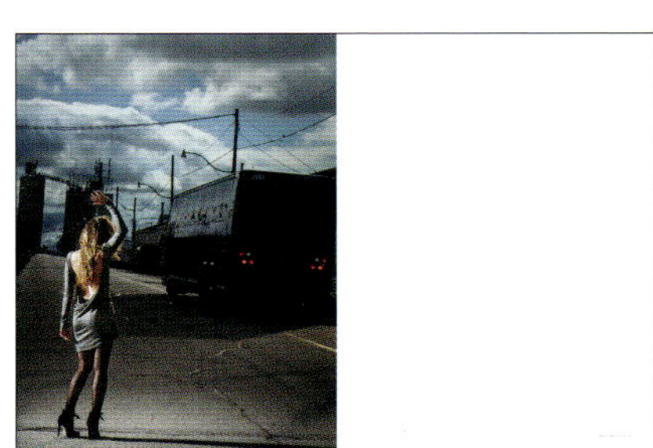
188 TWENTY4FIFTY1 I 2012

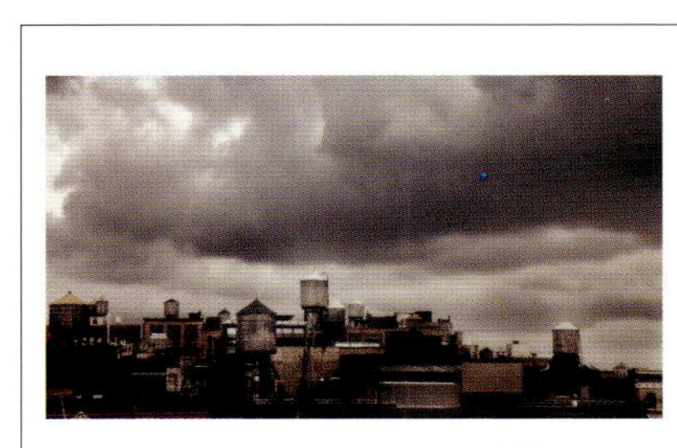
190 BALLOON OVER NYC I 2010

When we see a roadside disaster, we are compelled to look as we drive past. But when we see a beautiful disaster, it's so much more. We are drawn in. Hooked. Moving on is impossible. We can't look away and, if we're not careful, sometimes we get involved, even when we know we shouldn't. Whether we help or hurt depends on who we are and on her....

From songs to novels to masterworks of art, throughout history we have all found ourselves drawn to images of beautiful women who are fascinating and tortured, wild and genius, crazy and passionate, destructive and dangerous.

Who are these women? Who are they really? What drives them? What do they want? What do we want from them? What is it about them we desire—their bodies or their souls?

Are they heartbreakers or heartbroken?

Beautiful Disasters

David Drebin

Wenn wir an einem Unfall vorbeifahren, schauen wir unweigerlich hin. Aber wenn wir ein *Beautiful Disaster* sehen, verbirgt sich noch viel mehr dahinter. Wir spüren den Sog, sind gefangen. Weiterzugehen ist unmöglich. Wir können den Blick nicht abwenden, und wenn wir nicht aufpassen, geraten wir in etwas hinein, von dem wir wissen, dass wir besser die Finger davon lassen sollten. Helfen wir oder verletzen wir das Opfer noch mehr? Das hängt davon ab, wer wir sind – und natürlich von ihr...

Ob in Liedern, Romanen oder Gemälden, der Mensch fühlt sich seit jeher zu Darstellungen schöner Frauen hingezogen, die faszinierend und gequält wirken, wild und genial, verrückt und leidenschaftlich, destruktiv und gefährlich.

Wer sind diese Frauen? Wer sind sie wirklich? Was treibt sie an? Was wollen sie? Was wollen wir von ihnen? Was an ihnen begehren wir – ihren Körper oder ihre Seele?

Brechen sie uns das Herz oder wir ihnen?

Beautiful Disasters

David Drebin

Quand on foule en forêt des espèces vénéneuses, on ne peut s'empêcher de ralentir le pas pour les examiner... Mais croiser une beauté vénéneuse, c'est encore autre chose. Elle nous aspire. Nous harponne. Nous cloue sur place. Capte notre regard et, si on n'y prête garde, nous fait basculer dans son monde, alors même, on le sait, qu'il ne faudrait pas. Céder ou résister, à vous de voir... à elle aussi.

De la chanson au roman en passant par l'œuvre d'art, nous sommes depuis toujours attirés par les images de ces beautés fascinantes et torturées, rebelles et géniales, folles et passionnées, destructrices et dangereuses.

Qui sont ces femmes ? Qui sont-elles vraiment ? Quels sont leurs ressorts secrets ? Que cherchent-elles ? Qu'attendons-nous vraiment d'elles ? Que désirons-nous : leur corps ou leur âme ?

Brise-cœurs ou cœurs brisés ?

Beautiful Disasters

David Drebin

Cuando al circular por la carretera vemos un desastre en la cuneta, todos sentimos el impulso de observarlo mientras pasamos junto a él. Pero cuando vemos un hermoso desastre, el impulso es mucho más fuerte. Nos sentimos arrastrados, obnubilados, no es posible desentenderse de él. No somos capaces de apartar la mirada, y a veces, si no hemos sido cuidadosos, acabamos implicándonos, por mucho que sepamos que no deberíamos. Si con ello terminamos ayudando o haciendo más daño, depende de quienes seamos nosotros... y de ella.

Ya sea en canciones, novelas u obras maestras del arte, a lo largo de la historia nos hemos sentido siempre atraído por las imágenes de esas mujeres hermosas que aparecen ante nosotros a un tiempo fascinantes y atormentadas, salvajes y geniales, locas y apasionadas, destructivas y peligrosas.

¿Quiénes son esas mujeres? ¿Quiénes son realmente? ¿Qué es lo que las mueve? ¿Qué es lo que desean? ¿Qué queremos nosotros verdaderamente de ellas? ¿Qué es lo que deseamos de ellas, sus cuerpos o su alma?

¿Van a rompernos el corazón, o son ellas las que lo tienen roto?

Beautiful Disasters

David Drebin

Se mentre guidiamo passiamo davanti al luogo di un disastro, il nostro sguardo è inevitabilmente attratto. Ma se al centro del disastro c'è la bellezza, l'attrazione è ancora maggiore: veniamo travolti, ipnotizzati, immobilizzati. Non riusciamo a distogliere lo sguardo e, se non stiamo attenti, rischiamo di finire coinvolti, pur sapendo che non dovremmo farlo. Se aiutiamo o procureremo danno dipende da noi – e da lei...

Dalle canzoni ai romanzi fino alle opere d'arte, tutti noi nel corso della storia siamo stati attratti dall'immagine di donne belle, che sono affascinanti e al contempo tormentate, selvagge e genuine, folli e appassionate, distruttive e pericolose.

Chi sono queste donne? Chi sono veramente? Che cosa le spinge a comportarsi in certi modi? Che cosa vogliono? Noi cosa vogliamo veramente da loro? Che cos'è di loro che desideriamo – il loro corpo o la loro anima?

Sono delle spezzacuori o hanno il cuore spezzato?

Beautiful Disasters – I disastri della bellezza

David Drebin

ABOUT DAVID DREBIN

In a unique manner, David Drebin's work combines voyeuristic and psychological viewpoints. He offers the viewer a dramatic insight into emotions and experiences which many of us have doubtlessly felt at some point of our lives. After successfully completing the Parsons School of Design in New York City in 1996, David Drebin rapidly made a name for himself as an internationally successful art photographer.

Drebin's photographs are epic, dramatic and, above all, cinematic. In a unique and opulent way, Drebin stages femme fatales against the gigantic backdrops of cities such as Hong Kong, New York, and Paris. The panorama of the big cities, which, due to their format, are a tribute to cinema, serve as cinematic settings. With their impressive skyscrapers, they provide the viewer with a nearly infinite surface for the imagination. The distinctive tension and depth in his pictures arise from the free combination of such differing topics as humor and sex, melancholy and sex, and melancholy and humor. His andscapes, often feeling more like dreamscapes are collected around the world.

Having worked with mega stars in the world of Fashion, Sports and Entertainment, Drebin continues to be prolific in publishing books and having them distributed around the world followed by exhibitions in Paris, New York, Miami, Istanbul, Amsterdam, Brussels and many other cities internationally.

David Drebin is represented by the world's finest Art Galleries including Camera Work, Galerie de Bellefeuille, Contessa Gallery, Photographers Limited Editions, De Buck Gallery, Young Gallery and Fahey/Klein.

DAVID DREBIN

David Drebins Arbeiten vereinen auf eine ganz besondere Art voyeuristische und psychologische Sichtweisen. Er bietet dem Betrachter einen dramatischen Einblick in Gefühlswelten und Erfahrungen, wie sie fast jeder aus seinem eigenen Leben kennt. Nach dem Abschluss an der New Yorker Parsons School of Design 1996 machte sich Drebin rasch einen Namen als international erfolgreicher Fotograf.

Seine Bilder sind episch, dramatisch und vor allem cineastisch. Drebin inszeniert mit seinen Femmes fatales opulente Tableaus vor majestätischen Städtekulissen wie Hongkong, New York und Paris. Das Panorama der Großstädte liefert nicht nur den Hintergrund für die dramatischen Inszenierungen, sondern ist aufgrund des Bildformats auch ein Tribut an das Kino an sich. Imposante Hochhäuser bieten dem Betrachter eine fast unendliche Oberfläche, die es dem Betrachter ermöglicht, seine Fantasie frei schweifen zu lassen. Die charakteristische Spannung und Tiefe der Bilder entsteht aus der freien Kombination so unterschiedlicher Themen Humor und Sex, Melancholie und Sex sowie Melancholie und Humor. Drebins Landschaftsaufnahmen, die oft wie Traumlandschaften wirken, werden auf der ganzen Welt gesammelt.

Drebin hat mit den Megastars der Mode, im Sport und in der Unterhaltungsbranche zusammengearbeitet und erfolgreich mehrere Bildbände veröffentlicht. Dazu kommen zahlreiche Ausstellungen in Paris, New York, Miami, Istanbul, Amsterdam, Brüssel und anderen Städten.

Er wird von den renommiertesten Galerien vertreten, darunter Camera Work, der Galerie de Bellefeuille, Contessa Gallery, Photographers Limited Editions, De Buck Gallery, Young Gallery und Fahey/Klein.

À PROPOS DE DAVID DREBIN

Dans son travail, David Drebin associe avec originalité voyeurisme et psychologie. Il offre au spectateur une spectaculaire plongée dans des émotions et des expériences que beaucoup d'entre nous ont sans doute connues à un moment ou à un autre de leur vie. Après avoir obtenu le diplôme de la Parsons School of Design à New York en 1996, David Drebin s'est fait rapidement un nom comme photographe d'art de stature internationale.

Ses images sont grandioses, fortes et, surtout, cinématographiques. Dans un style unique et somptueux, il met en scène des femmes fatales avec, pour gigantesque toiles de fond, des villes comme Hong Kong, New York ou Paris. De par leurs dimensions, ces mégapoles constituent un hommage au cinéma, et ce sont leurs panoramas qui servent ici de décors de plateau. Avec leurs tours imposantes, les villes fournissent à l'imagination du spectateur un terrain de jeu presque infini. Leur tension et leur profondeur, les images de Drebin les doivent à une libre combinaison d'ingrédients aussi disparates que l'humour, le sexe et la mélancolie : humour et sexe, mélancolie et sexe, mélancolie et humour. Ses paysages, qui s'apparentent souvent plus à des lieux oniriques, séduisent les collectionneurs partout dans le monde.

Après avoir collaboré avec les plus grands noms de la mode, du sport et du spectacle, Drebin reste très prolifique en publiant des livres qui bénéficient d'une diffusion planétaire et sont suivis d'expositions, notamment à Paris, New York, Miami, Istanbul, Amsterdam et Bruxelles.

David Drebin est représenté par les meilleures galeries d'art du monde, dont Camera Work, la Galerie de Bellefeuille, Contessa Gallery, Photographers Limited Editions, De Buck Gallery, Young Gallery et Fahey/Klein.

SOBRE DAVID DREBIN

La obra de David Drebin combina personalísimas perspectivas voyeuristas y psicológicas. A través de ella, el artista permite al espectador acceder y comprender emociones y experiencias que muchos de nosotros hemos conocido en uno u otro momento de nuestras vidas. Tras completar con éxito sus estudios en la neoyorquina Parsons School of Design en 1996, David Drebin no tardó en darse a conocer internacionalmente como fotógrafo artístico.

Las fotografías de Drebin destacan por su carácter épico, dramático y, principalmente, cinematográfico. Con un estilo único, opulento, Drebin se sirve de grandes ciudades à la Hong Kong, Nueva York y París como colosales telones de fondo frente a los que escenifica las poses de sus *femmes fatales*. Los panoramas de la gran ciudad, por su formato homenajes en sí mismos al séptimo arte, aportan el componente cinematográfico a sus fotografías: los inmensos rascacielos ponen en manos del espectador una superficie casi infinita sobre la que dejar volar la imaginación. La tensión y profundidad palpables en las imágenes emana de la libre combinación de motivos tan divergentes como el sexo y el humor, la melancolía y el sexo y la melancolía y el humor. Sus paisajes, imbuidos a menudo de una fuerte carga onírica, han sido obtenidos en muy distintos puntos del planeta.

Tras trabajar con las más destacadas figuras de la moda, el deporte y el espectáculo, Drebin mantiene su prolífica actividad creadora: sus libros encuentran difusión en todo el mundo, a la estela de sus exposiciones en París, Nueva York, Miami, Estambul, Amsterdam, Bruselas y otras muchas ciudades de rango internacional.

La representación de David Drebin corre a cargo de algunas de las más destacadas galerías de arte del mundo, entre ellas Camera Work, Galerie de Bellefeuille, Contessa Gallery, Photographers Limited Editions, De Buck Gallery, Young Gallery y Fahey/Klein.

DAVID DREBIN

Le opere di David Drebin combinano in un modo del tutto unico prospettive voyeuristiche e psicologiche, offrendo allo spettatore la possibilità di gettare uno sguardo profondo nelle emozioni e nelle esperienze che molti di noi hanno indubbiamente vissuto a un certo punto della propria vita. Dopo aver terminato con successo gli studi alla Parsons School of Design di New York, nel 1996, David Drebin è riuscito in breve tempo a farsi un nome a livello internazionale nel campo della fotografia d'arte.

Le fotografie di Drebin sono epiche, drammatiche e, più di ogni altra cosa, cinematografiche. In un modo assai singolare e opulento, Drebin immette sulla scena personaggi femminili attraenti che si stagliano sullo sfondo maestoso di città come Hong Kong, New York e Parigi. Il panorama offerto dalle grandi città – che per le loro stesse dimensioni sono un autentico tributo al cinema - servono da sfondo scenografico: dominate da maestosi grattacieli, queste città offrono allo spettatore uno spazio praticamente illimitato in cui liberare l'immaginazione. Il caratteristico contrasto e la profondità che esprimono gli scatti di Drebin nascono dalla libera associazione di temi contrastanti come umorismo e sesso, malinconia e sesso, o malinconia e umorismo. I panorami che fanno da sfondo alle sue opere, e che spesso sembrano paesaggi onirici, provengono da ogni parte del mondo.

Drebin ha lavorato per nomi di fama internazionale nel campo della moda, dello sport e dello spettacolo, e continua a pubblicare e distribuire in tutto il mondo svariati volumi fotografici. Le sue opere sono state esposte a Parigi, New York, Miami, Istanbul, Amsterdam, Bruxelles e molte altre città di tutto il globo.

Le fotografie di David Drebin trovano spazio anche in alcune delle più prestigiose gallerie d'arte del nostro pianeta, tra cui spiccano nomi come Camera Work, Galerie de Bellefeuille, Contessa Gallery, Photographers Limited Editions, De Buck Gallery, Young Gallery e Fahey/Klein.

IMPRINT

All post production by Dan Ebert
All titles created by Darling and Darling productions
Foreword by Eric Colmet Daâge, Editor of Photo, France
Text by David Drebin
German translations by Heike Schlatterer, VerlagsService Dr. Ulrich Mihr; Beate Susanne Hanen
English translation by Ashley L. Brown, Romina Russo, WeSwitch Languages
French translations by Philippe Mothe
Spanish translations by Pablo Álvarez, Romina Russo, WeSwitch Languages
Italian translations by Romina Russo, Federica Benetti, WeSwitch Languages

Editorial coordination by Inga Wortmann, teNeues Verlag
Production by Nele Jansen, teNeues Verlag
Design by Iris Durie, teNeues Verlag
Color separation by Medien Team-Vreden, Germany

Published by teNeues Publishing Group

teNeues Verlag GmbH & Co. KG
Am Selder 37, 47906 Kempen, Germany
Phone: 0049-2152-916-0
Fax: 0049-2152-916-111
e-mail: books@teneues.de

Press department: Andrea Rehn
Phone: 0049-2152-916-202
e-mail: arehn@teneues.de

teNeues Digital Media GmbH
Kohlfurter Straße 41–43, 10999 Berlin, Germany
Phone: 0049-30-7007765-0

teNeues Publishing Company
7 West 18th Street, New York, NY 10011, USA
Phone: 001-212-627-9090
Fax: 001-212-627-9511

teNeues Publishing UK Ltd.
21 Marlowe Court, Lymer Avenue, London SE19 1LP, UK
Phone: 0044-20-8670-7522
Fax: 0044-20-8670-7523

teNeues France S.A.R.L.
39, rue des Billets, 18250 Henrichemont, France
Phone: 0033-2-4826-9348
Fax: 0033-1-7072-3482

www.teneues.com

Bibliographic information published by the Deutsche Nationalbibliothek.
The Deutsche Nationalbibliothek lists this publication in the Deutsche Nationalbibliografie;
detailed bibliographic data are available in the Internet at http://dnb.d-nb.de.

ISBN 978-3-8327-9658-7
Library of Congress Control Number: 2012941944

Printed in Italy

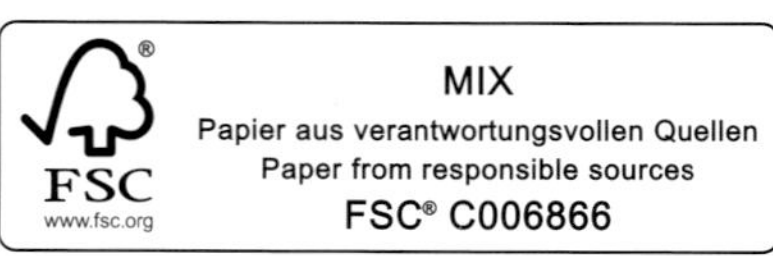

David Drebin is represented exclusively
in Europe by Camera Work Gallery, Berlin
www.camerawork.de

Galleries/Art Dealers

USA
Contessa Gallery
www.contessagallery.com

De Buck Gallery
www.debuckgallery.com

Fahey/Klein Gallery
www.faheykleingallery.com

CANADA
Galerie De Bellefeuille
www.debellefeuille.com

EUROPE
Amsterdam
Rize Art Gallery
www.rizeartgallery.com

Berlin
Camera Work
www.camerawork.de

Brussels
The Young Gallery
www.younggalleryphoto.com

Istanbul
EL'PS'SGALLERY
www.elipsisgallery.com

Paris
Acte2galerie
www.acte2photo.com

Vienna
Photographers Limited Editions
www.photographerslimitededitions.com

teNeues Publishing Group
Kempen
Berlin
Cologne
Düsseldorf
Hamburg
London
Munich
New York
Paris

teNeues